Series Editors

W. Hansmann
W. Purgathofer
F. Sillion

D. J. Duke
A. Puerta (eds.)

Design, Specification
and Verification
of Interactive Systems '99

Proceedings of the Eurographics Workshop
in Braga, Portugal,
June 2–4, 1999

Eurographics

SpringerWienNewYork

Dr. David Duke
Department of Computer Science,
University of York, York, U.K.

Dr. Angel Puerta
Red Whale Software,
Palo Alto, U.S.A.

© 1999 Springer-Verlag/Wien

Typesetting: Camera-ready by authors

Graphic design: Ecke Bonk

Printed on acid-free and chlorine-free bleached paper

SPIN: 10734677

With 89 Figures

ISSN 0946-2767
ISBN-13:978-3-211-83405-3   e-ISBN-13:978-3-7091-6815-8
DOI: 10.1007/978-3-7091-6815-8

Preface

This book is the formal proceedings of the Eurographics Workshop on Design, Specification and Verification of Interactive Systems, DSV-IS'99, which was held at the University of Minho, Braga, Portugal from June 2 to June 4, 1999. The previous events of this series were held at Pisa, Toulouse, Namur, Granada, and Abingdon; the theme this year was "Engaging the Mind by Enriching the Senses", emphasising the importance of the interface in making interaction both effective and enjoyable.

Presentations and discussions covered topics that included specification methods and their use in design, model-based tool support, task and dialogue models, distributed collaboration, and models for VR input. As in previous years, there was a strong emphasis on formal representations and modelling techniques, and their use in understanding interaction and informing the design of artefacts. However, the aim of the workshop is to encourage an exchange of views within a broad community, and other approaches, in particular tool support for model-based design, were also represented.

This book includes the papers of the two invited speakers (one as an abstract only), the fourteen full papers accepted for publication, two shorter position papers, and the reports from the working group discussions. The format of the workshop aimed to mix formal paper presentations with informal discussion sessions, with the two invited talks setting the tone for the meeting.

Mandayam Srinivasan launched the technical programme with a talk entitled "Haptic Interactions in the Real and Virtual Worlds". Just as visual and audio rendering build on our understanding of how the human visual and auditory systems operate, so too effective haptic rendering requires knowledge of the equivalent human haptic capabilities. After an overview of human haptics, covering biomechanical, neurophysiological, and pyschophysical mechanisms, Prof. Srinivasan gave a tour through the history of haptic feedback devices, leading up to the ongoing work at MIT. The talk concluded with an overview of the challenges currently being addressed in haptic research, in particular extending the "working space" in which a device can operate, and the potential to incorporate kinesthetic sensation through millimeter-scale devices.

The second invited talk, by Dr. Mike Hollier of BT Labs, UK concerned interaction on a much larger scale. Entitled "Matching Technology to People for Telepresence", the talk began on a light note by re-examining some of the visions of telecommunications from the 1960's. For example, while the idea of "faxing" a document using photographic plates placed over a television receiver may seem comic today, many of the ideas envisioned in the '60s have been developed, albeit utilising different technologies. More recent ideas such as "teleconferencing" have also continued to evolve, with for example animated avatars providing a socially more controlled alternative to real-time video links. The talk concluded with an outline of the visions for tomorrow, in particular a new level of "transparency" in interfaces, and Dr. Hollier explained why achieving this requires not just better technology, but a much better understanding of how people can interact with that technology.

Papers were presented in six sessions, organised as follows:

- Novel Interfaces
- Specification Techniques
- Architectures and CAD
- Distributed Cooperation
- Using Specifications in Design
- Tasks and Dialogue

A further four sessions were used for informal discussion within working groups, and for the outcome of the discussions to be presented in the closing plenary session.

We would like to thank the following organisations for sponsoring the event: Eurographics, FCT (Fundação para a Ciência e a Tecnologia), CPCIS (Companhia Portuguesa de Computadores Informatica e Sistemas, Lda), and Ordem Dos Engenheiros. We would like to express our sincere thanks to José Campos (York), and to Mário Martins, his colleagues, and students from the Department of Informatics at the University of Minho, for the excellent local organisation.

The programme chairs
David Duke and Angel Puerta

Contents

VIII

Haptic Interactions in the Real and Virtual Worlds

M A Srinivasan, C Basdogan, and C-H Ho
Laboratory for Human and Machine Haptics
Massachusetts Institute of Technology
77, Massachusetts Avenue, Cambridge, MA 02139 USA
e mail : srini, basdogan, chihhao@mit.edu

Abstract

In humans or machines, haptics refers to the use of hands for manual sensing and manipulation. Recently, haptic machines that enable the user to touch, feel, and manipulate virtual environments have generated considerable excitement. Synthesizing virtual haptic objects requires an optimal balance between the human haptic ability to sense object properties, computational complexity to render them in real time, and fidelity of the device in delivering the computed mechanical signals. In this paper, we primarily describe the progress made in our "MIT Touch Lab" over the past few years concerning the development of haptic machines, the paradigms and algorithms used in the emerging field of "Computer Haptics" (analogous to Computer Graphics), and experimental results on human perception and performance in multimodal virtual environments. Several ongoing applications such as the development of a surgical simulator and virtual environments shared by multiple users are also described.

1. Introduction

Virtual environments (VEs), generally referred to as virtual reality in the popular press, have caught the imagination of lay public as well as researchers working in a wide variety of disciplines. VEs are computer-generated synthetic environments with which a human user can interact to perform perceptual and motor tasks. A typical VE system consists of a helmet that can project computer-generated visual images and sounds appropriate to the gaze direction, and special gloves with which one can command a computer through hand gestures. The possibility that by wearing such devices, one could be mentally transported to and immersed in virtual worlds built solely through software is both fascinating and powerful. Applications of this technology include a large variety of human activities such as training, education, entertainment, health care, scientific visualization, telecommunication, design, manufacturing and marketing.

Virtual environment systems that engage only the visual and auditory senses of the user are limited in their capability to interact with the user. As in our interactions with the real world, it is desirable to engage the haptic sensorimotor system that not only conveys the sense of touch and feel of objects, but also allows us to manipulate them. In particular, the human hand is a versatile organ that is able to press, grasp, squeeze or stroke objects; it can explore object properties such as surface texture, shape and softness; it can manipulate tools such as a pen or a jack-hammer. Being able to touch, feel, and manipulate objects in an environment, in addition to seeing (and/or hearing) them, gives a sense of compelling immersion in the environment that is otherwise not possible. Real or virtual environments where one is deprived of the touch and feel of objects, seem impoverished and seriously handicap human interaction capabilities.

Haptic interfaces are devices that enable manual interactions with virtual environments or teleoperated remote systems. They are employed for tasks that are usually performed using hands in the real world, such as manual exploration and manipulation of objects. In general, they receive motor action commands from the human user and display appropriate tactual images to the user. Such haptic interactions may or may not be accompanied by the stimulation of other sensory modalities such as vision and audition. It is quite likely that much greater immersion in a virtual environment can be achieved by the synchronous operation of even a simple haptic interface with a visual and/or auditory display, than by large improvements in, say, the fidelity of the visual display alone.

Although computer keyboards, mice, trackballs, and even instrumented gloves available in the market can be thought of as relatively simple haptic interfaces, they can only convey the user's commands to the computer, and are unable to give a natural sense of touch and feel to the user. Recent advances in the development of force-reflecting haptic interface hardware as well as haptic rendering software have caused considerable excitement. The underlying technology is becoming mature and has opened up novel and interesting research areas. In this paper, we primarily describe the progress made in our "MIT Touch Lab" over the past few years on various aspects of haptics relevant to the development of multimodal VEs. In the next section, a basic introduction to *human haptics*, the study of the human hand-brain system relevant to manual exploration and manipulation, is provided. The subsequent section is on *machine haptics*, concerned with the electromechanical devices used as haptic interfaces. Next, the paradigms and algorithms used in the emerging field of *Computer Haptics* that deals with the software for haptic interactions are described. Subsequently, some of our recent experimental results on human perception and performance in multimodal virtual environments are summarized. Finally, several ongoing applications such as the development of a surgical simulator and virtual environments shared by multiple users are described.

2. Human Haptics

In order to develop haptic interfaces that are designed for optimal interactions with the human user, it is necessary to understand the roles played by the mechanical, sensory, motor and cognitive subsystems of the human haptic system. The mechanical structure of the human hand consists of an intricate arrangement of 19 bones connected by almost as many frictionless joints, and covered by soft tissues and skin.

The bones are attached to about 20 each of intrinsic and extrinsic muscles through numerous tendons which serve to activate 22 degrees of freedom of the hand. The sensory system includes large numbers of various classes of receptors and nerve endings in the skin, joints, tendons, and muscles. Appropriate mechanical, thermal or chemical stimuli activate these receptors, causing them to transmit electrical impulses via the afferent neural network to the central nervous system (of which the brain forms a part), which in turn sends commands through the efferent neurons to the muscles for desired motor action.

In any task involving physical contact with an object, be it for exploration or manipulation, the surface and volumetric physical properties of the skin and subcutaneous tissues play important roles in its successful performance. For example, the fingerpad, which is used by primates in almost all precision tasks, consists of ridged skin (about 1 mm thick) that encloses soft tissues composed of mostly fat in a semi-liquid state. As a block of material, fingerpad exhibits complex mechanical behavior -- inhomogeneity, anisotropy, rate and time-dependence. The compliance and frictional properties of the skin together with the sensory and motor capabilities of the hand enable both gliding over a surface to be explored without losing contact, as well as stably grasping smooth objects to be manipulated. The mechanical loading on the skin, the transmission of the mechanical signals through the skin, and their transduction by the cutaneous mechanoreceptors are all strongly dependent on the mechanical properties of the skin and subcutaneous tissues.

Tactual sensory information conveyed to the brain from the hand in contact with an object can be divided into two classes: (i) *tactile information*, referring to the sense of the nature of contact with the object, mediated by the responses of low threshold mechanoreceptors innervating the skin (say, the fingerpad) within and around the contact region; (ii) *kinesthetic information*, referring to the sense of position and motion of limbs along with the associated forces, conveyed by the sensory receptors in the skin around the joints, joint capsules, tendons, and muscles, together with neural signals derived from motor commands. Only tactile information is conveyed when objects are made to contact passive, stationary hand, except for the ever-present kinesthetic information about the limb posture. Only kinesthetic information is conveyed during active, free (i.e., no contact with any object or other regions of skin) motion of the hand, although the absence of tactile information by itself conveys that the motion is free. Even when the two extreme cases mentioned above are included, it is clear that *all* sensory and manipulatory tasks performed actively with the normal hand involve both classes of information. In addition, free nerve endings and specialized receptors which signal skin temperature, mechanical and thermal pain, as well as chemogenic pain and itch are also present.

The control of contact conditions is as important as sensing those conditions for successful performance of any task. In humans, such control action can range from a fast muscle or spinal reflex to a relatively slow conscious deliberate action. In experiments involving lifting of objects held in a pinch grasp, it has been shown that motor actions such as increasing grip force are initiated as rapidly as within 70 msec.

after an object begins to slip relative to the fingerpad, and that the sensory signals from the cutaneous afferents are critical for task performance. Clearly, the mechanical properties of skin and subcutaneous tissues, the rich sensory information provided by a wide variety of sensors that monitor the tasks continuously, and the coupling of this information with the actions of the motor system are responsible for the human abilities of grasping and manipulation. A brief summary of the psychophysical and neurophysiological results available on the human haptic abilities in real environments and the references to the corresponding literature is given in [1].

3. Machine Haptics

Machine haptics refers to the design, construction, and use of machines to replace or augment human hands. Although such machines include autonomous or teleoperated robots, here we focus on haptic interfaces to VEs. Haptic interfaces are devices composed of mechanical components in physical contact with the human body for exchange of information with the human nervous system. In performing tasks with a haptic interface, the human user conveys desired motor actions by physically manipulating the interface, which, in turn, displays tactual sensory information to the user by appropriately stimulating his or her tactile and kinesthetic sensory systems. Thus, in general, haptic interfaces can be viewed as having two basic functions: (1) to measure the positions and contact forces (and time derivatives) of the user's hand (and/or other body parts) and (2) to display contact forces and positions (and/or their spatial and temporal distributions) to the user. Among these position (or, kinematic) and contact force variables, the choice of which ones are the motor action variables (i.e., inputs to the computer) and which are the sensory display variables (i.e., inputs to the human) depends on the hardware and software design, as well as the tasks the interface is employed for. At present, most of the force-reflecting haptic interfaces sense position of their end-effector and display forces to the human user.

A primary classification of our haptic interactions with real or virtual environments that affects interface design consists of the following three basic elements: (i) free motion, where no physical contact is made with objects in the environment; (ii) Contact involving unbalanced resultant forces, such as pressing an object with a fingerpad; (iii) Contact involving self-equilibrating forces, such as squeezing an object in a pinch grasp. Depending on the tasks for which a haptic interface is designed, some or all of these elements will have to be adequately simulated by the interface. For example, grasping and moving an object from one location to another involves all the three elements. The design constraints of a haptic interface are strongly dependent on which of these elements it needs to simulate. Consequently, the interfaces can be classified based on whether they are force-reflecting or not, as well as what types of motions (e.g., how many degrees of freedom) and contact forces they are capable of simulating.

An alternative but important distinction in our haptic interactions with real or virtual environments is whether we touch, feel and manipulate the objects directly or with a tool. The complexity in the design of a haptic interface is seriously affected by which of these two types of interactions it is supposed to simulate. Note that an `ideal' interface designed to provide realistic simulation of direct haptic exploration and manipulation of objects, would be able to simulate handling with a tool as well. Such an interface would measure positions of, say, the user's hand and display forces, and would have a single hardware configuration (e.g., an exoskeleton) that could be adapted to different tasks by changes in software alone. For example, the act of grasping a hammer would be simulated by monitoring the position and posture of the hand and exerting the appropriate forces on the fingers and palm when the fingers and palm are in the appropriate positions. However, the large number of degrees of freedom of the hand, extreme sensitivities of cutaneous receptors, together with the presence of mass, friction and limitations of sensors and actuators in the interface make such an ideal impossible to achieve with current technology. In contrast, an interface in the form of a tool handle, where reconfigurability within a limited task domain is achieved through both hardware and software changes are quite feasible. Thus, one of the basic distinctions among haptic interfaces is whether they attempt to approximate the ideal exoskeleton or employ the tool handle approach.

Another set of important distinctions concerning haptic interfaces results from a consideration of the force display sub-systems in an interface. Broadly speaking, force display systems can be classified as either (1) ground-based or (2) body-based. Frequently, the distinction between grounding sites is overlooked in the literature. For example, exploration or manipulation of a virtual object requires that force vectors be imposed on the user at multiple regions of contact with the object. Consequently, equal and opposite reaction forces are imposed on the interface. If these forces are self-equilibrating, as in simulating the contact forces that occur when we squeeze an object, then the interface need not be mechanically grounded. However, if the forces are unbalanced, as in pressing a virtual object with a single fingerpad, the equilibrium of the interface requires that it be attached somewhere. A force-reflecting joystick attached to the floor would be a ground-based display, whereas a force reflecting exoskeletal device attached to the user's forearm would be a body-based display. If such an exoskeleton is used to simulate the act of pressing an object with a fingerpad while standing, the stesses that would have been normally experienced by the entire musculoskeletal system would be absent beyond the forearm. The perceptual consequences of such an alteration are not known and warrant investigation.

A survey of the haptic interface devices developed so far is beyond the scope of this paper, but a relatively recent one can be found in [1]. In our MIT Touch Lab, we have developed device hardware, interaction software and psychophysical experiments pertaining to haptic interactions with virtual environments (recent reviews can be found in [1] and [2]). Two specialized devices for performing psychophysical experiments, the linear and planar graspers, have been developed. The linear grasper is capable of simulating fundamental mechanical properties of objects such as compliance, viscosity and mass during haptic interactions. Virtual walls and corners were simulated using the planar grasper, in addition to the simulation of two springs within its workspace. The PHANToM, another haptic display device developed at the MIT Artificial Intelligence Laboratory [3], has been used to prototype a wide range of force-based haptic display primitives. A variety of haptic rendering algorithms for displaying the shape, compliance, texture, and friction of solid surfaces have been implemented on the PHANToM [2, 4]. All the three devices have been used to perform psychophysical experiments aimed at characterizing the sensorimotor abilities of the human user and the effectiveness of computationally efficient rendering algorithms in conveying the desired object properties to the human user.

4. Computer Haptics

Computer Haptics is a rapidly emerging area of research that is concerned with the techniques and processes associated with generating and displaying the touch and feel of virtual objects to a human operator through a force reflecting device. Analogous to computer graphics, it deals with models and behavior of virtual objects together with rendering algorithms for real-time display. It includes the software architecture needed not only for haptic interactions but also their synchronization with visual and other display modalities.

In order to develop effective software architectures for multimodal VEs, we have experimented with multi-threading (on Windows NT platform) and multi-processing (on UNIX platform) techniques and have successfully separated the visual and haptic servo loops. Our experience is that both techniques enable the system to update graphics process at almost constant rates, while running the haptic process in the background. We are able to achieve good visual rendering rates (30 to 60 Hz), high haptic rendering rates (more than 1 kHz), and stable haptic interactions. Although creating a separate process for each modality requires more programming effort, it enables the user to display the graphics and/or haptics on any desired machine(s), even those in different locations, as long as the physical communication between them is provided through a cable. Programming with threads takes less effort, but they are not as flexible as processes.

We have also developed a graphical interface that enables a user to construct virtual environments by means of user-defined text file, toggle stereo visualization, save the virtual environment and quit from the application. This application program was written in C/C++ and utilizes the libraries of   (1) Open Inventor (from Silicon Graphics Inc.) for graphical display of virtual objects, (2) ViewKit (from Silicon Graphics Inc.) for constructing the graphical user interface (e.g. menu items, dialog boxes, etc.), and (3) Parallel Virtual Machine (PVM), a well-known public domain package, for establishing the digital communication between the haptic and visual processes. The user can load objects into the scene, and assign simple visual and haptic properties to the objects using this text file. Following the construction of the scene using the text file, the user can interactively translate, rotate, and scale objects, and the interface will automatically update both the visual and haptic models.

Two types of haptic rendering techniques have been developed: point-based and ray-based. In point-based haptic interactions, only the end point of haptic device, also known as the end effector point or haptic interface point (HIP), interacts with objects

[5, 6]. Since the virtual surfaces have finite stiffnesses, the end point of the haptic device penetrates into the object after collision. In our laboratory, a set of rule-based algorithms has been developed for fast detection of collisions. We use a hierarchical database, multi-threading techniques, and efficient search procedures to reduce the computational time and make the computations almost independent of the number of polygons of the polyhedron representing the object. Each time the user moves the generic probe of the haptic device, the collision detection algorithms check to see if the end point is inside the virtual object. In ray-based haptic interactions developed in our laboratory, the generic probe of the haptic device is modelled as a finite ray whose orientation is taken into account, and the collisions are checked between the ray and the objects [7]. Both techniques have advantages and disadvantages. For example, it is computationally less expensive to render 3D objects using point-based technique. Hence, we achieve higher haptic update rates. On the other hand, the ray-based haptic interaction technique handles side collisions and can provide additional haptic cues for conveying to the user the shape of objects.

Once the software and hardware components were put together for integrating multiple modalities, we focussed on developing techniques for generating multimodal stimuli. Our interest in generating multimodal stimuli is three-fold: (a) to develop new haptic rendering techniques to display shape, texture, and compliance characteristics of virtual objects, (b) to utilize these techniques in our experiments on human perception and performance to study multimodal interactions, and (c) to explore a variety of applications of multimodal virtual environments where haptics adds value. Our progress in the area of haptic rendering is summarized under three headings: shape, texture, and compliance.

4.1 Shape

When smooth and continuous object shapes are approximated by polyhedra for haptic rendering, the user does not perceive the intended shape. Instead, the discrete edges between polygons as well as the planar faces of the polygons are felt. To minimize such undesirable effects, we have proposed *force shading* [8]. In this method, which falls within the general class of force mapping techniques, the force vector is interpolated over the polygonal surfaces such that its direction varies continuously. Consequently, the surfaces of virtual objects feel smoother than their original polyhedral representations. This technique is analogous to Phong shading in computer graphics.

4.2 Texture

Since a wide variety of physical and chemical properties give rise to real-world textures, a variety of techniques are needed to simulate them visually and haptically in VEs. Haptic texturing is a method of simulating surface properties of objects in virtual environments in order to provide the user with the feel of macro and micro surface textures. We have developed two basic approaches: *force perturbation*, where the direction of the displayed force vector is perturbed, and *displacement mapping*, where the microgeometry of the surface is perturbed [7]. Using these methods, we have successfully displayed textures based on Fourier series, filtered white noise, and fractals. But the display of haptic textures using the force perturbation technique was effective only in a certain range (0.5 mm to 5.0 mm in height). To extend the range of haptic textures that can be displayed, we have modified the algorithm to include the calculation of the location of the point closest to the object surface prior to collision detection. Using this additional information, we are now able to render macro textures (> 5.0 mm height) as well. We have also experimented with 2D reaction-diffusion texture models used in computer graphics and successfully implemented them for haptics to generate new types of haptic textures. The reaction-diffusion model consists of a set of differential equations that can be integrated in time to generate texture fields. Moreover, we have developed techniques to extend our work on 2D reaction-diffusion textures to three dimensional space. We have also studied some of the image and signal processing techniques frequently used in computer graphics to convolve 2D images of spots (i.e. simple 2D geometric primitives such as circles, squares, and triangles) with noise functions in order to generate a new class of haptic textures.

In summary, the following texture rendering techniques have been developed: a) force perturbation, b) displacement mapping. Using these rendering techniques, we can display the following types of synthetic haptic textures: a) periodic and aperiodic haptic textures based on Fourier series approach, b) noise textures (based on the filtered white noise function), c) fractal textures, d) reaction-diffusion textures (a set of differential equations are solved in advance to generate a texture field that can be mapped onto the 3D surface of the object), and e) spot-noise textures (the noise function is convolved with 2D images of spots to generate distorted spots that can be displayed haptically). In addition, we have developed image-based haptic textures (the grey scale values of an image are used to generate texture fields that can be mapped onto the surface of 3D objects) as well as methods to display static and dynamic friction.

4.3 Compliance

We have developed procedures for simulating compliant objects in virtual environments. The developed algorithms deal directly with geometry of 3D surfaces and their compliance characteristics, as well as the display of appropriate reaction forces, to convey to the user a feeling of touch and force sensations for soft objects. The compliant rendering technique has two components: (1) the deformation model to display the surface deformation profile graphically; and (2) the force model to display the interaction forces via the haptic interface. The deformation model estimates the direction and the amount of deformation (displacement vector) of each node (i.e. a vertex) of the surface when it is manipulated with the generic probe of the haptic interface device. We utilize a polynomial model or a spline-based model to compute the displacement vector of each node and to visually display deformations. In the force model, a network of springs is utilized to compute the direction and magnitude of the force vector at the node that is closest to the contact point. The techniques described here enable the user to interactively deform compliant surfaces in real-time and feel the reaction forces.

Using the user interface and haptic rendering techniques described in the previous sections, we have designed experiments to investigate human performance involving multimodal interactions in virtual environments. The user interface has enabled several experimenters to rapidly load virtual objects into desired experimental scenarios, interactively manipulate (translate, rotate, scale) them, and attach sophisticated material and visual properties to the virtual objects.

5. Experiments on Human Perception and Performance

Concurrent with the technology development that enables one to realize a wider variety of haptic interfaces, it is necessary to characterize, understand, and model the basic psychophysical behavior of the human haptic system. Without appropriate knowledge in this area, it is impossible to determine specifications for the design of effective haptic interfaces. In addition, because multimodal sensorimotor involvement constitutes a key feature of VE systems, it is obviously important to understand multimodal interactions. Furthermore, because the availability of force feedback in multimodal VE interfaces is relatively new, knowledge about interactions involving force feedback is relatively limited. In general, research in this area not only provides important background for VE design, but the availability of multimodal interfaces with force feedback provides a unique opportunity to study multimodal sensorimotor interactions.

5.1 Purely Haptic Interactions

Using the Linear Grasper, a haptic interface device, psychophysical experiments have been carried out to measure human haptic resolution in discriminating fundamental physical properties of objects through active touch. The subjects utilized their thumb and index fingers to grasp and squeeze two plates of the Linear Grasper, which was programmed to simulate various values of the stiffness, viscosity, or mass of virtual objects. During the experiments, haptic motor performance data in terms of applied forces, velocities, and accelerations were simultaneously recorded.

The Just Noticeable Difference (JND), a commonly accepted measure of human sensory resolution, was found to be about 7% for stiffness, 12% for viscosity, and 20% for mass. The motor data indicated that subjects used the same motor strategy when discriminating any of these material properties. Further analysis of the results has led to the postulation of a single sensorimotor strategy capable of explaining both the sensory resolution results and motor performance data obtained in the experiments. This hypothesis, called the "Temporal force control - spatial force discrimination (TFC-SFD) hypothesis," states that subjects apply the same temporal profile of forces to all stimuli and discriminate physical object properties on the basis of differences in the resulting spatial profiles of these forces. A special case of this hypothesis is that when humans discriminate stiffness, viscosity or mass, they do so by discriminating the mechanical work needed for actually deforming the objects. Implications of these results to the design of virtual environments include specifications on how accurately the dynamics of virtual objects need to be simulated and what parameter values will ensure discriminable objects.

To explore the possibility that multisensory information may be useful in expanding the range and quality of haptic experience in virtual environments, experiments have been conducted to assess the influence of auditory and visual information on the perception of object stiffness through a haptic interface, as described in the next two sections.

5.2 Haptic-Auditory Interactions

We have previously shown that when virtual objects are tapped through a haptic interface, contact sounds can influence the perception of object stiffness [9]. In another series of experiments, we investigated the effect of the timing of a contact sound on the perception of stiffness of a virtual surface. The PHANToM was used to display virtual haptic surfaces with constant stiffness. Subjects heard a contact sound lasting 130 ms through headphones every time they touched a surface. Based on our earlier work on stiffness discrimination, we initially hypothesized that presenting a contact sound prior to actual impact creates the perception of a less stiff surface, whereas presenting a contact sound after actual impact creates the perception of a stiffer surface. However, the findings indicate that both pre-contact and post-contact sounds result in the perceptual illusion that the surface is less stiff than when the sound is presented at contact.

5.3 Haptic-Visual Interactions

Previously we have shown how the perception of haptic stiffness is strongly influenced by the visual display of object deformation [10]. An important implication of these results for multimodal VEs is that by skewing the relationship between the haptic and visual displays, the range of object properties that can be effectively conveyed to the user can be significantly enhanced. For example, although the range of object stiffness that can be displayed by a haptic interface is limited by the force-bandwidth of the interface, the range perceived by the subject can be effectively increased by reducing the visual deformation of the object.

In continuing this line of investigation on how vision affects haptic perception, we have conducted two new sets of experiments to test the effect of perspective on the perception of geometric and material properties of 3D objects [11]. Virtual slots of varying length and buttons of varying stiffness were displayed to the subjects, who then were asked to discriminate their size and stiffness respectively using visual and/or haptic cues. The results of the size experiments show that under vision alone, farther objects are perceived to be smaller due to perspective cues and the addition of haptic feedback reduces this visual bias. Similarly, the results of the stiffness experiments show that compliant objects that are farther are perceived to be softer when there is only haptic feedback and the addition of visual feedback reduces this haptic bias. Hence, we conclude that our visual and haptic systems compensate for each other such that the sensory information that comes from visual and haptic channels is fused in an optimal manner. In particular, the result that the farther objects are perceived to be softer when only haptic cues are present is interesting and suggests a new concept of *haptic perspective*. To ensure that this result was not an artifact of the robot arm (i.e. position and force errors due to the kinematics of the haptic device) or our experimental design, we performed three different tests, but the result did not change.

5.4 Haptics Across the World Wide Web

In order to make haptics and our research studies accessible and transferable to the others, we opted to integrate haptics into the Web. A demonstration version of the visual-haptic experiment as described above using the PHANToM haptic interface was developed for use across the World Wide Web. The program was written in Java, using multi-threading to create separate visual and haptic control loops, thereby increasing the speed of the haptics loop to keep the program stable despite its graphics overhead. The application program was placed on the Laboratory of Human and Machine Haptics web page (http://touchlab.mit.edu), to be executed by any remote user with a PHANToM and a Windows NT computer running Netscape for WWW access. Remote users could download a dynamic link library and some Java classes from the web page to their computer, and then run the program in their web browser. Users were asked to discriminate the stiffness of sets of two springs, displayed visually on the screen and haptically with the PHANToM, and to send in their responses via an e-mail window in the web page. Thus, we now have the ability to perform perceptual experiments with multimodal VEs across the internet.

6. Applications

We describe below two examples of how multimodal virtual environment systems are being used in our laboratory to explore novel application areas.

6.1 Simulation of Minimally Invasive Surgical Procedures

Research in the area of computer assisted surgery and surgical simulation has mainly focused on developing 3D geometrical models of the human body from 2D medical images, visualization of internal structures for educational and preoperative surgical planning purposes, and graphical display of soft tissue behavior in real time. Conveying to the surgeon the touch and force sensations with the use of haptic interfaces has not been investigated in detail. We have developed a set of haptic rendering algorithms for simulating "surgical instrument - soft tissue" interactions. Although the focus of the study is the development of algorithms for simulation of laparoscopic procedures, the developed techniques are also useful in simulating other medical procedures involving touch and feel of soft tissues. The proposed force-reflecting soft tissue models are in various fidelities and have been developed to simulate the behavior of elastically deformable objects in virtual environments. The developed algorithms deal directly with geometry of anatomical organs, surface and compliance characteristics of tissues, and the estimation of appropriate reaction forces to convey to the user a feeling of touch and force sensations [12].

The hardware components of the set-up include a personal computer (300 MHz, dual Pentium processor) with a high-end 3D graphics accelerator, a force-feedback device (PHANToM from SensAble Technologies Inc.) to simulate haptic sensations. During the simulations, the user manipulates the generic stylus of the force-feedback device to simulate the movements of a surgical instrument and to feel its interactions with the computer generated anatomical organs. The associated deformations of the organs are displayed on the computer monitor and reaction forces are fed back to the user through the haptic interface. The software was written in C/C++, using multi-threading techniques to create separate visual and haptic control loops, thereby increasing the haptics servo rate (varies from 500 Hz to 2 kHz) while simultaneously satisfying the requirements of graphics update rate of at least 30 Hz. Recently, we have made progress in two areas:

Development of "thin-walled" models to simulate tissue deformations and to compute reaction forces: In the language of mechanics, the "thin-walled" structures are broadly classified into membranes, structures with essentially no bending stiffness compared to the in-plane stiffness, and shells, structures in which bending behavior is also important. We have used such structures as organ models to simplify the mechanistic computations while at the same time retaining some of the physics of tool–tissue interactions. In our implementation, triangular elements are used to represent the organ geometry and the virtual work principle is used to derive the incremental equations of motion [13]. The initial results suggest that "thin-walled" models can predict nonlinear behavior of tissues.

Development of algorithms to simulate tissue cutting and bleeding: We have developed computationally fast algorithms to display (1) tissue cutting and (2) bleeding in virtual environments with applications to laparoscopic surgery. Cutting through soft tissue generates an infinitesimally thin slit until the sides of the surface are separated from each other. Simulation of an incision through tissue surface is modelled in three steps: first, the collisions between the instrument and the tissue surface are detected as the simulated cutting tool passes through. Then, the vertices along the cutting path are duplicated. Finally, a simple elastic tissue model is used to separate the vertices from each other to reveal the cut. Accurate simulation of bleeding is a challenging problem because of the complexities of the circulatory system and the physics of viscous fluid flow. There are several fluid flow models described in the literature, but most of them are computationally slow and do not specifically address the problem of blood flowing over soft tissues. We have reviewed the existing models, and have adapted them to our specific task. The key characteristics of our blood flow model are a visually realistic display and real-time computational performance. To display bleeding in virtual environments, we developed a surface flow algorithm. This method is based on a simplified form of the Navier-Stokes equations governing viscous fluid flow. The simplification of these partial differential equations results in a wave equation that can be solved efficiently, in real-time, with finite difference techniques. The solution describes the flow of blood over the polyhedral surfaces representing the anatomical structures and is displayed as a continuous polyhedral surface drawn over the anatomy [14].

6.2 The Role of Haptics in Shared Virtual Environments

We have conducted a set of human experiments to investigate the role of haptics in shared virtual environments (SVEs). Our efforts were aimed at exploring (1) whether haptic communication through force feedback can facilitate a sense of togetherness between two people at different locations while interacting with each other in SVEs, (2) if so, what types of haptic communication/negotiation strategies they follow, and (3) if gender, personality, or emotional experiences of users can affect the haptic communication in SVEs. The experiment concerns a scenario where two people, at remote sites, co-operate to perform a joint task in a SVE. The experiments are abstractions from real situations in order to create a more controlled environment suitable for explanatory studies in the laboratory. During the experiment, subjects were not allowed to meet their remote partner, and did not know where their partner was located. The participants were in different rooms but saw the same visual scene on their monitor and felt the objects in the scene via a force feedback device, the PHANToM.

The goal of the task was to move a ring with the help of another person without touching a wire. A ring, a wire, and two cursors attached to the ring were displayed to the subjects. Haptic interactions between cursors as well as between cursor and the ring were modelled using a spring-damper system and a point-based haptic rendering technique [15]. Subjects were asked to move the ring back and forth on the wire many times, in collaboration with each other such that contact between the wire and the ring was minimized or avoided. If the ring touched the wire, the colors of the ring and the surrounding walls were changed to red to warn the subject of an error. They were changed back to their original colors when the subjects corrected the position of the ring. To hold the ring, both subjects needed to press on the ring towards each other above a threshold force. If they did not press on the ring at the same time, the ring did not move and its color was changed to gray to warn them. To move the ring along the wire, they each needed to apply an additional lateral force.

Two sensory conditions have been explored to investigate the effect of haptic communication on the sense of togetherness: (1) both visual and haptic feedback provided to the participants; (2) only visual feedback was provided to the participants. Performance and subjective measures were developed to quantify the role of haptic feedback in SVEs. Performance measure was derived from the following measurements: (1) total amount time takes to complete task, (2) the ratio of erroneous-time to total time. Several *subjective* questions were asked, through a questionnaire, in four categories including their (1) performance, (2) their sense of 'being together', (3) emotional reactions, and (4) personality profile. Each of the questions in categories 1,2, and 3 were rated on a 1-7 scale. Subjective measures were correlated with the performance measures to deduce conclusions on the effect of haptic feedback to the task performance and the sense of being with someone in SVEs . The results suggest that haptic feedback significantly improves the performance and contributes to the feeling of "sense of togetherness" in SVEs.

7. Future Research

Many of the issues concerning the development of haptic interfaces and computer haptics are summarized in [2]. Although both ground-based and exoskeletal force-reflecting haptic interface devices are available in the market, further improvements in range, resolution, and frequency bandwidth of these devices are needed to match their performance with that of the human user. In moving towards realistic haptic displays that mimic direct natural touch, tactile displays are probably the most challenging among the technologies that need to be developed. The emerging field of micro-mechanical systems holds promise for providing very fine arrays of tactile stimulators. In collaboration with researchers at Carnegie-Mellon University, we are developing electrostatic-pneumatic actuators for use in sensors and as surface-normal actuators. Although capable of relatively small forces and deflections, arrays of such actuators integrated with addressing electronics would be inexpensive, light-weight, and compact enough to be worn without significantly impeding hand movement or function.   In addition, the current technology makes feasible a 20 x 20 array of individually controlled stimulators on a 1 cm x 1cm chip.

In the area of computer haptics, the current models of virtual objects that can be displayed haptically in real-time are quite simplistic compared to the static and dynamic behavior of objects in the real world. Computationally efficient models and interaction techniques that result in real-time haptic displays that match the human perceptual capabilities in accuracy and resolution will continue to be a challenge, even with the current rate of increase in processing speeds. This is because the complexity of the models, such as in detecting collisions of moving multiple objects or in performing a mechanistic analysis of a deformable object in real-time, can be arbitrarily high. Synchronization of the visual, auditory and haptic displays can be problematic, because each modality requires different types of approximations to simulate the same physical phenomenon. Use of multiple processors with shared memory and/or multi-threading seems to be essential. To have haptics across the internet in a manner that is useful to a large number of users, standardized protocols for distributed VEs should include haptics explicitly.

Due to inherent hardware limitations, haptic interfaces can only deliver stimuli that approximate our interactions with the real environment. It does not, however, follow that synthesized haptic experiences created through the haptic interfaces necessarily feel unreal to the user. Consider an analogy with the synthesized visual experiences obtained while watching television or playing a video game. While visual stimuli in the real world are continuous in space and time, these visual interfaces project images at the rate of about 30 frames/sec. Yet, we experience a sense of realism and even a sense of telepresence because we are able to exploit the limitations of the human visual apparatus. The hope that the necessary approximations in generating synthesized haptic experiences will be adequate for a particular task is based on the fact that the human haptic system has limitations that can be similarly exploited. To determine the nature of these approximations, or, in other words, to find out what we can get away with in creating synthetic haptic experiences, quantitative human studies are essential to assess which types of stimulation provide the most useful and profound haptic cues for the task at hand.

Acknowledgements

This work was carried out under NAWC/TSD and ONR contracts. Authors would like to acknowledge Lee Beauregard, David Brock, Suvranu De, David DiFranco, Alexandra Hou, Hugh Morgenbesser, and Wan-Chen Wu for various parts of the work described in here. We also want to thank Ken Salisbury and his group at the MIT Artificial Intelligence Laboratory for their collaboration in various projects.

References

[1] Srinivasan, M A, Haptic Interfaces, In Virtual Reality: Scientific and Technical Challenges, Eds: N. I. Durlach and A. S. Mavor, Report of the Committee on Virtual Reality Research and Development, National Research Council, National Academy Press, 1995.

[2] Srinivasan, M A and Basdogan, C, Haptics in Virtual Environments: Taxonomy, Research Status, and Challenges, Computers and Graphics, Vol. 21, No. 4, 1997.

[3] Massie, T H and Salisbury, J K, The PHANToM Haptic Interface: A Device for Probing Virtual Objects. Proceedings of the ASME Dynamic Systems and Control Division, Vol. 55(1), pp. 295-301, 1997.

[4] Salisbury, J K and Srinivasan, M A, Phantom-Based Haptic Interaction with Virtual Objects, IEEE Computer Graphics and Applications, Vol. 17, No. 5, 1997.

[5] Ho, C-H, Basdogan, C and Srinivasan, M A, Haptic Rendering: Point- and Ray-based Interactions, Proceedings of the Second PHANToM User's Group Workshop, October, 1997.

[6] Ho, C-H, Basdogan, C and Srinivasan, M A, Efficient Point-based Rendering Techniques for Haptic Display of Virtual Objects, Presence, 1999 (in press).

[7] Basdogan, C, Ho, C-H and Srinivasan M A, A Ray-based Haptic Rendering Technique for Displaying Shape and Texture of 3D Objects in Virtual Environments, Proceedings of the ASME Dynamic Systems and Control Division, Ed. G. Rizzoni, DSC-Vol. 61, pp. 77-84, ASME, 1997.

[8] Morgenbesser, H B and Srinivasan, M A, Force Shading for Haptic Shape Perception, Proceedings of the ASME Dynamic Systems and Control Division, DSC-Vol. 58, pp. 407-412, ASME, 1996.

[9] DiFranco, D E, Beauregard, G L and Srinivasan, M A, The Effect of Auditory Cues on the Haptic Perception of Stiffness in Virtual Environments, Proceedings of the ASME Dynamic Systems and Control Division, Ed. G. Rizzoni, DSC-Vol. 61, pp. 17-22, ASME, 1997.

[10] Srinivasan, M A, Beauregard, G L and Brock, D L, The Impact of Visual Information on Haptic Perception of Stiffness in Virtual Environments, Proceedings of the ASME Dynamic Systems and Control Division, DSC-Vol. 58, pp. 555-559, ASME, 1996.

[11] Wu, W-C, Basdogan, C and Srinivasan, M A, Effect of Visual Perspective on the Visual and Haptic Perception of Size and Stiffness in Virtual Environments, Proceedings of the ASME Dynamic Systems and Control Division, 1999 (in press).

[12] Basdogan, C, Ho, C-H, Srinivasan, M A, Small, S D and Dawson, S L, Force Interactions in Laparoscopic Simulations: Haptic Rendering of Soft Tissues, Proceedings of the Medicine Meets Virtual Reality (MMVR'98) VI Conference, San Diego, CA, pp. 385-391, January, 1998.

[13] De, S and Srinivasan, M A, Thin Walled Models for Haptic and Graphical Rendering of Soft Tissues in Surgical Simulations, Proceedings of Medicine Meets Virtual Reality Conference 7, San Francisco, CA., January, 1999.

[14] Basdogan, C, Ho, C-H and Srinivasan, M A, Simulation of Tissue Cutting and Bleeding for Laparoscopic Surgery Using Auxiliary Surfaces, Proceedings of Medicine Meets Virtual Reality Conference 7, San Francisco, CA., January, 1999.

[15] Ho, C-H, Basdogan, C, Slater, M, Durlach, M, and Srinivasan, M A, The Influence of Haptic Communication on the Sense of Being Together, Workshop on Presence in Shared Virtual Environments, BT Labs, Ipswich, UK, June, 1998.

Matching Technology to People for Telepresence

M. Hollier

BT Labs, Martlesham Heath, Ipswich, UK
Email: mike.hollier@bt.com

Abstract. The first steps towards a multi-media telepresence revolution have already been taken. Ubiquitous network connectivity with variable bandwidth on demand will be available in the near future due to the evolution of Global IP-networks and fixed mobile convergence, e.g. UMTS. In order to efficiently deliver the radical variety of services that will become possible it is necessary to match the delivery technology to the end user's needs. It will be necessary to enable a range of communications tasks with a variety of bandwidths, local processing power, and user requirements. To do so the delivery systems will have to be adaptive and context sensitive. The network, middleware and delivery technology must be optimised using perceptual criteria. These criteria will be in terms of audio/video perception and communications task requirements. Perceptual models are being developed at BT Labs. For multi-media systems we require multi-modal models for which the influence of task is very significant. In order to account for this level of task dependency we are having to develop and evaluate cognitive models. Examples that illustrate the diversity of emerging service propositions and the complexity of the optimisation task they represent include: immersive telepresence environments, desktop video and video-graphic conferencing tools, portable multi-media terminal, and wearables.

An Analysis and a Model of 3D Interaction Methods and Devices for Virtual Reality

Charles Albert Wüthrich

CoGVis/MMC*, Department of Media,
Bauhaus-University Weimar, D-99421 Weimar, Germany.
caw@medien.uni-weimar.de

Abstract. The growing power of computing devices allows the representation of three-dimensional interactive virtual worlds. Interfaces with such a world must profit from our experience in the interaction with the real world. This paper corrects the early taxonomy of interaction devices and actions introduced by Foley for screen based interactive systems by adapting it to real world and to virtual reality systems. Basing on the taxonomy derived, the paper presents a model for a Virtual Reality system based on Systems Theory. The model is capable of including both traditional event-based interaction input devices, as well as continuous input devices. It is strongly device oriented, and allows to model mathematically all currently possible input devices for Virtual Reality. The model has been used for the implementation of a general input device library serving as an abstraction layer to a Virtual Reality system.

1 Introduction

The history of Computer Science has been strongly influenced by the often clumsy interfaces between man and computers. Until the point-and-click mouse-based interface was introduced at Xerox in the mid-seventies [26, 23], computers were regarded as mysterious devices operated by specialized personnel. Now they are ubiquitous in our society, thanks to their easier-to-use interfaces with humans, and their field of application has expanded from performing tedious calculations to tasks more related to our everyday life.

The "power under the hood" of today's computers permits us to interact in real time with three-dimensional computer-generated virtual worlds of growing complexity. However, if Virtual Reality (VR) wants to be accepted and used by laymen, there is the need for a profound rethinking of the way interfaces with three-dimensional worlds are done. Most available interfaces to the 3D world are ad-hoc application-oriented solutions [2, 29], and include only a few general considerations on interfaces. Only recently research has focused more and more on general interfaces for Virtual Reality Environments [20, 17, 24], as well as on models for interaction [7, 6]. In a recent survey paper on 3D interaction

---

* Computer Graphics, Visualization/Man Machine Communication Group

techniques [10], Hand has given a nice overview on the methods used up to now for this task.

Two things need to be done in order to develop generic 3D interaction techniques with Virtual Reality Objects. On one hand, it is important to observe how we interact with the real world, in the attempt of being able to find common factors that allow a reduction in complexity. In other words, a taxonomy has to be developed both for interaction devices and for actions with the world. In parallel, a model of an interactive system has to be found that allows its mathematical description. This includes a model for input devices and for actions based on the taxonomy deduced from observation.

This paper addresses exactly this problem, and, similarly to the early studies on human-computer interaction for computing devices, tries to analyze the type of interfaces and actions that we perform in everyday life. The analysis is strongly based on Foley's seminal work on human-computer interactions, and comes to similar conclusions about our interaction with the real world [8, 9], integrating them with observations on real-world situations as well as from readings of standard literature [21, 22, 15, 3, 19, 13, 4].

The paper then presents a model for an interactive system based on systems theory. Such model describes an interactive system as a 7-tuple. The model presented allows to include not only discrete but also continuous input and state changes. As opposed to broadly used finite state machines, it is therefore capable of representing also interactions where the input is ruled by a continuous function, such as a force varying in time continuously. It is therefore a generalization of current models. Finally, existing computer input devices are fitted into the system input model to prove the applicability of the model proposed and to show its expressive strengths.

2 Interfacing with the real world

The process of learning the possible interactions with the world is in general a lifelong process for a human being. We constantly learn how to use the new objects that we happen to encounter: a new car, a piece of machinery at work, the remote control of our video recorder, or a simple object such as a tennis racket. Previous experience suggests to a human being the first way of interacting with an object: if we see a round knob, we "instinctively" try to turn it around the imaginary axis passing through its center.

However, the number of basic actions, and the number of the atomic operations that we perform with any object are, in general, limited in number and do not require particular manipulation skills. Our environment is "designed" to ease our clumsy interaction with objects, so that we can accomplish easily our everyday tasks. This is why most manipulations with simple and complex objects are similar to each other, and why there is a limited number of possible interactions and manipulations that we usually do. On each object surrounding us, there are always recurring hooks that allow our interactions with the functionality of an object.

Foley classifies non-voice-based computer input hardware in *locators, key-boards, valuators*, and *choice devices*. Locators transmit to the system positional information. A keyboard is an input device delivering to the system a large set of characters. A valuator, such as a radio dial, is a device delivering to the system an absolute value. Choice devices are instead devices delivering to the system a series of values. The function keys of a keyboard are a typical example thereof.

Although this classification is reasonable for traditional computer systems, it is not suitable for the use in Virtual Reality, since for example the use of keyboards is often clumsy in virtual environments. Here a study of interface devices present in the real world is necessary.

In the real world, most of the interfacing devices boil down a handful. The simplest type are *switches*, which are devices capable of delivering one or more states, in any case a finite number of them. Switches can come either in linear or in circular form. Then there are *valuators*, which again come either in linear (sliders) or circular form (volume knobs). *Locators* are far less common in the real world, because usually location is signaled through acoustic, visual and tactile feedback. However, pointing sticks have always found application, for example, in teaching. Many devices are a combination or extension of the above mentioned types: for example an analogue joystick can be regarded as a bidimensional valuating device completed by some switches. Note that both of Foley's keyboard and choice devices can be seen as a combination of switches.

Devices are used to perform basic interaction tasks. For traditional interfaces, Foley classifies basic interaction tasks into *positioning, selection, text string input*, and *quantification*. These basic tasks are composited to perform complex tasks. These categories are restrictive if they have to be applied to the real world or Virtual Reality. and we extend these categories into a wider class.

As in computer interfaces, the number of actions that we perform can be reduced to a finite and well describable number of actions. In our observations, the atomic actions that have always recurred may be reduced to the following:

- *Selecting/Grabbing*: The action of grabbing secures a firm interaction with surrounding objects for comfortable manipulation.
- *Positioning*: Displacing things by rigid movements is the first modification that we are able to apply to the surrounding environment. Note that navigation can be seen as a particular form of positioning, namely reflexive positioning.
- *Deforming*: This action enables us to modify the shape of the surrounding objects to create new tools and, more in general, new objects.

These are the main mechanical interactions that we perform with the surrounding environment. To facilitate interaction, we use some additional cognitive processes to allow us satisfactory manipulation:

- *Controlling*: Clues delivered by the senses and coordination permit us to apply the appropriate forces and actions to the surrounding environment. While we learn basic actions, such as grabbing, we learn how to control these basic actions.

— *Letting objects interact*: In the most advanced actions that we perform with the surrounding world, we let things interact, learn the consequences of these interactions and use them for our purposes. This kind of interaction can be called *tool-based interaction*.

Note that all of these basic actions are performed in a continuous space on a continuous time scale.

Basic actions are then used in different contexts to obtain different outputs and to perform the variety of tasks of our everyday life. In other words, the *action* (i.e. pushing a pedal) is the same, but the *context* (i.e. which pedal we are pushing) is totally different. Only the mutual position of the pedals allows us to distinguish between them.

3 Fundamentals of System Theory

In order to model the interface with a system we refer back to classical cybernetics definitions. This has been recently proposed by M. Syrbe for Computer Science in general [25]; here we propose to start from system input to a Virtual Reality System, and more in general, to an Interactive System. In classical Systems Theory [1, 28, 16, 27, 32, 11, 12, 18] and in its most simple definition, a system is defined as a "black" box upon which a certain action is done that induces a response. In other words, a system receives external inputs and produces some sort of output. This means that in order to describe a system[1], first the sets U of the inputs and Y of outputs have to be chosen.

Once this is done, the time scale in which we want to analyze the system has to be determined. Here two choices are possible: if the inputs and the outputs vary continuously, such as, for example, in an electrically based system such as a transformer, then a continuous time scale has to be taken, since it is important to know the outputs at all positions in the time scale [5]. If, instead, the system evolution can be observed and described reasonably in discrete time slices, then the set of times can be taken as being a discrete subset of the continuous time scale. The choice of the set T of time is therefore fundamental to build an adequate model of a system.

Once inputs, outputs and time are defined, the input function $u : T \longrightarrow U$ which we want to apply to the system has to be specified. In the case of a system with discrete time, all possible sequences built on U can be presented to the system. In the case of continuous systems, instead, the type of the analysis performed depends on the continuity and differentiability of the input functions, and it is therefore useful to specify the set Ω of the admissible input functions.

In order to model the evolution of the system, and in the case of a deterministic system, such as ideally a virtual system should be, a set X of system states has to be defined. In direct relation to the system states, a state transition

---

[1] In the following we will use the same notation as introduced by P. Mussio and G. De Michelis in their lecture notes in Systems Theory given at the University of Milan in 1985.

function $\phi : T \times T \times X \times \Omega \to X$ has to be introduced, which associates to an initial state x_0 at an initial time t_0 and a certain input between t_0 and t_1 a new state x_1 at the instant t_1. At the same time, an exit function $\eta : T \times X \longrightarrow Y$ has to be defined which associates to a state x_1 at at a given time t_1 the output at the same instant. In symbols,

$$x(t_1) = \phi \left(t_1, t_0, x(t_0), u(t)_{[t_0, t_1)} \right)$$

and

$$y(t_1) = \eta(x(t_1)) .$$

The function ϕ must satisfy three conditions.

$$\phi(t_0, t_0, x', u) = x' \qquad \text{consistency}$$
$$\phi(t_2, t_1, \phi(t_1, t_0, x', u), u) = \phi(t_2, t_0, x', u) \qquad \text{congruence}$$
$$\phi(t_1, t_0, x', u) = \phi(t_1, t_0, x', u_1) \text{ if } u(t) = u_1(t) \text{ in } [t_0, t_1] \quad \text{causality}$$

Recapping, for the purpose of interface modeling, an interactive system can be therefore defined as 7-ple $S = <T, U, Y, X, \Omega, \eta, \phi>$, where

- $T \in R$ is the set of times of the system, which can be continuous or discrete,
- U is the set of inputs,
- Y is the set of outputs,
- X is the set of states of the system.
- The set Ω is the set of admissible input functions $u : T \to U$ to the system,
- $\eta : T \times X \to Y$ is the exit function, and
- $\phi : T \times T \times X \times \Omega \to X$ is the state transition function of the system, which associates to a final time, to a initial time, to a state and an input function a new state of the system.

4 Modeling 3D input to a VR System

The main advantage of using this sort of definition instead of commonly used finite state machines for modeling a 3D interactive system is the fact that this definition explicitly includes both continuous and discrete time. This allows not only to model event driven discrete system changes, such as changing a switch state, but also to model a broader class of interactions, requiring feedback and control, which are intrinsically continuous activities.

Let us start from the analysis of the time modeling relevant for such a system: in usual 2D human-computer interfaces, usually inputs are event driven, and, as such, occur at discrete instants t_i in the time scale. However, there are typical interaction activities that are not discrete, such as object dragging in a drawing program. In this case, a continuous time scale would be more adequate for input modeling. However, the computer system samples the actions at discrete (usually uniform) points t_i on the time scale, where $t_i - t_{i-1} = k$, $\forall i \in \mathbf{Z}$. As already mentioned, activities requiring feedback and control, instead, are continuous in real world activities. For example, an artisan modeling clay on a rotating machine in order to shape a vase applies a continuously varying force at continuous positions of space until the desired shape is achieved. Similarly, an artist playing a piano uses different types of finger strokes to obtain different sound modulations. Thus the time scale used for inputs in a generic interactive system can be at the same time a discrete one, a uniform sampling of the time axis and a continuous one. The appropriate time axis is therefore strictly dependent on the kind of input device being currently used and on the input action being performed.

We just affirmed that the type of input is dependent on the interface device. Let us analyze one by one the different input devices available and see what type of input they achieve. Note that in this analysis the stress is set in the input functions achieved, and it therefore includes time as a quantity delivered by the devices.

Switches can deliver to the system a finite number of states at certain points on the continuous time axis: therefore, their input is representable as a pair $d_s = (s, t)$ given by a state $s \in \{s_1, \ldots, s_n\}$ and an instant $t \in \mathbf{R}$.

Valuators are similar devices, except that their state space is a continuous one, i.e. in bijection with the $[0, 1]$ interval on the real axis. We can therefore represent their input as a pair $d_v = (s, t)$, where $s \in S$ and $S \leftrightarrow [0, 1]$, and, again, the instant $t \in \mathbf{R}$.

Locators, such as mice and tracking devices, have the purpose of delivering a position P in the two- or three-dimensional space in time. More complicated locating devices, such as data gloves, deliver the relative positions of the finger joins, i.e. a multidimensional vector in space[2]. Their input can be therefore modeled as a pair $d_l = (P, t)$, where the instant $t \in \mathbf{R}$ and $P \in \mathbf{R}^j$, ($j = 2, 3, \ldots, n$).

In general, an input device delivers therefore always a pair $D = \langle d, t \rangle$, where d is a device dependent quantity and $t \in \mathbf{R}$ is an instant on the time axis. Given an input device, the input delivered by it is therefore a function of time.

The set of the possible inputs to an interactive system depends therefore on the input devices available, and is the Cartesian product of all possible inputs delivered by the various devices. However, the model has to take into account the fact that input devices can also deliver no input to the system at certain times. For example, some switches only communicate to the system changes of their state, and nothing if nothing new happens. This can be modeled by allowing devices to deliver the empty set to the system. Thus, the input set to an interactive system is the set U of the possible t-uples of device deliveries

$$(D_{s,1}, \ldots, D_{s,h}, D_{v,1}, \ldots, D_{v,k}, D_{l,1}, \ldots, D_{l,m}),$$

where $D_{s,j} \in \{d_{ij}, \emptyset\}$, $D_{v,j} \in \{d_{vj}, \emptyset\}$ and $D_{l,j} \in \{d_{lj}, \emptyset\}$ indicate the deliveries of the j-th switch, valuator, and locator devices respectively, and where the delivery of $\emptyset$ by a certain device means that the device is not generating any input.

---

[2] The number of variables delivered by simple data gloves is mostly equal to 14, the number of independent falangae (joins) of the human hand

Note that the system input at a certain time is given by a t-ple of U and a time t on the time axis. It too, therefore, is a function of time determined by external input to the system. Depending on the nature of the input device, such function might be either a continuous function or a discrete one.

Note also that the set Ω of admissible input functions is not of importance in an interactive system, since illegal inputs are filtered out by the input devices due to their physical characteristics. The system input will therefore be given here by U instead of the admissible functions Ω.

5   Fitting actions into this model

The set of system states X, instead, depends on the specific system we are analyzing, and is therefore bound by the concrete example in study. Once system states are outlined, the state transition function $\phi : T \times T \times X \times \Omega \to X$ has to be defined. Actually, it is the function associating a new state to a final and initial time, looking at the current state and at an input. As stated before, the input at a given time is the set of states at the same time of all input devices. The transition from a state to another state is what usually is called an *action* on a system. In more detail, an action on a system is the act of transitioning from one state to another one induced by a series of inputs.

Actions are in general relevant for an object or for groups of them. Objects in a 3D Virtual Reality system are in general geometric entities defined in a three-dimensional coordinate system. As such, their state can be defined through a multitude of parameters: static rigid objects can be described through their 6 degrees of freedom (the position of a specific point and the orientation of the solid's axes with respect to the world coordinate system), moving rigid objects can be described in time through their equations of movement (through the use of quaternions), whereas skeleton objects can be defined by the mutual positions of their rigid components plus the position of the main body, and elastic objects are objects the geometry of which is modifiable through some continuous function of time. A generic object of the system is therefore nothing else but a list of parameters (variables) which can be interactively changed through input, and a selection binary state variable. A similar view has been proposed for Virtual Reality simulation systems in [14]. The set of the system states is thus given by the collection of the variables of the objects of the system.

Among the possible object states, an object (or a group of objects) has to be selected before any interaction can occur with it. *Selection* is an action on the system which changes the state of one or a group of objects to the binary variable "selected", and allows until deselection the interaction which this specific object or group of objects. Each object in the system with which an interaction is possible is selectable.

Once an object is selected, rigid motions and deformation can be applied to it. In rigid motion a sequence of one or more valuator inputs and the triggering of a finish action modify the state of the selected object[3]. From the point of view of input, rigid motion is the consequence of a vector $\mathbf{v}(t) = \{d_{v1}(t), \ldots, d_{vk}(t)\}$ of valuator inputs (in time) terminated by a terminating switch input d_s. It changes the state of the currently selected objects according to the state transition functions. The deliveries of the valuators in general are mapped to the parameters defining the virtual objects, either by directly associating a valuator to one parameter or by using some functional model of the motion [15]. Note that recently developed devices, such as the University of Brown *virtual tricoder* [31, 30], use a 3D locator instead of valuators as an impostor for the object that is being manipulated to simplify the interaction functional model.

Also in *deformation* the input function is, in general, a continuous function which results in the deformation of a selected object. Again, continuous valuator deliveries are mapped to the parameters defining the object geometry, and deformation is the consequence of a mapping of a vector $\mathbf{v}(t) = \{d_{v1}(t), \ldots, d_{vk}(t)\}$ of valuator delivers into modifications of the geometry of an object. Note that here too multidimensional locators can be used instead of valuators to simplify the interaction model. For example, two fingers of a data glove can control the resizing of one object in one direction, delivering the positions of its bounding box parameters.

Note that in general these continuous functions are sampled for system input due to the discrete system tick in a computer-based system. However, due to the continuous nature of the actions, and to the sampling problems present in discretization issues, it is more appropriate to model such actions in the continuous space.

Feedback, instead, is the combination of the input function and of user testing of the system states to modify in a desired way the state of one or more objects. Here, the user actions are directly influenced by system output to perform the desired modifications. The input function $u(t)$ is here therefore also a function of the output function $\phi(t)$. In symbols, in a discrete system allowing feedback, $u(t_0 + h) = f(\phi(t_0))$, whereby the function f is steered by the user.

Here it's important to spend a few words on system output: in a generic physical system, output is the "black box" product. In a Virtual Reality system, instead, since the system only produces output through its output devices, i.e. the system displays (which can be both visual or tactile, depending on the devices which are present on the system), output is in general only geared to provide the user with a feedback.

Last, but not least, consideration has to be given to *tool based interaction*. In this case, one object is used by the user to modify the state of one or more other objects of the system. This can be reconducted to normal interaction with one object from the point of view of input. The difference here is that the influence of input on the system states does not limit itself to the selected object itself, but can change also the state of other non-selected objects of the Virtual Environment. This means that the resulting system state after input is not only

---

[3] Note that navigation can be seen as a rigid motion of the entire world with respect to the observer.

a direct mapping of the input parameters, although it's a direct consequence of it. Instead, input is propagated throughout the system through interactions between the system objects, that is, the resultant of the state transition function depends on input and on the interactions between the Virtual Reality system objects.

The *exit function* η is not relevant in an interactive system, since in general the system runs indefinitely until some sort of exit input is delivered, which sets the system in exit state and terminates execution of the system. After this the system is terminated. This is mainly reflected in practical applications in the main loop of the program, which is usually an infinite loop terminated by a single exit condition.

6   Conclusions and Applications

With the model presented in the former chapters, the foundation has been laid for modeling an interactive deterministic system based on classical System Theory. The model bases on the observation that indeed input for Virtual Reality systems can be categorized in a handful of device and action types. Through this model, the binding to a general mathematical theory is insured, allowing the application of computability considerations and of mathematical results to Virtual Reality systems.

Moreover, the model can be directly implemented for input devices of a Virtual Reality system into an input library which is independent from the device used and which reduces input deliveries to a handful according to the type of device used. This enormously simplifies the writing of software for handling input to a VR system. This idea has been used in the AVToolkit currently in use at the Bauhaus-University for allowing input to such a system. AVToolkit is a hardware abstraction layer which interfaces hardware devices to a VR system, such as tracking devices, space mice, styluses, button boxes, virtual tricoders, even keyboards, and delivers to the system the hardware independent parameters which can be used for the system transition functions.

The abstraction layer of the toolkit saves direct programming of the single device drivers, which are indeed independent from the system being used and are more dependent on the (expensive) hardware available, and shifts the hardware oriented layer in the system to simple conversion functions from device data into the model data. The use of the toolkit therefore frees the programmer from the tedious daily fight with the device hardware manuals.

This model has more far reaching consequences than a "mere" library of input devices. It allows the deterministic analysis of an interactive system and of its state changes due to input. Moreover, it shifts the border between user action and the system to where input hardware devices interfaces to the user. It also constitutes the interaction basis for a new model for global VR systems, such as the VOODIE system described in [14].

Finally, the model presented lays the foundations for the integration of continuous input in interactive systems. This represents a strong generalization of the existing models, since it allows the integration, for example, of input modes which are important in computer-based music, where input dynamics plays an important role.

Of course, this work is only a first step in a new direction. Future work will concentrate in the modeling of VR output and display, so as to integrate user behaviour into the system. This is not easy, since users are in general no deterministic systems and usually interact in a context-sensitive way. Furthermore, a detailed analysis of the system transition functions is required, so as to be able to categorize existing VR systems into a taxonomy that allows an abstraction from the existing application oriented applications. This analysis is needed in order to understand what kind of system a VR system is and what is computable through it. Parts of this additional work are already under investigation and the first results are very promising. Finally, the internal consequences in the system state transitions due to continuous input have to be explored more thoroughly.

Acknowledgments

Thanks are due to the students and the assistants at the [atelier, virtual] Lab of the Bauhaus-University Weimar, in particular Holger Regenbrecht, Martin Kohlhaas and Jan Springer, who were misused as a dialectic testbed for the ideas of this paper. Andreas Mehlich and his diploma provided me with additional food for thought. Jan Springer conceived and implemented the AVToolkit, and Jo Thönes, of the "Franz Liszt" conservatory in Weimar, pointed me out to the use of dynamic input in music. Special thanks are due to Grit Thürmer, Thore Schmidt-Tjarksen, Christoph Lincke and Marko Meister of the CoGVis/MMC group at the Faculty of Media of the Bauhaus-University Weimar for proof-reading the manuscript and for their constructive suggestions.

References

1. W. R. Ashby. *Einfuehrung in die Kybernetik*. Suhrkamp, Frankfurt/Main, 1974.
2. P. Astheimer. Applied virtual reality - IGD's VR development environment and applications. In *Computers and their Applications '96. Proceedings of the International Conference on Computers and their Applications*, pages 107–112, San Francisco, 1996.
3. R. M. Baecker and W. Buxton. *Readings in Human Computer Interaction: A Multidisciplinary Approach*. Morgan Kaufman Publishers, 1987.
4. R. M. Baecker, J. Grudin, W. Buxton, and S. Greenberg. *Human Computer Interaction: Toward the Year 2000*. Morgan Kaufman Publishers, 1995.
5. A. G. Barto. Discrete and continuous models. *International Journal of General Systems*, 4:163–177, 1978.
6. D. Duke, P. Barnard, D. Duce, and J. May. Systematic development of the human interface. In *APSEC'95: Second Asia-Pacific Software Engineering Conference, 1995*. IEEE Society Press, 1995.
7. G. Faconti and D. Duke. Device models. In *DSV-IS'96: Eurographics Workshop on Design, Specification and Verification of Interactive Systems*, pages 73–91. Springer Verlag, Wien, 1996.

8. J. Foley and V. L. Wallace. The art of graphic man-machine conversation. *Proceedings of the IEEE*, 62(4):462–471, 1974.

9. J. D. Foley, V. L. Wallace, and P. Chan. The human factors of computer graphics interaction techniques. *IEEE Computer Graphics & Applications*, 4(11):13–48, Nov. 1984.

10. C. Hand. A survey of 3d interacton techniques. *Computer Graphics Forum*, 16(5):269–282, Dec. 1997.

11. J. E. Hopcroft and J. D. Ullman. *Introduction to Automata Theory, Languages and Computation*. Addison-Wesley, Reading, MA., 1979.

12. R. E. Kalman, P. L. Falb, and M. A. Arbib. *Topics in Mathematical System Theory*. McGraw-Hill, New York, N.Y., 1969.

13. D. Mayhew. *Principles and Guidelines of User Interface Design*. Prentice-Hall, Englewood Cliffs, NJ, 1990.

14. M. Meister, C. Wüthrich, and J. Springer. VOODIE: An object oriented distributed interactive environment. Research Report MSRR-98-002, Faculty of Media, Bauhaus-University Weimar, Weimar, 1998.

15. D. A. Norman. *The Psychology of Everyday Things*. Basic Books (Harper Collins), 1988.

16. L. Padulo and M. A. Arbib. *System Theory*. Saunders, Philadelphia, PA., 1974.

17. S. Rezzonico, Z. Huang, R. Boulic, N. M. Thalmann, and D. Thalmann. Consistent grasping interactions with virtual actors based on the multi-sensor hand model. In M. Göbel, editor, *Virtual Environments '95*, pages 107–118. Springer Verlag, Wien, 1995.

18. G. Ropohl. *Eine Systemtheorie der Technik*. Hanser, Wien, 1974.

19. G. Salvendy, editor. *Handbook of Human Factors*. J. Wiley and Sons, New York, 1987.

20. R. M. Sanso and D. Thalmann. A hand control and automatic grasping system for synthetic actors. *Computer Graphics Forum*, 13(3):C167–C177, 1994.

21. B. Shneiderman. Direct manipulation: A step beyond programming languages. *IEEE Computer*, 16(8):57–69, Aug. 1983.

22. B. Shneiderman. *Designing the User Interface: Strategies for Effective Human-Computer Interaction*. Addison-Wesley, Reading, MA, 1986.

23. D. Smith, C. Irby, R. Kemball, W. Verplank, and E. Harslem. Designing the Star user interface. *Byte*, 7(4):242–282, Apr. 1982.

24. M. Stark, M. Köhler, and P. ZYKLOP. ZYKLOP: Ein System für den gestenbasierten Dialog mit Anwendungsprogrammen. In D. W. Fellner, editor, *MVD'95: Modeling - Virtual Worlds - Distributed Graphics: Beiträge zum Internationalen Workshop MVD '95, 27-28. November 1995, Bad Honnef*, pages 69–82. Infix, 1995.

25. M. Syrbe. Über die Notwendigkeit einer Systemtheorie in der Wissenschaftsdisziplin Informatik. *Informatik Spektrum*, 18:222–227, 1995.

26. C. P. Thacker, E. M. Craig, B. W. Mapson, R. Sproull, and D. R. Boggs. Alto: A personal computer. In D. Siewiorek, G. Bell, and A. M. Newel, editors, *Computer Structures: Readings and Examples*. McGraw-Hill, New York, N.Y., second edition, 1981.

27. V. Turchin. *The Phenomenon of Science*. Columbia University Press, New York, 1977.

28. L. von Bertalanffy. *General System Theory. Foundations, Development, Applications*. George Braziller, New York, 1968.

29. G. Wesche, J. Wind, W. Heiden, F. Hasenbrink, and M. Gbel. Engineering on the responsive workbench. In *Proceedings of the Eighth Eurographics Workshop On*

Visualization in Scientific Computing, pages 41–48. Laboratoire d'Informatique du Littoral, Boulogne-sur-Mer, France, 1997.

30. M. Wlotka. Interacting with virtual reality. In J. Rix, E. Haas, and J. Texeira, editors, *Virtual Prototyping - Virtual Environments and the Product Development Process*. Chapman & Hall, 1995.

31. M. Wlotka and E. Greenfield. The virtual tricoder. Technical Report CS-95-05, Department of Computer Science, Brown University, Providence, RI, 1995.

32. E.-G. Woschni. *Informationstechnik*. VEB Verlag Technik, Berlin, 1974.

Towards Hybrid Interface Specification for Virtual Environments

Mieke Massink[1], David Duke[2], and Shamus Smith[2]

[1] CNR - Ist. CNUCE
Via S. Maria 36
I56126 Pisa - Italy
M.Massink@guest.cnuce.cnr.it

[2] Human-Computer Interaction Group
Department of Computer Science, University of York
Heslington, York YO10 5DD, U.K.
{duke, shamus}@cs.york.ac.uk

Abstract. Many new multi-modal interaction techniques have been proposed for interaction in a virtual world. Often these techniques are of a *hybrid* nature combining continuous interaction, such as gestures and moving video, with discrete interaction, such as pushing buttons to select items. Unfortunately the description of the behavioural aspects of these interaction techniques found in the literature is informal and incomplete. This can make it hard to compare and evaluate their usability. This paper investigates the use of HyNet to give concise and precise specifications of hybrid interaction techniques. HyNet is an extension of high-level Petri Nets developed for specification and verification of hybrid systems, i.e. mathematical models including both continuous and discrete elements.

1 Introduction

New technologies for virtual environments (VEs) have been eagerly embraced by VE users and developers. The process of diffusing this technology into a wider range of products has, in part, been enabled by the development of 'generic' virtual reality (VR) toolkits such as dVise and SuperScape. Unfortunately it is difficult to find reports that detail the *process* used to develop virtual environments. However it would seem reasonable, given the maturity of the technology, to suggest that prototyping and exploratory development play a significant role. Nevertheless, as the technology of virtual environments becomes adopted into mainstream software systems and products, exploratory approaches become rather less attractive.

Also, the increased processing power of computers has paved the way for the development of radically new multi-modal interaction techniques for interaction in virtual environments. The techniques used in these environments include the tracking of human behaviour such as eye gaze, hand and body gestures, facial expression and speech recognition as input techniques and continuous visual, audio or even haptic feedback as output techniques.

We feel that the interface technology and the complexity of interaction are two features of virtual environments that will be particularly problematic for software developers. The INQUISITIVE project [6] is a three year research effort between groups at The University of York and the Rutherford Appleton Laboratory (RAL). The aim of the project is to develop methods and principles that can be used to improve the design of interfaces for virtual environments, in particular by looking at how end-user requirements on the interface can be mapped, through a development process, onto facilities supported by an interaction toolkit.

However, the very nature of virtual environments contributes to the difficulty of describing and modelling interaction. Many VE interaction techniques share the fact that they consist of both continuous components and discrete components of interaction [23, 24]. For example, we may want to explore the virtual world projected around us by means of turning our head. To obtain this, the movement of our head should be rendered continuously in order to produce a realistic presentation of the scene we are looking at. At the same time we may want to select an object by means of pointing and clicking, which implies discrete interaction.

It is clear that for creating a sense of 'reality' for the user the interface has to 'behave' according to the expectations of the user that are founded on their experiences with the real world. The description of the behavioural aspects of a *hybrid interface*, i.e. an interface with both continuous and discrete aspects, is often a rather difficult task. It is common for new interaction techniques to be described in natural language text and/or presented as a video presentation of the techniques use. Although this may give a first impression of the technique, it gives very little support for rigorous analysis of its usability and usefulness, for its comparison with other techniques or for the combination of the technique with other techniques in, for example, different settings. One reason for the difficulty to describe the behavioural aspects of interaction techniques is that many interactions happen simultaneously, some in a continuous manner, others in a discontinuous discrete way.

In the area of concurrency theory, many formalisms have been proposed to deal with the description of behavioural aspects of concurrent systems and, more recently, formalisms are being proposed for the description of mathematical models of systems that consist of both continuous and discrete components, so called *hybrid systems* [1]. It is beyond the scope of this paper to give an overview of all the proposed formalisms to specify hybrid systems, but many of them are extensions of existing formal specification languages and comprise hybrid process algebras [7], hybrid automata [1, 5, 11] and hybrid high-level Petri Nets [28, 27]. All of these languages have a formal semantics. Specifications written in such a language would therefore be amenable to mathematical analysis. This analysis can in some cases be supported by automatic verification such as model checking [2, 19, 4, 10].

A formal model can only be developed when sufficiently detailed information is available. The descriptions of user interface techniques in the VE literature are often insufficient from this point of view. One of the aims of this paper is to investigate whether formalisms for the description of hybrid systems can be used to provide additional documentation of the behavioural aspects of hybrid interfaces. This documentation is not only important when the interface is completely implemented and working, but especially during the design and development of the interface when different design options have to be described and evaluated. That there is a clear need for such formalisms has been demonstrated in [8] that reports on the difficulties that design teams have to document and communicate their ideas during meetings in the early phases of design. Another indication for the need for more clarity and the possibility of rigorous and systematic analysis of a design are the results reported in [12]. In this article industrial software developers report empirical data on errors that get introduced during the various software development phases. One of their findings is that 40 percent of those errors get introduced during the design phase, but only 5 percent of those errors are discovered during that phase. It is well known that the later errors are discovered, the more difficult it is to correct them, leading to significantly higher costs [25].

The use of formalisms and models should however not be seen as an alternative to approaches for the development of interfaces such as rapid prototyping, but rather as a *complementary activity*. This activity allows for the early discovery of particular problems in the interface and helps in selecting the most promising design options that can consequently be used to develop a prototype.

Research on a proper graphical formalism that can assist interface designers during many phases of the design process is one of the topics studied in the European Union TMR project TACIT [26]. Such a formalism should ideally be suitable to express system oriented aspects of the interface as well as user oriented and cognitive aspects.

In this paper we specify a hybrid interaction technique for navigation in a virtual television studio by means of a virtual video camera [3]. The modelling language we use is HyNet [28, 27], a hybrid extension of High-level Petri Nets [9]. HyNet combines three promising concepts for the description of hybrid interfaces; a graphical notation to define discrete and continuous parallel behaviour, the availability of object oriented concepts and a high-level hierarchical description that allows the specification of reasonably complex systems.

Typical questions of interest in hybrid interfaces are:

- Are there states or situations reachable that are a consequence of continuous and discrete events and that should be avoided? For example states in which the user would lose control, or finds a surprising state of the system.
- Properties related to performance issues such as questions of latency, variance in output that interfere with the smooth use of the interface by the user or that distract them from the task that is to be performed.

In this paper we concentrate on questions of the first kind. Questions of the second kind require detailed information on the real-time aspects of an interface.

The specification language we use can express those aspects, but the documentation of the interface described in this paper did not provide details of this kind.

In Section 2 we motivate in more detail the study of what we call *hybrid interfaces*. In Section 3 an informal description is given of the navigation technique. Section 4 gives a summary of the graphical formalism HyNet. Section 5 gives a formal specification of the technique. Section 6 addresses the questions regarding the usability of the interaction technique and Section 7 discusses the use of HyNet as a formalism to model these kind of interfaces. Some conclusions are drawn in Section 8.

2 Hybrid Interfaces

Hybrid interfaces can be defined in analogy to hybrid systems as interfaces that have both continuous and discrete aspects. Many input techniques that are currently in use could be considered as a hybrid interface. For example a joystick to control the view of a scene that gradually changes (continuous change) in combination with pressing buttons to select objects (discrete selection).

In virtual environments, increasingly sophisticated interaction techniques have been proposed with sometimes intricate interaction between continuous and discrete parts. The description of the behaviour of this type of interface is hard to describe in natural language due to the parallelism and dynamicity of such interfaces.

Research into this unknown territory requires careful consideration. In the context of the current projects, we wish to be able to describe what is required, but at a level that is independent of a virtual environment implementation. This will hopefully lead to the development of portable modelling techniques which can then be specified at higher levels of rigour if required.

Informal descriptions of a number of new experimental virtual environment interaction techniques have been given in the context of CHIMP (Chapel Hill Immersive Modelling Program) [13, 16, 15, 14]. These are interaction techniques for navigation and manipulation of objects in an immersive virtual environment, as opposed to through-the-window (desktop) environments. Preliminary work on the specification of a number of interaction techniques based on two-handed interaction have been described in [23].

In this paper we study the specification of a navigation technique based on a through-the-window environment. The navigation technique is used to move a virtual camera through a virtual, three dimensional (3D) space. An informal description of the mouse based navigation technique is given in the next section.

3 Informal description of Mouse Based Flying

Mouse Based Flying is an interaction technique meant for navigation through virtual environments. The technique is based on the mouse as input device and the screen as output device. The technique described in this section is used in commercially available software [3] to operate a virtual flying camera in a 3D scene for planning the production of television programs. The mouse is supposed to have three buttons; the left, middle and right button. The screen is assumed to display a still image of a 3D architectural space in which the user can virtually move around and observe the space as through a virtual camera.

By default Mouse Based Flying is not activated. To activate it the middle mouse button has to be pressed once. At this point, a small square appears at the position on the screen where the cursor was at the time when the middle mouse button was pressed. The flying technique is now activated and when the cursor is moved away from the square, by means of the mouse, the space projected on the screen starts moving with a speed proportional to the distance between the cursor and the square. The square and the cursor are not moving together with the space, but remain on a fixed place on the screen, except that the cursor is reacting to the movements made with the mouse. The movement of the space can be stopped by moving the cursor back into the square, or by clicking the middle mouse button once, which deactivates the interaction technique and leaves the space projected in the state in which it was just before deactivation.

The position of the cursor with respect to the square defines both the velocity with which the scene moves on the screen and the way in which the scene is moved. The screen can be thought of as being divided into four sections by two imaginary lines, one horizontal and one vertical, that cross at the square. By default, the vertical position of the cursor with respect to the horizontal line through the square corresponds to seeing the scene as if one is looking through a camera that is moving forward (if the cursor is above the line) or backward (when it is below the line). In the horizontal direction it is as if one is looking towards the left (when the cursor is at the left of the vertical line) or right (when it is at the right of it).

A combined movement of the camera is obtained when the distance between the cursor and each of the lines is more than zero. To be more precise we should say that the imaginary lines have a width that is equal to the width of the square. The distance between the cursor and a line is actually the distance between the cursor and the nearest border of the line when the cursor is not on the line. When the cursor is on a line, the distance to this line is zero. This allows a user to move the scene in exactly one dimension only. With the other two mouse buttons different functionalities can be chosen. In Table 1 an overview is given of the combinations.

A formal specification of the behavioural aspects of the navigation technique is given in Section 5. The specification language used is summarised in the next section.

4 Hybrid High-Level Petri Nets

Hybrid High-Level Petri Nets (HyNet) is a description technique that integrates three established modelling approaches. The main underlying theory is that of

left mb	right mb	horizontal effect	vertical effect
released	released	look left/right	move forward/backward
pressed	released	look left/right	look up/down
released	pressed	move left/right	move up/down
pressed	pressed	look left/right	look up/down

Table 1. Selection of different navigation options

Petri Nets [18] and in particular its high-level hierarchical version [9]. This theory provides a formalism for the description of system behaviour in which independent processes are active in parallel and perform discrete steps. In order to accommodate the description of continuously evolving processes the formalism has been extended with differential algebraic equations. Object-oriented concepts such as inheritance, polymorphism and dynamic binding have been introduced to provide means for a more compact and clear structuring of the specification of a complex system. The underlying concept of time is that of discrete time, i.e. time evolves in discrete small time units. A detailed description of Hybrid High-Level Petri Nets can be found in [27, 28]. In this section we give a summary of the most important aspects of the language based on [27]. Further details on the formalism will be explained on the fly in Section 5.

Places, transitions and arcs
HyNet provides a graphical specification language. Specifications are directed graphs consisting of places, transitions and arcs. There are two types of transitions and four types of arcs. Their graphical representation is given in Figure 1 and Figure 2. The transitions can be discrete transitions or continuous transitions. The arcs can be divided into two groups; discrete directed arcs and continuous undirected arcs. The three discrete arcs are standard Petri Net arcs, enabling arcs and inhibitor arcs. Enabling arcs and inhibitor arcs can only go from a place to a transition. If the place of an enabling arc has a token then the transition is enabled, if the place of an inhibitor arc has a token then the transition is disabled. Enabling arcs can be recognized graphically by a small open circle on the arc while inhibitor arcs have a small black circle in the place of the arrowhead. There is only one type of continuous arc.

Inscriptions
In HyNet the net elements are labelled by what are called *inscriptions*. Places are labelled by a *place type* and a *place capacity*. The type defines the kind of objects that may reside on a place. These can be elementary objects such as Bool, Char or Token, or a user defined complex class defined in a syntax similar to that of C++. The capacity of a place defines how many objects can be held at the place at any moment.

Arcs are labelled by an *arc weight* and a *variable name*. The weight of continuous and inhibitor arcs is one by default. The weight of standard arcs and enabling arcs is a positive integer that defines how many objects have to reside on the incident place to enable the incident transition. The variable name at the arcs is used as a reference to the objects at the place.

Transitions are labelled by inscriptions that consist of five parts; the *firing capacity*(FC), the *activation condition*(AC), the *firing action*(FA), the *delay time*(DT) and the *firing time*(FT). The firing capacity specifies how often a transition can fire in parallel with itself. The activation condition is a Boolean expression that expresses further requirements to objects enabling a transition. The firing action consists of a sequence of executable statements in the case of discrete transitions and of a set of differential equations in case of continuous transitions. The delay time and firing time give respectively the time that passes between enabling of a transition and its execution and the amount of time that the execution of the transition takes. These two inscriptions can only be given to discrete transitions.

Semantics

For the purpose of this article it is probably most illustrative to explain the semantics of HyNet by means of small examples in the following paragraphs. HyNet specifications change states over time by firing discrete and continuous transitions. Since discrete transitions may take time to fire, the beginning and ending of a firing are considered as separate events. With this in mind, the evolution of a HyNet specification can be summarized as follows:

1. Execute all events belonging to discrete transitions that can be executed at the current time. Time does not proceed in this step.
2. Change the values of objects bound in all enabled continuous transitions until:
   - a discrete event can be performed or
   - a continuous transition becomes enabled or disabled.
   Time will elapse in this step, also in case no continuous transitions are enabled.
3. Continue with step 1.

Whether a transition is enabled and can fire depends on the markings, i.e. the objects residing on places surrounding the transition, the inscriptions of the transition, the places around it and the arcs. We describe the firing conditions of discrete and continuous transitions separately.

Discrete transitions

An example of a discrete transition is given in Figure 1. It shows a small HyNet specification with one discrete transition and four places together with the inscription of the transition. Place $p1$ has a marking of two integer objects; 2 and 5. Place $p1$ can have infinitely many integer objects, as is described in its inscription $[Int, Omega]$. Place $p2$ can have a marking of type $Token$ and can have at most one token at any time. Place $p3$ can have at most one integer and place $p4$ one Boolean object. The text next to the picture gives the inscription of transition t. The arc from place $p1$ to transition t is labelled by $2x$. This means

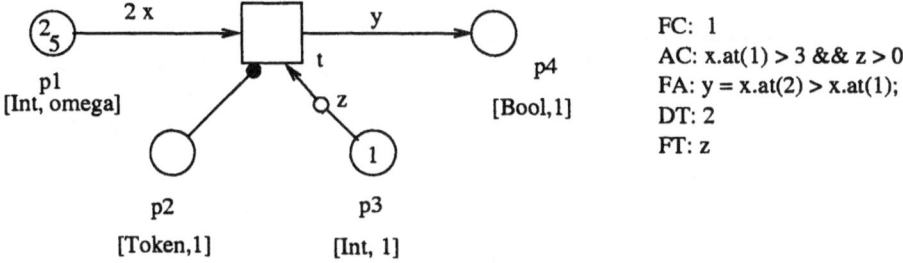

Fig. 1. Example of discrete transition

that two objects, named $x.at(1)$ and $x.at(2)$ can be bound. The arc from place $p2$ is an inhibitor arc, while the arc from place $p3$ is an enabling arc. Arcs from $p1$ and to $p4$ are standard arcs.

In order for a transition to take place, its *precondition* has to be fulfilled. This means that all places connected to inhibitor arcs have to be empty, every variable of an ingoing arc be bound by an object and the activation condition (AC in the transition inscription) has to be fulfilled by the bounded objects. If all this is satisfied, then the transition starts its delay period indicated at DT in the transition inscription. After the delay time has passed completely and without interruption, the transition can be fired as soon as it is enabled. This means that not only does the precondition have to be fulfilled, but the transition must have free firing capacity and that the places that are going to receive objects (the postset of the transition) can receive all the tokens that the transition will produce.

In the example, transition t could be fired with $x.at(1) = 5$, $x.at(2) = 2$ and $z = 1$, resulting in $y = false$ on place $p4$.

If a transition could fire in more than one way at a time there is a conflict situation. These situations are solved non-deterministically.

All objects have a unique identification number and are labelled with a time-stamp of the time of their instantiation. We have omitted this information in the example.

Continuous transitions
Figure 2 shows an example of a continuous transition. Continuous transitions are graphically denoted by a double box. Places can only be connected to it by continuous arcs, enabling and inhibitor arcs. Places that are connected by continuous arcs can only be marked with objects of type Real. A continuous transition is enabled if all places at inhibitor arcs are empty, every variable of an incident arc can be bound to an object and the activation condition (AC) is fulfilled by the bound objects.

The set of differential equations in the firing action (FA) of the transition inscription defines how the objects bound by x and y change in every time tick. In our example, variable x is increased by $0.5 * z$ in every clock tick. Variable y instead, is decreasing by a constant 1.

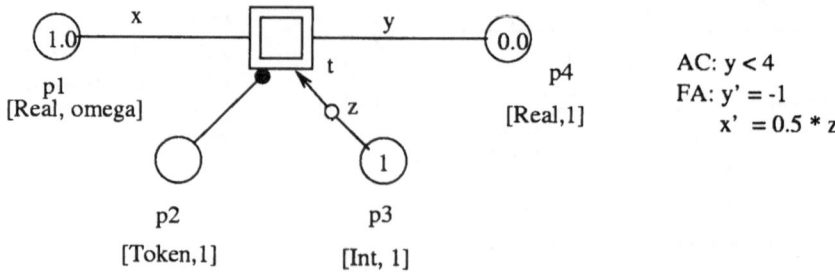

Fig. 2. Example of a continuous transition

Continuous transitions can become disabled in two ways. Firstly, if the activation condition (AC) is no longer fulfilled, or, secondly due to other parallel activity in the net, an object bound by a variable is being consumed by a discrete transition or an object is produced on a place connected via an inhibitor arc.

The activation condition and the firing action are often written directly inside the graphical box that represents a transition.

Conflict handling

In general conflicting transitions are dealt with as follows. Discrete events have precedence over continuous transitions. In the case of continuous transitions that are changing the same object, the new value of that object is the sum of the changes.

Hierarchy

The HyNet language allows the use of transition refinement or macro expansion as a concept for building hierarchical specifications. Details on this concept can be found in [21]. We explain this concept on-the-fly when describing the specification.

5 Formal specification of the navigation technique

For the formal specification of the navigation technique an object oriented approach is followed. Relevant objects in the interface are used to structure the specification. Although HyNet provides a number of concepts to specify real-time behaviour, the informal description of the interface did not provide information about this aspect. Therefore the time aspects have been modelled in a symbolic way and could be seen as parameters of the model. The same approach has been followed for other missing information such as the exact relation between mouse displacement and cursor movement and the size of the square indicating the activation of the interaction technique.

The mouse is operated directly by the user and the displacement of the mouse is translated into displacement of the cursor on the screen. This gives us two other objects; the cursor and the screen. The navigation technique is used to navigate through a virtual 3D scene, that is projected on the screen (2D). This projection depends fully on the view point from which the scene is being observed by the user. It seems therefore useful to also model the scene and the view point as separate objects.

The next step is to establish the relations between the objects. The input for the navigation comes from the mouse that is operated by the user. We model this in an abstract way by the abstract transition 'mouse movement' that regulates the movement of the mouse and the pressing and releasing of the mouse buttons.

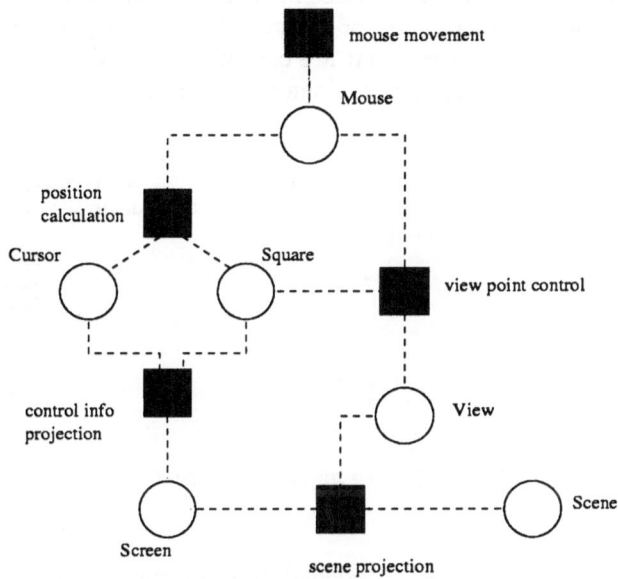

Fig. 3. Abstract HyNet model of the navigation interface

The movement of the mouse has a direct relation with the movement of the cursor on the screen. It also defines where the square is projected on the screen when the middle mouse button is pressed. These two activities have been modelled as the abstract transition 'position calculation' connecting the mouse with the cursor and the square.

The square and the cursor are projected on the screen by means of the abstract transition 'control info projection' modelling the projection. When the square is still visible the change in the view of the scene is fully defined by the displacement of the mouse and the buttons that are pressed or released. This is modelled by the abstract transition 'view point control' connecting the mouse, the square and the view.

Finally, the scene, seen from a certain view point, has to be projected on the screen. This is modelled by the abstract transition 'scene projection' connecting the view, the scene and the screen.

This gives us an initial abstract sketch of the navigation interface presented in Figure 3.

In the following refinements of the abstract transitions more details of the specification are given.

Mouse operation

At the top of the abstract net is the mouse and the abstract transition modelling the operation of the mouse, i.e. its movement and the pressing and releasing of buttons. Figure 4 shows the subnet dealing with the mouse operation. The mouse itself is modelled as an object of the class *Mouse*. Its attributes are the position of the mouse (x and y), the velocity of the mouse in x and y direction modelled as two Real numbers (vx and vy) that are continuously updated, and three bits (l, m and r) that indicate the status of the mouse buttons.

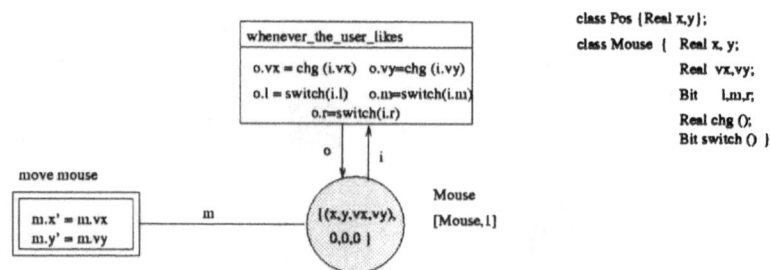

Fig. 4. Mouse movement subnet

The movement of the mouse is modelled by a continuous transition that uses the values for the velocity (i.e. displacement per time unit) of the Mouse object. This continuous transition is not restricted by an activation condition, so the position of the mouse is continuously updated at every clock-tick.

The change of the values for the velocity and the pressing and releasing of buttons is modelled by a discrete transition that a user can activate "whenever_the_user_likes". This condition is left informal in this specification of the interface but it could be refined into a model of user behaviour that one would like to analyse in combination with the specification of the interface.

The method *chg* models the change in velocity and direction of mouse displacement that the user performs in operating the mouse. The method *switch* models the operation of the buttons by the user. This method gives the value that models the position of a button, where 1 stands for the button being pressed and 0 for the button being released.

Position calculation

The displacement of the mouse is in direct relation to the position of the cursor on the screen. Figure 5 shows the subnet for this abstract transition.

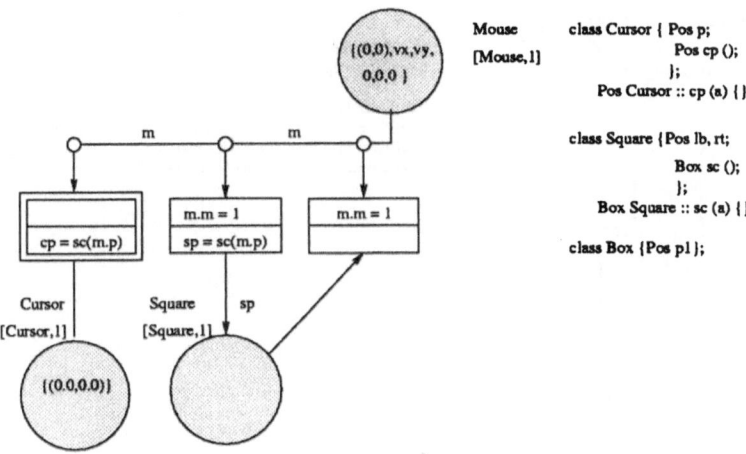

Fig. 5. Position calculation subnet

The cursor is an object of type *Cursor* and has as attribute the position of the cursor (p) on the screen. The method *cp* calculates the cursor position as a function of the mouse displacement.

The position of the mouse also defines the position of the square on the screen that indicates the activation of the navigation technique when the user presses the middle mouse button. The square is an object of type *Square* and has as attributes the position of the square, *lb* and *rt*, which stand for left bottom position and right top position of the square.

When the navigation technique is not activated, no object resides on place *Square*. When the middle mouse button is pressed once, an object of type *Square* is produced as result of a discrete transition. When the middle mouse button is pressed again, the object disappears from the place, indicating that the navigation technique is not activated. Note that at most one object can reside at place *Square* as is indicated by the place inscription.

Control info projection
The cursor and the square, if it is there, have to be made visible on the screen. This is done by means of a continuous transition that projects the two objects on the screen. The subnet is given in Figure 6.

The screen is an object of type *Screen* which is modelled as a 2D coordinate space. The methods *prjcr* and *prjbx* project the cursor and the box on the screen. The method *proj* projects a view of the scene on the 2D screen and is used in the subnet given in Figure 10.

View point control
A more interesting part of the specification is the control of the view point with respect to the 3D scene through which the user is supposed to navigate. Depending on which buttons are pressed by the user, the navigation technique

42

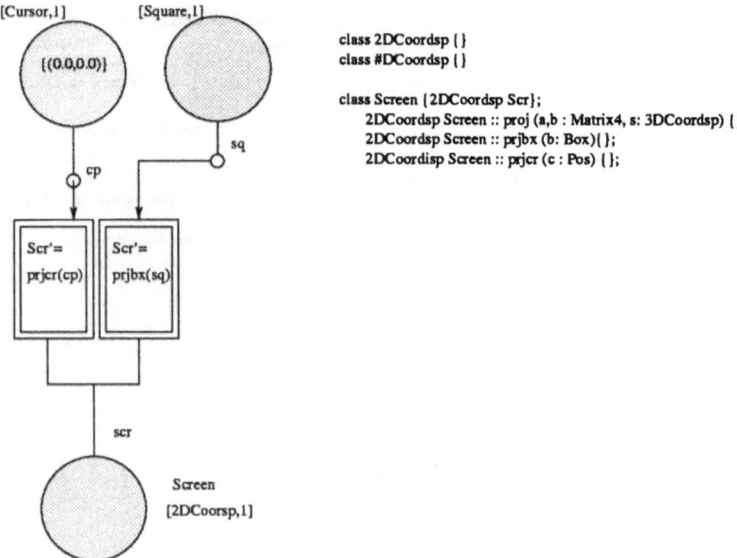

```
class 2DCoordsp { }
class #DCoordsp { }

class Screen {2DCoordsp Scr};
    2DCoordsp Screen :: proj (a,b : Matrix4, s: 3DCoordsp) { }
    2DCoordsp Screen :: prjbx (b: Box){ };
    2DCoordisp Screen :: prjcr (c : Pos) { };
```

Fig. 6. Control info subnet

operates in different modes. The user can only get indirect information on the mode in which the navigation technique is operating by trial and error. The view point control transition is further refined by the abstract subnet given in Figure 7 which introduces a place for an object modelling the mode.

The refinement of the two new abstract transitions are given in the Figure 8 and Figure 9.

The mode is an object of class *Mode* and has as attributes a number of variables. Two variables of type *Real*, *distx* and *disty* contain the distance between the cursor and the square on the screen. This distance is calculated by method *p* and updated continuously whenever the navigation technique is active.

When the user presses the middle mouse button a *Mode* object is created on place *Mode* and the distance is initialised to 0. The initial mode of operation in the horizontal direction is the observation of the scene with a camera that is turning left or right. The vertical direction gives a view equal to moving the camera forward and backward. The mode for the horizontal and vertical directions are changed when the left and or right button of the mouse are toggled.

The increase and decrease of the distance between the cursor and the square (a continuous transition) is calculated directly as a function of the displacement of the mouse per time unit.

Note the difference in the use of the mouse buttons illustrated in Fig. 5 and Fig. 8. The middle mouse button works with a 'clicking' rule: each mode change requires a press-and-release sequence. The left and right mouse buttons work with a 'status' rule: the status, up or down, of the button at any time defines the way of navigation.

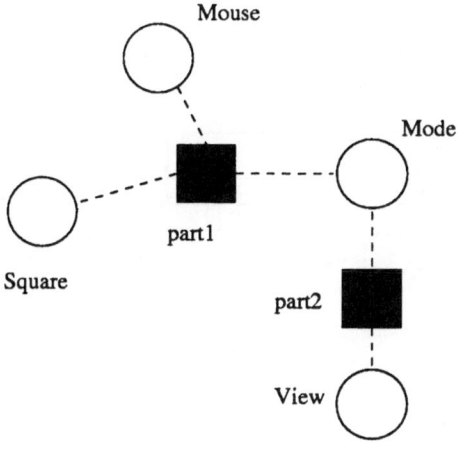

Fig. 7. View point control subnet, abstract

In Figure 9 the updating of the parameters of the view matrix are specified. The activation conditions of the continuous transitions specify at any moment which of the transformations are active. Whenever the navigation technique is enabled, two modes of transformation are active, one corresponding to the functionality in horizontal direction, the other corresponding to that in vertical direction. The amount of change of the view matrix parameters is a function of the value of the distance attribute of the *Mode*.

The object *View* is an object of class *Matrx*4 denoting a 4 × 4 matrix. On this matrix basic transformations are defined as methods, such as rotation in x direction (*rotvwx*), rotation in y-direction (*rotvwy*) and translation of view point in x, y and z direction (*trnsvwx*, *trnsvwy* and *trnsvwz* respectively). Further, there is a function that creates the initial view matrix (*create*).

Scene projection
The final step in the interaction is the projection of the 3D scene onto the 2D screen. For navigation we can assume that the scene is only observed from different view points, but not changed. The scene can therefore be modelled as a 3D coordinate space. Further a projection matrix is necessary that contains the information on the kind of device that the scene is projected on. The projection itself is a continuous transition that is always activated (at least when the navigation technique is active) and continuously updates the *Screen* (see Figure 10).

The user
The specification in this section does not contain an explicit model of user behaviour, but simple models of user behaviour could be investigated by refining the discrete transition in the mouse movement subnet. This refinement could

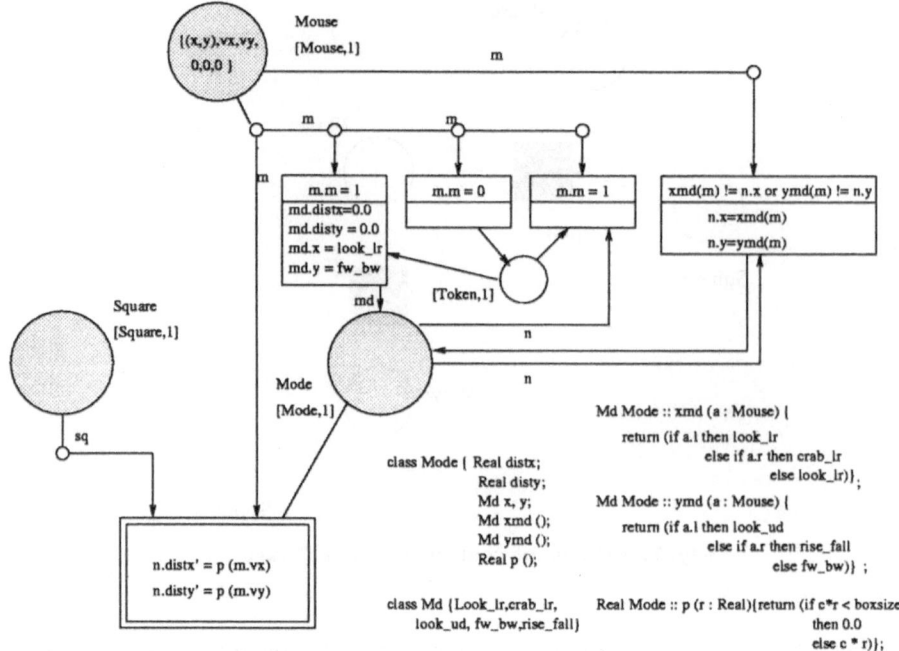

Fig. 8. View point control subnet, part1

make use of what is made visible to the user via the screen by adding for example an enabling transition from the screen to the user. But also without an explicit model of the user we can perform a first analysis of the interaction technique because the kind of inputs and feedback of the technique have been made explicit. In the following section we discuss a number of usability issues based on the formal specification.

6   Reasoning about the formal specification

The formal specification can tell us more about the interface than the informal description of the interaction technique. Although informal descriptions may be appropriate for general descriptions of environments, systematic implementation and analysis of systems require more detailed and better defined specification. In particular, informal descriptions tend to simplify the operation and often do not describe what happens in many somewhat extraordinary situations. For example the explanation of the navigation technique in the manual [3] did not mention the existence of the invisible area of two bands as broad as the square in which the change of the view is only subject to *one* of the selected view transformations, which makes it much easier to navigate strictly in one direction. Further, the description in the manual said that the little square had to be placed in the *middle* of the screen. It turned out that the navigation technique also starts

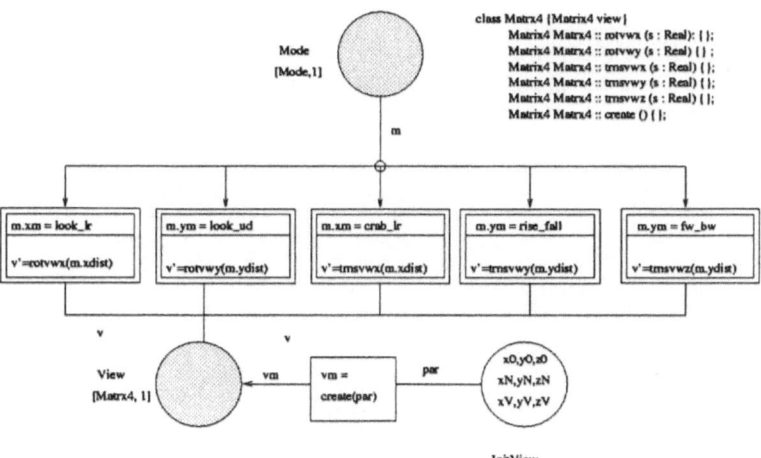

Fig. 9. View point control subnet, part2

with the square at any place on the screen. When the square is placed close to the border of the screen this only reduces the distance that can be created between the cursor and the square in some direction.

Although the description in Section 3 might be a bit more precise on these issues, it is again not complete and precise enough. Try to find out, based on the text, what would happen if a user would first push the left mouse button and after that push the middle mouse button to start the navigation. Maybe one could guess the result, but to what degree of certainty? The formal specification gives an unambiguous answer to this question. This illustrates that this level of specification allows better informed decisions to be made for the application of VE technology to support the particular interaction techniques. Many "what if" questions can be answered in an unambiguous way based on the formal specification, especially cases that represent somewhat unusual patterns of interaction.

Software developers must be concerned with making use of the most appropriate technology in a way that meets the requirements of the client, including quality criteria such as usability, robustness, maintainability, error-tolerance, etc., see for example [25].

In this section we discuss a number of questions related to the usability of the navigation technique. We assume that the technique is used to navigate through an architectural 3D virtual space that is projected on a 2D screen. The list of discussed usability requirements is not meant to be complete. We discuss some variations of common usability requirements of interfaces, see for example [17, 22]. Problems related to mode and mode confusion [20] are also discussed in the context of continuous interaction. The discussion serves the purpose to show that many of these usability questions can be properly and systematically addressed when having a formal, precise specification of a (hybrid) interface.

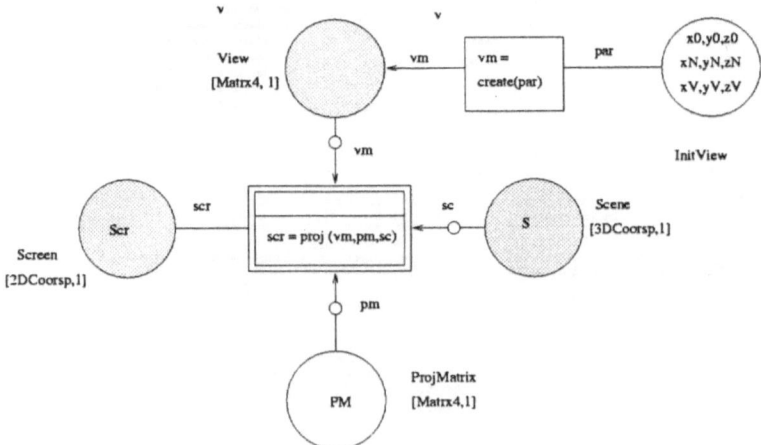

Fig. 10. Scene projection subnet

Active actors
Whether an object in the specification is changed or not and under which conditions can be seen in the specification from the kind of arcs that are connecting the object. The first observation that can be made concerning the interface is that what is visible on the screen is fully determined by the user's interaction via the mouse. This means that the virtual environment that the user is exploring, the scene, does not change by itself. Even stronger, the virtual environment does not change at all, only the point of view from which the user looks at the environment changes.

Type of interaction
The continuous and discrete parts of the interaction are clearly recognizable from the discrete and continuous transitions in the HyNet specification. The kind of interaction that takes place is both of a continuous and discrete nature. The continuous part is the update of the screen to the view point chosen by the user (continuous output) and the movement of the mouse (continuous input). The discrete part is the pressing and releasing of the mouse buttons that switch the navigation techniques into different modes of operation. As we mentioned earlier, the specification shows that the operation of the mouse buttons is not the same for each button. The middle mouse button must be operated using a 'clicking' rule whereas the left and right buttons work in a 'status oriented' way.

Mode changes
One of the problems that may occur in user interfaces are mode changes that escape the attention of the user and that may lead to confusion. We have seen that in this interaction technique the user has full control over the point of view from which he observes the virtual space. However, the only feedback that is given about the mode of operation is the way in which the screen is changing

over time. The difference between the view from a camera that is slowly crabbing left (or right) or one that is slowly turning to the left (or the right) may be noticed only after a while.

More interesting is the change in functionality when the left button is already being pressed by the user. If he also decides to press the right button, no change in functionality occurs. However, if the left button was in released position, pushing the right button would have caused a change in functionality. This exact behaviour can be found in the definition of the methods xmd and ymd in class $Mode$. Although this problem could have been found in other ways and is probably not difficult to solve, it is the detailed systematic specification that draws our attention to these kind of design choices. Unfortunately the language HyNet does not provide automatic support for the analysis of properties of the specification, in which case it would have been much easier to verify a large number of requirements one would like to hold of an interface. Currently, we are modelling parts of an interface as an automata specification and can perform the analysis by automatic verification of a number of temporal logic formulas that formalise important usability requirements.

Possibilities to 'undo' an operation
We have seen that a user may change mode accidentally by pressing a mouse button. This brings to the question whether it would be necessary for a user to 'undo' a certain action and what this implies in a continuous interaction technique like navigation. In principle the user could turn back to a previous point in the virtual space by navigating 'backwards' through the space. However, this is not very easy; the cursor has to be moved to the opposite quadrant and the user has to guess from what he sees in the screen whether he reached a previous position. There are no precise indications about the position of the view point available like for example a set of numeric coordinates.

If an accidental mode change occurred the user has no fast and precise way to return to the point at which the mistake was made.

Even worse, when a mode mistake is made while the distance between the cursor and the square is large, the accidental movement may be quite disrupting and confusing. One possibility is whether it would be more user friendly to automatically move the cursor to the square whenever a mode change is made.

A third possible problem that may occur is if a user got suddenly confused about the place in which he is navigating and would like to go back to a well-known point of reference. This is also not provided by the currently described navigation technique.

Shortcuts
The described navigation technique does not provide any shortcuts in order to navigate fast to certain positions. One could think of a user inserting marking points to which it would be easy to return, or the possibility to record a certain trajectory in order to follow it a second time later on.

What is the cognitive load?
The user certainly has to remember the various modes of operation that are related to combinations of pressed and released mouse buttons. Also the way to leave the interaction technique is not indicated. This can be seen from the information that is projected on the screen (only the control objects *Cursor* and *Square* are provided).

How to exit?
Although the user has to remember by heart how to exit the navigation technique, he can exit at any moment. When leaving the navigation, the user is left exactly at the place where he arrived.

Indication of errors
There doesn't seem to be any specific errors that are reported to the user.

7 Evaluation of HyNet for the specification of hybrid interfaces

The combination of object oriented concepts, concurrency, discrete and continuous transitions, hierarchy and graphical notation makes HyNet quite a powerful language for the description of hybrid interfaces. The object oriented concepts provide means for a structured organisation of a specification and hierarchy provided as transition refinement allows the structuring of rather large specifications. The concurrency concepts are useful to describe the behavioural aspects of the objects involved in the interface, and the graphical presentation may be helpful to discuss specifications in a more interdisciplinary setting.

Unfortunately no computer tool support has yet been developed for the simulation or automatic verification of properties, although there are plans for the development of an interactive interpreter for animation and validation of HyNet models [27]. The availability of these tools would make it much easier to analyse the specification in a formal and systematic way and to compare different options.

The HyNet language, although it is powerful, is also rather complex. The inscriptions of discrete transitions consist of many components and the rule for firing transitions is also rather complex. This is a disadvantage when the specification is used as the basis of an interdisciplinary discussion. The intuitively appealing pictures may describe a much more complicated behaviour than at first sight one would be expected. This, together with the lack of tool support, may make the specifications less accessible to a wide interdisciplinary audience than it could have been.

Currently we are studying the use of automata based specification formalisms that appear to have a simpler semantics and for which verification tools are already available. Automata based formalisms for the description of hybrid systems currently do not provide object oriented concepts or means for structuring specifications in a hierarchical way.

The use of formal modelling techniques for hybrid interfaces is a step towards more accurately defined descriptions of interaction within virtual environments. This provides a way of describing and understanding what particular interaction techniques support, and consequently, how or whether they are appropriate for supporting given tasks in an application. The development of a design process for mapping requirements to the implementation of virtual environments is part of the ongoing work in the current projects. The use of HyNet allows the behaviour of hybrid interfaces to be defined and the interaction to be concisely mapped and can be used to support arguments about human factors issues.

8   Conclusions

Interfaces for virtual environments are highly dynamic and based on a combination of discrete and continuous interaction techniques. This makes them hard to describe in a sufficiently precise way in natural language. However, in order to compare and analyse the usability of the interfaces in an early stage of design more precise specifications are needed. Such specifications can form the basis for rapid prototyping but also for mathematical models of the interface that are amenable to computer aided verification of properties concerning its usability.

The importance of both discrete and continuous aspects of interaction techniques in interfaces means that they can be considered as hybrid systems. The development of suitable formalisms for the specification of hybrid systems has recently become an important area of research.

In this paper we have investigated the use of HyNet for the specification of dynamic aspects of an interface for navigation in a virtual, 3D space. HyNet is a formalism based on High-level Petri Nets and developed within the area of hybrid systems design. It provides a number of concepts that are useful to deal with the complexity of hybrid interfaces. We used transition refinement to split the specification into smaller components. Objects have been defined for the main concepts in the interface and both discrete and continuous transitions have been used to model the behavioural aspect of the interface.

The resulting specification turned out to be very useful to answer specific questions about the functionality of the interface. The different role of the mouse buttons and the way they are used to interact with the system have been made explicit. Further a preliminary analysis of the usability of the interface was performed by checking a number of standard usability requirements such as those related to mode confusion, the possibility to 'undo' an action and the availability of adequate feedback.

Unfortunately there are no software tools yet available that allow for the automatic verification of properties of the specification. The current specification may serve, however, as a basis for the development of other models which are supported by automatic verification tools such as hybrid automata. The construction of such models and the formalisation of usability requirements for the purpose of model checking are some of the important areas of future research.

9 Acknowledgements

This work was supported by the TACIT network under the European Union TMR programme, contract ERB FMRX CT97 0133 and in part by the UK EPSRC INQUISITIVE project, Grant GR/L53199.

References

1. R. Alur, C. Courcoubetis, N. Halbwachs, T. A. Henzinger, P.-H. Ho, X. Nicollin, A. Olivero, J. Sifakis, and S. Yovine. The algorithmic analysis of hybrid systems. *Theoretical Computer Science*, 138:3–34, 1995.
2. E. Clarke and E. Emerson. Synthesis of synchronization skeletons for branching time temporal logics. In *Logic of Programs: Workshop, (Yorktown Heights, NY)*, volume 131 of *Lecture Notes in Computer Science*, pages 52–71. Springer Verlag, 1981.
3. ColtVR. *Virtual Production Planner*. BBC/Colt International, 1997.
4. Z. Har'El and R. Kurshan. Software for analytical development of communications protocols. *AT&T Bell Lab. Tech. J.*, 69(1 (Jan.-Feb.)), 1990.
5. T. A. Henzinger. The theory of hybrid automata. In *Proceedings of the 11th Annual IEEE Symposium on Logic in Computer Science (LICS 96)*, pages 278–292, 1996.
6. INQUISITIVE homepage, 1999.
   http://www.cs.york.ac.uk/~shamus/inquisitive/.
7. H. Jifeng. From csp to hybrid systems. In *A Classical Mind : Essays on Honour of C. A. R. Hoare*, pages 171–189. Prentise Hall, 1994.
8. S. Jones and J. Sapsford. The role of informal representations in early design. In P. Markopoulos and P. Johnson, editors, *Design, Specification and Verification of Interactive Systems*, pages 117–133. Springer, 1998.
9. J. K and G. Rozenberg, editors. *High-level Petri Nets — Theory and Applications*. Springer-Verlag, 1991.
10. R. P. Kurshan. *Computer-Aided Verification of Coordinating Processes*. Princeton University Press, Princeton, NJ, 1994.
11. K. G. Larsen, B. Steffen, and C. Weise. Continuous modeling of real-time and hybrid systems: from concepts to tools. *International Journal on Software Tools and Technology Transfer*, (1):64–85, 1997.
12. P. Liggesmeyer, M. Rothfelder, M. Rettelbach, and T. Ackermann. Qualitätssicherung Software-basierter technischer Systeme – Problembereiche und Lösungsansätze. *Informatic-Spektrum*, (21):249–258, 1998.
13. M. Mine. Virtual environment interaction techniques. Technical Report TR95-018, University of North Carolina, 1995.
14. M. Mine. *Exploiting Proprioception in Virtual Environments Interaction*. PhD thesis, University of North Carolina, 1997.
15. M. Mine. Chimp: Chapel hill immersive modeling program. http://www.cs.unc.edu/~mine, 1998.
16. M. Mine, F. P. Brooks Jr, and C. H. Sequin. Moving objects in space: Exploiting proprioception in virtual-environment interaction. In *Proceedings of SIGGRAPH 97*, pages 19–26, 1997.

17. J. Nielsen. *Usability Engineering*. AP Professional, 1993.
18. C. A. Petri. Kommunikation mit automaten. Schriften des iim nr. 2, Institut für Instrumentelle Mathematic, 1962. English translation: Technical Report RADC-TR-65-377, Griffis Air Base, New York, Vol. 1, Suppl. 1, 1966.
19. J. Queille and J. Sifakis. Specification and verification of of concurrent systems in ceasar. In *Proceedings of Fifth ISP*, 1982.
20. N. B. Sarter and D. D. Woods. How in the world did we ever get into that mode? mode error and awareness in supervisory control. *Human Factors*, 37(1):5–19, 1995.
21. S. Schöf, M. Sonnenschein, and R. Wieting. Efficient simulation of thor nets. In G. D. Michelis and M.Diaz, editors, *Applications and Theory of Petri Nets, 16th International Conference*, volume 935 of *LNCS*, pages 412–431. Springer, 1995.
22. B. Shneiderman. *Designing the User Interface*. Addison-Wesley, 1987.
23. S. Smith and D. Duke. Virtual environments as hybrid systems. In *Proceedings of the Eurographics UK 17th Annual Conference, EG-UK'99*, pages 113–128. Eurographics UK Chapter, 1999. Cambridge, UK.
24. S. Smith, D. Duke, and M. Massink. The hybrid world of virtual environments. In *Accepted for publication at Eurographics '99*, 1999. Milan, Italy.
25. I. Sommerville. *Software Engineering*. Addison-Wesley, fifth edition, 1996.
26. TACIT homepage, 1999.
http://kazan.cnuce.cnr.it/TACIT/.
27. R. Wieting. Hybrid high-level nets. In D. B. J.M. Charnes, D.J. Morrice and J. Swain, editors, *Winter Simulation Conference*, pages 848–855, 1996. Coronado, California.
28. R. Wieting and M. Sonnenschein. Extending high-level petri nets for modeling hybrid systems. In A. Sydow, editor, *Proceedings of the IMACS Symposium on Sytems Analysis and Simulation*, 1995. Berlin, Germany.

Contrasting Models for Visualisation
(Seeing the wood through the trees)

Chris Roast and Jawed Siddiqi

Sheffield Hallam University
Sheffield, S1 1WB, UK
Email: C.R.Roast@shu.ac.uk
Tel: +44 (0)114 253 3763

Abstract. It is widely recognised that design quality is influenced by the perspective adopted by developers. In the case of formal methods such perspectives are frequently offered by identifying and/or developing appropriate models, from which requirements and systems can be expressed and even verified. In addition, to this there is a growing recognition that selecting and employing a model is an activity which is less dependent upon formal adequacy and more dependent upon ease of use. In this paper we examine and assess factors relevant to design quality that are apparent in comparing two alternative modelling approaches. The specific case study used is that of a system for visualising and manipulating a logical tree.

1 Modelling and Specification

When examining the use and adoption of formal specification it is valuable to recognise two forces that appear to influence their use. The first is that formal specification notations normally embody very powerful abstraction facilities which encourage the modelling of a domain and its requirements, this enables specific problems to be treated as specialisations of more generic frameworks. The second is that the representation itself (i.e. the formal specification) becomes a precise account of a unqiue artifact that will satisfy a specific set of requirements. When one considers the specification process of some artifact these two forces (*modelling* and *specifying*) (see [6]) can be in opposition, the cost of developing, or identifying, a valid abstraction may not be seen as directly contributing to the specification of the artifact under consideration. By contrast, if modelling is ignored, then often inappropriate abstractions are adopted and, not suprisingly, the resulting specification can be of poor quality and possibly error-prone. One consequence of this is that *modelling* (i.e. development of generic models), as opposed to *specification*, can be seen as a legitimate activity in itself.

The effective use of abstract models in HCI clearly can benefit development in numerous ways, at its most general level it can characterise highly generic properties such as usability requirements [7, 17, 12]. In contrast to identifying and using generic usability requirements to guide development, a considerable amount of work focused upon providing verifiable architectural models [9, 8]. The work of [6, 10] suggests and illustrates an inter-mediate approach for which specific domain and application oriented models are used, enabling the articulation of focused usability requirements as well as supporting formal development.

The development and effective use of formal methods is a concern evident within the work described above, and within the formal methods community in general. In particular, there is a growing awareness that expressive power and adequacy is only of value if it can be accessed effectively.

Cohen [4] and Wing [19] both identify the absence of pragmatic considerations, such as, guidelines on how formal methods should be used, as major issues for utility. One example of guidelines could be the "ten commandments" drawn from experience by Bowen and Hinchey [2]. However, their commandments relate to activities that would form part and parcel of any good software engineering process model, the identified processes that "thou shall carry out" include: estimate costs, document thoroughly, reuse, etc.. Similar concerns have been raised by Leveson [11] with the proposal for the realistic treatment of formal specifications as central representations within development. Hence, it is argued that formal specifications are managed effectively by employing structures and concepts common to software development. Moreover, surveys of the use of formal methods add further weight to the argument that human factors within formal methods are not adequately considered. For example, [1, 5, 13] concur that the mathematical notations used are not accessible, and are difficult to understand for different individuals in design teams.

2 Method

In this paper we are interested in examining what influence the adoption of a modelling perspective can have upon the activity of specification. Specifically, within user centred system development modelling is widely advocated as a means of ensuring a good understanding of how a system is likely to be used. Moreover, the specification produced is based on a model having a high degree of co-incidence betwen the users' conceptual view of the problem domain requirements and physical behaviour of the artifact or tasks supported by the system specification. Therefore here we wish to examine the inter-relationships between the *problem domain* of the specification and the *tasks* supported by the specification.

We conduct this examination through the analysis of an example specification problem, comparing two alternative approaches to the modelling upon which specifications are based, these differing characterisitics or "mind-sets" are based on two different modelling perspectives characterised as follows:

- An abstract domain centered perspective
- A concrete device centered perspective

In contrast to comparing distinct specification structures, such as those considered by [3], the concern here is with the level of abstraction employed in articulating formal specification. Our central focus of examination is a human factors one relating to the ease or complexity of four specific factors:

- visualisation of the implied output,
- the process of specification construction,
- reasoning about the specification,
- and the specification itself.

3 Case Study

The case study chosen for examining different styles of specification is motivated by a network service directory structure and its visualisation. The service supports the organisation of network resources using a logical tree structure within which each resource can be located and manipulated.

- individual resources are represented by leaf nodes,
- the root node represents the organisation in its entirety, and
- below the root are various organisational unit nodes which themselves can contain further sub-organisational units, or leaves.

The two different specifications of the system considered are based on alternative strategies to modelling termed *abstract*, i.e. domain centered, and *concrete*, i.e. device centered ([16] illustrates a formal evaluation of similar, but less general specification alternatives). In simple terms, the *abstract* strategy reflects a desire to delay commitment to details which are not evident within the problem setting, whereas the *concrete* approach reflects a common strategy of adopting familiar interface styles & strategies.

the abstract strategy In this case the the model is constructed in terms of the stated problem domain elements, that is simply taking a perspective that is driven by the notion of presenting and manipulating a logical tree and therefore making the minimal necessary assumptions to obtain a precise specification. The motivation for minimal commitment is to avoid unwarranted assumptions limiting the space of design alternatives.

the concrete strategy In this case the problem domain is modelled as a 'subclass' of a familiar model structure based upon viewing a concrete visualisation of the logicial tree. This perspective can be thought of as one which is the product of relying upon cartesian space which is familiar to both the designer and the user.

The Problem Context

Specify a system for visualising and maniplauting an arbitrary tree structure as specified below. Manipulation is to be managed by operating on individual tree nodes, the operand of any operation will be the 'current' node.

The specified visualisation should fulfil the following general requirements:

- *Uniqueness:* for any tree the view of it should be uniquely defined.
- *Observability:* it should be possible to observe all parts of any tree.
- *Bounded output:* the amount of information displayed is parameterised to within a specific bound.
- *Cursor view:* at all times the current node should be in view.

The tree structure is given by the following Z, the initial types used are: node identifiers, node-sort identifiers and node-names, given respectively by

$$[ID, Sort, Name]$$

Node types are distinguished by whether or not they are 'container nodes', container nodes *can* have nodes below them (whereas non-container nodes must be leaf nodes). Hence, some node sorts are classed as containers:

$$\begin{array}{|l}
containers : \mathbb{F}\, Sort \\
\hline
containers = \ldots
\end{array}$$

The schema *Directory* defines a tree of unqiue nodes (*ID*'s) each of which is attributed a name and sort. (The details of *Tree* are given in the appendix.) The definition of *Tree* introduces $\_ \searrow \_$ as an 'offspring' relation in the tree. In addition, all parent nodes are of sorts included in the class *containers*. Reflecting the requirement for a current node, the variable *current* : *ID* is required to be present in the tree.

$$\begin{array}{|l}
\_\_ Directory _____ \\
Tree \\
name : ID \nrightarrow Name \\
sort : ID \nrightarrow Sort \\
current : ID \\
\hline
\mathrm{dom}\ sort = \mathrm{dom}\ name = nodes \\
\forall\, i, j, p : ID \bullet \\
\quad ((p \searrow i) \wedge (p \searrow j) \wedge (name(i) = name(j))) \\
\quad \Rightarrow i = j \\
sort(\!|\ parents\ |\!) \subseteq containers \\
current \in nodes
\end{array}$$

With this initial structure, the two approaches to modelling and specifying solutions are described.

3.1   The Concrete Model and Solution

The *concrete visualisation* is structured with the aim of distinguishing the levels
of functional and graphical elements of the directory view. Given the tree, the
visualisation: *Render* maps this onto a representation based upon the Cartesian
plane, in terms of labels, icons and line segments:

[*Label, Icon*]

$Loc == \mathbb{N} \times \mathbb{N}$

Render _____

   Directory

   $map : ID \rightarrowtail Loc$

   $line : Loc \leftrightarrow Loc$

   $label : Loc \twoheadrightarrow Label$

   $icon : Loc \twoheadrightarrow Icon$
   ―――――――――

   . . .

A key element in this approach to specification is the definition of the *map*
function which determines where each node is positioned on the plane. Since
many alternative definitions of *map* would provide adequate visualisations, we
have omitted a specific instance in this discussion. ([14] provides an illustration
of how a definition of *map* could proceed.)

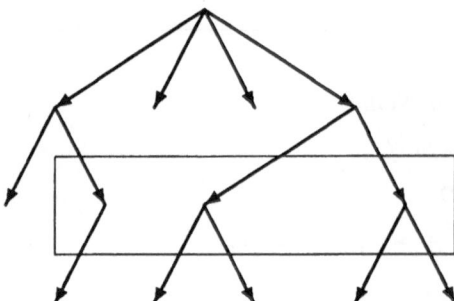

Fig. 1. An illustration of a window on a rendered tree

The last level of the concrete visualisation is given by *Window* which models
the familiar output constraints of limiting the visualisation to a parameterised
rectangle of the rendering. (See figure 1.)

$\boxed{\begin{array}{l} \textit{Window} \underline{\hspace{6cm}} \\ \textit{Render} \\ \textit{displayLine} : Loc \leftrightarrow Loc \\ \textit{displayLabel} : Loc \nrightarrow Label \\ \textit{displayIcon} : Loc \nrightarrow Icon \\ \textit{top, bottom, left, right} : \mathbb{N} \\ \textit{area} : \mathbb{F} \, Loc \\ \underline{\hspace{6cm}} \\ \forall\, x,y : \mathbb{N} \bullet (x,y) \in \textit{area} \Leftrightarrow \\ \quad (x \leq \textit{right}) \wedge (x \geq \textit{left}) \wedge (y \leq \textit{top}) \wedge (y \geq \textit{bottom}) \\ \textit{displayLabel} = \textit{area} \lhd \textit{label} \\ \textit{displayIcon} = \textit{area} \lhd \textit{icon} \\ l \in \textit{displayLine} \Leftrightarrow (\exists\, m : (ID \leftrightarrow ID) \bullet l = \textit{clipped}(m, \textit{area})) \\ \textit{map}(\textit{current}) \in \textit{area} \end{array}}$

Here, *displayLine*, *displayLabel* and *displayIcon* are defined to reflect *line*, *label* and *icon* respectively, restricting the locations and clipping the lines to *area*. In addition, the schema encodes the requirement that the current node should be within the view defined.

This specification is structured in a conventional manner restricting the abstract structure in order to define a visualisation. Reasoning about this style of specification is easy for some purposes but particularly hard when we wish to consider what information about the tree is visible to the user. This complexity arises from having to accurately identify how the lines within the specified view relate to the $\searrow$ relation of the tree.

The Abstract Model and Solution

The alternative model describes a view of the tree based on the same core *Directory*. However, the visualisation in this case is defined on the tree structure, and not on the Cartesian plane. Instead of modelling a rendering, this approach focuses upon identifying the part of the tree that is to be viewed. Numerous abstract views of the tree can be considered, for the example here, we consider the 'part' of the tree to be viewed at any time to be a connected subset of nodes providing a locality within the tree. This view is a sub-tree within the directory that is pruned to give a bound to its complexity. This view makes different demands upon the specifier and since it promotes the explicit consideration of what domain information is shown to users.

The specification of the pruned sub-tree has to fulfil the criteria set out in the problem: **uniqueness, observability, bounded output.** Although the idea of a pruned sub-tree is a relatively straightforward abstraction, specifying it to a degree that satisfies these criteria is complex. The following scheme represents one approach which was motivated by minimising the parameters used to identify any specific view.

The solution chosen assumes that there is a breadth $(2 \times Width)$ which is the maximum number of sibling nodes within a view. The parameters determining a view are nodes *PSRoot* and *PSLimit* which identify the upper and lower limits of a path within the tree.

$$\mid \quad Width : \mathbb{N}$$

$$
\begin{array}{|l}
\hline
\textit{PSTree} \underline{\hspace{6cm}} \\
\textit{Directory} \\
\quad \_ \searrow_v \_ : ID \leftrightarrow ID \\
\quad \textit{PSRoot}, \textit{PSLimit} : ID \\
\hline
(a \searrow_v b) \Leftrightarrow (\exists\, y : ID;\; \textit{left}, \textit{right} : \text{seq}\, ID \bullet \\
\quad (\textit{PSRoot} \searrow^* a \searrow y \searrow^* \textit{PSLimit}) \wedge \\
\quad (a \searrow b) \wedge \\
\quad \textit{tree}(a) = (\textit{left} \frown \langle y \rangle \frown \textit{right}) \wedge \\
\qquad (b = y \vee \\
\qquad b \in \text{ran}((1..\,\textit{Width}) \lhd \textit{right}) \vee \\
\qquad b \in \text{ran}(((1 + \#\textit{left} - \textit{Width})..\#\textit{left}) \lhd \textit{left}))) \\
\textit{current} \in \text{dom}(\searrow_v) \cup \text{ran}(\searrow_v) \\
\hline
\end{array}
$$

For the specified view $\searrow_v$, *PSRoot* is the root of the sub-tree; *PSLimit* is a node below the root which identifies a unique path within the tree and; *Width* defines the number of branches off nodes on the path are included in the view. Specifically, the offspring pair (a, b) appear in the view $(\searrow_v)$ provided: the node a is on the path between *PSRoot* and *PSLimit*; a has the offspring y on the path; and b is a sibling of y which is not further than *Width* from y. (See figure 2.)

Since, *PSRoot* and *PSLimit* represent limits of a path within the tree, different values of *PSRoot* and *PSLimit* are capable of covering the tree, hence ensuring *observability*. In addition, the path length and constant width ensure *bounded output*.

As with the concrete case we have not detailed how pruned sub-tree is to be rendered, however the criteria of *bounded output* ensures that the rendering is not technically infeasible. The complete system would specify the relationship between $\searrow_v$ and some rendering for some output method.

3.2 Operation Examples

Having developed the two alternative views an operation in each is considered — in this case adding a new node. The operation is initially specified for *Directory*

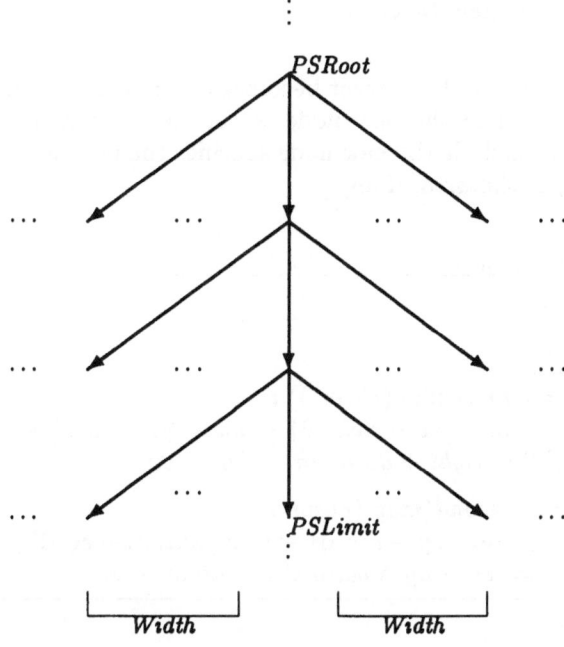

Fig. 2. The abstract view illustrated

and then the necessary updates to the two views are considered. The key influence on the specification of the view update is the that of ensuring that the current node remains in view. Adding a new node involves inputting a new node name (n?), node sort (s?) and *ID* (i?), the node is placed as an offspring of *current*.

$$
\begin{array}{|l}
\hline
\underline{\text{\textit{ADDMain}}} \\
\Delta \textit{Directory} \\
n? : \textit{Name} \\
s? : \textit{Sort} \\
i? : \textit{ID} \\
\hline
\forall j : \textit{ID} \bullet (\textit{current} \searrow j) \Rightarrow (\textit{name}(j) \neq n?) \\
\textit{sort}(\textit{current}) \in \textit{containers} \\
\textit{tree}' = \textit{tree} \oplus \{\textit{current} \mapsto \textit{insert}(\textit{tree}(\textit{current}), i?)\} \\
\textit{name}' = \textit{name} \oplus \{i? \mapsto n?\} \\
\textit{sort}' = \textit{sort} \oplus \{i? \mapsto s?\} \\
\textit{current}' = i? \\
\hline
\end{array}
$$

ADD for the concrete view

When adding a node the current becomes the new node, the concrete view need only be moved when the new node is outside the window *area*. To move the window *area* to include the new node specifies the necessary horizontal shift and vertical shift, of the *area*, if any.

_ADDWindow_____
ADDMain

Δ Window

---

let $cx == first(map'(cusor'))$ •
let $dx == max\{cx - right, 0\} - max\{left - cx, 0\}$ •
$\quad right' = right + dx \wedge left' = left + dx$

let $cy == second(map'(cusor'))$ •
let $dy == max\{cy - top, 0\} - max\{bottom - cy, 0\}$ •
$\quad top' = top + dy \wedge bottom' = bottom + dy$

This ensures that the *current* node stays in view, shifting the area to include any addition which takes the current node right or left of the area, and above or below the area.

ADD for the abstract view

For the abstract visualisation the view update for when the new nodes goes out of view has to be expressed in terms of the pruned sub-tree and involves less familiar considerations than the concrete case. In particular the nature of the update has to accommodate three conditions:

- When the new current position is in view, the view parameters (*PSLimit* and *PSRoot*) stay the same.
- When the new current position is not in the view and is an offspring of *PSLimit*, then the path viewed is shifted down the directory tree so the new current node comes into view.
- Finally, when the new current position is not in the view and it is not an offspring of *PSLimit*, then the path is moved laterally to lead to the new current node.

The first of the above cases is 'obvious', the two others offer the simplest approach to ensuring that the new current node comes into view, in both of these cases the new current node is the new view limit.

```
┌─ ADDPSTree ──────────────────────────────────────────────
│ ADDMain
│
│ ΔPSTree
├────────────────────────────────────────────────────────
│ if (PSRoot↘'*x ↘'y↘'* PSLimit) ∧
│     tree(x) = (left ⌢ ⟨y⟩ ⌢ right) ∧
│         (current' = y ∨
│         current' ∈ ran((1..Width) ◁ right) ∨
│         current' ∈ ran(((1 + #left − Width)..#left) ◁ left))
│     then
│         (PSLimit = PSLimit' ∧ PSRoot = PSRoot')
│ else if (PSLimit ↘' current')
│     then
│         (PSRoot ↘' PSRoot' ∧ PSRoot'↘'* PSLimit' ∧
│         PSLimit' = current')
│ else (PSRoot = PSRoot' ∧ PSLimit' = current')
└────────────────────────────────────────────────────────
```

The first condition covers the case when the view paramters do not need updating. The second case concerns when the new node is out of view and is positioned below the end of the old path, the root is moved to its offspring on the path and the limit is moved to the new node. In the final case the root stays the same but the limit is made the new node, thus the path viewed is shifted laterally.

4 Discussion

The specification approaches illustrated in this paper are intended to be illustrative of alternative approaches to development. The case studies focus on the highly pertinent problem of considering the interplay between the requirements of the problem domain and the tasks supported by the system. Specifically, the focus of the illustrations has been that of tree visualisation and operations on trees. From the case study, we can compare how the domain requirement of adding a node to a tree is articulated in terms of the two models and the contrasting features of the approaches. The comparison focuses on the human factors issue of complexity of the following: visualising the display, the process of specification construction, the process of reasoning about the specification, and the specification itself.

In the concrete case, the visualisation operation can only be expressed purely in terms of the display as specified by *Rendering* and *Window*. Hence, the updated view necessary corresponding to the addition of a node has to be expressed as an update to the rectangle *area* that is shown. In doing so, there is minimal association with the problem domain requirements, in fact the only domain association in the updated view is that the general requirement *cursorview* (i.e. the current node is in view at all times) is satisfied. Hence, an implementation in which the window area were always shifted so that only the new node is in

62

view would be satisfactory in this concrete framework. Additional constraints characterising perferred properties of the function *map*, which determines where each node is positioned on the plane, would be required to reason any more about the domain characteristics of the display.

By constrast the abstract approach to adding a new node involved expressing operations in terms of the domain, as opposed to an intermediate alternative representation. As a consequence, the definition of how the view may be updated is in terms of the pruned sub-tree and thus, questions regarding requirements about what structures are in view can be expressed and reasoned about. The abstract model thus benefits our understanding of how the visualisation can support problem domain requirements. For example, for any operation (including adding a node) the abstract model will enable the resulting view to be specified in problem domain terms. For instance, the abstract approach enables us to articulate questions about requirements regarding whether the new offspring relation were visible following adding a node:

$$ADDPSTree \vdash (current \searrow_v current')$$

The same question regarding such a requirement simply cannot be expressed in the concrete case.

Furthermore, the fact that the concrete approach to defining a view is based less on the domain is evident from the fact, we can construct concrete displays which are uninformative about the domain features. For example, windows depicted in figure 3 show views that hide the node inter-relationships, such views in the abstract model are impossible. Hence we can speculate as to the more formal relations between two the visualisations which may be indicative of their distinct natures:

- For any specific tree, the number of possible *Window* views is greater than or equal to the number of possible *PSTree* views.
- Treating the visualisation in terms of arcs and nodes, *PSTree* is always 'complete' in the sense that every arc has end nodes. The same cannot be said of *Window*.
- Treating the visualisation in terms of arcs and nodes, *PSTree* is always 'fully connected' in the sense that for every pair of nodes their is a series of arcs connecting them. The same cannot be said of *Window*.

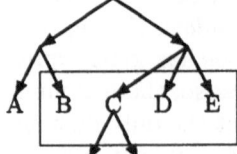 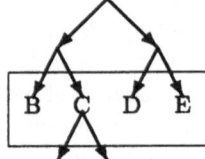 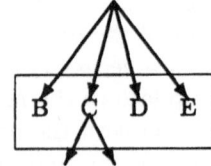

Fig. 3. Ambiguity of structure for a concrete view

In relation to the process of specification construction we make two observations. First, the context in which visualisation was specificied was sufficiently concrete to be easily related to familiar GUI styles and behaviours. Hence, the question as how to update the view was not problematic, familiarity with GUI's and window managers suggested a straightforward approach to the construction of an operation to update the view. Second, the available functions and operations on integer and natural numbers enabled a concise form of expression to be achieved. No specific auxillary functions or abstractions were required to articulate the solution. Therefore it can be observed that the specification construction process was relatively straightforward.

Despite the benefits of the domain oriented perspective illustrated, it has its own difficulties. First, delaying commitment and maintaining the abstract view results in specification which does not have the characteristics of familiar user interfaces, as a consequence decisions made regarding the view update are speculative. The three conditions defining the update are thought to be reasonable, but there is no informal reference model to support this judgement. Second, in contrast with the concrete view, the abstract updated view is considerably more complex to articulate. It is possible that the 'right abstraction' may ease expression and representation, but there is limited support for this from the available specification mechanisms.

Taking our observations regarding the two modelling approaches we can consider their general merits and limitations.

The development of a valid specification is of obvious importance to system development. In the case of two approaches considered, we can ask to what extent they support reasoning about requirements and tasks so as to support validation. In the concrete case, the specification of view and its update immediately divorces itself from the problem domain of the directory tree. Hence, the reasoning possible within the concrete model cannot be related to user requirements within the domain. The user requirements which the specification does suggest are those of navigating the Cartesian plane with limited regard for what is represented on it. This is not to say that the concrete perspective makes the consideration of domain tasks impossible, but domain oriented tasks are not made available by the model. In the abstract approach, the view developed does not involve an alternative representation to that of the domain — the pruned sub-tree is itself a tree in which $\searrow_v \subseteq \searrow$. This ensures that reasoning about the view provided relates directly back to the directory tree domain. As a consequence, deliberations about specific details of the abstract view relate directly to requirements and tasking concerning the domain. Thus, the abstract approach can be seen to offer stronger support for validation because of its higher level of co-incidince with the domain.

Although the abstract modelling approach has close cohesion with the domain of requirements and user tasks, it also promotes a highly specific view of the domain, in our example, emphasising pruned sub-trees within the directory tree. The approach focuses upon tasks expressed in terms of the tree, hence, it can be envisaged that view navigation tasks suggested by the model would involve the manipluation of the path delimited by *PSRoot* and *PSLimit*. The resulting approach to view navigation can be seen as overly prescriptive in nature, especially when compared with that of the concrete approach. Similar speculation about the concrete approach suggests that view navigation would employ the generic GUI techniques of scrolling on a two-dimensional plane. In this case, the approach to navigation is far more descriptive, allowing users to "roam freely".

Comparing the complexity two specifications for the *ADDNode* operation we can see that the one based on the concrete view *ADDWindow* is the simpler of the two because the constituent elements (Caretsian integer co-ordinates and the respective arithmetic operations) are simpler than the elements in the *ADDPSTree* because all the elements and subsequent operators are in terms of representation of the tree in modelling notation.

In the current context what is meant by user centred, since the designer is producing the software for some intended user, which of the two models would be considered more user-centred? One may argue that the directory tree rendered in a two dimensional Cartesian plane as a series of horizontal and vertical lines is what most devices use to display directories and therefore it is user-centred, however this would be akin to arguing that a QWERTY keyboard is user-centred. Strictly speaking, such a perspective is more accurately described as device centred in that the designer has incorporated within the specification certain aspects of the device. One might also argue the converse that is that the abstract model is more user-centred in that no decision have been made as to its rendering and on determining what rendering is user-centred then one can adapt the design to meet the requirements. However, a more accurate characterisation of the abstract model would be to describe it as designer centred, because it meets the needs of the designer in not fixing the representation until it is known what rendering is user-centred [18].

There is clearly a subtle interplay between the concerns that the two approaches provoke. Within the context of a specific design we can see that these issues are posing questions about a broader context of use, such as the extent to which users will engage in identified domain tasks as opposed to a broad range of activities and possibly emergent tasks. (In the former case the abstract approach is likely to be more applicable.) This suggests that the effective use of formal modelling and specification within interface development is dependent upon a thorough and valid understanding of context. The issues raised also support the view that modelling is highly influential upon the nature of solutions developed, and that the notations employed cannot be used in a 'value free' manner. In general, we conclude that the use of formal notations is reliant upon an understanding of factors examined in this paper and the identification of contextual information that would help prioritise them for specific cases.

A   Trees

The tree is represented by a mapping from nodes to sequences of nodes, the intention being that the sequence a node maps to is all the immediate offspring of that node.

```
┌─ Tree ────────────────────────────────────────────────
│  tree : ID ⇸ seq ID
│
│  nodes, parents, children, leaves : 𝔽 ID
│
│  root : ID
│
│  _ ↘ _ : (ID ↔ ID)
├────────────────────────────────────────────────────────
│  ↘ = {x, y : ID | y ∈ ran tree(x)}
│
│  (id_{[ID]} ∩ ↘⁺) = emptyset
│
│  parents = dom ↘
│
│  children = ran ↘
│
│  nodes = (dom ↘) ∪ (ran ↘)
│
│  leaves = (ran ↘) \ (dom ↘)
│
│  {root} = (dom ↘) \ (ran ↘)
└────────────────────────────────────────────────────────
```

In summary, parents within a tree are all those nodes which map to something and children are all those mapped onto. The leaves of a tree are those children which are not parents, and the converse identifies the trees root. An offspring (↘) of a specific node is defined as an element of the set that node maps to. Finally, a path within a tree is any sequence of nodes where adjacent pairs in the sequence are parent child pair.

References

1. S. Austin and G I Parkin. Formal methods: a survey. Technical report, 1993. National Physical Laboratory, UK.
2. Jonathan P. Bowen and M. Hinchey. Ten commandments of formal methods. *IEEE Computer*, April 1995.
3. C. Britton, S. Jones, and W. Lam. Separating the system interface from its internal state: an alternate structure for Z specifications. In Siddiqi [15], pages 87 – 102. ISBN 0 86339 7948.
4. B. Cohen. A rejustification of the need for formal notations. *IEE Software Engineering Journal*, 1989.
5. D. Craigen, S. Gerhart, and T. Ralston. An international survey of industrial application of formal methods. Technical report, 1993. NISTGCR 93 626.
6. A. M. Dearden and M. D. Harrison. Abstract models for HCI. *The International Journal of Human-Computer Studies*, (46):151–177, 1997.
7. A. J. Dix. *Formal Methods for Interactive Systems*. Academic Press, 1991.
8. D. Duke, G. Faconti, M. Harrison, and Paterno F. Unifying views of interactors. In *Advanced Visual Interfaces '94*, pages 143–152. ACM Press, 1994.
9. D. J. Duke and M. D. Harrison. Mapping user requirements to implementations. *Software Engineering Jounal*, 10(1):13–20, 1995.

66

10. P. Kotze. A generic modeling framework for interactive authoring support environments. In Siddiqi [15], pages 14 – 31. ISBN 0 86339 7948.
11. N. G. Leveson. Intent specification: An approach to building human-centered specification. In *ICRE'98*, pages 204–213. 1998.
12. P. Markopoulos. Comparing non deterministic models of tasks and devices. In Siddiqi [15], pages 70 – 85. ISBN 0 86339 7948.
13. A. F. Monk, M. B. Curry, and P. C. Wright. Why industry doesn't use the wonderful notations we researchers have given them to reason about their design. In D. J. Gilmore, R.L. Winder, and F. Detienne, editors, *User-centred requirements for software engineering*, pages 185–188. Springer-Verlag, 1994.
14. C. R. Roast and J. I. Siddiqi. Using the template model to analyse directory visualisation. *Interacting with Computers*, 9(2):155–172, 1997.
15. J. I. Siddiqi, editor. *BCS-FACS Workshop on Formal Aspects of the Human Computer Interface, Sheffield Hallam University, 1998*. SHU Press, 1998. ISBN 0 86339 7948.
16. J. I. Siddiqi and C. R. Roast. Formally assessing visual and textual notations for supporting program modification. Technical report, Sheffield Hallam University, 1998.
17. B. Sufrin and J. He. Specification, refinement and analysis of interactive processes. In M. D. Harrison and H. W. Thimbleby, editors, *Formal Methods in Human Computer Interaction*, pages 153–200. Cambridge University Press, 1990.
18. H. W. Thimbleby. Delaying commitment. Technical Report YCS 90, University of York, Computer Science Dept., 1987.
19. J.M. Wing. A specifier's introduction to formal methods. *IEEE Computer*, pages 8–22, 1990.

This article was processed using the LaTeX macro package with LLNCS style

Towards User Interfaces Prototyping from Algebraic Specification

M. Cabrera; J.C. Torres; M. Gea

Dpto. Lenguajes y Sistemas Informáticos. University of Granada

E.T.S.I. Informática. Av. Andalucía, 38. 18071. Granada. Spain.

mcabrera@goliat.ugr.es; jctorres@goliat.ugr.es; mgea@goliat.ugr.es

Abstract: This paper describes the use of an algebraic specification language GRALPLA [1,2,3], to specify User Interface. In order to obtain a description at a high level of abstraction, the specification language has been enriched with such concepts as Interactive Objects, and user actions. A description of a prototyping tool based on this language has been given.

1 Introduction

Software engineering using a variety of techniques and tools helps us to develop most systems. These tools support the complete process, from specification to maintenance. However, when we have to develop the connection of this software with the user (the interface), only a few techniques sustain this development.

Because a growing demand for access to computers exits, it is necessary to create human-computer interfaces that provide a better, easier, and quicker access mechanisms (WIMP, multimodal and 3D Interfaces). User Interfaces have become more complex and consequently its development process has also become more important.

In this task, interactive tools allow us to define the look and feel of the interface based on toolkits such as Motif or Open Look [TM]. These tools generate the User Interface code and the designer has to make the connection with the non-interactive part of the application.

We can specify the User Interface and the rest of the application using the best specification technique for each part, and create a prototype linking these parts. However, using this method of specification different techniques and languages are used to specify both parts where no relationship exists between them. Thus, it is difficult to check the properties of the whole application.

There are several tools to specify User Interfaces. Most of them are model-based, and only some generate prototypes from specifications. Examples of these tools are:

- UIDE [4] uses parameters, pre-conditions and post-conditions to specify the application model. An extension of UIDE [5] provides an interface model that specifies the operational constraints of the tasks specified in the application model. It can be used to support the end-user (e.g. automatic generation of context-sensitive text). UIDE uses its own notation and runtime system.

- HUMANOID [6,7] provides a declarative modelling language that consists of five semi-independent parts: the application semantic, the presentation, the behaviour, the dialogue sequencing and the action side effects. HUMANOID uses its own notation and runtime system like UIDE.

- TRIDENT [8,9] uses an Activity Chaining Graph to specify the task model and an entity-relationship diagram to represent the application model. TRIDENT uses its own notation and generates a textual description of the User Interface that can be used as an UIMS entry.

- ADEPT [10] incorporates tasks and user modelling components with a rapid prototyping User Interface design tool. The task modeller provides a graphic environment to construct and edit task models described in terms of Task Knowledge Structures. The output of this component is used to feed the Abstract Interface Model to generate a high-level specification of the interaction, expressed in terms of the dialogue structure and abstract interaction objects. A generator tool creates a default Concrete Interface Model (CIM) that can be edited by the designer. The CIM can be translated into a platform dependent implementation based on a standard set of widget as Open Look [TM].

- JANUS [11] uses the JANUS Definition Language as input format, generated from object-oriented analysis tools or from plain text. The output of the JANUS system is a file matching the internal data structure of existing UIMS. The full functionality of the UIMS can therefore be used.

- TADEUS [12,13] is a task-oriented and user-centred methodology to develop User Interfaces. TADEUS bases the generation of specifications on Dialogue graphs, a most general form of the Petri Net. The output of this approach is a prototype that can be used as input of an existing UIMS.

- FUSE [14] system consists of three components BOSS, FLUID, and PLUG-IN. These tools can be used independently. In FUSE-system, the specification of the user and task models is the input of the FLUID system. FLUID output is a formal specification of the logical User Interface. BOSS takes this specification and generates the prototype of the User Interface. PLUG-IN produces the on-line documentation of the interface. BOSS employs a specification technique called HIT (Hierarchic Interaction graph Templates).

- TLIM [15,16] is a method for the design, specification and verification of interactive systems. TLIM uses a diagrammatic notation (an extending set of LOTOS operators); a task specification to drive the design and implementation of interactive applications; the interactor concept as an abstract model; and the use of model checking techniques to reach conclusions about the properties of the specification.

- MECANO [17,18] system defines a generic Interface Model (MIM) that is described using MIMIC, an object-oriented modelling language, based on C++. MIMIC can describes the user, user-task, domain, presentation, dialog and design models. In a second phase, MECANO uses a software environment MOBI-D, which supports the design, implementation and execution of a user interface, based on MIM. MOBI-D is an open architecture composed by U-Tel, TIMM, MOBILE and Models Editors.

These tools have several common features:

- They use an explicit model to represent the application domain. The model is described using a notation at a high level of abstraction using formalism based on declarative semantic.
- In model-based tools, the user tasks are translated to the model. There must be a closer relationship between tasks and the selected model.
- There are tools for automating prototyping as runtime environments or code generations.

Our approach differs from this model architecture because we focuses in the use of property-oriented specification based on algebraic specification. The advantages of such approach can be summarised as follows:

- It allows us to describe the interface (interactive objects) at a high level of abstraction without entering on low level details, or fixing an explicit representation.
- In this framework, formal properties of interactive system can be studied and verified [19].
- We have developed a specification language GRALPLA and translation tools for automatic code generation.

The objective of the work is the study of the whole system with the same formalism, integrating the specification language with interactive layout design tools.

In this paper, we define the structure of a property-oriented tool based on algebraic specification. The use of mathematical formal models in the development process can help us in the design of the system, obtaining a better communication and organisation of ideas, and a more rigorous reasoning about the properties of the system. However, we must keep in mind that it is difficult to define the quality of a User Interface, because there is no global quantitative measure to use in this context.

We propose the use of an algebraic specification language, GRALPLA, to specify the complete application. The specification is based on a new kind of element included in the language, Interactive Object, which is an abstraction of a User Interface component. The prototyping tool designed for GRALPLA has been extended in order to generate a prototype for the interactive part of the application in a widely used language (Tcl/Tk or Java).

2   Interactive Objects

The functional structure of the application is completely based on algebraic specification. However, the interactive elements must be distinguishable from the rest of the application, because they have special characteristics that need to be specified without ambiguity. It should be possible for the user to handle these elements which should also be represented graphically. Thus, it is necessary to include a new class of object in our algebraic language: *Interactive Object*.

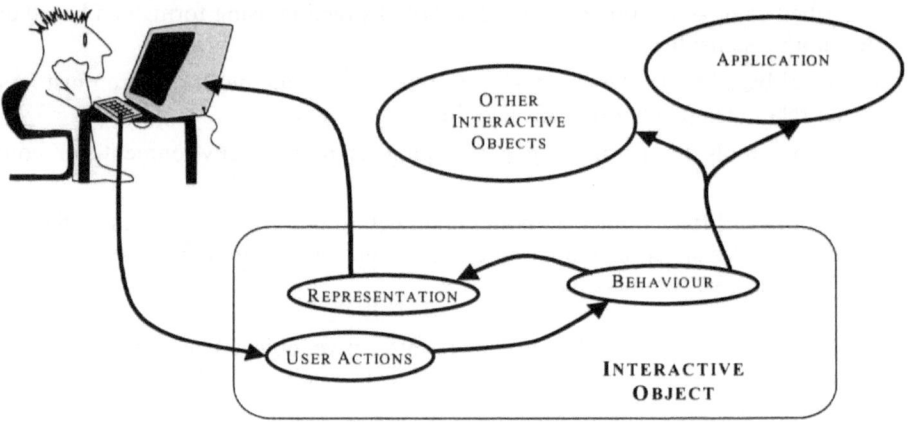

Figure 1. Interactive Object

Interactive Objects (Figure 1) represent components of the user interface. They have some special attributes: a representation, a mean to be manipulated by the user and a connection with the internal part of the application.

The representation expresses the structure of the Interactive Object and determines its visualisation, allowing us build complex Interactive Objects through the composition of simpler ones. The representation of an Interactive Object is an aggregate of predefined Interactive Objects. It also describes the graphic appearance of the object. Note that no layout, or low-level detail of the representation, is given. This information will be described interactively using a layout design tool at a later stage.

Other new elements are user actions. *User actions* are functions that are activated by user operations on the interface, in a standard way. There is a predefined set of user actions, whose elements are similar to events in Tcl/Tk or Java. Including some of them in the object definition implies that they must be allowed for this object. The behaviour of the object when these functions are performed is described using axioms in the usual way. Some user actions have a predefined semantic, which is assumed when the function is not redefined.

Our main goal is to generate a prototype from the specification; therefore, the code generation should be based on standard User Interface toolkits, all of which are event based. The input devices of the system produce these events; the window manager takes these events and sends them to applications that are already waiting for them.

After these events arrive, the application must react according to its actual state. Input events affect the system by modifying the application and User Interface states. These changes are represented in the functional history of the specification.

Why have we decided to introduce a new object instead of using the standard GRALPLA language? We found that the specification in GRALPLA language was complex to write and understand when we were trying to specify a User Interface, because it was necessary to include a lot of low level details, in order to describe the User Interface using graphic objects and asynchronous functions. Therefore, we propose this new object in order to produce clear and readable specifications, and an optimal code generation for the prototype, permitting the establishment of a link between these objects and standard User Interface toolkits in the code generation.

The application actions are defined using function calls, as in the standard version of GRALPLA. The application may be imported by the Interactive Object, allowing in this way, application functions to be called from it. It is also possible to import the user interface objects from the application allowing it to govern the interface.

The last new element is termination function, which allow us destroy or inactivate the object where necessary. This mechanism is described as predefined termination functions, allowing a function call as argument, or as a set of ending functions, which destroy the object after been executed. Note that in any case, the termination mechanism does no change the meaning of the Abstract Data Type defined. But it is needed in order to express destruction of components at the prototype level, as there is no clear scope notion at the specification level.

In Figure 2, we can see the specification of SetValue object. SetValue is part of an input form to set an integer variable. This object displays a text and an integer value that can be changed using the up and down buttons. The Reset button discards the changes made and restores the initial value. The OK button returns the value and the control to the application. Figure 3 shows a possible visualisation of this object.

In Figure 4, we can see the specification of a simple dialog window, as an interactive object. The MessageWindow object is used to display questions that can have a positive or negative answer. It shows a text message, and two buttons. The Yes button express the positive answer of the user, and the No button the negative one.

Figure 5 shows an example of specification module using this interface, to demonstrate how the connection is achieved. This specification is part of an example that uses the MessageWindow object to erase an element. The Delete function erases an element asking for confirmation to the user. The Confirm function returns true or false, depending on the user answer. The ConfirmedbyUser function returns true if the user has confirmed the action. The RemoveConfirmation is used to avoid a future

Interactive Object SetValue;

Import Label, Button;

Constructors	SetValue:	string,
		int,
		Object,
		AcceptCB: func (Object, int → Object)
	→ SetValue;	

Representation   SetValue (Str, I, O, Acc) =
                                Label (Str) +
                                Label (I) +
                                Button ("ArrowUp", Up) +
                                Button ("ArrowDown", Down) +
                                Button ("OK", Accept) +
                                Button ("Reset", Reset);

DestroyAfter: Accept;

User Actions

Functions	Up:	SetValue → SetValue;
	Down:	SetValue → SetValue;
	Accept:	SetValue → SetValue;
	Reset:	SetValue → SetValue;
private	Set:	SetValue, int → SetValue;
private	Get:	SetValue → int;
private	GetObject:	SetValue → Object;

Axioms	**Var**	S: SetValue;
		Str: string;
		I: int;
		O: Object;
		Acc: func (Object, int → Object);

Up (S) = Set (S, Get (S) + 1));
Down (S) = if (Get (S) > 0) Set (S, Get (S) - 1));
Accept (S) = AcceptCB (GetObject (S), Get (S));
Reset (Set (S, I)) = Reset (S);
Get (Set (S, I)) = I;
Get (SetValue (Str, I, O, Acc)) = I;
GetObject (SetValue (Str, I, O, Acc)) = O;

Figure 2. Specification of SetValue

delete action as result of a previous confirmation. The DoDelete function performs the delete action without checking.

The remainder of this section comments this example. We will refer to the user interface specification as the interactive object and to the non-interactive component as the application.

The specification contains a special section (which does not appear in previous versions of the specification language): "User actions". *User actions* are asynchronous functions (events) that are triggered when the user performs specific operations on the user interface. There is a predefined set of user actions, which can be included in every interactive object. The functions chosen are those of the Java Window Tool Kit. User actions that are not defined for a given object can not be performed on it. For instance, objects that do not accept the Move event can not be moved.

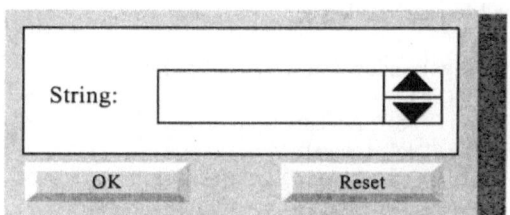

Figure 3. SetValue

The semantic of user actions is explained using axioms, as is the case for normal functions. Some actions have a predefined behaviour. In the example of Figure 4, there are three user actions: Move, FocusOn and FocusOff. The first, Moved, does not appear on the axioms sections and so has no special semantic for this object. FocusOn and FocusOff are used to highlight the interface object. These are the only actions the user can carry out at this level with this object. This implies that, for instance, the interface can not be resized.

There are two mechanisms to build complex components from simpler ones. The first is inheritance, which is used, in the normal sense [2,17]. The second is aggregation, which is specified using the representation mechanism included previously in the language to capture the graphic representation of graphic non-interactive object. The inclusion of a representation section for an interactive object means that the object contains some simpler interactive objects. In the example of Figure 6, a message window has been built using two buttons and a label.

The connection between the interactive object and the application is expressed using callbacks. The constructor of the interactive object has an argument indicating the application functions that must be called from the interface. The constructor on the example uses three arguments. The first is the text that must be shown in the window, the other two arguments are the application functions to be called when the user pushes the Accept and Cancel buttons. When it is necessary to provide complex data to the application, the communication can be performed in two steps. In the first the control is passed to the application, in the second the application calls a query function of the user interface object to obtain the data.

Interactive Object MessageWindow;

Import Label, Button;

Constructors   MessageWindow: String,
                                       Object,
                                       AcceptCB: func (Object →Object),
                                       CancelCB: func (Object →Object)
             → MessageWindow;

Representation   MessageWindow (Str, O, Acc, Can) =
                       Label (Str) +
                       Button ("Yes", Accept) +
                       Button ("No", Cancel);

DestroyAfter: Accept, Cancel;

User Actions

FocusOn: MessageWindow → MessageWindow;
FocusOff: MessageWindow → MessageWindow;
Move: MessageWindow, Point → MessageWindow;

Functions

            Accept: MessageWindow → MessageWindow;
            Cancel: MessageWindow → MessageWindow;
Private   GetObject: MessageWindow → Object;

Axioms

Var   M: MessageWindow;
          S: string;
          O: Object;
          Acc, Can: func (Object → Object);

FocusOn (M) = Highlight (M);
FocusOff (M) = UnHighlight (M);
Accept (M) = AcceptCB (GetObject (M));
Cancel (M) = CancelCB (GetObject (M));
GetObject (MessageWindow (S, O, Acc, Can)) = O;

Figure 4. Specification of a Message Window

The connection between the user actions and the application functions is expressed using the representation and the axioms. We use the representation of the object to indicate which functions of the object must be called from its components interactive objects. In the example, we use two buttons.

Object Example

Import MessageWindow, Element;

Constructors   Example: ➔ Example;

Functions

	Delete:	Example, Element ➔ Example;
	Yes:	Example ➔ Example;
	No:	Example ➔ Example;
private	Confirm:	Example, Object ➔ bool;
private	ConfirmedByUser:	Example ➔ bool;
private	RemoveConfirmation:	Example ➔ Example;
private	DoDelete:	Example, Element ➔ Example;

Axioms

Var   P : Example;
                 O: Object;
                 E: Element;

Delete (P, E) =
    if (Confirm (P, MessageWindow ("Do you really want to delete it?", *P, *Yes, *No)))
               DoDelete (RemoveConfirmation (P), E)
               else RemoveConfirmation (P);
ConfirmedByUser (Yes (P)) = True;
ConfirmedByUser (No (P)) = True;
ConfirmedByUser (Example ()) = False;
Confirm (Yes (P), O) = True;
Confirm (No (P), O) = False;
RemoveConfirmation (Yes (P)) = P;
RemoveConfirmation (No (P)) = P;

Synchronization

do Confirm (P, O) when ConfirmedByUser (P);

Figure 5. Specification of an example use of MessageWindows

Buttons are predefined interactive objects, whose constructor allows us to indicate a label to be written on the button, an a function to be called when the button is pressed.

The first button on the example, labelled Accept, calls the function *Accept*. The second one, Cancel button, calls the function *Cancel*. Cancel and Accept are normal functions of the object, and so their semantic can be expressed using axioms. In the example, we would like to point out that these functions call an application function, and then destroy the interactive object. This mechanism is summarised in Figure 7.

To express the termination of the object we have included a destroy clause, which destroys the object after calling the functions *Accept* or *Cancel*.

Figure 5 is the skeleton of the specification of a module, showing the connection with *MessageWindow*. The function *Delete* is assumed to ask for confirmation. The generic axiom describing *Delete* evaluates the function *Confirm*, which, as a side effect creates the *MessageWindow* object (see Figure 7). *Confirm* is true whether function *Yes*, which is called from MessageWindow when the accept button is pressed, has been executed. *Confirm* appears in the synchornization section, having as guard the function *ConfirmedByUser*, which is true only when the user have pressed

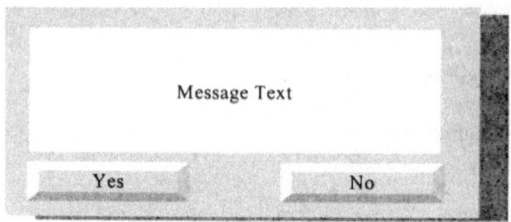

Figure 6. Message Window

some button in the *MessageWindow*, that is, functions *Yes* or *No* have been performed. Note that to carry out the deletion operation it is necessary to use an extra function *DoDelete*, which performs the operation without checking. The *RemoveConfirmation* function is used to eliminate the information about the confirmation, avoiding that a future *Delete* function calls may use the result of a previous confirmation.

A hierarchical structure of Interactive Objects based on the composition of basic elements has been created to define the User Interface. GRALPLA is Object-Oriented, so new Interactive Objects can be derived from existing ones, where only the definition of the special characteristics of the new element would be necessary.

Once it is specified the Interactive Object, it could be append to a library and redefined or used in other specifications. This library would will be used as base of an Interface Builder that generates the specification of the interactive application interactively.

1. Delete function is called on Example. Delete calls Confirm.

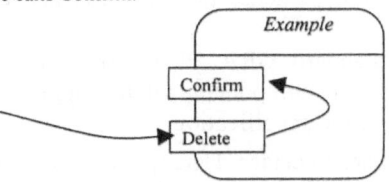

2. Message Window is created by Delete. This implies creating its UI representation.

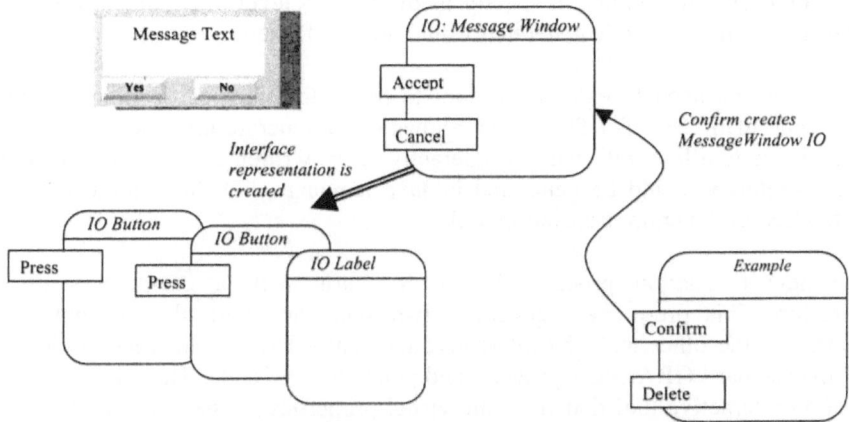

3. The user presses the Accept button. The IO of Accept button calls function Accept on MessageWindow, which call the Yes function on Example object.

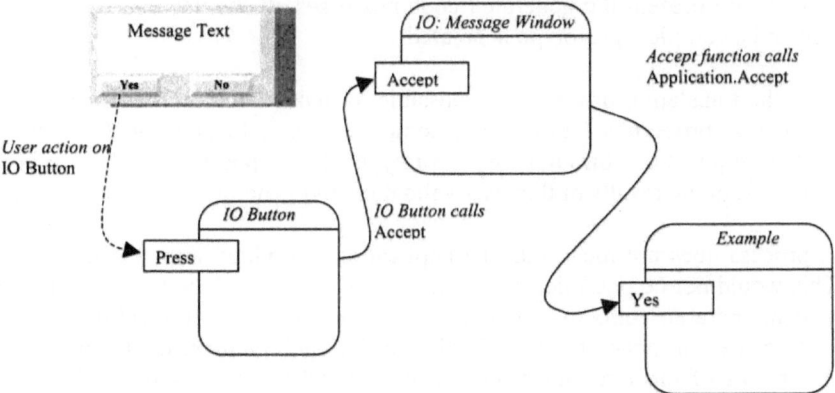

Figure 7. Connection schema of objects from Figures 4 and 5.

3   Translation Process

Our goal is to produce a prototype from User Interface specification. We are working on the development of a new prototyping tool based on GRALPLA prototyping tool.

The prototype generation process has been divided into two branches:

- The standard GRALPLA tool, that generates C++ code, translates the non-interactive components of the application and verifies the properties of these parts of the specification.
- The User Interface design, that generates Java or Tcl/Tk code, where the designer fixes the visual aspects of the User Interface and verifies its properties.

It would be possible to translate the interactive part of the application with the standard tool, but this implies to specify them at a low level of abstraction, near the code layer, and the C++ code generated would not be efficient.

Therefore, we need to extend this tool to translate this specification in a more suitable code than C++. Tcl/Tk or Java allows us to generate this code and make it possible to create a link with the non-interactive part, written in C++. Of course, the complete prototype could be generated in Java language, but this would imply the reconstruction of the entire translation tool.

The new translation process (Figure 8) starts with a pre-process of the specification. This pre-process generates two files, one with the non-interactive elements, and the other with the interactive elements. The non-interactive elements follow the standard GRALPLA process, and generate C++ code. The other file is the input of an interactive tool that fixes the visual properties of the elements (position, colour, and size).After this definition, the tool verifies whether any changes are in agreement with the specification and the code can be generated. Because all the specifications are present the generated code possesses all the necessary links to the C++ code and a complete prototype is created.

During the translation process, it is possible to make automatic verifications[19] of the specification properties (correctness, completeness...). In addition, the user can validate the application through the prototype. It is possible to redesign the specification from the results of this user validation and generate a new prototype.

This process does not mean that the application is divided into two independent parts. This would not be possible. A high-level specification of the User Interface has been created, and a post-process has been designed to fix the low-level details. With this structure, we can generate an optimal code for each element of the application. Several versions of the User Interface can be created from the same specification, because the visual aspects will not influence the specification if we do not change the functionality. This characteristic allows the users to manually tailor their own interface layout, and enable the use of different input and output devices with the same specification. The possibility of adapting the User Interfaces could be of great importance, especially for users with special needs.

The elements of the User Interface have an initial state that the user can change interactively, but the user can not modify the basic properties of these elements, which implies that the specification does not change in this process. The user chooses the appearance, the place and order of these elements on the screen.

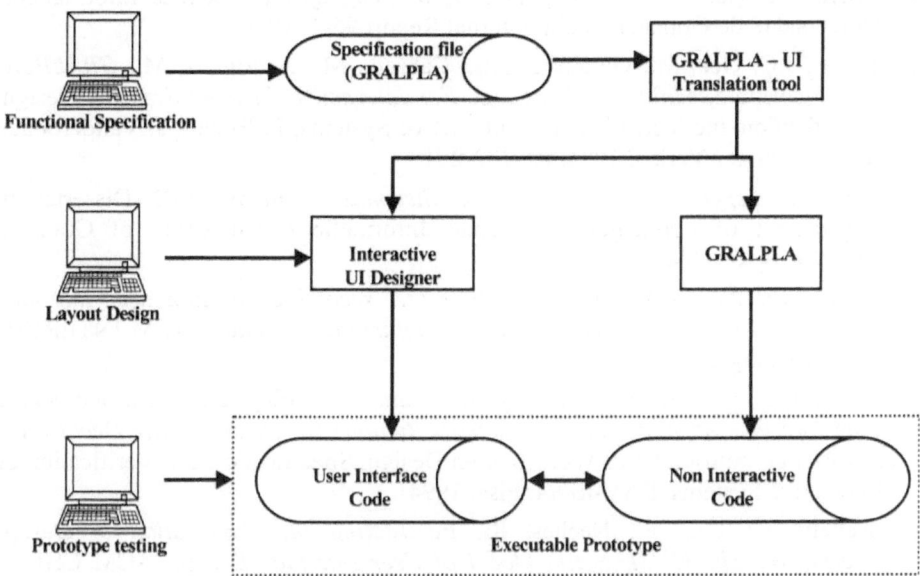

Figure 8. Translation Process Schema

4 Conclusions and Future Works

In this work, we present the structure of a powerful tool of specification. We can specify a complete application and verify its properties from an algebraic specification.

This approach poses some advantages: automatic verification from specification, executable prototypes (first version of the application), reusability of the specification, different versions of the User Interface from one specification.

We are currently developing this integrated system, and studying the application of this technique to multimodal and 3D interfaces.

5 Acknowledgements

This research is funded by the Comisión Interministerial para la Ciencia y la Tecnología (CICYT), grant number TIC98-0973-C03-01, where we are specifying the User Interface of GIRT [20], an object-oriented rendering system.

80

6 Bibliography

1. Torres, J.C.; Gea, M.; Gutiérrez, F.L.; Cabrera, M.; Rodríguez, M.: *The GRALPLA Specification Language*. Dpto. Lenguajes y Sistemas Informáticos, Universidad de Granada, Spain. Internal Report 96-1, 1996.

2. Torres, J.C; Gea, M.; Gutiérrez, F.L.; Cabrera, M.; Rodriguez, M.: *GRALPLA: An Algebraic Specification Language For Interactive Graphic Systems*. Design, Specification and Verification of Interactive Systems, F. Bodart, J. Vanderdonck (eds.). Springer Verlag, 1996. pp. 272-291

3. Gea, M. *Especificación Formal de Sistemas Gráficos*. PhD Dissertation, Department of Lenguajes y Sistemas Informáticos, University of Granada, Granada, Spain. June 1997.

4. Sukaviriya, P.; Foley, J.D.; Griffith, T.: *A second generation user interface design environment: The model and the runtime architecture*. ACM INTERCHI 93 Proceedings. ACM, 1993.

5. Sukaviriya, P.; Muthukumarasamy, J.; Frank, M.; Foley, J.D.: *A Model-based User Interface Architecture: Enhancing a Runtime Environment with Declarative Knowledge*. Eurographics Workshop on Design, Specification and Verification of Interactive Systems, DSV-IS'94. Pisa. 1994

6. Szekely, P.; Luo, P.; Neches, R.: *Facilitating the Exploration of Design Alternative: The HUMANOID Model of User Interface Design*. ACM CHI 92 Proceedings. ACM 1992.

7. Szekely, P.; Luo, P.; Neches, R.: *Beyond Interface Builders: Model-Based Interface Tools*. InterCHI'93, pp 383-390.

8. Bodart, F.; Hennebert, A.M.; Leheureux, J.M.; Provot, I.; Vanderdonckt, J.: *A Model-Based Approach to Presentation: a Continuum from Task Analysis to Prototype*. Eurographics Workshop on Design, Specification and Verification of Interactive Systems DSV-IS'94. 1994

9. Bodart, F.; Hennebert, A.M.; Leheureux, J.M.; Provot, I.; Sacré, B.; Vanderdonckt, J.: *Towards a Systematic Building of Software Architectures: the TRIDENT Methodological Guide*. Eurographics Workshop on Design, Specification and Verification of Interactive Systems DSV-IS'95. 1995

10. Markopoulos, P.; Pycock, J.; Wilson, S.; Johnson: *Adept – A task based design environment*. Eurographics Workshop on Design, Specification and Verification of Interactive Systems CADUI'96. 1996.

11. Balzert, H,: *From OOA to GUI – The JANUS-System*. Proceedings Interact'95. 1995.

12. Schlungbaum, E.; Elwert, T: *Automatic User Interface Generation from Declarative Models*. Proceedings of the 2nd International Workshop on Computer-Aided Design of User Interfaces CADUI'96. Namur, Belgium, 1996. J. Vanderdonck (Ed.) Presses Universitaires de Namur, 1996. pp.3-18.

13. Schlungbaum, E.; Elwert, T: *Modelling and Generation of Graphical User Interface in the TADEUS Approach*. P. Palanque, R. Bastide (eds.): Designing,

Specification, and Verification of Interactive Systems. Wien, Springer Verlag, 1995. Pp. 193-208.

14. Lonczewski F.; Schriber S.: *The Fuse-System: an integrated User Interface Environment*. Proceedings of the 2nd International Workshop on Computer-Aided Design of User Interfaces CADUI'96. Namur, Belgium, 1996. J. Vanderdonck (Ed.) Presses Universitaires de Namur, 1996. Pp. 39-56.

15. Paternò, F.; Meniconi, S.: *TLIM, a Systematic Method for the Design of Interactive Systems*. Palanque, P; Paternò, F. (eds.). Formal Methods in Human-Computer Interaction. Springer Verlag, FACIT Series, ISBN 3-540-76158-6, 1997. pp 241-260.

16. Paternò, F.; Santoro, C.; Tahmassebi, S.: *Formal Models for Cooperative Task: Concepts and an Application for En-route Air Traffic Control*. Markopoulos, P.; Johnson, P. (eds.). Design, Specification and Verification of Interactive Systems'98. Springer Verlag. 1998. pp 71-86.

17. Puerta, A: *The MECANO Project: Comprehensive and Integrated Support for Model-Based Interface Development*. Proceedings of the 2nd International Workshop on Computer-Aided Design of User Interfaces CADUI'96. Namur, Belgium, 1996. J. Vanderdonck (Ed.) Presses Universitaires de Namur, 1996. Pp. 19-35.

18. Puerta, A.; Eisenstein, J.: *Interactively Mapping Task Models to Interfaces in MOBI-D*. Proceedings 5th Eurographics Workshop on Design, Specification and Verification of Interactive Systems, DSV-IS'98. Abingdon, United Kingdom, June 1998.

19. Gutiérrez, F.L.; Gea, M.; Torres, J.C.: *Verification of Interactive Systems using Algebraic Specification*. Proceedings 5th Eurographics Workshop on Design, Specification and Verification of Interactive Systems, DSV-IS'98. Abingdon, United Kingdom, June 1998.

20. Ureña, C.; *Designing an Object-Oriented Rendering System*. Proceedings 6th Eurographics Workshop on Programming Paradigms in Graphics. Budapest, Hungary. September 1997.

7 Appendix. GRALPLA Specification Language Syntax

More detailed information about GRALPLA can be obtained in our Web page
http://giig.ugr.es/inv/lineas/formales/index-uk.html

<Module_espec> ::= <Header> [<Dependencies>] <Constructors> [<Representation>]
[<Destroy>] [<User_Actions<] [<Functions> <Axioms>] [<synchronization>]

<Header> ::= [**interface**] [**parametric**] [**interactive**] [**graphic**] **object** *object_name*
  [<Parameter_id> { , <Parameter_id> }] [: <object_id> {, <object_id> }] ;

<Parameter_id> ::= *param_id* [: *type_id*]
| *fn_id* : **func** (*type_id* { , *type_id* } -> *type_id*)

<Dependencies> ::= [**import** { *object_id* [<Parameter_id> { ,<Parameter_id> }]] } ;]

<Constructors> ::= [**Constructors**]
  { [**private**]*function_id* : [*type_id* { , *type_id* }] -> *object_id* [<Explicit_rep>]; }

<Explicit_rep> ::= [**where graphic_rep** `(` *function_id* [*var_id* { , *var_id* }] `)'* = <Term>]

<Representation> ::= **Representation** *function_id* : [*type_id* { , *type_id* }]) =
                 object_id ([*type_id* { , *type_id* }])
                 { + *object_id* ([*type_id* { , *type_id* }]) } ;

<Destroy> ::= **DestroyAfter:** *function_id* { , *function_id* } ;

<User-Actions> ::= **User Actions** { *function_id* [< *selector_id* { , *selector_id* } >] :
{ *type_id* { , *type_id* } } -> *type_id* { , *type_id* } ; }

<Functions> ::= **Functions** { [**private**] [**process**] [**asynchronous**]
function_id [< *selector_id* { , *selector_id* } >] :
{ *type_id* { , *type_id* } } -> *type_id* { , *type_id* } [<error_description>] ; }

<error_description> ::= **:= error** [(<type_error> [, " comment "])]

<type_error> ::= **warning** | **fatal**

<Axioms> ::= **Axioms**
[**var** { *var_id* { , *var_id* } : *type_id* ; }]
{ *function_id* (<Term> { , <Term> }) [. *selector_id*] = <Expresion>

<Expresion>::=<Sentence> | (<Expresion>) | <Expresion> '|' <Expresion>

<Sentence> ::= <Term>
| if (<Term>) <Expresion> [else <Expresion>]

<Term>::= <Term> <Operation> <Term> | not <Term>
| function_id [(<Term> { , <Term> }) [. selector_id]]
| var_id | int_cte | real_cte | char_cte | true | false

<Operation> ::= + | - | * | / | and | or | < | > | >= | <= | <> | =

<Synchronization> ::= Synchronization
{ do function_id (var_id { , var_id }) when <Expression> ; }

Computer-Aided Design of Menu Bar and Pull-Down Menus for Business Oriented Applications

Jean Vanderdonckt

Université catholique de Louvain
Place des Doyens, 1 - B-1348 LOUVAIN-LA-NEUVE (Belgium)
Phone: +32 (0)10 47.85.25 - Fax : +32 (0)10 47.83.24
E-mail: vanderdonckt@qant.ucl.ac.be
Web: http://www.qant.ucl.ac.be/membres/jv/jv.html

Abstract. Building a usable menu bar, related pull-down menus and submenus or cascaded menus remains an important design activity in the development of interactive applications, especially in the domain of business oriented ones. To provide some assistance to designers who are responsible for achieving this task, a two-phased design method for a menu bar and related pull-down menus is presented. Based on a entity-relationship model of the final application, a first phase automatically generates an initial menu tree; a second phase enables designers to interactively perform refinement operations on the initial tree to obtain a final menu tree. This tree can be finally exported to a graphical editor for free editing and adaptation. This method covers the selection and the positioning of menu items, a first proposal for mnemonics and accelerators that are intrinsically based of menu design guidelines.

Keywords. Automated Generation of User Interfaces, Computer-Aided Design of User Interfaces, Entity-Relationship Model, Guidelines, Menu bar, Model-based approach, Pull-down menu, Specification, Task model.

1   Introduction

Many aspects such as dialogue design, window or dialog boxes have been addressed in model-based approaches for user interface (UI), whereas the building of a menu bar, related pull-down menus and cascaded menus have received little attention. This situation is somewhat puzzling when the following are considered:

1. The usability of menu design is probably the most advanced in research and development, e.g. [5,6,9,12]. In particular, Norman has written a complete book about the trade-offs involved in menu design based on experimental research that have produced practical menu design guidelines [6].
2. Some techniques have been introduced to guide menu design in a structured way and various aspects such as the optimal number of items per menu [9], the traversal time of a menu, the depth and length of menu are well known [6]. Some techniques were developed to systematically produce usable menu structures manually.
3. Nearly all these contributions can be embodied in a software tool that automate parts of menu design. This could be very efficient since most relevant information to be exploited to significantly initiate a menu design can be found in traditional models (a task, a data or a domain model).

In a context where rapid application development is imposed by time and resource constraints, it could be appropriate to provide some assistance to designers who are responsible for designing a menu for an interactive application by developing a complete method for such a design.

The rest of this paper is structured as follows: section 2 will review the state of the art in the area of computer-aided design of menus by reporting on experiences on both methods and software tools; section 3 will present a method for producing a complete menu tree for a business oriented interactive application based on windows, icons, menus and popup (WIMP) technology; section 4 will highlight how this method can be applied on a small medical case study; section 5 will explain the complete design process supported by a software tool that works on a specification repository of models; section 6 will conclude by discussing some open issues resulting from the experience gained with this method and by summarising some future work.

2 Related work

MENUDA [10] was an experimental knowledge-based menu design assistant to aid the design of menu systems. Its knowledge base is structured as a semantic network of menu design guidelines collected from the literature in the domain of experimental research. Although this tool can identify relevant guidelines for each linguistic level (e.g., semantic, syntactic, lexical, physical), it does not produce any menu nor does it specify how these guidelines should be used.

MIKE [7] is probably the first research that followed a model-based approach. This software tool automatically generates a Unix graphical UI by exploiting the declarations of procedure signatures. These declarations, contained in the foreword of a Pascal unit, are exploited to automatically generate items on a menu bar and its resulting pull-down menus. The programmer writes the Pascal code of a unit containing the semantic functions of the application and adds comments for each signature from which MIKE will derive information to generate a menu. The signature

```
procedure Search_customer_by_id(customer,id,results);
        (* Menu='Customer' Item='Search customer by id.'*)
```

will generate a "Customer" item on the menu bar associated with a menu item labelled "Search customer by id."; all other procedures associated with the same menu bar item will appear in the same pull-down menu. In its Macintosh version, Mickey [8], the menus are generated in an equally straightforward manner.

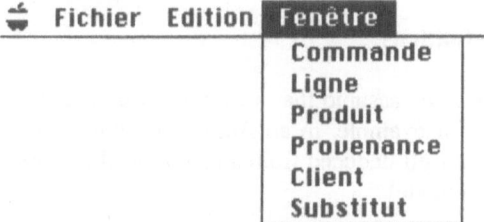

Fig. 1 Example of menu generated by MACIDA.

MacIDA [11] automatically generates MacApp code for a Macintosh graphical UI from functional specifications contained in an information structure model (graphically depicted as an entity-relationship model) and a dynamic model (graphically depicted as an activity chaining graph [2]). This tool extracts the names of entities and relationships found in the information structure model and generates a "Window" item on the menu bar containing these names associated with related windows or dialogue boxes (fig. 1).

JANUS [1] automatically generates a Windows'95 graphical UI from an object oriented model obtained from object-oriented analysis. The designer manually transforms this model into requirements stored in a JANUS Definition File (JDF) manipulated by a Computer-Aided Software Engineering (CASE) tool. This file is then exploited to map objects and their relationships (such as *is_a* or *is_part_of*) onto menu bar and pull-down menu items according to transformation rules (fig. 2).

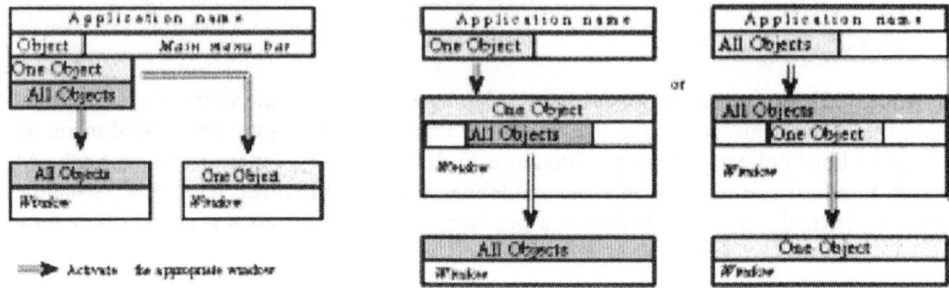

Fig. 2 Example of menu generated by JANUS.

These three last examples show that some significant parts of the menu tree can be automatically generated in a model-based approach where models result from software engineering. They are all based on the "object-action" paradigm frequently found in WIMP UIs: the task objects fill the menu bar as items and the actions which are performed on a particular object (or set of objects) fill the pull-down menus and sub-menus as items.

We can note that IBM *Common User Access* de facto standard is based on the "action-object" inverse paradigm, where the ordering of menu bar items is recommended as: File, Edit, Actions, View, Options, Help. Our proposed method will rely on the first paradigm, which is more commonly used.

3 A Method for Systematic Menu Tree Building

3.1 Hypothesis and definitions

As preliminary hypothesis, we assume that a designer has already performed some functional analysis resulting, for example, in an Activity Chaining Graph (ACG) as function dynamics model, which is itself deduced from a hierarchical task model [2], and an entity-relationship model as data model.

The set of items found on a menu bar, the related pull-down menus and sub-menus can form a menu tree structure whose leaf nodes are *terminal items* whereas all non-terminal items are *selection items*. The user will be able to initiate an action as soon as he or she has selected a terminal item. Terminal items may appear at every level, although menu bar terminal items are not recommended [6], except if they are presented in a distinctive manner, such as Item!. Selection items are provided to guide the user in navigating through the menu tree and triggering semantic functions.

A *dialogue function* is a semantic function including input/output of information pertaining to the user's interactive task via interaction media such as screens, keyboards (for instance, "Search a customer by its identification"). A *service function* is an auxiliary function not directly appearing the ACG, but deduced from its configuration to improve the usability of the task (for instance, "List existing customers alphabetically" may not appear in an interactive task "Record an order for a customer", but can be deduced from its semantics). The *control* of a function can be *implicit* if it is triggered by the interactive application (for instance, when an order is placed in a pool, a summary of ongoing orders are periodically printed) or *explicit* if the user is responsible for its triggering (for instance, to record an address change in the customers' database).

A function with explicit control is said *global* when it can be triggered through any menu items wherever the use is in carrying the interactive task. It is said *local* if it is triggered in a local context which is only valid during a defined period of time in the interactive task (for instance, by a "Validate" push button in a dialog box).

3.2 Definition of the method

The method consists in traversing two phases: the first phase, producing an initial tree, can be completely automated by a software tool whereas the second should be computer-aided, thus providing designers more flexibility on the final tree.

3.2.1 Phase 1: Automated generation of a initial menu tree

1.1 Automated generation of a menu bar

Since the data model is considered to be a complete already existing entity-relationship model, we assume that all entities and relationships are known with their attributes. Although the rest of this paper will derive items based on entities and relationships properties, the strategy remains valid for objects and relationships properties from an object-oriented model serving as data model.

- Define E = set of all entities related to the application semantics.
- Define R = set of all relationships related to the application semantics.
- Sort entities in E by decreasing order of number of attributes, then alphabetically for entities having a same number of attributes.
- Sort relationships in R by decreasing order of main connectivity, then alphabetically for relationships sharing a same connectivity.
- Generate a first menu bar whose items are elements of E followed by elements of R. The items labels are the default names of entities and relationships found in the functional specification, with underscores removed and words uncapitalised.

The rationale behind these choices is that a menu bar should contain application objects which have associated semantic functions [13].

1.2 Automated generation of pull-down menus

- Define $P = P_E \cup P_R$ where P_E = set of interactive tasks (or phases in the application decomposition) sorted according the order of appearance of entities in E and P_R = set of interactive tasks (or phases in the application decomposition) sorted according the order of appearance of relationships in R.
- Sort P_E and P_R by order of function appearance as specified in the main ACG.
- For each entity or relationship in the menu bar, generate a pull-down menu whose items are the related interactive tasks. If there are no such tasks, no menu is generated. The labels of menu items are the default names of interactive tasks found in the functional specification with underscores removed and words uncapitalised.

Each interactive task consequently appears one time in P partitioned into P_E and P_R, while non-interactive tasks are not concerned. In these interactive tasks, functions with explicit control are particularly considered, whether they are global dialogue function or local service functions. The rationale behind these choices is that the menu tree should be organised according to the functional structure of an application and should reflect the user's task model [6]; all functions based on a user dialogue should appear in the menu tree. The ordering of menu bars items by order of importance is derived from the guideline stating that such an order is known to improve usability [5,6]. Basic actions should appear on pull-down menus [6]: therefore, interactive tasks that can be decomposed into dialogue functions will appear as such.

1.3 Automated generation of cascaded menus

	Level 1	Level 2	Level 3
Selection item	Attachment = pull-down menu Presentation = Item	Attachment = cascaded menu Presentation = Item...	Attachment = list of values Presentation = Itemʋ
Terminal item	Attachment = dialog box, secondary application window, function Presentation = Item..., Item, Item!	Attachment = dialog box, secondary application window, function, toggle Presentation = Item..., Item, Item!, Item√	Attachment = dialog box, secondary application window, function Presentation = Item..., Item, Item!
Abstract Interaction Object [3]	Menu bar	Pull-down menu	Cascaded menu
Labels	Names of entities and relationships	Names of interactive tasks	Names of dialogue and service functions
Structure	Guided by data model	Guided by Activity Chaining Graph	Guided by Activity Chaining Graph
Ordering	By importance	By sequence	By sequence

Table 1 Summary of design options for generating the initial menu.

- For each interactive task p appearing in P, define F_p in extension the set of dialogue functions and service functions which are not local.
- Sort each F_p first with dialogue functions sorted by order or appearance in the task ACG, then with service functions with no particular order.
- For each interactive task, generate a cascaded menu whose items are the F_p elements if $F_p \neq \varnothing$. The labels of cascaded menu items are the default names of functions found in the functional specification.

The rationale behind these choices is that actions and sub-actions of an application should appear in sub-menus [6,13] and preferably sorted by sequential order [6]. After performing these three steps, we conclude that each level 1 menu item is a selection item if there is a pull-down menu attached or a terminal item if there are not. Each level 2 menu item is a selection item if there is a cascaded menu attached or a terminal item if there are not. Each level 3 menu item is a selection item if a list of values is presented or a terminal item if there are not (table 1).

3.2.2 Phase 2: Computer-aided design of a final menu tree

2.1 Eliminating degenerated menus

At level 1 of the initial menu tree, we have $length$(level 1)= # items = # application objects (entities and relationships); we also have $length$(level 2)= # interactive tasks and $length$(level 3)= # non-local dialogue and service functions. Consequently, we can have at level 1 an item appearing in the menu which is attached with no pull-down menus if all tasks were attached to other items. Moreover, if a selection item at level 1 or 2 is attached with a single terminal item at the subsequent level, then the selection becomes no longer appropriate. The first item is then called *quasi-terminal item* and the menu is called a *degenerated menu*. The designer is then asked whether he or she would prefer to delete the terminal item to have a quasi-terminal item or to keep it as it is (fig. 3).

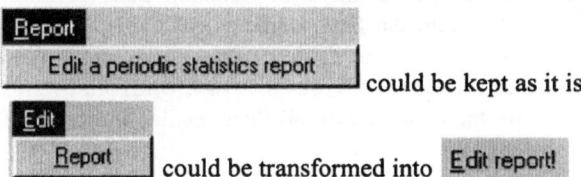

Fig. 3 Example of eliminating degenerated menus.

2.2 Unifying menu items

It is likely that two dialogue functions could lead to two different items in a menu. For instance, "Search a customer by its id." and "Search a customer by first name, last name" can generate multiple items in different menus. These two functions belonging to the same interactive task could be unified to have a unique item. On the other hand, two such items can be relevant from the user's task viewpoint. Thus, a confirmation is asked to the designer to see if two such functions should be grouped in the same task, thus appearing in a single item, or if a separation should be maintained.

2.3. Re-eliminating degenerated menus

This step results from the previous one: unifying two items into one can lead to a degenerated menu. In this case, it could be deleted with designer's confirmation.

2.4 Balancing the menu tree

Although the initial menu tree mirrors the structure and sequence of functions within interactive tasks, it is not necessarily balanced in terms of both depth and length. Kiger [5] recommends that the optimal tree depth is 2 whereas the optimal menu length is 8. A menu having few items, 2 or 3 for instance, could be embedded in a parent menu by replacing it with selection items assembled in a visual group delimited by two horizontal separators to denote the task visual disclosure. Balancing the tree consists in an iterative process from which a wider, yet less deep, tree is expected. Obviously, the resulting tree can become different from what has been derived from the ACG. It is thus required to ask designer's confirmation before applying any balancing operation. To guide the designer, the current depth and length could be provided.

2.5 Formatting the items

The labels of menu items are the defaults names of entities, relationships, and functions stored in the functional specification repository (for instance, "Search_cust_id" for "Search a customer by identification". Since each selection item should possess a meaning that mirrors the selection process and since each terminal item should mirror a task action, these default names are not necessarily appropriate or usable. Thus, the current label is reviewed for each item by the designer for editing and "..." is added for each terminal item attached to a dialogue box, "!", for each level 1 terminal item. Before editing, all underscores appearing in default names can be replaced by spaces under the designer's control, thus producing "Search cust id.".

2.6 Adding standard menus

According to the designer's need, standard menus can be selected and automatically added. Two alternatives are proposed: the IBM *Common User Access* norm and the Microsoft Windows standard. While the first promotes standard menus attached to a menu bar like Workplace or Selected, Edit, Actions, View, Options, Help, the second standard tends to prefer File, Edit, Objects, View, Options, Windows, Help or ?. Theses standard menus are then added with all their regular and reserved mnemonics and accelerators.

2.7 Adding a Help menu

This feature is embodied to support the future implementation of a help system for the interactive application. If such a system will be implemented and if the Help has not been added during the previous step, a standard Help menu is then added. If no help system will be implemented, the Help menu is restricted to one item "About...".

2.8 Adding a Quit menu item

If a File standard menu has not been added previously, the item Quit responsible for quitting the interactive application is added as the last menu item of the first pull-down menu after a separator, as it is often the case [6].

2.9 Selecting the mnemonics

During this step, menu mnemonics are proposed to the approval of the designer: if an item is attached to a standard menu, then the standard mnemonic is selected (e.g., "Q" for Quit); if an item is not attached to a standard menu, the label initial is proposed. If this letter is already used as mnemonic in the same pull-down menu thus inducing a conflict, the next consonant of each word is proposed until the conflict vanishes. If such a conflict still exists after examining all consonants, the same process is reiterated on vowels and special characters, e.g., *,@,-.

2.10 Selecting the accelerators

During this step, menu accelerators are proposed to the approval of the designer: if an item is attached to a standard menu, then the standard accelerator is selected (e.g., Ctrl-P for Print). If an item is not attached to a standard menu, it would be appropriate for find relevant accelerators for the most frequently used functions. Since this information should come from other sources, only the functions located at the beginning of a task path on an ACG are subject to an accelerator proposal. It basically consists of a control key (Ctrl, Shift) along with the initial, a consonant or a vowel extracted from the label, preferably the mnemonic, if it has been determined before.

2.11 Including a menu tree map and help

When novice or intermittent users are interacting with the interactive application, a first guidance could be included as a map representing the menu tree associated with explanations for each item. This explanation is the default description of each task and function appearing in the ACGs. When the interactive application is used by experienced, frequent users, a list of keyboard or mouse accelerators could be automatically added as soon as the accelerators have been chosen.

3.2.3 Phase 3: Manual editing of a final menu tree

The final menu tree can finally be edited within the software tool itself: item editing, grouping, pull-down menus restructuring, item transferring from one pull-down menu to another. For this purpose, a three-view approach is followed (fig. 4):

1. An *individual view* displays all editable properties of each item, such as label, mnemonic, accelerator, activity,...
2. A *textual view* where the hierarchy of menu bar, pull-down menus and cascaded menus are displayed textually for fast item moving.
3. A *graphical view* where the menu tree can be directly manipulated as in a real UI.

In this manual editing, the designer is able to perform any traditional modification on the menu bar and the pull-down menus. This facility therefore provides room for defining customisable menus at design time. There is no support for modifying user-customisable menus at execution time.

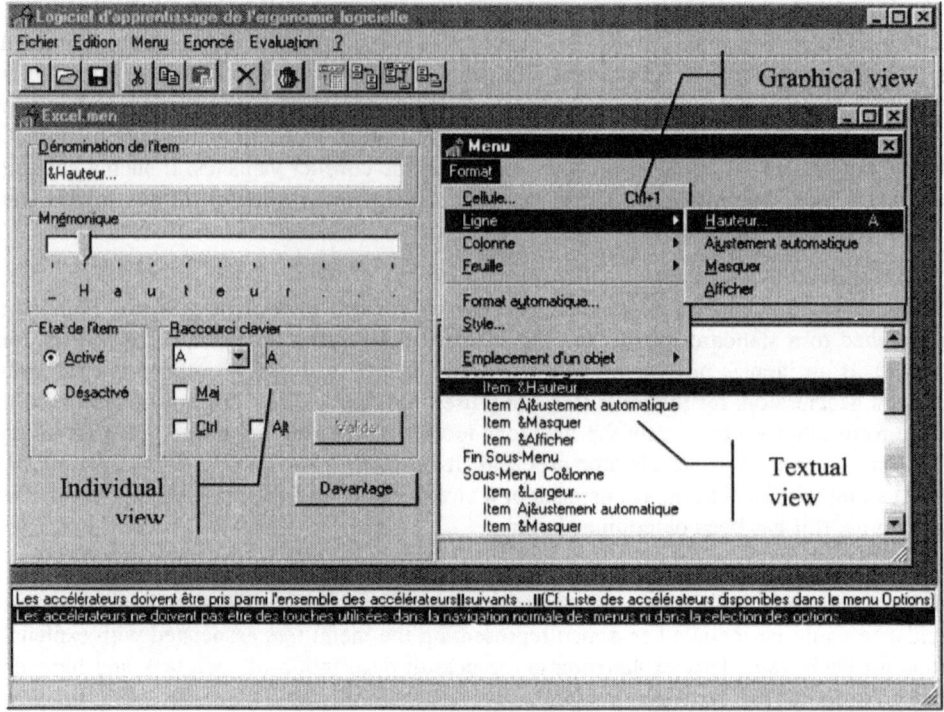

Fig. 4 Manual editing of the final menu tree.

4 An Example of Method Application

To exemplify the previous method, we apply it on a case study related to patient management in a hospital. From the entity-relationship model of this case study, we can extract E = {Patient, Care, Regimen, Room, Service, Hospital, Doctor, Prescription} and R = {Care_Prescription, Regimen_Prescription, Destination, Origin, Reimbursement, Room, Affiliation, Belonging, Movement, Perform, Is_part_of, Reimbursement_Prestation}. The first automated phase produces P = {Admission, Input_Transfer, Input_Exit, Prescription_Care, Prescription_Prestation, Cancel_Prescription, Recall_Prescription, Change_Regimen, Ask_Info_Patient_1, Ask_Info_Patient_2, Ask_ Info_Old_Patient, Select_Patient, Meals list}.

Interactive tasks are then distributed as follows:
$P_{E\_Patient}$ = {Admission, Input_Transfer, Input_Exit, Ask_Info_Patient_1, Ask_Info_ Patient_2, Ask_info_old_patient, Select_Patient}.
P_{E_Care} = {Prescription_Care, Prescription_Prestation, Cancel_Prescription, Recall_ Prescription}
$P_{E\_Regimen}$ = {Change_Regimen, Meals list}
P_{E_Room} = $P_{E\_Service}$ = $P_{E\_Hospital}$ = ... = $P_{E\_Prescription}$} = $\varnothing$

All other P_E are empty since their related interactive tasks have already been chosen. Similarly, all $P_R = \varnothing$. The decomposition of interactive tasks into functions gives:

$F_{Admission}$ = {Verify_patient_existence, Verify_patient_not_recorded, Verify_no_movement, Record_patient, Update_patient, Validate_doctor, Validate_service, Validate_ category, Validate_regimen}

$F_{Input\_Transfer}$ = {Validate_doctor, Validate_patient, Validate_source_bed, Validate_ target_bed, Verify_no_move, Verify_patient_in_bed, Check_free_beds, Record_ transfer}

F_{Input_Exit} = {Validate_doctor, Validate_patient, Validate_source_bed, Verify_no_ move, Verify_patient_in_bed}

$F_{Prescription\_Prestation}$ = {Validate_prescription, Cancel_prescription}

$F_{Cancel\_Prescription}$ = {Validate_prescription, Cancel_prescription}

$F_{Recall\_Prestation}$ = {Recell_prestation}

$F_{Change\_Regimen}$ = {Validate_doctor, Validate_patient, Validate_Regimen_ record_change_regimen}

F_{Meals_List} = {Meal_List}

$F_{Ask\_Info\_Patient\_1} = F_{Ask\_Info\_Patient\_2} = F_{Ask\_Info\_Old\_Patient}$ = {}

After accepting all default design options, the software tool produces the menu bar and pull-down menus depicted in fig. 5. The labels of menu items are the names of functions as stored in the functional specifications repository with underscores removed and names uncapitalised.

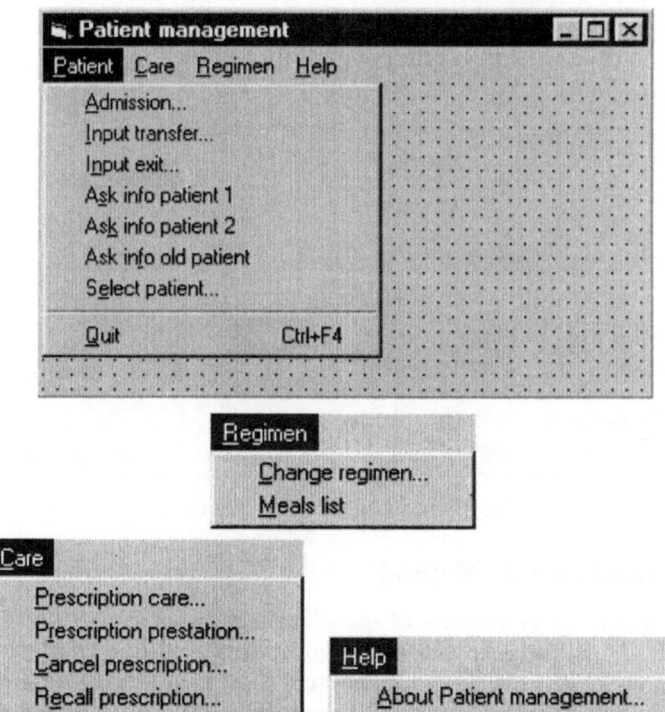

Fig. 5 Final menu tree with default options.

94

When all options are requested during generation, various facilities are added, such as the menu map and a list of generated accelerators (fig. 6). Of course, if these accelerators are edited manually outside the tool, the final menu tree is no longer consistent with the previous results. The designer is entirely responsible for checking that consistency is preserved and that no conflict is appearing. An inconsistency may appear between the initial model and the final menu as soon as a manual function introducing some inconsistency is operated on the menu tree.

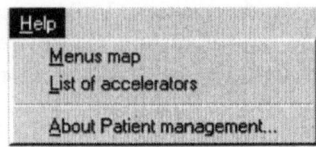

Fig. 6 Final help menu with complete options.

From these menus, it should be possible for the designer to easily change the labels of items, the mnemonics, the accelerators and the positioning of separators. Anyway, as much as possible is done to provide an initial menu tree that would be regarded as a good starting point for computer-aided completion. Designers are allowed to perform other manual operations such as (fig. 7): the changing of menu labels, choosing other mnemonics or accelerators, or introducing separators between groups of items.

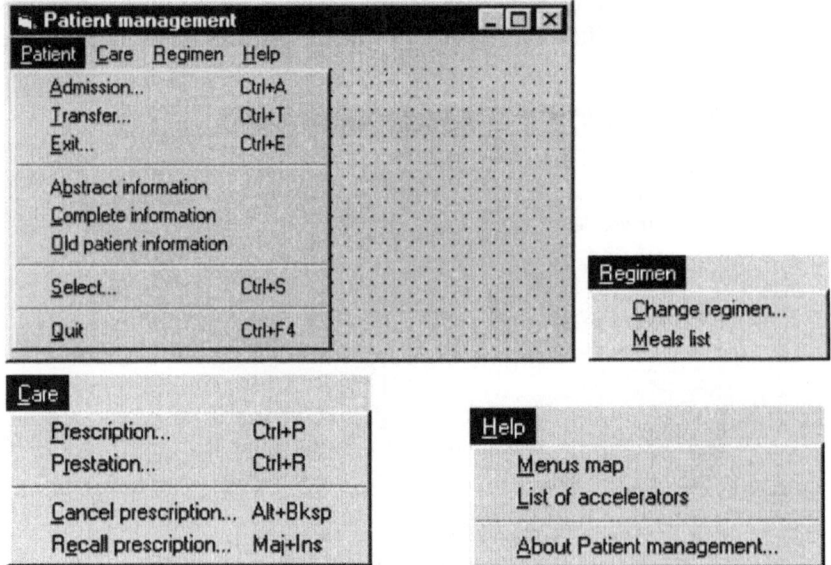

Fig. 7 Final menu tree after editing.

5   Tool Support for this Method

A software tool that scans a repository of specifications written in Dynamic Specification Language (DSL) [2] supports the above method. In this repository, various models are stored as textual declarative statements in different files: entity-relationship model, function structuring model, Activity Chaining Graph model… DSL is the related specification language to declare these models. Models can consequently be input graphically with the model editor (fig. 8) which automatically produces the DSL specification from the graphical model or with the textual editor that directly produces the DSL specifications. The menu generator exploits these textual specifications to progressively generate a menu tree and to enable designers to interactively edit it within the tool. When manual editing operations are finished in the tool, it automatically (fig. 8):

1. Stores the resulting definition of menu as new DSL specifications for the presentation model [2]; it is expressed as instances of Abstract Interaction Objects [3].
2. Generates a .FRM file containing the definition of menus according to Visual Basic V5.0 format. This ASCII flat file can be easily manipulated since it contains concrete specifications like

```
VERSION 5.00
Begin VB.Form Essai
    Caption          =    "Patient management"
    ClientHeight     =    2550
    ClientLeft       =    165
    ClientTop        =    735
    ClientWidth      =    4980
    LinkTopic        =    "Form1"
    ScaleHeight      =    2550
    ScaleWidth       =    4980
    StartUpPosition =    3    'Windows Default
    Begin VB.Menu MenuPatient
        Caption          =    "&Patient"
        Index            =    1
        Begin VB.Menu ItemPatientAdmission
            Caption       =    "&Admission..."
            Index         =    11
            Shortcut      =    ^A
        End
    ...
```

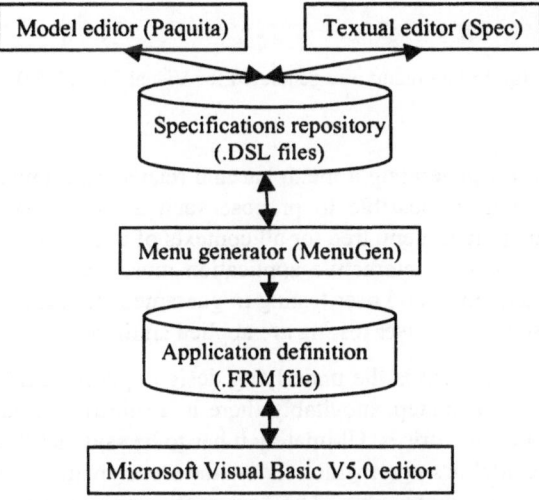

Fig. 8 The menu production process.

The designer is then able to perform any manual operations on the results within the Microsoft Visual Basic V5.0 editor (fig. 9) with the potential risk of loosing consistency with what has been previously generated in the menu generator. The menu resulting from this stage can be different with respect to the presentation model stored in the specifications repository, thus introducing some inconsistency. The designer is therefore responsible for updating the presentation model accordingly.

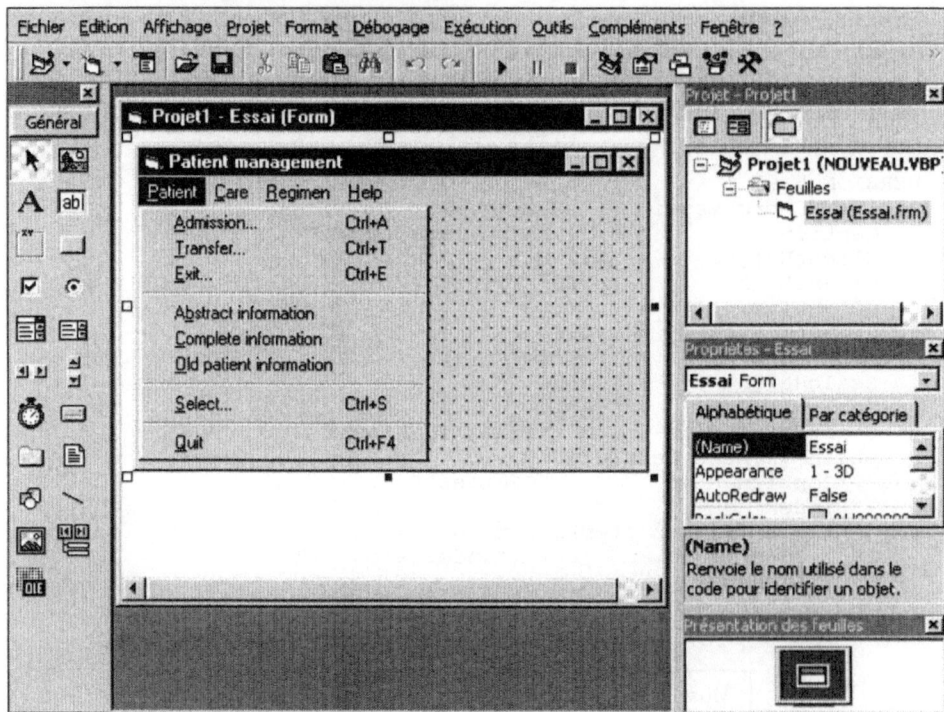

Fig. 9 Final menu tree generated for Visual Basic V5.0.

6   Conclusion

The proposed method for generating a menu bar and related pull-down menus is probably sub-optimal, but it seems impossible to propose such a method which uniformly and univocally leads to an optimal menu tree for all contexts of use. Moreover, determining the optimal menu for a particular interactive application must involve a range of activities, such as referring to guidelines, and user testing to guarantee that these guidelines is appropriate and that the results of the user testing are applied similarly.

What is interesting to note here is the underlying design options and guidelines that have been explicitly used for each step. Inevitably there is a selection process of these guidelines, and the problem of bias arises. Ultimately it has to be said that there are biases in this method, but that the guidelines upon which the method was created was described openly. Those biases are therefore discernible. The best protection against bias in this kind of method to have the process conducted independently by more than one team, and to be subjected to expert review. Although we informally conducted such a process, complete method validity cannot be ensured. Many extensions are possible, depending on the adopted usability targets and the potential of translating existing menu design guidelines into operational rules and ergonomic algorithms. Seven possible extensions will be studied in the near future:

1. To look for new heuristics for positioning horizontal separators to visually identify blocks of related items into a group. For instance, such separators can surround menu items related to interactive tasks which can be grouped or which are semantically related to each other; moreover, similar heuristics might be created to group or ungroup sub-tasks according to the task model structure.

2. To design a command language that is syntactically equivalent to menus for frequent users (or to use some more sophisticated techniques to identify appropriate mnemonics and accelerators). Such research is already ongoing elsewhere [4,14]; fig. 10 shows how mathematical curve plotting commands in GNUPLOT can be typed after a command prompt or selected from the pull down menus to complete a command. In this case, the items selectable from the pull-down menus form a menu selection context which is completely equivalent to a command language. Each command can be initiated either by selecting it from the menus or by typing it as a command or both together.

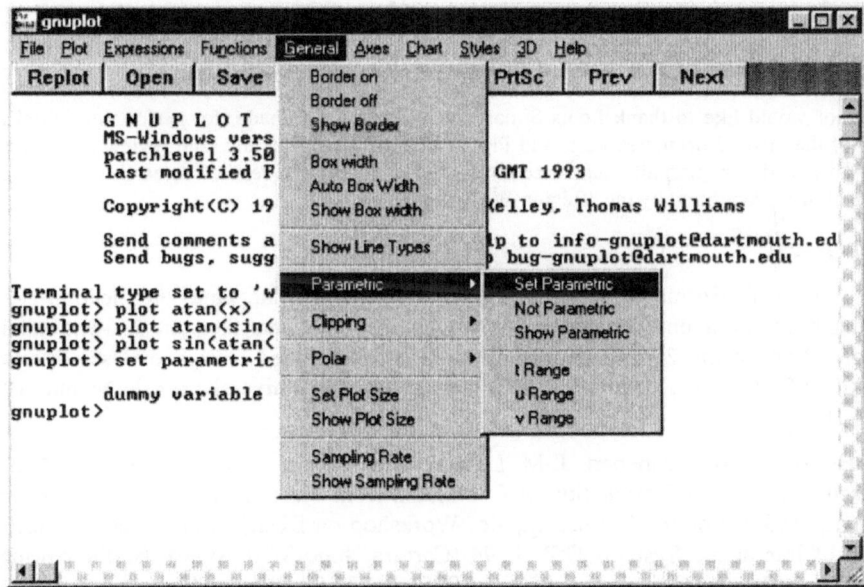

Fig. 10. Menu selection equivalent to a command language in GNUPLOT.

3. To generate a set of sub-trees when the number of items becomes critical: this situation particularly arises when the entity-relationship model contains many entities and relationships that are relevant to specific interactive tasks; the risk here is to generate a menu bar with too much items.

4. To define a variable UI by separating menu items into two categories: *fundamental items* which are frequently selected, processed or which are important for the application and *infrequent items* which are less frequently operated. This is aimed to introduce short and complete versions of a menu both novice and expert users, respectively.

5. To develop new heuristics for mnemonics selection: the mnemonics which are proposed in the current method are mainly based on a conflict resolution between letters without considering the letters in the menu items themselves. It is intended to develop heuristics which consider initial letters, phonetics aspects (especially for shortcuts) and significant letters (e.g., other letters than those which have poor underlining such as 'i', 'j', 'l').

6. To embody menu design guidelines which can be automatically tested on the current menu tree (e.g., guidelines for ensuring consistency, unique mnemonics and shortcuts, appropriate wording) to provide on-line critiques.

7. To explore how user-customizable menus can be supported: currently, all menu items are generated and determined at design time. To support user-customizable menus, a menu item should be generated and determined as the results of a run time procedure. A further analysis is required to determine how this kind of menu item can be generated in Visual Basic V5.0 and on what kind of model this generation can rely upon. For example, a simplified user model can be exploited to select a particular pull-down menu or any particular item depending on the user profile.

Acknowledgements

The author would like to thank Louis Simon, from Teleglobe Canada, for performing initial user testing of the method presented here, and Prof. Gilbert Cockton for his kind review of this manuscript. This work was partially supported by a belgian "FIRST-Université" research program, convention n°1407, supported by the "Région Wallonne".

References

1. H. Balzert, F. Hofmann, V. Kruschinski, C. Niemann. The Janus Application Development Environment-Generating More than the User Interface. In J. Vanderdonckt (ed.): Proc. of the 2nd Int. Workshop on Computer-Aided Design of User Interfaces CADUI'96 (Namur, June 5-7, 1996). Namur: Presses Universitaires de Namur, 1996, pp. 183-206.

2. F. Bodart, A.-M. Hennebert, J.-M. Leheureux, I. Provot, J. Vanderdonckt: A Model-based Approach to Presentation: A Continuum from Task Analysis to Prototype. In F. Paternò (ed.): Proc. of 1st Eurographics Workshop on Design, Specification, Verification of Interactive Systems DSV-IS'94 (Carrara, June 8-10, 1994). Berlin: Springer-Verlag: Focus on Computer Graphics 1995, pp. 77-94. Available at http://www.info.fundp.ac.be/cgi-publi/pub-spec-paper?RP-94-023.

3. D.A. Duce, M.R. Gomes, F.R.A. Hopgood, J.R. Lee: User Interface Management and Design. In Proc. of the Workshop on User Interface Management Systems and Environments (Lisbon, June 4-6, 1990). Berlin: Springer-Verlag 1991.

4. W.K. Horton. Designing & Writing On line Documentation - Help files to Hypertext. Chichester: John Wiley & Sons, 1990.

5. J.I. Kiger. The depth/breadth tradeoff in the design of menu driven user interfaces. International Journal of Man-Machine Studies. Vol. 20. No. 2. February 1984, pp. 201-213.

6. K.L. Norman. The Psychology of Menu Selection: Designing Cognitive Control at the Human/Computer Interface. Norwood: Ablex Publishing Corp. 1991.

7. D.R. Olsen. MIKE: The Menu Interaction Kontrol Environment. ACM Transactions on Graphics. Vol. 5. No. 4. Octobre 1986, pp. 318-344.

8. D.R. Olsen. A Programming Language Basis for User Interface Management. In K. Bice, C. Lewis (eds.): Proc. of the ACM Conf. on Human Factors in Computing Systems CHI'89 (Austin, 30 April-4 May 1989). New York: ACM Press 1989, pp. 171-176.

9. K.R. Paap, R.J. Roske-Hofstrand. The Optimal Number of Menu Options per Panel. Human Factors. Vol. 28. No. 4. August 1986, pp. 377-385.

10. K.A. Parng, V.S. Ellingstad. Menuda: A Knowledge-Based Menu Design Expert System. In M. Galer, S. Harker et J. Ziegler (eds.): Proc. of the 31st Annual Meeting of the Human Factors Society HFS'87. Santa Monica: Human Factors Society 1987, pp. 1315-1319.

11. I. Petoud, Y. Pigneur: An Automatic and Visual Approach for User Interface Design. In G. Cockton (ed.): Proceedings of the IFIP TC 2/WG 2.7 Working Conference on Engineering for Human-Computer Interaction EHCI'89 (Napa Valley, 21-25 August 1989). Amsterdam: Elsevier Science Publishers B.V., 1990, pp. 403-419.

12. P. Shoval. Functional Design of a Menu-Tree Interface within Structured System Development. International Journal of Man-Machine Studies. Vol. 33. No. 5. November 1990, pp. 537-556.

13. J.L. Sibert, J.D. Foley. User-Computer Interface Design. Tutorial #1, Conference on Human Factors in Computing Systems CHI'90. Seattle, April 1, 1990.

14. J. Whiteside, S. Jones, P.S. Levy, D. Wixon. User Performance with Command, Menu, and Iconic Interfaces. In L. Borman & B. Curtis (eds.): Proceedings of the ACM Conference on Human Factors in Computing Systems CHI'85 (San Francisco, 14-18 April 1985). New York: ACM Press 1985, pp. 185-191.

Presentation Models by Example

Pablo Castells
E.T.S.I. Informatica
Universidad Autonoma de Madrid
Ctra. de Colmenar Viejo km. 17
28049 Madrid, Spain
pablo.castells@ii.uam.es

Pedro Szekely
Information Sciences Institute
University of Southern California
4676 Admiralty Way, #1001
Marina del Rey, CA 90292
szekely@isi.edu

Abstract Interface builders and multi-media authoring tools only support the construction of static displays where the components of the display are known at design time (e.g., buttons, menus). High-level UIMSs and automated designers support more sophisticated displays but are not easy to use as they require dealing explicitly with elaborate abstract concepts. This paper describes a GUI development environment, HandsOn, where complex displays of dynamically changing data can be constructed by direct manipulation. HandsOn integrates principles of graphic design, supports constraint-based layout, and has facilities for easily specifying the layout of collections of data. The system incorporates Programming By Example techniques to relieve the designer from having to deal with abstractions, and relies on a model-based language for the representation of the displays being constructed and as a means to provide information for the tool to reason about.

Keywords User interface development tools, model-based user interfaces, direct manipulation, programming by example, data visualization, graphic design.

1. Introduction

Visual tools for GUI development have greatly contributed to alleviate the effort involved in interface construction [7], and one can hardly conceive GUI development nowadays without the assistance of a graphical editor of some sort. Visual builders save time, require very little knowledge from the developer, and help improve the quality of displays. However, the tools we know today are confined to the construction of the static portion of presentations and provide very little or no support for the dynamic aspects of interface displays. The main reason for this is that the level of abstraction of the visual languages these tools provide is very low, which on the one hand favors their ease of use, but on the other makes it very hard to specify procedural information.

Research in the field of Programming By Example (PBE) has shown that it is possible to overcome these limitations by including inference capabilities and domain knowledge to make it possible to build abstractions by manipulating concrete objects [5, 8]. However the results achieved to date tend to lack the reliability required for a wide implantation in GUI technology. Inference entails unpredictability and lack of control when the user is not provided with all the relevant information about the state of the application and the steps taken by the system. The difficulty resides in finding the appropriate form to convey this information.

On the other end, certain high-level systems like UIMSs and model-based tools support sophisticated interface features [2, 3, 12, 13, 14] but they are hard to use as they require learning a particular specification language and understanding non-trivial abstract concepts. While some of these tools have been complemented with graphical editors, the interaction with the developer tends to be based on menus, property-sheets, and the like. Typically, direct manipulation is supported for the customization of displays after they are generated, but the designer is not provided with adequate control over the generation process itself. Carrying the kind of abstract and complex underlying concepts and mechanisms as these systems use to an intuitive visual environment is a difficult problem in general.

Even for the static part of displays, interface builders and multimedia authoring tools do not provide adequate support. While graphic design has become an essential part of the development of GUI products, few if any tools support it, or they do in a very limited way. The layout facilities are patterned after the layout facilities of drawing editors where groups of elements can be left-aligned, right-aligned, etc. Graphic designers often work by defining guides and grids to organize page layouts [1, 15].

Our research aims at extending the expressive power of existing visual tools for the construction of a significant range of dynamic displays while retaining the ease of use of direct manipulation, providing facilities for constructing well structured and visually appealing screen layouts. Our approach consists of a) using the model-based paradigm for the internal representation of the constructed displays, with models that support dynamic presentation functionalities, b) developing an extended visual language with the appropriate level of abstraction, that incorporates PBE techniques for the interactive specification of dynamic presentations by manipulating interface presentation objects in a visual tool, c) allowing the developer to create examples of application data at design-time, and to use them to construct concrete presentations that are generalized by the system, and d) incorporating high-level graphic design facilities that help improve interface quality and simplify the construction of complex layouts. These ideas have been carried to a GUI development tool, HandsOn (Human-Amiable tool for building Neat Display Structures by working ON examples), for the interactive construction of presentation models [5].

Figures 1 through 3 show examples of displays built in HandsOn. Figure 1 is the famous Minard chart showing Napoleon's march to Moscow. The thickness of the line encodes the number of troops in Napoleon's army, the line darkness encodes the temperature (darker is hotter). The squares and labels indicate places where battles took place. The input data consists of two lists of records. One containing information about latitude, longitude, number of troops, and temperature, and the other list containing records of the time and places where battles took place. This figure is an example of a custom designed display that cannot be produced by any charting program. Sage [10, 11] can automatically generate this chart from the relational data, but it requires that each tuple provide the two end-points of each line. In HandsOn this display can be modeled independently of the format in which the data comes in (list of points or list of intervals).

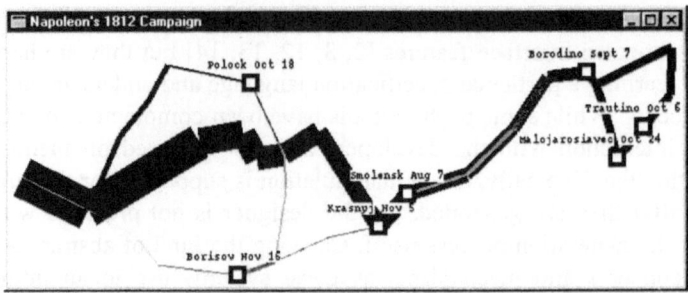

Fig. 1. Napoleon's march to Moscow

Figure 2 shows a composite bar-chart. The input data is a list of three records one for each person. The record for each person itself contains a list of records about the activities that the person is managing. This chart cannot be produced by charting programs, but can be produced by Sage. The difficulty in generating this display is that it consists of two charts put side by side in a coordinated way, and each chart itself is a hierarchical composition of an outline display (the data for each person) with a chart (the activities managed by each person).

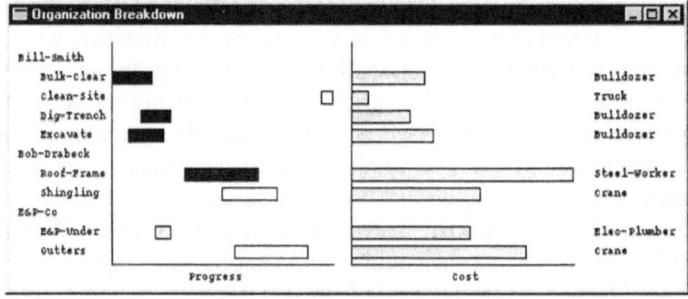

Fig. 2. Complex bar-chart

Figure 3 shows a tree structure where the width of each node is dependent on the information contained in that node. This figure is interesting because it shows that HandsOn supports recursively defined models.

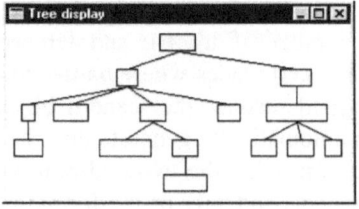

Fig. 3. Tree display

The rest of the paper is organized as follows. The next section gives a quick description of the main components of the system. Section 3 gives an overview of the underlying interface model used for the construction of displays, and how models are visualized graphically. Section 4 describes the PBE techniques used in our system to define constraints and control structures, which are illustrated in section 5 by showing a complete example.

2. System overview

HandsOn takes its presentation model from previous work in Mastermind (see [4]). The model language has been conceived to be easily amenable to interactive specification and bridges the gap between the declarative descriptions obtained from a graphical tool and the procedural information needed to execute the interfaces described in the model. Visual languages are well suited for the description of static shapes, i.e. declarative information, but it is hard to obtain procedural information this way. The model-based approach helps by providing a declarative representation to model dynamic display behavior. Declarative models are constructed in a graphical environment, and executable presentations are generated from the information collected in the model. Figure 4 shows the architecture of the HandsOn presentation generation system.

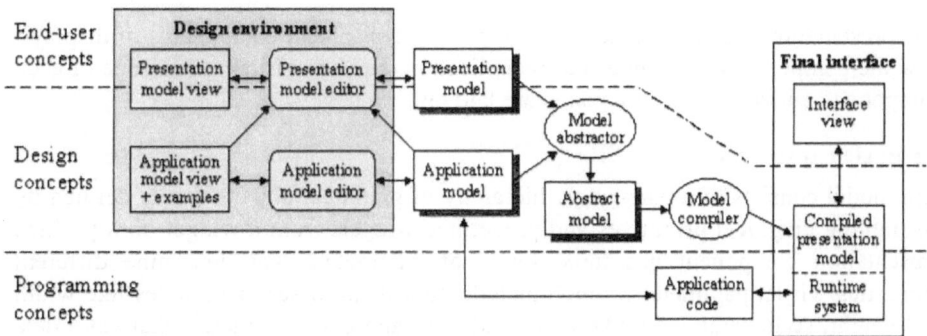

Fig. 4. HandsOn architecture

The HandsOn development environment consists of a graphical presentation editor and an application data builder (see fig. 6). The latter is used to create examples of application data, and the former to construct presentations. The developer uses data examples to provide values at design-time for the construction of interface presentations that display application data at run-time. The designer can browse the classes that are defined in the application, select classes, create instances of the classes in the application data builder and edit their contents to construct application object examples.

The data builder displays data as a tree where composite data (objects and lists) can be expanded or collapsed. HandsOn provides direct manipulation facilities for connecting data from the application examples built by the designer to graphical components of the presentation. Rather than building a generic display, the designer constructs specific displays using specific data and the system generates abstract constructs by generalizing the examples. Data examples provide the designer with concrete objects to refer to, and they provide the system with information that the system uses to infer the designer's intent.

Tightly integrated in both the visual language and the presentation model, HandsOn provides graphic design tools like movable guides and dynamic grids for global screen space organization. These tools are not provided merely as passive visual aids, but in the form of design objects that interact actively with other objects of the display, playing a central role in defining the dynamic behavior of presentations.

The output that results from the presentation editor is a model of the interface presentation containing references to application data examples. From this model a generic model is generated by generalizing from the examples, inferring data characterizations to parameterize presentations. The abstract model is translated into an executable representation that is given to the run-time system to generate and manage displays at run-time. The run-time system maps the compiled abstract model to actual application data to generate the final display that is presented to the end-user.

3. The model

The presentation model specifies the structure and graphical components of displays, how the components are connected to application data, the visual appearance of each component, and how the components are laid out.

3.1 Basic constructs

The model consists of a part-whole hierarchy of graphical objects that is defined by assembling graphical primitives and predefined widgets from a widget library. Each presentation component has three kinds of parameters that determine different properties: visual parameters, which include guides and other magnitudes like width and height, style parameters like color and font, and data parameters that store data from the application. Components can serve as prototypes to create instances, i.e. copies that dynamically inherit properties from the prototype.

Predefined components have their own set of primitive parameters that control their basic graphic properties, but new parameters can be added by the designer. All components have at least four natural guides (the bounding box) that define components' size and position. Other guides can be added, like middle guides, a baseline for text labels, or other arbitrary guides. Two of these guides define the origin of coordinates for all the other guides and sub-parts of the component.

The model supports one-directional constraints on parameters with respect to other parameters and/or application data. Constraints are themselves model objects with their own parameters that can in turn be constrained, allowing for the incremental construction of complex constraints. Predefined components usually have default constraints on some of their parameters and guides (e.g. the width parameter of graphic primitives depends on left and right).

Other dynamic constructs supported by the model include iterative displays that show variable amounts of application data. Iterative constructs are described by a presentation component and a collection of application values. They are created at run-time by creating one replica of the component per value in the sequence of data. Typically, certain settings of the copies depend on the corresponding values of the list. If the list of values changes, the replication is automatically updated accordingly. The presentation model also allows the specification of conditional displays whose structure, layout and visual appearance depends dynamically on the data to be presented or the presentation context (e.g. available screen space).

The application model includes standard types, sequences, object class definitions, and specific example objects created by the developer. Application examples are the keystone for constructing abstract control structures without using an abstract (visual or textual) language. Our application model requires the application to be written or wrapped in a programming framework that supports dynamic object creation, object browsing, dynamic method invocation and a mechanism for the notification of changes in object attribute values. In our prototype implementation we have assumed that the part of the application that is relevant for the interface is written in Amulet [6], but a more general platform like CORBA would meet our requirements as well, and would impose less restrictions on the application programmer.

3.2 Visualizing the model

Presentation models are visualized in the graphical editor under a representation that is very similar to the final resulting interface. When abstract constructs are visualized that depend on application data, data examples are used to provide the designer with a concrete representation.

Certain elements appear in the editor that are not part of the final interface. It is the case of guides, grids and parameters. Guides and grids are represented by vertical or horizontal lines and sets of lines respectively. Non-guide parameters are visualized as a box showing the name of the parameter. When selected, their value is shown and can be edited if it is not constrained. To avoid clutter, these auxiliary objects are hidden most of the time, but there are (implicit and explicit) commands to bring them up for selected objects. Figure 5 shows a portion of the presentation editor work area where a text label, a rectangle, and a line have been created. The parameters of all three objects are being visualized; label *WIDTH* and line *THICKNESS* are selected. The bounding-box guides of the rectangle are visible, and other guides are hidden.

Guides and parameter icons are shown in blue when they are not constrained, and in red otherwise (this cannot be seen in the grayscale figure). Free guides can be moved and free parameters' value can be edited, so that dependent guides and parameters, if any, are updated accordingly. Constrained guides and parameters cannot be altered directly unless the designer wants to customize the constraint by demonstration, as we will describe in section 4.1.

Constraints involving selected parameters can be visualized in the editor as red arrows that connect an output variable to one or more input variables. In figure 5, the top guide of the rectangle is constrained to be placed a fixed offset above the

106

horizontal guide near the bottom of the figure. The designer can free parameters and guides, change input variables or constrain other parameters by moving constraint-arrow ends to different objects. Selected constraints can be copied and pasted in the editor, so that new unconnected arrows appear that can be linked to other objects, defining new constraint instances that take their settings after the original constraint.

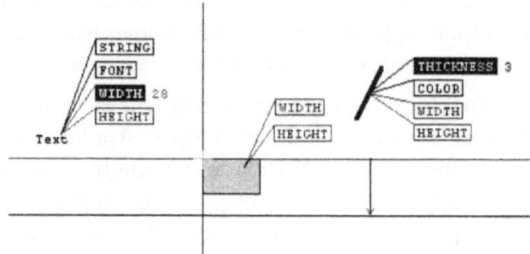

Fig. 5. Visualizing model objects in the presentation editor.

4. Building presentations by example

The designer creates display components by selecting graphical primitives and predefined components from a widget library. The graphical editor allows grouping components, adding guides, grids or new parts to aggregate components, visualizing component parameters and editing their value, and other common usual facilities of graphical editors. The designer can define constraints visually and customize them by demonstrating the desired effects. By manipulating application data examples the designer can define data dependencies and abstract control structures.

4.1 Defining constraints

HandsOn supports one-directional constraints that consist of the composition of a set of standard functions like linear functions and max/min, application object attribute access expressions (data constraints), and invocation of object methods. The designer can set constraints visually on presentation parameters by dragging or pointing at parameters, guides, and application data, within or across the presentation and application models. We use the generic term *link operation* to refer to all gestures that indicate a direct association between two presentation elements, like dragging a guide onto another guide, which sets an equality constraint on the moved guide with respect to the other guide when *guide-snapping-mode* is on. A more general way to perform link operations is to press the *link* command button, point at a guide, a parameter or a presentation component, and drag the mouse onto a guide, a presentation parameter or a value being displayed in the application area. A rubber-band red arrow from the object to the mouse pointer provides interim feedback for the operation.

The meaning of these gestures and the kind of constraints that result depend on the nature and characteristics of the variables involved, and a few global environment settings like guide-snapping-mode and *constraint-demonstration-mode*. The action to be taken in response to the designer's manipulations often involve other operations besides creating constraints, and is determined by a set of heuristics that examine the presentation and application objects involved each time the designer performs a link operation. Also certain restrictions apply that prevent the creation of illegal constraints like the ones that would cause circularities.

For instance in the construction of the Minard chart shown in figure 1, if the designer links the *THICKNESS* parameter of a line segment to the *TROOPS* attribute of an object of type *Stage* constructed in the data area, the system defines an equality constraint from the value of the attribute to the thickness of the line, if constraint-demonstration-mode is off. This means that the thickness of the line will be equal to the troop size at the corresponding march stage, which will probably range over several hundred thousands units. In this case, this is probably not what the designer wants. Rather, the constraint should include a scaling factor to adjust the application data to the desired dimensions of the chart on the screen, as is usually the case when displays take numeric magnitudes from application data. This is why the system automatically defines a linear transformation constraint when the designer links numeric values if demonstration mode is on. The linear transformation is defined to conform to the current values of the variables being connected, giving default values to underdetermined coefficients. In the previous example, in demonstration mode the system sets $THICKNESS = a \cdot TROOPS + b$ where b is assigned the default value 0 and a is assigned the quotient of the current values of *THICKNESS* and *TROOPS*.

The designer can modify the coefficients of linear constraints by demonstration by editing the constrained values. This mechanism is activated when the constraint demonstration mode is on. A constraint is customized by creating a copy of the constraint and connecting it to a new set of variables. The new set of values plus the original one provide two equations involving the coefficients of the constraint. By repeating the operation, more equations are obtained. Linear constraints keep track of the maximum consistent set of most recently provided equations obtained in this way so that the coefficients of the linear transformation can be determined by solving the system of equations (if there are not enough equations, the appropriate number of coefficients are taken as constants). Once the equations are solved, the result is applied to all instances of the constraint. By editing values involved in one of the constraint instances, the corresponding equation is modified accordingly and the coefficients are recalculated. Value sets can also be provided without copying constraints by detaching a constraint from its variables, modifying the value of the variables and reattaching the constraint.

When HandsOn is not in constraint demonstration mode, constraint output variables cannot be changed, and when input values are modified, the constrained parameters are automatically adjusted to enforce the constraint.

4.2 Control structures

Each time a presentation parameter is mapped to a data value, HandsOn examines the data structure containing the value, all the way up to the top-level of the structure, looking for structural properties like recursivity, iteration, pre-existing links to presentation objects, and other characteristics of the data. This analysis provides the system with hints to infer control structures to display the data, like replications, recursive presentations and conditionals.

Replications are collections of variable amounts of components that correspond to sequences of application data. To build a replication the designer needs to describe a generic component and how it maps to application data, and then specify how the remaining copies should be created using a list of data, and how they should be laid out. In HandsOn the designer builds replications for specific examples of data sequences, and the system generalizes the constructed presentation for lists of values of the same type.

The simplest way to define a replication is to link a guide or a parameter of a presentation component to a value displayed in the application model area that belongs to a list or to a data structure contained in a list. When the designer does so, upon confirmation the system assumes that a replication is being defined. The component to which the guide or parameter belongs is the component to replicate, and the data sequence is the list that contains the value to which the presentation was linked. Each replication component will have a constraint to its associated application data as defined by the link operation between the original component and the data. HandsOn is able to generate nested replications for nested data lists, but does not handle more than two nesting levels at a time. Treating more than two nestig levels at once would produce a cluttered construct almost impossible to handle for the designer.

By using example values the designer can see at design-time how the replication will look like. By manipulating the generated replicas, the designer defines how the replication should be laid out. The designer can also refine the presentation of replicas by editing the first one, changing its visual settings and defining more constraints to data, so that the system automatically propagates changes to the remaining replicas. How actions on individual replicas are translated to remaining replicas is determined by a set of heuristics that select iteration variables and constants among the elements involved.

For example, to build the chart shown in figure 1, the designer creates a list of objects of type *Stage* in the data area (assuming the data is organized as a list of intervals rather than a list of points), and draws a line segment in the presentation area. Then the designer links the *THICKNESS* parameter of the line to the *TROOPS* attribute of the first *Stage* (see fig. 6). Because the stage object appears inside a list, HandsOn infers a replication of line segments with respect to stages, with line thickness constrained to stage troops. Now the designer links the guides that determine the x and y coordinates of the start point of the first replicated line to the attributes *LATITUDE* and *LONGITUDE* of the *START_POINT* of the first stage. Automatically every replicated line's start point takes its coordinates from the corresponding stage. Line end points are constrained to stage *END_POINTs* coordinates in a similar way. Were the data given as a list of points, the designer would attach the end point of the first segment to the second point in the data sequence, so that replicated segments would be associated to two instead of one element of the sequence.

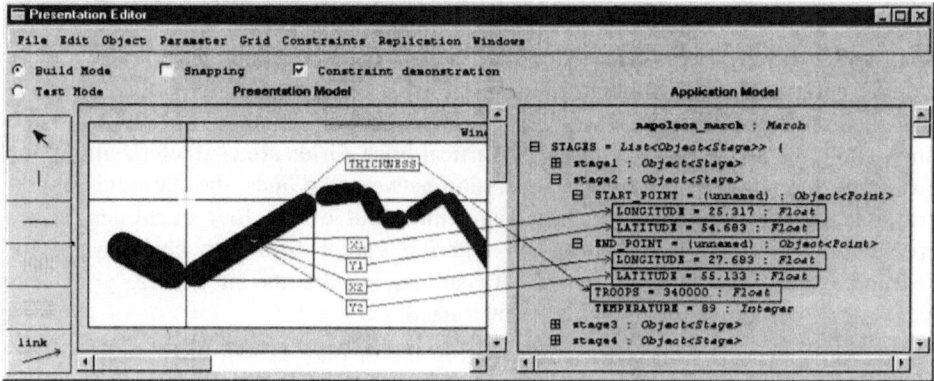

Fig. 6. The HandsOn environment: data constraints and replication of line segment

HandsOn is also able to infer presentations for recursive data structures like trees and networks. The system detects a recursive presentation when the designer links two presentation objects of the same type to two respective objects in the application area that have a containment relationship, i.e. one object can be accessed from the other through a traversal of successive object attributes and list members. After asking for the designer's confirmation, the system builds a recursive presentation by defining an abstract component prototype that consists of grouping the two graphical objects plus other related components, and taking the whole abstract prototype as the model for the second graphical object involved in the recursion. The recursion prototype has an input parameter that is assigned successive values from the recursive data structure until an empty list or a NULL object is reached, or until an object is reached that has already been displayed in the recursive presentation. Related components to be included in the recursion prototype, like arcs between nodes of a tree, are determined by heuristics that check for constraint relationships with the two initial objects used to define the recursion. These additional components can be added before or after the recursion is defined.

If the containment relationship in the recursive data structure involves list membership, recursion is combined with replication, as is the case in the tree display shown in figure 3 (recursion over tree levels and iteration over node children). HandsOn does not currently handle the case where recursion involves nested lists.

A limited form of conditional presentation is also currently supported in the visual environment. When the designer links two variables that have different types, the system first tries to find an appropriate transformation that is compatible with the types (see section 4.4 below). If no defined transformation function is applicable, HandsOn creates a conditional definition for the constrained value based on a switch-like statement that is defined by tuples of value correspondences. A more general mechanism for the specification of conditional presentation constructs is currently under development.

4.3 Layout

The MASTERMIND layout facilities are based on the grid design techniques used in graphic design. By manipulating guides and grids the designer determines the size and positioning of presentation objects. Guides are horizontal or vertical reference lines, and grids are sets of horizontal or vertical lines. Grids are characterized by four quantities: the number of lines, the separation between the lines, the start and the end positions. A grid is defined by specifying three out of the four quantities. Other presentation parameters are edited by entering values from the keyboard or by defining constraints to other values. By setting constraints on guides, grids and parameters, self-adjusting layouts are constructed.

For example, a horizontal grid can be used in the display shown in figure 2 for the layout of labels and bars. The grid spacing can be defined in terms of the font size of the text being displayed, and the top and bottom of the grid can be defined to match horizontal guides at the top and bottom of the window. Interface builders do not provide this kind of facilities for good page design. Some interface builders provide grids, but they are used just for initial placement of the items. It is not possible, for instance to specify the grid size based on font size, so that if the font size is changed at run-time, the design doesn't break apart.

Guides and grids are also crucial for defining the layout of replicated parts. In the simplest case, a replication can be assigned to a grid, meaning that consecutive replicas are placed in consecutive grid-lines. The designer attaches the primary replica to one or more grid lines and the system infers the positioning of the rest of the objects across the grid. HandsOn includes heuristics for the adjustment of the layout strategy by manipulating individual replicas: it is possible to specify the grid-line index for the first replica, to specify the number of grid-lines to be occupied by each replica, to specify that each replica should go to the next free grid-line, etc. Nested replications can be assigned to a common grid, so the elements are placed sequentially on the common grid (see fig. 7). Recursive presentations can also be laid out with respect to a single grid, as in the tree display (fig. 3).

4.4 Data descriptions

To infer the appropriate effects from the designer's actions, HandsOn uses information obtained by examining model properties and design context information. The system analyzes value types, visual properties and geometric relationships among the objects being manipulated, structural patterns of the data being used, existing mappings from data to presentations, and data visualization context. This information is used to generate automatically presentation constructs and to produce generalizations from the examples provided by the designer. The latter involves generating abstract references to data values and presentation objects, and substituting concrete values by presentation variables whose value is computed at run-time according to the way data references are described.

Data reference descriptions involve describing the data structure traversal and the transformation functions that have to be applied in order to compute values. These descriptions are generated when the designer assigns data examples to presentation parameters. Transformation functions can be specified by the designer or inferred by the system by examining the types of involved variables. When the designer links two variables that have different types, HandsOn tries to construct a compatible constraint by considering object method calls (if an application object is involved) and standard conversion functions (like string to color or number to string) that agree with the types. The designer is asked for a choice if more than one function is possible (if none is found by the system or provided by the designer, a conditional is defined as explained in 4.3). This is how, for example, progress bars in figure 2 can have their left and right (integers) attached to task start and end dates respectively, if *Date* objects have a *date_to_int* method. In demonstration mode, if the return value of the constraint is a number, a linear transformation is added for scaling as described in 4.1.

Structure traversal specifications are generated to match the structure of the data being displayed in the application area. When a value being assigned to a presentation is nested in a higher-level data structure, HandsOn infers a data description for the value that involves accessing the nested value from the top-level data structure displayed at this time. References to application examples are used to parameterize presentations. Some of the data examples give rise to presentation input arguments and others become data access expressions. Whether a data reference is generalized in one way or the other depends on the context in which the data is displayed at design-time. An input parameter is created for objects that are displayed at the top-level in the application example builder at the time when the designer connects presentations to data, and all other values become internal parameters that take their value from input parameters, which states a natural rule that should be easy to understand for designers.

5. An example

The bar-chart display (fig. 2) is a good example of the use of replications, grids and guides. The display consists of two nested replications. The outer replication corresponds to the list of workers that perform a work like repairing a building, and the inner replication corresponds to the list of tasks that each worker performs. For each task the display shows its name, a bar that indicates the start and end dates of the task and its status (different colors for finished, on course, cancelled), a bar that corresponds to task cost, and a label showing the resource used for the task.

5.1 Top-level replication

The designer starts by creating the labels that display worker names. S/he creates a window in the presentation design area and adds a label to the window client area. Then the designer creates an object of type *Works* in the application area, gives it the name *repair_building* and fills it in with example values down to the innermost levels, creating a complex data structure of nested objects and lists (see fig. 7).

At the top-level, *repair_building* has a single attribute whose value is a list of objects of type *Worker*. The designer links the *STRING* parameter of the label to the attribute *NAME* of the first worker, *bill_smith*. The object *bill_smith* appearing inside a list of objects, HandsOn, upon confirmation, automatically replicates the original label with respect to the list of workers, attaching labels' text to worker names.

The original label's position did not have any constraint for the system to propagate, so the replicated labels are given a default arbitrary positioning close to the first label. The designer adds a horizontal grid to the window, and adjusts grid line spacing as desired. S/he activates guide snapping and drags the first label's top guide onto the first grid line, defining a constraint that is automatically propagated to the remaining replicas, attaching each label's top to successive grid lines.

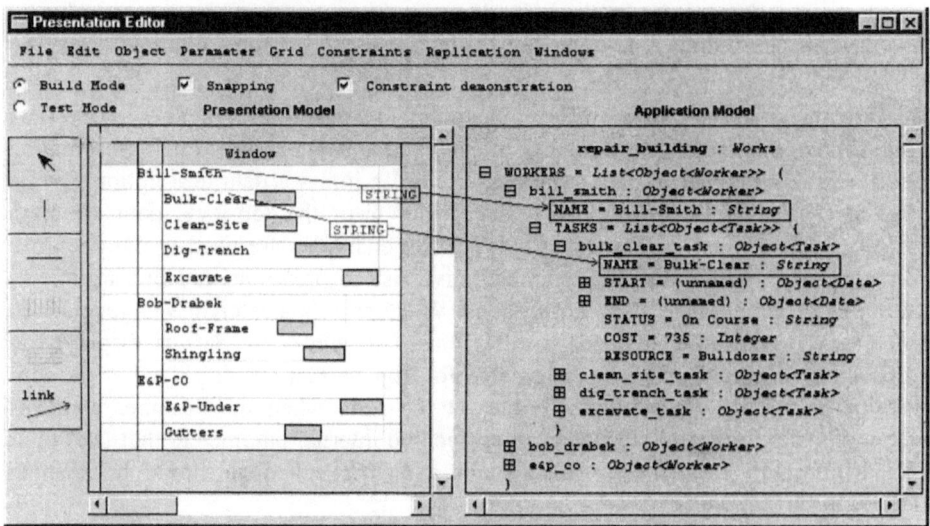

Fig. 7. Building and laying out nested replications in the HandsOn environment

In order to make room for the worker's tasks display, the designer moves the second label down by two grid lines. This modifies the replication layout rule so that replicas are placed every three grid lines. The designer left-aligns the labels by adding a vertical guide to the window and linking the first label's left guide to it, so that all labels take this constraint.

5.2 Editing replications

Now the designer adds labels for the tasks performed by each worker: the designer adds a label next to the first worker name label, and groups both labels. HandsOn propagates this operation so now the replication is made of groups of two labels. Groups are visualized as gray-border rectangles that comprise their components.

Worker objects have a *TASKS* attribute that is a list of the tasks the worker performs. The designer links the new label's *STRING* parameter to the attribute *NAME* of the first task of *bill_smith*, *excavate_task*. The system notices that *excavate_task* belongs to a list, so a replication of labels is created showing the name of tasks performed by *bill_smith*. Because the replicated label belongs to a replica associated to *bill_smith*, similar replications are generated in the remaining replicas of the top-level iteration, substituting *bill_smith* by the value (the worker) that corresponds to each replica.

The designer now attaches the first label's top to the grid line immediately below the *bill_smith* label. Task labels of all workers are laid out vertically in response, taking one grid line per label starting after each worker's name label grid line. To avoid overlapping and wasted space between worker groups, the designer moves down the second group to the grid line immediately below the first group. As a consequence, the worker replication is laid out according to the rule "take as many grid lines as needed". The designer left-aligns task name labels by adding a vertical guide and linking the first label's left to it (see fig. 7).

5.3 Constraint customization

Bars for task progress and task cost, and labels for task resources are added for all task replicas just by adding them to the first replica. The left and right position of progress bars should correspond to the start and end dates of the corresponding task. The designer links the left guide of the *bulk_clear_task* progress bar to the *START* attribute of the *bulk_clear_task* object. Types do not match so upon designer's acceptance HandsOn creates a constraint using the *date_to_int* method of the *Date* object class, followed by a linear transformation that is given default coefficients, as described in 4.1. The constraint is tuned under demonstration mode by copying and attaching it to the bar's right and the task end date, and by manually manipulating date values and bar ends to obtain the desired effect. As before, settings are transmitted to the corresponding replicated parts.

Cost bars are left aligned using a vertical guide, and their width is linked to task costs, customizing the linear constraint for scaling. Progress bar color is defined as a conditional property by linking different color values to different corresponding status string values.

When the running presentation is generated, the example object *repair_building* turns into an input parameter that is added to the chart top-level widget (i.e. the window). This parameter has to be supplied at run-time with an object of type *Works*, and all the parameters that were linked to data inside *repair_building* are constrained to compute their values from the object stored in the input parameter.

The construction process described is only one of many possible ways to build the display. For instance, it is possible to create all the components that correspond to one particular task (name label, progress bar, cost bar, resource label), group them, replicate the group for all tasks of one particular worker, and then replicate again for all workers. The way we have shown the construction of the example, the display is constructed by columns, paying little attention to the nested structure, whereas in the latter approach the chart is seen as a set of rows and the design is a more direct mapping to the nested data structure.

6. Related work

HandsOn's presentation model is based mostly on Mastermind [4]. One can think of HandsOn as a graphical editor built on top of the Mastermind presentation system in which the designer can construct presentation models by direct manipulation of display objects without being concerned with how the underlying model is being represented. The main improvement with respect to the Mastermind model is the incorporation of application data examples into the model at design-time, from which generic models are abstracted by the system.

Our model of presentation is similar to Humanoid's templates [12], which also have constructs for replication and conditionals, though Humanoid does not support layout based on grids and guides, and the way they are used in our system for the layout of replications. Humanoid includes a graphical environment for the construction of interfaces, but the designer works mainly on an abstract representation of the model. The designer is provided at design-time with a view of the resulting display, though the direct manipulation facilities supported on this view are intended for browsing rather than for editing the model.

Peridot [8] supports creating sets of widget copies by using examples of data sequences at design-time. Unlike HandsOn, Peridot requires the designer to specify explicitly input parameters for presentations. Peridot uses a very simple data model consisting basically of lists and simple types, whereas HandsOn supports more elaborate relationships involving complex data structures. Peridot automatically infers the layout for sets of widgets by requiring very little information from the designer, but it does not support the construction of complex layouts.

In many respects, HandsOn is similar to automatic presentation planners such as Sage [10, 11] and Gold [9]. These systems allow the designer to associate specific data values to presentation settings, and they analyze characteristics of the data in order to infer properties of the display. However, Gold and Sage can only produce presentations from relational data, whereas HandsOn can model a much larger variety of displays.

HandsOn borrows the idea of using constraints for propagating values in the component tree from Amulet [6]. HandsOn is implemented using Amulet, and the generated models are translated into Amulet objects, making extensive use of the Amulet constraint system.

7. Conclusions

HandsOn combines the expressive power of a model-based system with the ease of use of a programming by example tool. Demonstrational techniques benefit from the model-based paradigm because the model provides an explicit declarative representation of the interface the tool can reason about. HandsOn infers presentation constructs by analyzing model information describing value types, structural properties of data, and spatial relationships in the presentation. The system also uses information about how the designer visualizes and handles data examples.

The direct manipulation techniques supported are qualitatively more powerful than those provided by interface builders and multi-media authoring tools in that they allow the specification of abstract constructs, which are used to create both static and dynamic displays. Balance between expressive power and ease of use is achieved by a) keeping limited the amount and complexity of model abstraction the developer has to deal with and b) mapping underlying model abstractions to visible presentation objects, reducing the mental transformation effort required from the developer between different representations of the interface.

HandsOn is currently under development, though most of the features described here have been essentially completed. The system has been implemented in C++ using Amulet [6], both for the design environment and for running the generated interfaces. The generated interfaces and the interface constructs visualized in the environment at design-time share a great part of their functionality —the designer works on presentations that have the same dynamic behavior as the executable display that results. However the generation of interface code from the model is still only partially implemented.

We are also improving the conditional presentation mechanism described in this paper to support displays whose structure and appearance depends on arbitrary conditions on data values, presentation parameters, and platform characteristics. The action side of the conditionals will consist of alternative presentations that can be specified by the designer either by constructing each one from scratch or by successively applying the desired modifications for each condition to a single component. Mastermind provides a model for this kind of constructs [4, 13]. The main difficulty now resides in specifying the model by demonstrating the conditions that determine the presentation to be applied.

Our work so far has focussed on the visual part of interface design and does not currently address aspects related to the dialog with the end-user. Our plans for the near future include the extension of our work to a more comprehensive environment that provides support for interactive aspects based on user task modeling.

Acknowledgements

Our thanks to the anonymous reviewers for their detailed feedback and helpful comments. The work reported in this paper was partially supported by the *Plan Nacional de Investigación,* Spain, Project Number TIC96-0723-C02-02.

References

1. R. Ballinger. *Layout and Graphic Design*. Van Nostrand Reinhold, New York, 1970.

2. Bauer, B. *Generating User Interfaces from Formal Specifications of the Application*. Proceedings of 2nd International Workshop on Computer-Adied Design of User Interfaces (CADUI'96). Presses Universitaires de Namur, 1996.

3. F. Bodart, A.-M. Hennebert, J.-M. Leheureux, I. Provot, B. Sacre, J. Vanderdonckt. *Towards a Systematic Building of Software Architectures: the Trident Methodological Guide*. Proceedings of 2nd Eurographics Workshop on Design, Specification, Verification of Interactive Systems (DSV-IS'95). Springer-Verlag, 1995.

4. P. Castells, P. Szekely and E. Salcher. *Declarative Models of Presentation.* Proceedings of International Conference on Intelligent Interfaces (IUI'96). Orlando, Florida, 1997.

5. P. Castells and P. Szekely. *HandsOn: Dynamic Interface Presentations by Example.* To appear in Proceedings of 8th International Conference on Human-Computer Interaction (HCI International ' 99). Munich, Germany, 1999.

6. A. Cypher (ed.). *Watch What I Do: Programming by Demonstration.* The MIT Press, 1993.

7. B. A. Myers et al. *The Amulet 2.0 Reference Manual.* Carnegie Mellon University Tech. Report, 1996.

8. B. A. Myers. *User Interface Software Tools.* ACM Transactions on Computer Human Interaction, v2, n1, March 1995, pp. 64-103.

9. B. A. Myers. *Creating User Interfaces by Demonstration.* Academic Press, San Diego, 1988.

10. B. A. Myers, J. Goldstein, M. Goldberg. *Creating Charts by Demonstration.* Proceedings of the CHI'94 Conference. ACM Press, Boston, April 1994.

11. S. F. Roth and J. Mattis *Data Characterization for Intelligent Graphics Presentation.* Proceedings of SIGCHI'90 Human Factors in Computing Systems. ACM press, Seattle ,WA, April 1990, pp. 193-200.

12. S.F. Roth, J. Kolojejchick, J. Mattis, and J. Goldstein. *Interactive Graphic Design Using Automatic Presentation Knowledge.* Proceedings of the CHI'94 Conference. ACM Press, Boston, April 1994, pp. 112-117

13. P. Szekely, P. Luo, and R. Neches. *Beyond Interface Builders: Model-Based Interface Tools.* Proceedings of INTERCHI'93, April 1993.

14. P. Szekely, P. Sukaviriya, P. Castells, J. Muthukumarasamy and E. Salcher. *Declarative Interface Models for User Interface Construction: The Mastermind Approach.* In Engineering for Human-Computer Interaction, L. Bass and C. Unger (eds.). Chapman & Hall, 1996.

15. A. Wiecha, W. Bennett, S. Boies, J. Gould and S. Greene. *ITS: A Tool For Rapidly Developing Interactive Applications.* ACM Transactions on Information Systems 8(3), July 1990, pp. 204-236.

16. R. Williams. *The Non-Designer Design Book.* Peachpit Press Inc., Berkeley, California, 1994.

Refinement of the PAC model for the component-based design and specification of television based interfaces

Panos Markopoulos, Paul Shrubsole and John de Vet
Philips Research Eindhoven
The Netherlands
{panos, psh, devet}@natlab.research.philips.com

Abstract. Componentisation of software promises to deliver cost efficiency that has not been achieved through object orientation [19]. PAC [5] is a popular conceptual architecture for structuring user interface software in an object oriented fashion. This paper reports our experience of adapting and refining PAC as a component architecture in the context of consumer electronics, and On-screen Displays in particular. The paper describes a structured scheme for the specification of user interface software components, distinguishing 'look' and 'feel' specific components, and fostering their modular development and re-use.

Keywords. PAC, user interface, software architecture, on-screen display, specification.

1   Introduction

This paper discusses a component architecture and a specification scheme for On-Screen Displays (OSD), i.e. graphical user interfaces for consumer electronics devices. The OSD may be supported, e.g., by a 'Set-Top Box' which is a device that displays, on an analogue television-set, a graphical user interface, e.g., for controlling its own signal processing functionality, a video recorder or electronic-program-guide (EPG) information provided by broadcasters, etc.

The component architecture discussed is an application and refinement of the Presentation Abstraction Control (PAC) model of graphical user interface software [5]. The architecture addresses the following requirements, which are typical for the consumer electronics domain:

- The user interfaces specified will be supported on a variety of platforms with different graphical output abilities: e.g., text only output, pixel based graphics, and different refresh rates for animation. The same 'feel' should be supported on all platforms, although the 'look' must adapt to the target platform. This may range from text only to animated, 3-D graphics. Thus, 'look' and 'feel' specific components should be specified and implemented independently.

- User interfaces are typically made for product families of possibly hundreds of variants supporting different languages and features. To support product variations at the architectural level, components should be treated as binary entities (i.e. not as source code) which can be composed by third parties relying only on their interface descriptions [19]. The composition of components relies on the specification of component interfaces (the concept is explained in more detail below).

- There are limited computing resources available for graphical user interfaces. Low to middle end products have processing abilities comparable to those of personal computers 10-12 years ago. High-end products can match current (low-end) personal computers in processing power, but they can only use 10-20% of their processing power to support graphical interaction. Most processing power is dedicated to signal processing.

- Implementations are mostly in C and are not object oriented. To avoid memory and computational overheads binding of messages to methods (or more generally procedure names to procedures) is static, as opposed to run-time binding which characterises object oriented systems.

- For current graphical user interfaces for OSD, the user input device is a remote control (rather than, e.g., a mouse) and there is no 'free moving cursor' supported. The implication is that the user interface architecture can be simpler than that required for direct manipulation interfaces. The focus of user actions changes through a 'jumping hilight' between large 'blocks' on the screen, which are accessed through constrained remote control events. Graphical objects are not dragged and dropped and no 'fine grain semantic feedback' is required. The latter requirements have been quite influential in shaping user interface software architectures for desktop computers (including the PAC model), but currently they are not necessary in the OSD domain.

- Early descriptions of the PAC model, e.g., [3,5], can be seen as a set of guidelines for structuring applications. To render the model operational, a specification technique is required that maps in a straightforward manner to implementation constructs.

- OSD interaction designers are mostly non-software engineers. Their specifications should be transparent to implementation concerns but it should be possible to relate them to specifications used by software designers. The specification of software components is therefore associated with a 'designer oriented' specification of the design concept proposed. This was based on the Interaction Styles template [9] which is discussed briefly and exemplified in the following sections.

The remainder of the paper discusses an architectural model that is shaped to address these requirements. Section 2 discusses related work. Section 3 presents the architectural model and the specification scheme derived. Section 4 discusses an example. Section 5 discusses the contributions and limitations of this work and current work.

2   Related Work

The refinement of PAC discussed here is an architectural model which can be used *prescriptively* to design, specify and implement interactive software components, and has been applied *descriptively*, to classify software components that support advanced graphics (advanced refers here to the state-of-the-art OSD). The intended users of this model are software engineers who design and implement graphical interface software. The aim is to encourage the modular development of software components, their inventorisation and systematic re-use.

The requirement for separating dialogue and functionality related components from presentation components is well served by the PAC model. However, this model needs to be articulated more clearly in an architectural framework (as argued by Coutaz [7]). This paper undertakes this effort within the limiting requirements of the consumer electronics domain outlined in section 1. Related work is [5], which provides a thorough tutorial description of the PAC model as a design pattern and provides guidance for its object oriented implementation. Also the AMF model [20] is a rendition of PAC as a design pattern, that focuses on the composition of PAC agents.

Earlier formal renditions of the PAC model have used formal modelling languages such as Z to capture the essence of the model but were not intended for constructive use, e.g., [2, 11]. The intention of the current approach is not towards analysis of the model itself or of systems built following the model, but to provide a blueprint for the implementation of the actual software and to guide the componentisation of the software produced.

The interaction techniques also need to be described independently of their implementation. Such a description is called here *designer oriented*. It uses the interaction styles template [9] used within Philips to specify user interfaces. The interaction styles templates is a variant of the User Action Notation [10]. It is simpler than UAN as it only describes single interactions steps. (In OSD systems interaction is via the remote control, individual interaction steps should be intuitively designed and specified and long interaction sequences are unlikely). The effect of each action is described through illustrations showing the display before and after the user action.

[15] compares the specification of user interface software from a software architecture viewpoint and a user, task-oriented viewpoint. The formalisms compared were both informal specifications structured in tables to reflect elements of the ADC formal interactor model [14] and the User Action Notation [10]. Although the comparison reflected the experience gained from a small case study, it shows that architectural and user action oriented descriptions provide complementary viewpoints at a similar level of abstraction. In the approach reported here, interaction styles specifications were paired up with component specifications, thus providing complementary descriptions of the user interface software. This practice is illustrated in the example of section 4.

The specification scheme presented is not formal. Formal specifications of user interface architecture are well served by interactor models as documented in earlier events of the DSV-IS series. From an architectural viewpoint, a criticism that applies to formal interactor models is that they do not help the developer determine the actual software structure: they rely on semantic constructs of the specification language used which do not necessarily map to the actual programming language constructs used. For example, LOTOS [12] used in [14], supports a synchronous communication of events. In the context of the study reported hereby, software components communicate with method calls. The exact nature of the method invocation mechanism in the target implementation platform is normally abstracted away in a typical formal specification but is an important concern for the structure and the content of the component architecture.

A range of communication schemes may be envisaged to model component interactions, e.g., streams of data, data sharing, constraints between the states of two objects, message sending, etc. The most modular approach requires the asynchronous selective broadcast of events which *implicitly invoke* methods inside objects [18]. Unfortunately, implicit invocation incurs prohibitive computational costs for current consumer electronics platforms. For this reason we assume that components comprising the user interface communicate with each other and with the application directly via method calls. Asynchronous user events are assumed to be serialised by some input manager. Processing individual user events can thus proceed in a serial fashion: all processing caused by one event must be completed before another one is processed. Exceptions to this rule may be necessary as a result of the asynchronous nature of user input, e.g., reversing the direction of movement within an animated menu structure. Such behaviour is encoded within individual components.

3 A component based architecture for interactive software for the next generation OSD

3.1 Scope of the model

The scope of the model discussed spans the presentation and interaction toolkit layers of the Slinky/Arch reference model [4]. Device drivers and input libraries provide device independent interpretations of user input to the components discussed here (e.g., a typical interpretation of a button press on the remote control would be "North" or "South"). Device drivers map abstract descriptions of output to invocations of graphics software (e.g., function calls to a graphics library). We assume the existence of an input manager handling the dispatch and serialisation of input events and a screen manager which merges the output of interactive objects. Thus, we model the display at an object by object basis rather than how the displays of individual interactive objects are merged together at runtime. This (quite standard) approach is consistent with the macroscopic software architecture for our target platforms.

3.2 'Look' and 'Feel' specific components

Interactors are characterized in terms of their presentation, their abstract functionality and their reactive behaviour. Figure 1, illustrates the decomposition of an interactor into a *behaviour component* and a *presentation component*. The intention of this division is that the presentation component captures the 'look' of the interactor while the 'feel' is defined by the behaviour component. This division encourages their independent design and implementation and allows for multiple presentations to be connected to the same behaviour component as long as they have consistent interfaces.

The notion of a *behaviour component* is introduced to describe a software component encapsulating the display-independent intrinsic behaviour of an interactor that supports a *basic user task*. By basic user task we mean a simple and recurring operation that the user performs and which is generic over the application-domain studied - in the present context TV-based and VCR-based graphical user interfaces. Examples of basic user tasks are: 'input a string' (e.g., a programme or channel name), 'set a value' (e.g., the volume) and 'choose among options' (e.g., selecting a channel). The display dependent data and functionality of an interactor are supported by a *presentation component*. This definition de-couples the notion of a behaviour component from the description of the *presentation* which visualises the data of the behaviour component. The presentation component implements a *design concept* which is particular to the behaviour component.

As an example, consider the task of selecting one of a small number of options supported by a vertical linear on-screen menu. To describe the corresponding design concept it is assumed that generalised "next" and "previous" interactions support navigation within the menu. The design concept directly concerns the visualisation of the menu and the "item in focus". How one should implement this idea is of no importance to the design concept. On the other hand, the behaviour component definition for (say) a pull-down menu, determines what data is held by the menu (e.g., a list of options), how the input received (e.g., a button press on the remote control) is interpreted to make a selection. The presentation component details how the information held by the behaviour component relates to the one on the display (e.g., that there is only one item in focus), it visualises this data and controls the animations for pulling down the menu, or for scrolling through its items.

Generally the separation of behaviour and presentation in graphical interaction is problematic: the interpretation of user input is normally display-based (see ., e.g., [13]). However, in OSD interfaces, there is no pointing device used and in the majority of cases the separation of behaviour and presentation is feasible (and desirable for the reasons mentioned in section 1).

3.3   Components and interfaces

Components and their interconnections are specified using elements of the graphical notation introduced with the Koala system [17]. Koala is a tool that supports the 'gluing' of components, implemented in C, at configuration time (i.e. before compilation). Given the source code for components and glue modules, which bind components together, and a specification of the composition structure for putting these components together, Koala matches procedure calls to their definitions, taking care of issues such as diversity between members of a product family and optimises the source code. The present approach does not use the Koala system as such. Only the architectural description language of Koala is used to take advantage of the familiarity of Philips staff with this formalism. The intention is to support a similar graphical formalism for the composition and the deployment of pre-fabricated binary components. Some elements of the Koala notation are summarised below.

Blocks represent components (see figure 1). Squares containing triangles represent interfaces. Interface squares are placed on the boundaries of component boxes. We

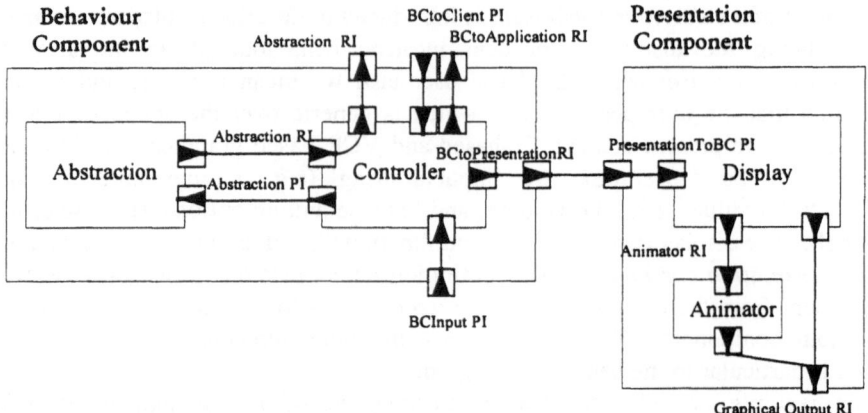

Fig. 1. The decomposition of interactors to a 'behaviour' and a 'presentation' component.

note the following conventions concerning interfaces and their specification in the remainder of this document:

- An interface makes some part of the encapsulated functionality of a component available to its environment.

- An interface will be described as a set of method calls, where each method is described by: the name of the method, the type of its arguments in round brackets, followed by the return type, *e.g., add(integer, integer):integer.* Parameter and return types may be omitted if there are none associated with the method call. In the specifications that follow we rely on the naming of these parameters and functions to convey their meaning – i.e. the types mentioned are not defined further.

- An inward pointing triangle represents a *provides interface (PI)*, which means that the component can provide a service to its environment.

- An outward pointing triangle represents a *requires interface (RI)* which models functionality the component requires from the environment.

- Connections between interfaces are restricted to directed connections from one or more requires interfaces to a single provides interface.

- Components can be nested to model compound components (see for example figure 1). Where interface connections cross boundaries of nested components we assign a unique name for the interface so as not to clutter the description (see for example the *Abstraction RI* interface in figure 1).

Note that the direction of an interface (provides or requires) is not directly associated with the data flow, but expresses dependency relationships between software components, i.e. the direction of method calls. For example, figure 1 stipulates that in order to operate successfully an interactor requires some graphical output functionality. Similarly the presentation provides some functionality to the behaviour component, etc.

Abstraction	Encapsulated data and its invariants.
Abstraction RI	Operations to initialise/modify the abstraction with data from the application or other interactors.
Abstraction PI	Operations upon the encapsulated data. They describe functionality that the behaviour component provides to its environment through the controller.
BCInput PI	The set of method-calls implementing input to the interactor. Usually reserved for user input which the behaviour component must interpret or for user initiated interrupts.
BCtoClient PI	Functionality the interactor provides to its environment. The receiver of this information has the initiative for calling the relevant method.
BCtoClient RI	Functionality the interactor provides to its environment. The BC keeps the initiative for calling the required methods to convey its results to other components.
BCtoPresentation RI	Method calls to visualise the abstraction data in the display and to control the display and its animators.
Control	Sequencing constraints implemented by the controller.

Table 1. Structured specification of a behaviour component.

3.4 Behaviour component: internal structure and specification

The behaviour component comprises of an abstraction component and a controller component. The controller component is responsible for handling user and system events to interrupt the currently executed method. User interrupts override or cancel the current control task, e.g., when the user reverses the current direction of movement within an animated menu. Interrupt messages should be translated to the presentation component in the form of method calls to affect the relevant aspects of the display, e.g., pausing or canceling an icon based animation.

The controller localises control, i.e. some temporal sequencing on its communications with its environment. As mentioned already, the provides and requires relations describe static dependencies between software components. The control specification captures dynamic behaviour. In general, the behaviour component drives the interaction with the presentation, while no assumptions are made with respect to whether it controls an application or vice versa (mixed internal/external control of the interface by the application is possible).

- *BCinput PI* models input in the form of method calls originating from the user through logical input devices or through other interactors mediating with the user. This interface includes methods for interrupt handling.
- The *Abstraction* is modelled as an abstract data type (ADT) and may be implemented as a module. The controller can access the abstraction state through its provides interface (*Abstraction PI*), which is a set of query and modification operations.

Display	Data and its visualisation and where applicable correspondence of abstraction to display features.
PresentationToBC PI	Provides interface to the behaviour component: a set of methods and their arguments.
Graphical Output RI	Requires interface for the graphical output (i.e. some subset of the target GDI called from within the presentation component).
Animator RI	A requires interface for the animator components (which are not specified explicitly in this paper).

Table 2. Structured specification of a presentation component

- The abstraction receives data for its initialisation from the application through the controller and specifically through the *Abstraction RI* interface.
- *BCtoClient PI* and *BCtoClient RI* communicate the result of the interaction to the application. If the behaviour component in question has the initiative for outputting some data it will do so through the RI to the PI of some other behaviour component or the application. If not, it will provide this data through its RI.
- The behaviour component reads and modifies data of the presentation component through *BCtoPresentation RI*. In doing so it ensures that changes are propagated from the abstraction to the presentation and vice versa. Also, it includes methods for interrupting the presentation.

A structured scheme for the specification of behaviour components is shown in Table 1. The first three rows define the abstraction data encapsulated by the behaviour component: the data it encapsulates, the operations to initialise/modify it and inquiry operators for reading its value. The interface to the presentation is a requires interface: the behaviour component requires some functionality for its visualisation. The control specifies the dynamic behaviour of the interactor, i.e. how it maps user input to invocations of functionality in the presentation and application.

3.5   Presentation component: internal structure and specification

The presentation is broken down into the *display component* and one or more *animator components* (see fig. 1). The display component encapsulates data and behaviour related to the presentation of data on the screen. One or more animator components can be invoked by the display, visualising some transient effect between display states. The display component controls the animators, i.e. it triggers them, it can interrupt them, reverse them, etc. Presentation components can be specified as in Table 2.

- *Display data* describes the data which is visualised by the presentation component, its visualisation and, where appropriate, the correspondence of features of the visualisation to the abstraction of the behaviour component.
- *PresentationToBC PI* is a set of methods that the presentation provides to the behaviour component. It serves the communication of data to and from the behaviour component when it is connected to the *BCtoPresentation RI* of the latter and the interruption of current animations by the behaviour component.

Fig. 2. The wheel selector design concept. Screen shot from non-interactive prototype.

- *Graphical Output RI* is the set of methods required for graphical output. These methods are left unspecified in the specifications of this document, to avoid unnecessary implementation bias in the absence of a generic graphical device interface for the candidate target platforms (e.g., the G+4 UIMS [1], Windows CE). The specification and implementation of a generic graphical device interface for all the target platforms is currently developed.

- *Animator RI* describes the interfaces of the display to animator components in terms of the start and the end state of the animation. States for the animation can be described by, e.g., some spatial/geometrical attribute of the display, the frame number in a sequence of frames/bitmaps.

At any moment an animator component maintains (at least) three variables: its start state, its current state (alias 'ist' state) and its target state (alias 'soll' state). In order to ensure a flexible user interface architecture animators are interruptible. This allows the user to cancel, or halt animators so as to allow other interactors to take precedence. It is the responsibility of the animator component to deal with interrupts: it may speed up the animation, it may stop it instantly or it may choose to reverse the animation by recursively instantiating itself with its *ist* state as a *start* parameter and its original *start* state as a *soll* parameter. In the tabular specifications of this paper we do not specify the animator components as they reflect detailed implementation concerns.

4 Example: the Wheel Selector

4.1 The design concept and the components to support it

As an example of the component architecture presented, this section discusses the architecture and the specification of software components to implement the 'wheel

Pre	User Action	System Reaction	Post
6 7 News Sports Music Films Documentary Talk Show	OK	Set currently selected variable to the value on the front of the wheel.	6 7 News 7 Sports Music Films Documentary Talk Show
6 7 News 7 Sports 6 Music 5 Films 4 Documentary 3 Talk Show 5	S (similar for N)	Move the wheel down (or up) to the next (or previous) variable on the list.	News 7 6 7 Sports 6 Music 5 Films 4 Documentary 3 Talk Show 5
6 7 News 7 Sports 6 Music 5 Films 4 Documentary 3 Talk Show 5	E (similar for W)	Turn the wheel bringing the next (or previous) value to the front	7 8 News 7 Sports 6 Music 5 Films 4 Documentary 3 Talk Show 5

Table 3. Specification of the wheel-selector design concept using the interaction styles template.

selector' design concept. Figure 2 is a screen-shot from the original designers' non-interactive prototype. The general idea is that the user can construct a 'profile' of television-programme-preferences by assigning values to each category of programmes displayed. The user can navigate up and down the programme categories and can turn the wheel left and right to change the value assigned to a particular category. The interaction with this component is specified in Table 3 using the interaction styles template of [9].

Each row of the table represents a single interaction step. A row is read left to right, but contrary to UAN [10], top-down ordering of the rows does not reflect sequence of user actions. The content of the display before and after the user action is shown on the Pre- and Post- columns of the template, while the system reaction corresponds to the 'connection to computation' column of UAN. This template form has been successfully applied by non software engineers in Philips for documenting and standardising interaction designs.

Figure 3 illustrates a composition of software components implementing the wheel-selector design concept. The *Value List* behaviour component holds a copy of the list of variables and their values (see specification of Table 4). *Value List* is independent of the presentation (whether for example tthe values are displayed on a wheel or on an array, etc). The list is initialised (say by the application) with *init(List)*.

Remote control events *N, S, E,* and *W* are mapped by the controller to invocations of *previousVar, nextVar, previousVal* and *nextVal* respectively. Event *OK* invokes the

127

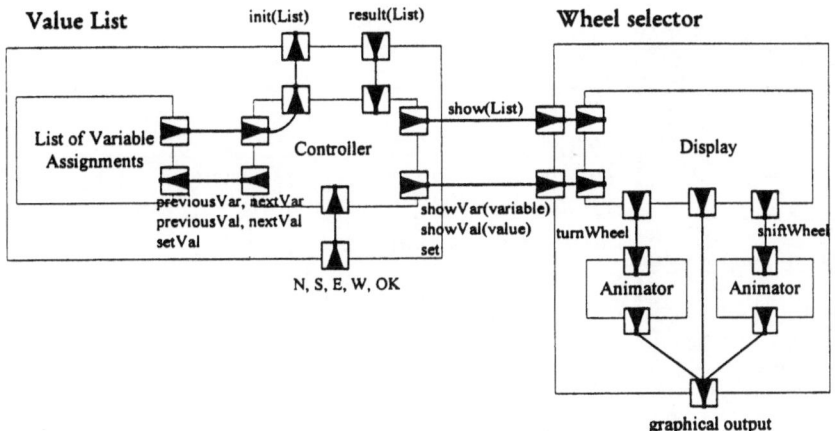

Fig 3. The architecture of the selector wheel interactor.

method *setVal* which assigns the *currentVar* to the *currentVal*. Method *result* returns the list of variables and their values.

4.2   Component weight and presentation independence

Supporting multiple views for the same abstraction data may lead to an excessively complex control component. This problem can be overcome by using the Observer design pattern [8] (supported by the MVC model [13]). Using PAC the observer pattern can be supported by hierarchical composition: a single behaviour component (an abstraction-controller pair) with many dependent controller-presentation pairs. The controllers would handle change notification and invoke updates of the dependents.

The approach adopted supports the requirement for presentation independence in nearly all cases except where the semantics of the behaviour component are *solely* dictated by its visualisation. An example of this is text input via a virtual keyboard, where the meaning of user actions for text entry is dictated solely by the visualisation of the character set on the screen (as a keyboard, sheets of characters, wheel selectors, etc.). Another example (which has always been outside the scope of the present work) is direct manipulation user interfaces found currently on desktop computers.

There is a danger that if we attempt to rid the behaviour component of any 'presentation bias' it may become contrived and of trivial size. Presentation independence and display mediated interaction set conflicting requirements for componentisation. The trade-off suggested with the component model discussed above is most appropriate for OSDs of consumer electronics where input is achieved via a remote control. In these cases the user navigates with a small set of buttons between interactive objects of significant size.

128

Abstraction	A list of variable-value pairs (i.e. a list of variable assignments). A pointer to the current variable and the current value is maintained.
Abstraction RI	*Init(list)* Operations to set the abstraction list of variable – value pairs with application data.
Abstraction PI	*NextVar, prevVar, nextVal, prevVal* support navigation with the list data structure. *getList* returns the current list. *setVal* sets the current variable to the current value.
BBInputPI	*N, S, E, W* and *OK*.
BBtoClient PI	*Result(list)* The result of the interaction is a list of variable assignments which can be read by the application or higher level components.
BBtoPresentation RI	*Show(list)* Sends list to the presentation component (the wheel selector). *ShowVar(Var)* sends the current variable to the presentation component. *ShowValue(Value)* sends the current value to the presentation component. *Set* tells the presentation component that the current variable is set to the current value.
Dialogue	*N, S* invoke the *nextVar* and *prevVar* methods of the abstraction and subsequently the *showVar*. *E, W* invoke the *nextVal* and *prevVal* methods and then the *showVal* method. *OK* invokes in order the methods: *setVal, set,* and *result(getList)*.

Table 4. The value list behaviour component.

4.3   Implementation

A selection of design concepts using advanced graphics for OSD, were implemented on an Windows NT based PC system using Win32 GDI, DirectX and OpenGL for the visualisation components. The choice of prototyping platform was based on the grounds of flexibility and performance.   As the infrastructure for using the component model is not yet in place, component composition was achieved using the Microsoft COM model [16].   Microsoft COM is a de facto industry standard component model, which facilitates run-time instantiation and binding of components along with extensive support for 3D graphics. Central differences with the Koala model for component composition [17] discussed earlier are:

- COM specifies only *provides* interfaces and not *requires* interfaces, and
- COM components are binary entities rather than units of source code.

The issues of porting user interface components from the PC to platforms for Philips consumer electronics (WinCE, MG and G+4 [1] based systems, particularly with

Display	*list*: The array of variables manipulated. A segment of this list is displayed at any time. *Wheel*: A circular list of values (the range of values for all the variables in the list). The list is rendered as a 3D hexa-hedron, placed next to the current variable and whose front face always shows the current value.
PresentationToBC PI	*Show(List) initialises the display data with the list to display.* *ShowVar(var) updates the current variable.* *ShowVal (val) updates the current value.* *Set* shows feedback of the assignment of the current variable to the current value.
Graphical Output RI	Methods for compressing/blitting bitmap resources.
Animator RI	*TurnWheel*. Turns the wheel ±60 degrees at a time, depending on which is the new current value. *ShiftWheel*. Shifts the wheel up and down depending on the relative position of the current variable.

Table 5. The wheel selector presentation component.

respect to 3D and general performance/resource issues, is under investigation. A few components for text entry have been ported to G+4 [1] providing a relatively advanced appearance within the resource limitations and graphics capabilities of G+4. Table 6 summarises implementation issues regarding components to support the task of creating a preference profile. Preference profiles are set up by television viewers with the purpose to filter Electronic Program Guide (EPG) information about television broadcasts. The components implemented have been created as both stand-alone demonstrations and as ActiveX control widgets for re-use within authoring environments such as Visual Basic and web authoring tools.

5 Discussion

The architecture presented in this paper is a refinement of the PAC [5] model. Contrary to PAC, this architecture does not prescribe a pattern for the composition of interactors comparable to the tree hierarchy supported by PAC. A PAC-like hierarchical composition of interactors is consistent with the present architecture but it is not the only possible way of component connection. The configuration of interactor compositions is currently under investigation.

The architectural model presented in this paper is more specific than PAC regarding the connections between the components, and the P,A,C constituents of PAC agents. It defines the interfaces between behaviour component, presentation and their environment, essentially 'componentising' the PAC model. This refinement is necessary to make the model operational and, also, it ensures the independence of the behaviour component from its presentation component, which was one of the primary aims of the modelling effort.

Component	Visualisation	Visualisation Implementation details
Image List Scroller		Basic 2D GDI calls to perform bitmap blitting (bit block transfers) where the number of image items is too great to display at once. The semantic choice of bitmaps (based on resource identifiers) is determined by the scrolling direction of the user.
Polygon Twister		Real-time 3D animation using OpenGL : 3D implementation allows for much greater flexibility with little coding overhead for alternative visualisations and animations. This comes at the expense of computation. Pre-stored bitmaps with image stretching are an alternative means for visualisation.
Wheel Selector (TV profiler– a compound component)		Combination of above components: The semantics of the image list in this case pertain to categories of TV programs whilst the Polygon Twister refers to the desired rating of the category. A Record of the current preferences is displayed in another image list (shown on the right).

Table 6. Software components for creating a preference profile.

PAC was introduced with the primary aim to support the implementation of direct manipulation graphical user interfaces. In this paper, considerable simplifications have been obtained for OSD interfaces with no free moving cursor.

[15] reports a similar tabular specification of interactors with a direct correspondence to a formal interactor model [14]. That interactor model and the specification scheme were not appropriate in our context as they assumed event based communication and do not help ensure the separability of behaviour and presentation components.

The component interface specifications recommended in this paper consist only of syntax. The robustness, clarity and correctness of interface specifications can be enhanced by some increased formality, e.g. by enriching interface descriptions with pre- and post- conditions [19], or even by specifying the temporal sequencing of method invocations as in [15]. This possibility, while not ruled out for future work, conflicts with current industry wide standards such as COM [16].

6 Conclusions

This research has focused on the definition of components and their interfaces. Not sufficient emphasis has been put on higher order architectural issues, such as the protocols applied for the communication between components, patterns of their composition and the roles components play in such composition patterns. These questions are the topic of current work which aims to provide notational and tool support for the composition of components.

Our experience is that design concepts for basic interaction tasks are very succinctly described using the interaction styles template [9]. To move from design to development, this design oriented description needs to be matched with a specification of the software components that implement the design concept. This paper has outlined a software architecture for the specification and implementation of graphical interaction design concepts. This architecture, which is a refinement and a 'componentisation' of the PAC model, distinguishes components supporting the 'look' and the 'feel' for a particular design concept.

This paper has reported part of our work in the area of componentising user interface software. Much of the difficulty arose because of the special requirements of the application domain and the limitations of the target platforms, e.g., memory limitations and the requirement for separable behaviour and presentation components. Further, the paper has discussed how the trend towards componentisation of software affects the application standard object oriented architectures such as PAC.

7 References

[1] Jansen, A. (1998). User interface management systems for consumer electorings products: The G+4 Approach. 4th Philips Software Conference, June 1998, Eindhoven, The Netherlands, Philips Internal Report.

[2] Abowd, G. (1992). *Formal aspects of human computer interaction.* Ph.D.Thesis, University of Oxford.

[3] Bass, L & Coutaz, J. (1991). *Developing software for the user interface.* Addison Wesley.

[4] Bass, L., (1992). A Metamodel for the run time architecture of an interactive system, *SIGCHI Bulleting, 24(1).*

[5] Buschmann, F., Meunier, R., Rohnert, H., Sommerlad, P. and Stal M. (1996) *A system of patterns. Pattern-oriented software architecture.* Wiley.

[6] Coutaz, J., (1987). PAC, an object oriented model for dialog design. In Bullinger, H.J. & Shackel, Eds., *INTERACT'87,* North Holland, Elsevier, 431-436.

[7] Coutaz, J., (1997). PAC-ing the user interface architecture. In M.D.Harrison and J.-C.Torres, Eds., *Design Specification and Verification of Interactive Systems '97,* Springer, 13-28.

[8] Gamma, E., Helm, R., Johnson, R. & Vlissides, J. (1994). *Design Patterns. Elements of Reusable Object-Oriented Software*. Addison Wesley.

[9] Hamberg, R, ter Horst, H., de Ruyter, B., & de Vet, J., (1998) Menu Interaction Styles, An information model and editor, *Nat.Lab. Technical Note 042/98*, Philips Internal Report.

[10] Hartson, R., Siochi, A.C., Hix, D., (1990). The UAN: A user - oriented representation for direct manipulation systems, *ACM Transactions on Information Systems*, 8, 181-203.

[11] Hussey, A. & Carrington, D (1996). Using Object-Z to compare the MVC and PAC architectures. In Roast, C & Siddiqi, J (Eds.) *Formal Aspects of the Human Computer Interface*, BCS-FACS workshop, Springer, eWiC series.

[12] ISO(1989). Information processing systems-open systems interconnection. – LOTOS A formal description technique based on the temporal ordering of observational behaviour. *ISO/IEC 8807*, International organisation for Standardisation, Geneva.

[13] Krasner, G.E. & Pope, S.T. (1988). A cookbook for using the Model-view-controller User Interface Paradigm in the Smalltalk-80 System. *Journal of Object–Oriented Programming*, 1(3), 26-49.

[14] Markopoulos, P. (1998). Formal architectural abstractions for interactive software. *Int. Journal of Human Computer Studies*, 49, 675-715.

[15] Markopoulos, P., Papatzanis, G., Johnson, P. and Rowson, J. (1998). Validating semi-formal specifications of interactors as design representations. In Markopoulos, P. and Johnson, P. (Eds.) Design, Specification and Verification of Interactive Systems '98, Springer, 102-133.

[16] Microsoft COM homepage. *http://www.microsoft.com/com*

[17] Ommering Van, R., (1998). Koala: a Component Model for Consumer Electronics Product Software. In Van der Linden, F., (Ed.). *Development and Evolution of Software Architectures for Product Families*. Springer, LNCS 1429, 76-86.

[18] Shaw, M. and Garlan, D. (1996). *Software Architecture. Perspectives on an emerging discipline*. Prentice Hall (New Jersey).

[19] Szyperski, C., (1997). *Component Software. Beyond Object-Oriented Programming*. Addison-Wesley.

[20] Tarpin-Bernard, F., David, B.T. (1997) AMF: a new design pattern for complex interactive software? In Smith, M.J., Salvendy, G., and Koubek R.J. (Eds.) *Design of Computing Systems: social and ergonomic considerations. Proc. HCI International '97*, Elsevier, 351-354.

Flexibly Mapping Synchronous Groupware Architectures to Distributed Implementations

Tore Urnes
Telenor Research and Development
P.O. Box 83
N-2007 Kjeller
Norway
Tore.Urnes@telenor.com

T.C. Nicholas Graham
Department of Computing and
Information Science
Queen's University
Kingston, Ontario, Canada
graham@cs.queensu.ca

Abstract

Design-level architectures allow developers to concentrate on the functionality of their groupware application without exposing its detailed implementation as a distributed system. Because they abstract issues of distribution, networking and concurrency control, design-level architectures can be implemented using a range of distributed implementation architectures. This paper shows how the implementation of groupware applications can be guided by the use of *semantics-preserving* architectural annotations. This approach leads to a development cycle that involves first developing the functionality of the application in a local-area context, then tuning its performance by setting architecture annotations. The paper concludes with timing results showing that architectural annotations can dramatically improve the performance of groupware applications.

1 Introduction

In recent years, a number of software architecture styles have been proposed to support the development of synchronous groupware systems. These include *PAC** [3], *ALV* [15], *C2* [25] and the *Clock* architecture style [12]. Such design-level architecture styles allow developers to specify the high-level structure of their applications while abstracting the low-level details of distributed implementation.

Tools supporting the development of groupware applications differ in the architectural abstractions that they present to developers. Low-level toolkits expose the underlying distributed system to the developer. For example, the highly successful *GroupKit* toolkit [21] is based on a fully replicated architecture with no concurrency control. Developers must therefore be aware that different participants' views may become inconsistent [14]. *GroupKit's* low-level implementation approach is part of the reason for its great success – programmers need to know that they are programming a distributed system, but have great control over the implementation of their application.

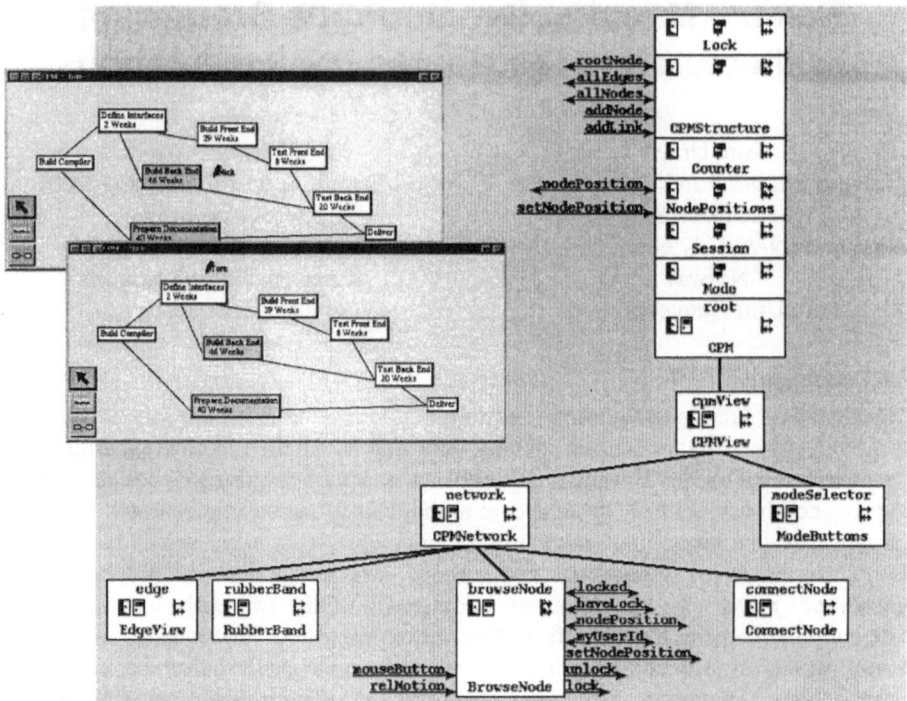

Fig.1. A critical path planning application and its design-level architecture.

High-level toolkits take the approach of automatically implementing a design-level architecture provided by the programmer. This approach simplifies the development of groupware applications by abstracting the details of networking, distribution and concurrency control, but at the cost of implementation flexibility. The *Rendezvous* toolkit [15] demonstrated that it was possible to automatically implement the high-level *ALV* architecture. *Rendezvous* provides only a purely centralized implementation, however, leading to problems with performance. Our own *Weasel* system [11] showed how high-level architectures could be mapped to a semi-replicated distributed implementation. In *Weasel*, the user interface is represented on the client machines and the functional core of the application is implemented on a server. As with *Rendezvous*, however, *Weasel* provided programmers with only one implementation strategy.

An alternative approach is to combine the advantages of high and low-level toolkits by providing both high level abstractions and the opportunity for low-level tuning. The *Suite* system [4] first demonstrated this approach by showing how a semi-replicated implementation of the model-view-controller (MVC) architecture [18] can be manually tuned by using peer to peer communication to bypass the model. The *GEN* system [19] provides shared objects as a high-level abstraction, and facilities for specifying how these shared objects should be implemented. The *Prospero* system [5] provides a *meta-object protocol*, allowing the developer to specialize the toolkit's mechanisms for managing shared data. *AMF-C* [24] provides groupware frameworks that can be customized following implementation.

In this paper, we demonstrate that it is possible to completely separate the functional design of a groupware application from the design of its distributed implementation. A design level architecture in the style of *PAC* [3] or *Rendezvous* [15] provides a conceptual framework for developing the application's functionality. This architecture is then annotated to guide its implementation as a distributed system. A toolkit provides a default implementation of the architecture, suitable for testing. To achieve production quality performance, architectures are tuned via *semantics-preserving annotations*. These annotations select between a variety of distribution styles, concurrency control methods, caching algorithms and replication strategies.

We have demonstrated this approach of separating the development of an application's functionality from the specification of its distributed implementation, using the *Clock* groupware development toolkit. Clock provides an architecture style based on layered MVC [18]. A distributed implementation of a Clock architecture is considered correct if it adheres to Clock's formal semantics [8]. As with other high-level architecture styles, Clock permits a wide range of implementations. The effect of a semantics-preserving annotation is therefore to specify to the Clock runtime system that a particular implementation is desired. Therefore, annotations do not change the functionality of the application, just its runtime performance.

Annotations can lead to dramatic improvements in the performance of groupware applications. As shown in section 4.1, the Clock implementation of a highly interactive project planning application runs with instantaneous response time, even when the participants are located in Canada and New Zealand. Over a wide area network, the annotated version of this application ran ten times faster than the automatically derived implementation.

This paper is organized as follows. We briefly introduce the *Clock* architecture style and show how this style can be used to implement a simple synchronous groupware application. We then introduce the architecture annotations that are used to control the distributed implementation of the architecture, and show the effects of applying the annotations on the runtime performance of the application.

2 The Clock Architecture Style

Clock architectures are used to design the structure of synchronous groupware applications. Like other groupware architecture styles, *Clock* architectures consist of a hierarchy of components representing the application's compositional structure. *Clock* architectures hide low-level implementation issues such as distribution policies, networking protocols and concurrency control.

Clock has been used to build a number of substantial applications, in our research group and elsewhere. These applications include a user interface design tool [2], a tool for recording design rationale [22], a multiuser web browser [9] and a multiuser video annotation tool [12].

2.1 An Example Groupware Application

To motivate how *Clock* architectures are designed, we use the example of a simple project scheduling application written in *Clock*. As shown in figure 1, the application allows multiple users to simultaneously create nodes in a critical path network, connect them, and rearrange them. The critical path through the network is shown in white. Telepointers allow people to see who else is present in the session, and what they are doing. Each participant sees the effects of other participants' actions in real time. Participants have private copies of the project toolbar, so that, for example, one person can be moving a node while another is connecting two nodes. The application is therefore relaxed WYSIWIS (what you see is what I see).

When a participant clicks on a node in the critical path, he/she implicitly locks the node so that others cannot move it. Thus, two participants can concurrently move different nodes, but cannot concurrently move the same node.

2.2 Clock Architecture for the Critical Path Application

Clock architectures are structured as trees of components. The root of the tree (the *CPM* node) implements the functional core of the application, in this case representing the structure of the project network and the critical path. A set of abstract data types (*ADT's*) is attached to the functional core, representing application data. In figure 1, ADT's implement the positions of the nodes in the project plan (*NodePositions*), the dependencies among the nodes (*CPMStructure*), and what users are currently participating in the project planning session (*Session*).

The architecture tree represents the hierarchical composition of the user interface. The root *CPM* node creates one instance of the user interface (*CPMView*) per participant. The *CPMView* is in turn composed of the project plan (*CPMNetwork*) and the project toolbar (*ModeButtons*). Components communicate via messages. For example, a *BrowseNode* responds to *mouseButton* and *relMotion* user inputs. A *BrowseNode* may make requests (e.g., using *nodePosition* to request the position of the node), and updates to change state (e.g., moving a node with the *setNodePosition* message.)

Clock architectures can be viewed as implementing a layered model-view-controller [18] structure, where the ADT's implement the model, and the components further down the tree implement the view/controllers.

To aid with concurrency control, *Clock* guarantees atomicity of input transactions. An *input transaction* describes the sequence of computation that is required to process a user input, i.e., to read in the input, modify the user interface and application state, and update the views of all users. Therefore, *Clock* implementations may process input transactions concurrently, but only if they can guarantee that the transactions will not conflict. Atomicity of input transactions provides a powerful, low-level concurrency control mechanism from which higher-level concurrency control policies can be implemented.

Clock architectures are developed using the *ClockWorks* visual editor [10]. In this editor, components can be easily added, moved, deleted and grouped into aggregate components. When *Clock* programs run, participants may enter or leave dynamically from any location on the Internet. Participants use a version of the *GroupKit* session manager [21] to enter a session. The current session information (i.e., the names and IP addresses of all participants) is automatically maintained in the *Session* ADT.

By default, *Clock* architectures are implemented using a fully centralized architecture. The complete application runs on a single machine, posting the view of each participant to his/her client machine. *Clock* architectures, however, can be implemented in a wide variety of styles, ranging from fully centralized to fully replicated, with a range of hybrid styles in-between. The next section shows how semantics-preserving architecture annotations can be used to map design-level architectures to a wide range of distributed implementations.

3 Annotations

Developing groupware applications is a challenging task. As with all interactive software, development is iterative, requiring rapid change in response to usability testing. At the same time, developers must contend with the complexities of implementing an efficient distributed system. In *Clock*, we have taken the approach that developers should be able to work first on getting the functionality of their application correct, and then on tuning the application to obtain acceptable performance. As outlined earlier, the *Clock* architecture style permits developers to implement their application without worrying about issues of concurrency control, distribution or networking. The *Clock* toolkit automatically provides a purely centralized implementation of the architecture that correctly implements the application's functionality.

This default implementation, however, typically fails to provide acceptable performance for more than a few users or over a wide-area network. In order to improve performance, the developer can place *annotations* on the architecture. These annotations give hints to the runtime system as to how the architecture should be implemented as a distributed system. Annotations are *semantics-preserving*, meaning that they are allowed to affect the performance, but not the functionality of the application. Annotations are therefore not considered to be part of the program, but rather are information to be used for runtime tuning.

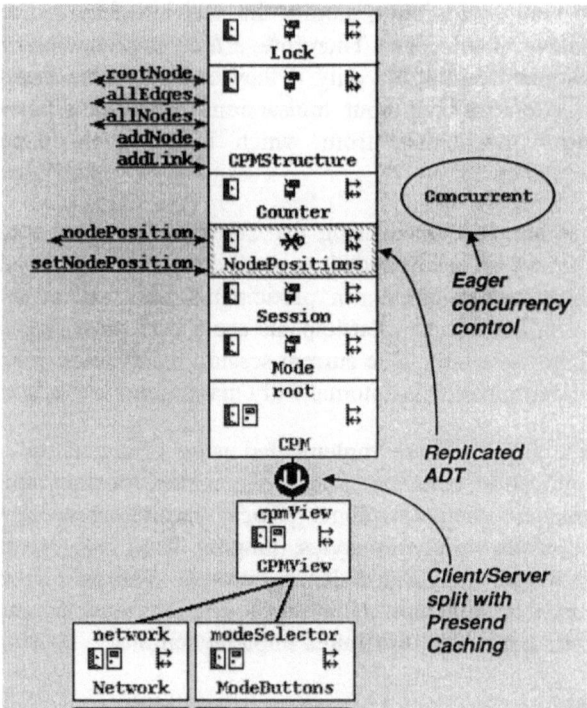

Fig. 2. The architecture of figure 1 annotated to improve performance.

In order to validate this two step approach to developing groupware applications, we have provided a set of annotations in *Clock*. Figure 2 shows the architecture of the critical path planner with annotations. Annotations are used to control the distribution of the application across multiple machines, the caching algorithms employed, replication of ADT's, and the concurrency control strategy.

The remainder of this section explains the effects of these annotations, motivating that a large space of possible implementations can be derived from a single *Clock* architecture. The timing results presented in the section 4 demonstrate that different choices of annotations can have a dramatic effect on the runtime performance of an application, particularly when running in a wide area context.

3.1 Annotations for Distribution
At runtime, an architecture leads to a set of code and data that must be distributed among the machines used to support the groupware session. One possible implementation is *purely centralized* (as used in *Rendezvous* [15]), in which all code and data is represented on a central server, while displays are posted to participants machines. Another common implementation is *semi-replication,* as used in *Weasel*

139

Fig. 3. Annotations specifying caching strategies: presend, prefetch, simple caching and no caching [13].

[11] and *Suite* [4]. In semi-replicated implementations, the shared context (or *functional core*) of the application is represented on a server machine, while each participant's user interface is represented on his/her own machine. Semi-replication has the advantage of supporting improved scalability [11], as the load of an increasing number of numbers of participants is distributed to the participants' own machines. However, semi-replication brings increased communication costs in that the user interfaces must communicate over the network in order to access data in the shared context. Which approach is best depends on the cost of network communication, the number of participants in the groupware session, the speed of the server, and the communication patterns of the application itself.

In Clock, annotations are provided which allow the architecture to be split between a server and client machines. As shown in figure 2, this annotation is attached to links in the architecture tree. Everything above the annotation is represented on the server machine; everything below is represented on the client machine. All update and request messages are automatically routed over the network boundary, transparently to the programmer. Developers can therefore easily experiment with different client-server split points without any reprogramming. Normally, the client-server split is made such that the shared context is placed on the server and the user interface on the client machines.

In summary, by using the client-server split annotation, developers can specify how their code is to be split among the machines being used in the groupware session. The annotations are changed simply by pointing and clicking in the *ClockWorks* environment [10]. Changing the client-server split requires no programming whatsoever.

3.2 Annotations for Caching
The primary disadvantage of semi-replicated implementation is that client machines must communicate over a network to request data from the shared context. These requests may be synchronous, requiring the client to block. Even in a local area context, clients may spend most of their time blocking [13]. Caching algorithms can be employed to reduce the number of remote requests that clients make. *Simple caching* records what requests have been made in the past, and what responses were received; if the client makes a request, the cache is consulted before making a remote request to the server. As is shown in section 4, simple caching can dramatically improve response times. More sophisticated schemes such as *prefetch* and *presend* caching [13] attempt to predict future requests and asynchronously service the

requests so that the responses will be available in the cache when the requests are actually made.

These schemes carry costs, however: simple caching costs memory at the client to maintain the cache entries, and introduces extra computation in order to test whether requests are already in the cache and to maintain cache coherence. Prefetch and presend caching introduce computation to predict future requests, and can tie up the server and network in computing and communicating requests that may never be made. The correct choice of caching algorithm therefore depends on network and machine speeds and the characteristics of the application itself.

Clock provides four annotations to control the caching strategy (figure 3). These annotations correspond to providing no, simple, prefetch and presend caching. To change the caching strategy, programmers simply click on the annotation, and select the desired strategy from a dialogue box.

3.3 Annotations for Concurrency Control
Participants in a groupware session can perform actions concurrently. The system must react in some reasonable way when participants perform conflicting actions.

Numerous concurrency control schemes for groupware have been proposed. These schemes trade off three properties: speed of resolving local reads/writes, intuitiveness of handling conflicts, and burden placed on the groupware application developer. Some of these tradeoffs are summarized by Greenberg and Marwood [14]. Pessimistic schemes (such as the use of locks) determine whether it is safe to access shared data before the access is made. The overhead of these checks means that users suffer a penalty of accessing shared data even if all the shared data is available locally on their own machine. Pessimistic schemes guarantee, however, that concurrent inputs will never lead to inconsistent state or unintuitive undoing of user actions.

Optimistic schemes are based on the assumption that conflicts are rare, and that it is therefore preferable to detect and repair conflicts after they have occurred. Our own *eager* concurrency control strategy uses a transparent rollback scheme [26]. Other approaches require the programmer to provide correct *rollback* functionality to undo erroneous actions (such as in Bayou [6]) or *operation transforms* that allow updates to be applied in different orders at different sites [7]. Optimistic approaches allow local operations to proceed without consulting with other sites, but may lead to unintuitive user interface behavior when user actions are undone or transformed. Optimistic approaches may require the programmer to provide special purpose code to detect and/or repair conflicts, increasing the development effort.

Fig. 4. Annotation specifying replication.

It is usually preferable to use a pessimistic scheme if acceptable performance can be obtained and move to an optimistic scheme as network latencies degrade. The choice of concurrency control schemes ultimately depends on the characteristics of the groupware application, the speed of the available network, and the availability of programmer time to devote to customizing concurrency control support.

In order to demonstrate that multiple concurrency control schemes can be supported within the same toolkit, we have included two algorithms in *Clock*: a locking scheme and the optimistic *eager* [26] concurrency control scheme. As shown in figure 3, programmers may select which scheme to use by clicking on the *locking/concurrent* annotation in the architecture.

3.4 Annotations for Replication

Groupware applications may be implemented with shared data represented on a central server [4,11,15], or replicated to the machines of the participants [1,14,17,21]. The primary benefit of replicating data is that response time can be improved, as local inputs can be processed without communicating with other machines. As discussed in the last section, however, replication requires sophisticated concurrency control schemes to ensure that replicas remain consistent. Additionally, replication may not be possible for some sorts of data (e.g., files or proprietary data) [20].

In *Clock*, we provide a flexible approach to replication, where developers can choose to replicate individual ADT's (figure 4). This way, the developer can choose to replicate those ADT's for which there will be a performance improvement, and centralize those for which no improvement will result. Replicated ADT's in *Clock* have no concurrency control associated with them. It is therefore incumbent on the developer to ensure that replicated ADT's have the property that applying updates in different orders will not cause consistency problems.

For example, in figure 3, the *NodePositions* ADT is replicated. This ADT keeps track of the positions of the nodes in the critical path network. The developer of this application knows that in practice, only one participant can be moving a given node at any given time. (Recall that clicking on a node locks the node.) It is therefore safe to turn off concurrency control on this ADT. In our experience, many applications contain important ADT's where concurrency control can be safely turned off, allowing replicated implementation with no overhead. As will be seen in the next section, replicating such crucial ADT's can result in dramatic speedups.

Copies of replicated ADT's are maintained on the server. The server is responsible for multicasting updates to all replicas, and maintaining a central copy of the current ADT state that can be used to allow late joiners to enter a session.

The use of annotations for replication differs from the use of annotations we have seen up to now. Annotations for distribution, caching and concurrency control are optimizations that can be applied to any architecture. By specifying those ADT's where concurrency control can be safely turned off, replication annotations allow the developer to specify application-dependent knowledge that the runtime system could not deduce. That is, the developer is specifying that in this case, the replication annotation is semantics-preserving. As argued by Edwards et al. [6], application-specific knowledge can dramatically improve the performance of concurrency control.

Replicated ADT's can be combined with centralized locks, allowing programmers to develop concurrency control strategies that are customized for their application. For example, in the critical path planner, the *Lock* ADT assigns locks for nodes. This ADT is centralized, so that requests for locks will be serialized. Manual locking of parts of the shared artifact can allow safe replication of parts of the shared context without the overhead of concurrency control.

4 Implementation

Annotations are automatically implemented by the Clock runtime system. Clock applications are divided into a server and a client part. The server is responsible for maintaining shared data, implementing concurrency control and notifying clients of changes in the shared context. Clients are responsible for implementing the user interface of a single user.

Clients include a cache and a replica store, while the server contains a concurrency control unit and a server side cache. Annotations are implemented by making a runtime decision as to how these cache, replica and concurrency control units are used.

Figure 5 shows the implementation of the critical path planner following application of the annotations of figure 3. This implementation is derived automatically by the Clock runtime system from the annotated design-level architecture. The server contains the ADT's implementing the structure of the critical path plan. The client replica store contains a copy of the *NodePositions* ADT.

The clients and server communicate via the Clock protocol [26], a networking protocol running over TCP/IP. The Clock protocol has been formally specified using the PROMELA protocol specification language, and validated through simulation and model checking [16], as well as through implementation in the Clock toolkit. Full details of the Clock protocol are provided elsewhere [26]. To give a flavour of the protocol, we consider how the protocol implements requests made by the view:

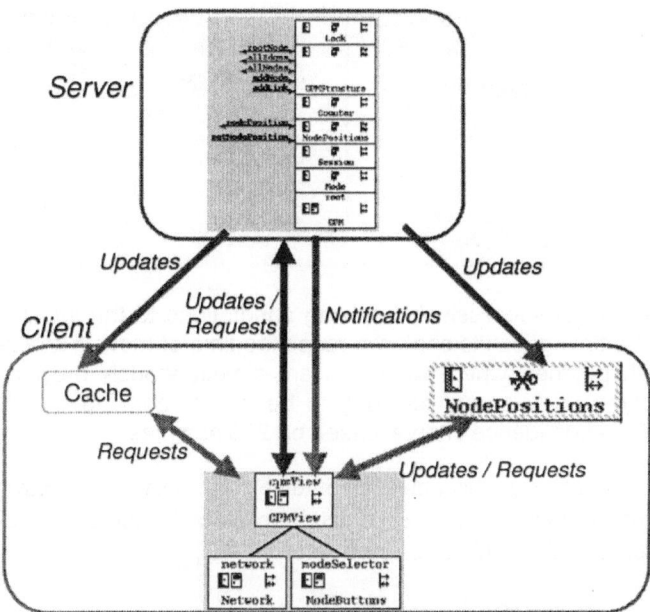

Fig. 5. Implementation architecture resulting from annotations of figure 2.

Requests to the shared context are first routed through the cache and the replica store, and only sent to the server if necessary. In practice, almost all requests are handled locally. Consider, for example, that during view computation, a client makes a request *r* with parameters *p*. The view computation unit issues a message *request(rqId,r,p),* where *rqId* is some unique id. The Clock runtime system routes this message first to the cache; if this request has been cached (with value *v*), a response message *response(rqId,v)* is returned to the view computation unit. If the value has not been cached, the request message is forwarded to the replica store. If one of the replicated ADT's is capable of handling the request, the response is computed, and the *response(rqId,v)* message is returned. Finally, if the replica store does not contain an ADT capable of handling the request, the *request(rqId,r,p)* message is forwarded to the server, which computes and returns the *response(rqId,v)* message. The view computation code is not aware of where the response is generated; view code simply issues the *request* message, and handles the *response* when it is returned. Therefore, distribution, caching and replication decisions do not impact view computation code. Similarly, the implementation of input-handling code is not impacted by changes in the distribution architecture.

Communication from server to client is also handled through the Clock protocol. Whenever actions by one user change the shared context, the caches and replica

	1ms Latency	10ms Latency	350ms Latency
Centralized	71±2 ms	126±2 ms	992±119 ms
Semi-Replicated	1,245 ±60 ms	24,523 ±2277 ms	∞
Presend Cache	131±4 ms	256±12 ms	∞
Eager Conc. Ctl	123±5 ms	193±15 ms	543±21 ms
Replication	89±3 ms	86±2 ms	86±2 ms

Fig. 6. Results of successively applying annotations to the architecture of figure 1. The timing results show the response time of moving a node in the critical path planner, when two users are simultaneously moving nodes. Times labeled as "∞" were too long to be measured. The given ranges specify a 90% confidence interval based on 275 samples.

stores on other clients may become out of date. The server asynchronously sends updates to the other clients. The level of detail provided by these updates depends on what form of server-side caching has been selected [13].

4.1 Effect of Applying the Annotations

We now consider how the use of annotations can greatly improve the performance of groupware applications. Figure 6 shows the results of successively applying annotations to the architecture of figure 1. These numbers were obtained through a set of experiments on both local and wide-area networks. All experiments used TCP/IP over the standard Internet. The experiments measured the response time of moving a node in the critical path planner in a two user session where both users are simultaneously moving nodes. The response time is defined as the time from which the user performs an input action (i.e., moving the mouse) to the time at which the display is updated. The local area experiments used three PC's, PII 300MHz, running Linux, with a round-trip latency of 1 ms between the machines. The first wide area experiments involved PC clients at Queen's University, and a SparcStation 10 server located at York University, with a 10 ms latency between the server and client machines. (Queen's and York Universities are separated by 250 km.) The second set of wide area experiments used two PC clients located at Queen's University, Kingston, Canada, and a Sun Ultra 1 server located at the University of Wellington, New Zealand; the round-trip latency between client and server was 350 ms.

As shown in figure 6, the default centralized implementation gives acceptable performance in the local area context, but slows in the wide area context to an unusable 1-second response time. Simply performing a client/server split gives unacceptably poor performance, even in the local area context (1.25 seconds response time.) Adding presend caching gives a substantial speedup, bringing response times to usable levels, except in the widest area context. Moving to eager concurrency control brings statistically insignificant improvement in the local area context. Over wide area, the overhead of obtaining locks is higher, and therefore eager concurrency control has a more significant effect. Finally, replicating the *NodePositions* ADT brings a significant speedup in both local and wide areas.

5 Analysis

The timing results presented in the last section show that annotating an architecture can result in dramatic speedup of applications. In the wide area case, the annotations made the difference between unusable and instantaneous response time, even in the case when two users are simultaneously interacting with the application. The best implementation is hybrid, combining centralized and replicated data and selective application of concurrency control. Such a hybrid implementation would be hard to derive automatically, but was easy to derive through architectural annotations.

According to Shneiderman [23], humans perceive response times of approximately 50 – 150 ms as instantaneous. The annotated implementation achieved response times in this range, even with participants as far separated as Canada and New Zealand. We have obtained similar results from other applications we have developed in *Clock* [26], such as a collaborative video annotator [12] and the *GroupScape* web browser [9].

We have shown that annotations allow programmers to develop applications without being concerned with their distributed implementation, then later tune the application to its distributed context. One possible criticism of design-level architectures is that they may be biased towards a client/server implementation, where the shared context is represented on the server machine. Even when components are replicated, a centralized component is involved in multicasting the client updates. In fact, annotations allow us to move very close to a pure replicated model if we choose. Replicated implementations typically must retain some central component to help in concurrency control, maintain session information, and deal with late joiners. If all ADT's from the shared context are replicated and caching is turned off, the server devolves to simply maintaining session information, dealing with late joiners, and multicasting updates between client machines. Most pure replicated implementations handle these functions through some centralized service.

The approach of using annotations has allowed us to experiment with a range of implementation algorithms to gauge their effectiveness. We have found presend caching [13] to be generally highly successful despite the burden it places on the server machine. Optimistic concurrency control [26] is generally preferable to locking, although in the local area context, its overheads may be as large as its benefits. It is important to be able to turn off these optimizations, however, as they are based on heuristics which may not be appropriate to every application.

The two-stage approach of first implementing a design-level architecture and then tuning it works well. We have had little difficulty tuning architectures after their completion, and in gaining significant speedups through this tuning.

6 Conclusions

In this paper, we have argued that it is possible to separate the design-level architecture for synchronous groupware systems from its ultimate implementation. We have shown how a single design-level architecture can be mapped to a wide range of implementation architectures, ranging from centralized to replicated. We have argued that in practice, hybrid architectures combining some centralized and some replicated data may be the most effective.

To validate these ideas, we presented our experiences with the *Clock* groupware development toolkit, in which design-level architectures can be optimized through semantics-preserving annotations. We showed how the application of annotations can lead to a hybrid implementation architecture, tuned to the specific properties of the groupware application and the hardware environment in which it is running.

The major shortcoming of our approach is that the annotations do not permit applications to be tuned on a per-client basis. We are continuing research into generalizing the annotation concept, developing hybrid concurrency control and caching algorithms, and dynamic reconfiguration of implementation architectures.

Acknowledgements

The work described in this paper was supported by the Natural Science and Engineering Research Council. Thanks also to Saul Greenberg and Mark Roseman for permitting us to use the *GroupKit* session manager [21].

References

1. J. Begole, C.A. Struble, C.A. Shaffer, and R.B. Smith. Transparent Sharing of Java Applets: A Replicated Approach. *UIST '97,* pages 55-64, 1997.
2. J. Brown and S. Marshall, Sharing Human-Computer Interaction and Software Engineering Design Artifacts. In *Proc. OZCHI'98*, Dec. 1998.
3. G. Calvary, J. Coutaz, and L. Nigay. From Single-User Architectural Design to PAC*: a Generic Software Architecture Model for CSCW. In *Proc. CHI '97*, pages 242-249. ACM Press, 1997.
4. P. Dewan and R. Choudhary. A High-Level and Flexible Framework for Implementing Multiuser User Interfaces. *ACM TOIS,* 10(4):345-380, Oct. 1992.
5. P. Dourish. Consistency Guarantees: Exploiting Application Semantics in a Collaboration Toolkit. In *Proc. ACM CSCW,* 1996.
6. W.K. Edwards, E.D. Mynatt, K. Petersen, M.J. Spreitzer, D.B. Terry, and M.M. Theimer. Designing and Implementing Asynchronous Collaborative Applications with Bayou. In *Proc. ACM UIST '97.* ACM Press, 1997.
7. C.A. Ellis and S.J. Gibbs. Concurrency Control in Groupware Systems. In *Proc. SIGMOD '89,* pages 399-407. ACM Press, 1989.

8. T.C.N. Graham. *Declarative Development of Interactive Systems.* Volume 243 of Berichte der GMD. Munich: R. Oldenbourg Verlag, July 1995.
9. T.C.N. Graham. GroupScape: Integrating Synchronous Groupware and the World Wide Web. In *Proc. INTERACT'97*, pp. 547-554, July 1997.
10. T.C.N. Graham, C.A. Morton, and T. Urnes. ClockWorks: Visual Programming of Component-Based Software Architectures. *J. Visual Lang. & Comp.*, 7(2):175-196, June 1996.
11. T.C.N. Graham and T. Urnes. Relational Views as a Model for Automatic Distributed Implementation of Multi-User Applications, *CSCW'92*, 59-66, 1992.
12. T.C.N. Graham and T. Urnes. Integrating Support for Temporal Media into an Architecture for Graphical User Interfaces. In *Proc. ICSE '97*, 1997.
13. T.C.N. Graham, T. Urnes, and R. Nejabi. Efficient Distributed Implementation of Semi-Replicated Synchronous Groupware. In *Proc. UIST '96*, pp. 1-10, 1996.
14. S. Greenberg and D. Marwood. Real Time Groupware as a Distributed System: Concurrency Control and its Effect on the Interface. *CSCW '94*, 207-217, 1994.
15. R.D. Hill, T. Brinck, S.L. Rohall, J.F. Patterson and W. Wilner. The Rendezvous Language and Architecture for Constructing Multi-User Applications. *ACM TOCHI*, 1(2):81-125, June 1994.
16. G.J. Holzmann. Design and Validation of Computer Protocols. Prentice Hall, 1990.
17. T. Kindberg, G. Coulouris, J. Dollimore, and J. Heikkinen. Sharing Objects over the Internet: the Mushroom Approach. In *Proc. IEEE Global Internet '96*, 1996.
18. G.E. Krasner and S.T. Pope. A Cookbook for Using the Model-View-Controller User Interface Paradigm in Smalltalk-80. *JOOP*, 1(3):26-49, Aug./Sept. 1988.
19. T. O'Grady. Flexible Data Sharing in a Groupware Toolkit. M.Sc. Thesis, Department of Computer Science, University of Calgary, 1996.
20. J.F. Patterson, M. Day, and J. Kucan. Notification Servers for Synchronous Groupware. In *Proc. ACM CSCW '96*, pages 122-129. ACM Press, 1996.
21. M. Roseman and S. Greenberg. Building Real Time Groupware with GroupKit, A Groupware Toolkit. *ACM TOCHI*, 3(1):66-106, March 1996.
22. M. Sage and C. Johnson, Pragmatic Formal Design: A Case Study in Integrating Formal Methods into the HCI Development Cycle. In *Proc. DSVIS'98*, 1998.
23. B. Shneiderman. *Designing the User Interface: Strategies for Effective Human-Computer Interaction, Third Edition.* Addison Wesley, 1998.
24. F. Tarpin-Bernard, B. David and P. Primet, Frameworks and patterns for synchronous groupware: AMF-C approach, *EHCI'98*, 1998.
25. R.N. Taylor, N. Medvidovic, K.M. Anderson, E.J. Whitehead Jr., J.E. Robbins, K.A. Nies, P. Oreizy, and D.L. Dubrow. A Component- and Message-Based Architectural Style for GUI Software. *IEEE Trans. SW Eng.*, 22(6), June 1996.
26. T. Urnes. *Efficiently Implementing Synchronous Groupware.* Ph.D. Thesis, Department of Computer Science, York University, October 1998.

Using TRIO Specifications to Generate Test Cases for an Interactive System

Bruno d'Ausbourg and Jacques Cazin

ONERA-CERT
2,Avenue Edouard Belin
B.P. 4025
31055 Toulouse Cedex 9, France
{ausbourg,cazin}@cert.fr

Abstract : User Interface Systems (UIS) are quite an important part of many current applications involving human end-users. Testing such open reactive systems requires an interaction with the end-user which must be carefully guided so as to avoid inherent non-determinism and combinatorial problems. In this paper we propose an approach based on a formal expression of UIS expressed in the temporal logic TRIO which uses a process of model generation to produce significant test cases and oracles. Moreover, we show how this approach can be integrated into a general validation and verification process in which the UIS is still informally developed.

Keywords : Interactive systems specification, verification, validation and testing, temporal logic, synchronous flow languages, TRIO, Lustre, model generation, model checking.

1 Introduction: Testing interactive systems

User interface systems (UIS) are becoming quite an important part of applications. They ensure the correct understanding of the internal state of those applications. They make communication between users and such applications easier. So, this increasing part must behave as expected. This point is particularly important when those interactive systems drive critical applications or widely distributed applications.

Software engineering methods and techniques were devised to help computer scientists or computer engineers in producing systems that work as intended. But, in fact, these methods and these techniques are not really applied in the area of UIS. Indeed, the development process of interactive systems requires the end user to participate in the specification, design and test stages. So, traditional software engineering frameworks are not well suited to deal with the resulting development process. Empirical practices are substituted to more methodological or more formal practices as they are defined by the software engineering rules.

So, the final system must be intensively tested because its behavior was not precisely defined. Then it is necessary to check that this system works, and that it works as intended. Tests are generally performed by putting end users in front of the developed system, by looking at how they play with this system, and by registering the interactive sessions. This test process may last indefinitely because the objectives of tests are not well defined in advance. So, one does not know exactly what must be tested, neither how that can be tested. Moreover, one does not know when test can be stopped because objectives are met.

This test strategy, or more exactly, this lack of test strategy, can generate very long interactive sessions that contain redundant sequences of interactions and that do not address properly the requested properties. So the cost of these steps of test is finally very expensive.

Moreover, tests are performed to ensure that the system behaves in accordance with some ergonomic rules. These rules are not easy to be checked by a human operator : in particular, if the operator is not systematically guided. For instance a rule that says *"the user can reach any screen$_x$ from any screen$_y$ by performing less than z actions"* is very difficult to check if the user has not a guide at his disposal ; this guide must explain exactly which actions must be performed and which are the expected results of these actions.

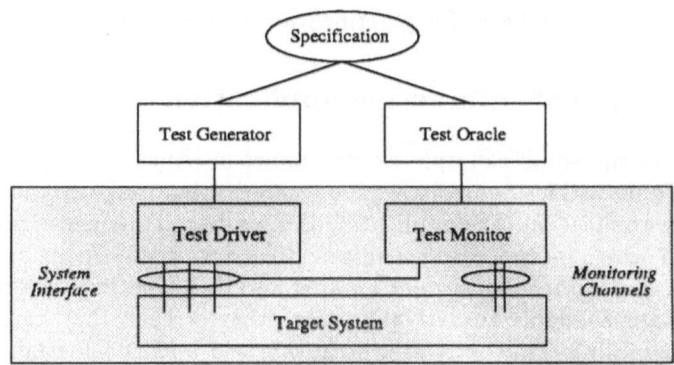

Fig. 1. Building blocks of a test automation system from [PS97]

Nevertheless, some works tackle the problem of testing interactive systems on the basis of systematic or formal approaches. For example, MacColl and Carrington[MC99] extended the Test Template Framework [SC96] in order to derive, from specifications, testing information for interactive systems. Peleska and Siegel gave in [PS97] the main building blocks allowing to automate testing of reactive systems. These blocks are represented on figure 1 and may be commented as follows:

- a formal *specification* is the starting point of the approach,
- the *Test Generator* creates from the specification the test cases i.e. the set of actions to be applied to the final system,

- the *Test Oracle* provides the expected results for each test cases, that is the expected reaction of the system,
- the *Test Driver* applies the test cases to the real target system,
- the *Test Monitor* observes the system under test and compare its reaction with the expected one.

The approach we present in this paper aims at producing relevant data for the Test Generator and Test Oracle on the basis of specification expressed in TRIO, a real time temporal logic. The paper is organized as follows: an illustrative example is used as the driving line of the paper. It is introduced in section 2. The main aspects of TRIO logics and the associated model generation technique are presented in section 3, and the use of this framework for test case and oracle generation in section 4.

Unfortunately, as we argued before, it is the never the case that UIS are produced in a top-down systematic way starting with a formal specification. In section 5, we show how we used a retro-engineering approach to abstract such a specification from UIS programs. This was done in a different context where we used Lustre model checking to prove properties of the UIS. Nevertheless, we show in section 6 that Lustre and TRIO based approaches can be formally linked and constitute alternate bases for a verification and validation environment.

2 An example of interactive application

We review here the small example we developed in [Aus98]. The application is depicted on figure 2. This figure shows four screens, that make up the mockup of an interactive application. The application is intended to manage bank accounts.

The main screen is the *Control* screen. The text field *Client* and *Account Number* are used to enter the account number and the client identification. Three pushbuttons are available to activate three other screens that correspond to particular operations. This activation is authorized and is achieved only if the user entered some data in a text field.

The *Credit* pushbutton activates the *credit* screen. This screen displays a text field *Amount* that accepts the value to credit on the selected bank account. The *Notification* toggle button indicates, if set, that the credit operation must be notified to the client by surface mail. The *QUIT* pushbutton validates the credit operation and erases the screen.

Similarly, the *Debit* pushbutton activates the *debit* screen. This display shows a text field *Amount* that accepts the value to debit on the selected bank account. The *QUIT* pushbutton validates this debit operation and erases this display.

The *QUIT* pushbutton on the *control* screen activates the *QUIT* message box to confirm the user wants to quit. The message box presents three options. The *YES* pushbutton confirms that the application must be exited. The *NO* pushbutton returns to the control screen. The *HELP* pushbutton does no operation: this function is not implemented inside the mockup.

The application functionalities are sketchy and a more realistic application would proceed quite differently. But it is not very important. In fact, we do not

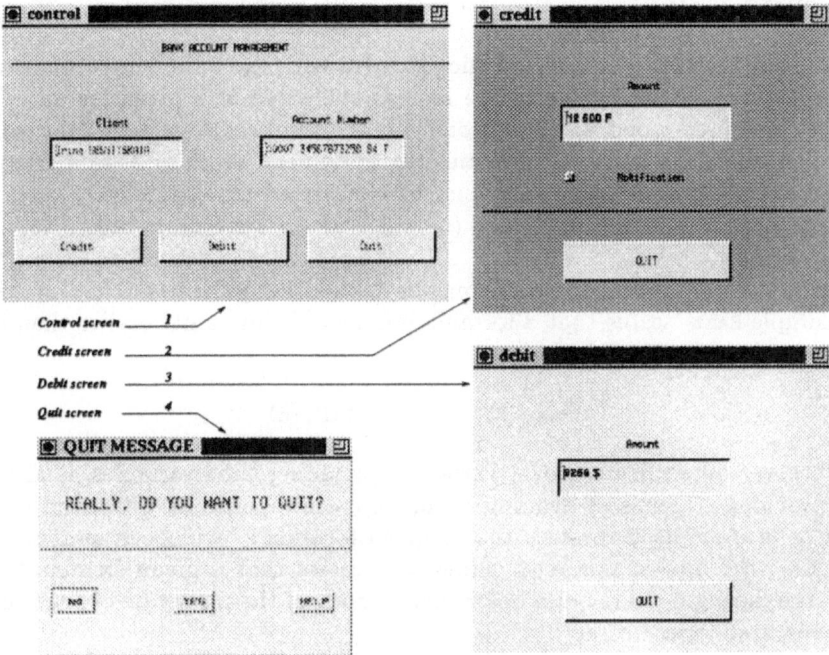

Fig. 2. A bank account management application

try to devise a proper application but we want to use this existing mockup (or prototype) of an application as an example to illustrate our approach.

3 An Overview of TRIO

TRIO is a framework allowing to model real time systems. It basically consists of a temporal logic supported by a set of tools such as a model generator (MG) and an history checker. We chose to use TRIO because of its underlying model of time which is linear and discrete. We consider this point as an advantage with respect to other real time based approaches. Indeed, we are more especially interested in the reactive side of UIS : the usability of UIS is related to properties of interactions with this UIS. And interaction is, by essence, a structure on events and states. These structures can be captured elegantly in systems built on discrete time models.

In the following, we shall introduce only some aspects of TRIO logic and model generation relevant for our work. More details can be found in specific papers such as [GMM90,MMG92] for the language definition, [Mor91,CCM94] for its use in specification and [MMSP96,CCO+96] for its use in test case generation.

152

3.1 TRIO logic

The logic of TRIO is a first order logic extended with one basic temporal distance operator `Dist` . Each formula of the logic is evaluated at a given instant which is implicitly understood as `Now` . Moreover, the temporal operator `Dist` allows reasoning about the truth of a formula at a moment which is distant from `Now` of several time units. `Dist(F,d)` must be considered true, implicitly `Now` , iff `F` will be true `d` time units after `Now` (or was true `-d` time units before `Now` , if `d` is less than 0).

A variety of temporal operators may be defined using the basic `Dist` operator: for example `Past` states that a formula was true d time units earlier than `Now` ; it is defined as:

$$\text{Past(F, d)} \stackrel{\text{def}}{=} \text{Dist(F,-d)}$$

Moreover quantification over variables, including time variables, is allowed. This provides a means of defining usual temporal operators. For example, the operator `SomF` is used to state that a given formula `F` will be true sometimes after `Now` ; the operator `Lasted` allows to express that a given formula `F` has been true during d time units before `Now` . Both of them may be defined, using the basic `Dist` operator as[1]:

$$\text{SomF(F)} \stackrel{\text{def}}{=} \text{ex d (d>0 \& Dist(F,d))}$$
$$\text{Lasted (F,d)} \stackrel{\text{def}}{=} \text{all a (0<a<d -> Dist(F,-a))}$$

As we still said, time in TRIO is considered linear and discrete. That means that each time instant is separated from the next one and the previous one by exactly one time unit. As a consequence, the user must define an interpretation of this time unit depending on the phenomena he is modeling.

Decidability of the validity of formulae is not possible in the general case where the temporal domain is infinite. To overcome this problem, the TRIO tools explore only a finite interval, a *temporal window*, in which the number of time points is, a priori, known and finite.

3.2 An example of TRIO specification

To highlight some possibilities of TRIO, we shall first use a rather high level specification of the example introduced in section 2. We use an abstraction level in which we only consider the absence or presence of the various screens on the display and the events allowing to make them appear or disappear. This specification is given in figure 3.

In this specification, the set of screen names is defined as the enumerated domain `screens` . The events corresponding to the user actions are modeled as time

---

[1] The following syntactical elements are useful for understanding the examples: logical conjunction &, disjunction |, negation ⁓, implication -> equivalence <-> , universal and existential quantifiers `all, ex`

```
signature
        temporal domain: 0..12 ;
domains
        screens:{control_scr, debit_scr, credit_scr, quit_scr};


TD Items
   propositions
                ev_start_control; ev_stop_control;
                ev_show_credit; ev_hide_credit;
                ev_show_debit;  ev_hide_debit;
                show_credit_authorized;
                show_debit_authorized;
   predicates
                displayed(screens);


formulae
axioms

control_on :  (Becomes(displayed(control_scr))-> Past(ev_start_control,1));
control_off : (Becomes(~ displayed(control_scr)) -> Past(ev_stop_control,1));

credit_on :  (Becomes(displayed(credit_scr))
                 -> Past(show_credit_authorized & ev_show_credit,1));
credit_off : (Becomes(~ displayed(credit_scr)) -> Past(ev_hide_credit,1));
credit_auth: show_credit_authorized <-> displayed(control_scr);

debit_on :  (Becomes(displayed(debit_scr))
                 -> Past(show_debit_authorized & ev_show_debit,1));
debit_off : (Becomes(~ displayed(debit_scr)) -> Past(ev_hide_debit,1));
debit_auth: show_debit_authorized
                 <-> (displayed(control_scr) & SomP(displayed(credit_scr)));

spec: Alw (control_on & control_off
           & credit_on & credit_off & credit_auth
           & debit_on & debit_off   & debit_auth );
```

Fig. 3. A high level specification of the bank account management application

dependent propositions ev_start_control , ev_show_credit , etc, and the current status of the interface is modeled by means of a single predicate, displayed , which will apply to any screen.

Changes in the interface status occur as consequences of user actions. This is modeled by a set of named formulae. For example, the formula named debit_on states that the debit_scr screens becomes displayed (i.e. it was not displayed just before Now , and Now it is) if, at the previous instant, the event ev_show_debit occurred, and this display was authorized.

Constraints may also be expressed by named formulae. For example `debit_auth` gives the definition (a logical equivalence `<->`) of `show_debit_authorized` as: the control screen is displayed and the credit screen has been displayed at least once in the past.

Finally the specification `spec` of the whole system is given as the conjunction of all these formulae which must be true on each instant of the temporal window.

3.3 Model generation

A model is, classically in logic, an assignment which makes a formula true. As TRIO is a temporal logic, this assignment is concerned with all the time dependent or independent items on which the formula depends. The assignment is defined at a given moment, and may also involve other assignments relative to other moments, due to the `Dist` operators.

For example, a model of the formula `Past(P,2) & P & SomF(Q)` at instant 2 may be P is false at 0, is true at 2, and Q is true at 10. This model is clearly not a model of the same formula at 4 . The previous model will be noted as a sequence of elementary events, each of which being an assignment of one variable at one instant :

```
not P   : 0
P       : 2
Q       : 10
```

A model is generally not unique, as several assignments may be used to turn a formula true at the same moment. For example

```
not P   : 0
P       : 2
Q       : [0..8]
```

in which Q is true from 0 to 8 is another model of the same formula at 2. It is the role of the Model Generator to compute one, several or all the models of a given formula at a given moment. This generation may be constrained by so-called histories which are also sequences of elementary events. In this case any generated model must contain all the events present in the history.

3.4 An example of model generation

Let us go back to our small abstract example, we may use the model generator to compute blindly models for the whole specification. As the specification is the same at each instant of the temporal window, the models may be computed at any instant.

If we proceed this way, we shall obtain a lot of "uninteresting models" like the one shown in figure 4 which may be interpreted as "the control screen was open at the beginning of the temporal window and nothing happens till the end of the window"

```
displayed(control_scr) :[0..12]
not displayed(credit_scr) :[0..12]
show_credit_authorized :[0..12]
not displayed(debit_scr) :[0..12]
not show_debit_authorized :[0..12]
```

Fig. 4. An uninteresting model

Instead, we have the possibility to be more precise in what we want to observe. For example if we are interested in situations in which the application does not work at the beginning (the screen is not displayed) and in which the debit screen is displayed at the end, we can express this as an history:

```
not displayed(control_scr):0
displayed(debit_scr) :12
```

and use it to constrain the model generation. Doing so, we shall get models like the one of figure 5 (end of lines have been numbered only for making comments easier).

```
not displayed(control_scr)    :0          (1)
not displayed(credit_scr)     :[0..9]     (2)
not show_credit_authorized    :0          (3)
not displayed(debit_scr)      :[0..11]    (4)
not show_debit_authorized     :[0..10]    (5)
ev_start_control              :0          (6)
displayed(control_scr)        :[1..12]    (7)
show_credit_authorized        :[1..12]    (8)
ev_show_credit                :9          (9)
displayed(credit_scr)         :10         (10)
ev_hide_credit                :10         (11)
not displayed(credit_scr)     :[11..12]   (12)
show_debit_authorized         :[11..12]   (13)
ev_show_debit                 :11         (14)
displayed(debit_scr)          :12         (15)
```

Fig. 5. A useful model

We may notice that the generated model extends the initial history which is in lines 1 and 15. No screens are displayed at the beginning (lines 1 to 4). The event **ev_start_control** occurs at 0 (6) then the control screen is displayed from 1 to the end (7). The credit screen is displayed at 10 after the event **ev_show_credit** has occurred (9 and 10). After that, the debit screen is allowed to be displayed (13), and it is what occurs following the event **ev_show_debit** occurrence (14 and 15).

4 Using TRIO for UIS Verification

The TRIO technology, as introduced in the previous section allows us to express a formal specification of a UIS. Moreover the model generation may be used as a kind of animation of this specification, and the resulting models may be interpreted as expected traces of the future system. In this section we show how we can use model generation to produce data for the test generation and the test oracle.

4.1 Refining the specification

First, we have to produce, and start with, a specification at an "adequate" level of refinement. By adequate, we mean that the specification refers to elements (user actions, interface status) which can be interpreted directly as actions and observations on the final system.

If we consider the abstract specification given in figure 3 this is not the case, as events like ev_show_credit , ev_show_debit etc are not defined in terms of user interaction with the final system. So we have to produce a more detailed specification like the one described in appendix A in which:

- various areas of the screens have been described as being screens , buttons, toggle buttons, text fields ,
- the status of the UIS is given by a set of predicates which apply these areas displayed for a screen, ticked for a toggle button, filled for a field,
- a designator (think such as a mouse) has been introduced to select one area, or another,
- end user actions as supported by the UIS are elements of the specification: the user may move_selector_on a given area[2], click on a button, typein a text field, etc.,
- as in the abstract specification, the effects of each user action on the UIS status are described by a set of named formulae. act_push_display_credit , for example, explains that the credit screen becomes displayed if the user click s when the condition selected_display_credit is met. This condition is described as the conjunction of:
  - the presence of the control screen,
  - the position of the selector on the display_credit button,
  - if needed, preceded by a move of the selector on this button, if it were not yet on this position.
- the constraint has been strengthened: the text fields account and client must have been filled and the credit screen must have been displayed in the past.

---

[2] the lack of polymorphism in TRIO leads to the splitting of this into 3 actions depending on the type of the area the selector is moved on

4.2   Defining test objectives

Test objectives, in the approach, describe a situation that we want to reach by a sequence of user actions on the system (we don't claim that this informal definition is general). As it has been shown in section 3 we have at our disposal two different means:

- using the notion of *history* we can describe *extensionally* the situation we want to reach, eventually the intermediate state we want to observe, as a sequence of elementary, dated, events concerned with variables describing the UIS status,
- using a *TRIO formula* we can describe the situation in an *intentional* way. This is the purpose of the prop1 formula which can be found at the end of the specification in appendix A: indeed SomF(displayed(debit_scr)) says that we want the debit_scr screen to be displayed at some moment in the future, without being more precise.

The advantage of this second way of formulating test objectives is that it requires the user to be less precise in the process of formulation. Practically, we use more often a combination of the two methods: an intensional expression of test objectives by means of logical formulae, and the definition of initial conditions of test by means of histories.

4.3   Using model generation

Once we have defined the test objectives in one of the ways mentioned above, we may use the model generator to provide us with test case generation. To do that, we have only to ask for the generation of models of the specification, at a chosen instant, and constrained either by an history, or by a logical formula describing the test objectives.

For the example of appendix A , we have asked for model generation of spec & dc_constraint at the initial instant, constrained by the test objective prop1 . One of the model we have obtained from the Model Generator is given in appendix B. This model has been manually rearranged to be easier to comment:

- lines 1 to 7 give the sequence of actions that must be performed by the user to reach the situation described by prop1 . They may be directly interpreted as a test sequence:
  - click anywhere at 0 (to start the application),
  - do nothing till 7
  - move selector on account field at 7,
  - type in (the account) at 8,
  - move selector on client field at 8,
  - type in (the client name) at 9,
  - etc...
- lines 16 to 27 describe the status of the display at different instants. They represent the expected results of the sequence of actions and, as such, play the role of the oracle:

- the control screen is not displayed at 0,
- it is displayed at 1, and from 8 to 11 (meanwhile, it does not matter)
- the credit screen becomes displayed at 11,
- ...
- the field account is not filled from 0 to 8,
- then it is filled from 9 to 11,
- etc...

5 Getting a formal specification of an UIS

The previous section showed how test sequences and test oracles can be generated from a formal specification expressed in TRIO. But these techniques can not be used to test UIS because it is practically never the case that UIS are developed with a formal specification. So, the problem is now to get such a formal specification of an UIS. We were yet faced to this problem. To solve it, we developed and experimented a retro-engineering approach to abstract and to build the specification from programs of an UIS mockup such as the example described in section 2.

Indeed, we take account of the fact that, in practice, UIS designers make use of software mockups and of prototypes and do not make use of written specifications. Therefore, it is crucial to verify exhaustively that these mockups and prototypes describe an UIS that behaves in accordance with some behavioral constraints that capture the user requirements. In case of no, mockups and prototypes must be corrected and re-designed iteratively until the requirements are satisfied. To enforce this approach, we devised and implemented [ASDR98] the prototype of a software environment devoted to the validation of interactive systems.

The techniques used to perform automated verification in the environment make explicit use of formal languages. These languages permit to describe and to operate computations on formal models of user interfaces ; note that in that case, the term *model refers now to an abstract and formal description of a system*. Such a model can be used and considered as a the inquired formal specification of the UIS.

5.1 Automatic generation of a model of the UIS in Lustre.

Some semantic analysis techniques, that are described in [Aus98], are used to build mechanically a formal model of the mockup of an UIS by analyzing the C and UIL codes of this mockup. A *model generator*, that is the heart of the environment, takes as an input the codes that are generated by an interface generator and outputs a formal model as a text written in the formal language Lustre.

Reading ([HCRP91]) will give a full description of language Lustre. In fact, a text in Lustre is a set of declarations expressed in an unordered list of equations. An equation $X = E$ where E is a Lustre expression of flows specifies that the flow variable X is always equal to the value of flow denoted by E. A flow variable is a function of time which is assumed to be isomorphic to the set of natural numbers. So a flow variable denotes the sequence of values that it takes at each instant. Expressions on flows are made of variable identifiers, constants (considered as constant functions), usual arithmetic, boolean and conditional operators, and only two specific operators: the *previous* operator *pre* and the *followed_by* operator $\rightarrow$.

Lustre equations can be structured into *nodes*. A node is in fact the declaration of a particular function of input flow variables onto output flow variables. The functional part of the node is declared by a set of equations that involve possibly local flow variables. Once declared, a node can be used as a functional operator inside any Lustre expression. Lustre nodes permit to model the behavior of *interactors*. It is now well accepted that interactor is the basic component and actor of interactions ([FP90],[DH93]). Theoretical models of interactors were suggested in [DH95] or [DFHP94]. The Lustre model describes an UIS as a network of nodes.

5.2 Verification of properties of the UIS by checking the Lustre model.

The model generator produces a formal model of the UIS. The objective is to be sure that the UIS satisfies some required behavioral properties. These properties may be formally checked on the model if the user has at disposal some formulas that capture the required properties. The environment provides the user with some *generic* formulas that express the definition of some various properties. These formulas are automatically instantiated to check the property on particular interactors of the UIS. For instance, a generic definition of *reachability_of_screen_X* is provided. To check that *Debit screen* of figure 2 is reachable, the user requires, by navigating through menus, to check the *reachability* property on the *Debit* interactor.

The user can build his own instantiated formulas by using a graphic property editor. This property editor allows the user to build schemes of logical and temporal relations between interaction objects that are involved in the UIS. It offers a set of palettes that permit the user to draw a graphical representation of the property he wants to check on the UIS. This graphical representation is translated into a Lustre formal expression by interpreting semantically the graphical produced constructs.

A key point is that the Lustre model can be transformed into a logical model, a state graph for instance. So, properties that are captured by Lustre formulas are checked on this logical model [ASDR98]. When a property P is not satisfied on the model, counterexamples can be generated. These counterexamples may be used as a diagnosis by the designer.

5.3 Limit of the approach when generating tests.

The ability to produce counterexamples is an effective means of producing tests. The principle of generation is the following. Assume that a test for a property P must be generated. Let C be a configuration of the UIS that satisfies P. Let $exp(C)$ be a formal expression in Lustre that denotes this configuration. An attempt to check that C is unreachable is done by checking $\neg exp(C)$. This fails and any counterexample can be viewed as a test of P.

The main problem, with this approach, is in getting the formulas $\neg exp(C)$ that permits to generate tests for P. These formulas are easy to produce when the expression for P is simple or trivial. Assume P is expressed as $(a \rightarrow b)$. Then three configurations C_1, C_2 and C_3 satisfy P : $(a \wedge b)$, $(\neg a \wedge \neg b)$ and $(\neg a \wedge b)$. Nevertheless, it may be difficult to exhibit exhaustively these configurations when the expression of P is more complex, and involves combinations of logical and temporal operators. We are faced with a real difficulty of this approach : generating tests is not a very easy job for any property P. In that case, using TRIO in place of Lustre may be helpful to overcome this problem.

6 Extending the approach by integrating and using TRIO to generate tests.

6.1 Why using TRIO is easier to get tests

TRIO brings an interesting and easy solution to the problem of getting tests. Assume a TRIO specification can be derived from the equivalent Lustre model (spec$_{Lustre}$). Assume also that a TRIO formula (P$_{Lustre}$) can be derived from the Lustre expression of a property P.

Then, generating test cases for P consists in generating models of the TRIO formula Alw(spec$_{Lustre}$ & P$_{Lustre}$). This is a quite natural and elegant way to generate these tests and this technical approach permits to overcome the problem of finding configurations that satisfy P. This search is automatically done by TRIO tools.

But the problem comes now to translate Lustre models and Lustre formulas into TRIO specifications and TRIO formulas. It is the job of a tool of the environment: Lus2trio.

6.2 Translating Lustre to TRIO.

The translation process is fully described in [AC98]. We just give an overview of this process to get an idea of how it works.

Briefly speaking, assume that a Lustre model is a set of declarations of boolean variables and of equations. It incorporates always some declarations of input and output variables of flows, and it incorporates eventually some declarations of local variables. All these declarations are translated into declarations of TRIO propositions. Equations of flows are translated into TRIO axioms A_i.

A last axiom *Spec* is added : $Spec = Alw(\bigwedge_i A_i)$. Consider the following Lustre node.

```
node uis(i1,i2:bool) returns (o1,o2:bool);
let o1 = not (i2 and i1);
    o2 = i2 or i1;
tel
```

It may be translated into the following TRIO declarations;

```
TD items
propositions
i1; i2; o1; o2;
formulae
axioms
A1 : o1 <-> ~(i2 & i1);
A2 : o2 <-> (i2 | i1);
Spec : Alw (A1 & A2);
```

The translation process is in fact a bit more complex, because expressions on flows may involve other syntactical constructs and various other operators. In particular the *followed_by* operator introduces some complexity in this process. But the principle given here stays the same and is easy to understand.

This process permits to build a new environment that works, in fact, on a unique object: the formal specification of the UIS. This specification can be equivalently expressed in Lustre or in TRIO.

6.3 Architecture of the whole environment

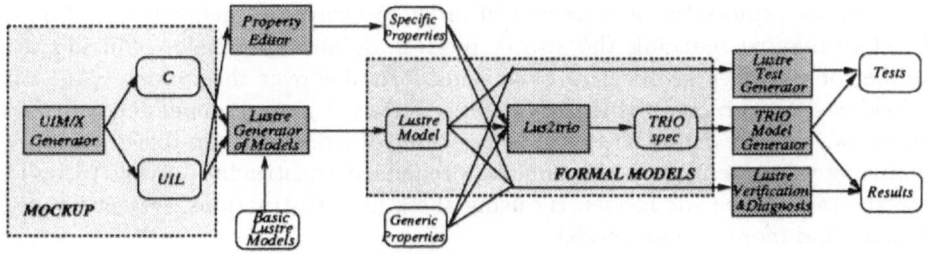

Fig. 6. The whole environment

The whole environment, that incorporates Lustre and TRIO technologies is depicted by figure 6. It shows that two formal models with two formalisms may be used to represent the behavior of a unique mockup of an UIS. Both permit to operate verification of properties on models and to generate tests related to the checked properties. The user can choose one technology or the other, depending on various parameters : for example, the type of operation he wants to perform or the complexity of formulas that capture properties he wants to test, and, of course, performance.

7 Conclusion

In this paper, we first showed how tests for an UIS can be generated from a formal specification of the UIS, expressed in the TRIO formalism. The objectives of tests are given by TRIO expressions of properties that capture the intended behavior of the UIS. Generating tests consists in generating models for the specification in conjunction with the property.

The problem is to get or to build such a specification. Practically, it does not exist, but mockups or prototypes are generally used in place of it. A possible approach consists in exerting some techniques of retro-engineering in order to get a formal and abstract representation of the UIS by analyzing the codes of mockups. We implemented the prototype of a validation environment around a Lustre model generator. We showed how a Lustre text may be translated into a TRIO specification. This translation tool permits the environment to be multi-formalism.

The example we used in this paper and that was described by section 2 is a windowing interface. But this validation process can be used to validate on other classes of UIS. We feel that such a process may be suitable for UIS that interface commercial systems or critical applications. In particular, we experimented this approach on UIS as : mobile telephones, the flight desk of an aircraft, the control subsystem of a satellite.

Nevertheless, the involved operations may be intrinsically very complex and may rapidly cause combinatory explosion problems both for TRIO and Lustre tools. So, we explore two approaches in order to overcome this problem. A first objective may be reducing the size of models, or more precisely, reducing the number of variables involved in evaluating formulae over the model. This can be achieved by two complementary means. Firstly, by using dependence analysis, we can remove definitions and declarations of irrelevant variables. An other promising way attempts to group some predefined constructs in order to build new abstractions on the model. By using these new abstractions, we get a more abstract and more concise model.

Moreover, we feel that the techniques and tools we presented can not be used without any method. Building or generating a big monolithic model, and running some tools on it does not work and is not a good approach. It is necessary to find some new approach that permits both to structure models and to decompose problems into subproblems that can be treated by tools. In other words, we need to devise some rigorous method that permits to achieve a form of modular verification.

We envisage also to extend the use of the TRIO model generator in order to perform some kind of *history checking*. This approach permits to check some properties on traces (encoded as histories). Traces may be extracted from some registered runs of an existing UIS. This technique is interesting because it would permit to evaluate a still existing UIS and to extend the use of our environment to evaluation of existing products.

References

[AC98]   B. Ausbourg(d') and J. Cazin. Validating Man Machine Interfaces : models and specifications. Technical Report 3.3709.00/DTIM, ONERA-CERT, Toulouse, France, July 1998.

[ASDR98]   B. Ausbourg(d'), C. Seguin, G. Durrieu, and P. Roché. Assisting the Automated Validation Process of User Interfaces Systems. In *Proceedings of the International Conference on Software Engineering, ICSE 98*, Kyoto, Japan, April 1998.

[Aus98]   B. Ausbourg(d'). Using Model Checking for the Automatic Validation of User Interfaces Systems. In P. Markopoulos and P. Johnson, editors, *Proceedings of Design, Specification and Verification of Interactive Systems '98*, Abingdon, UK, June 1998. Eurographics, Springer-Verlag.

[CCM94]   E. Ciapessoni, E. Crivelli, and M.Migliorati. Functional specification of the control system of a pondage power plant. Technical report, ENEL/CRA, 1994.

[CCO⁺96]   J. Cazin, E. Ciapessoni, W. Osnowycz, E. Ratto, and C. Seguin. An experience in the specification and test of an electrical flight control system using a temporal logic framework. In *DASIA Conference*, 1996.

[DFHP94]   D.J. Duke, G. Faconti, M.D. Harrison, and F. Paterno. Unifying views of interactors. In *Proceedings of Advance Visual Interface'94 Workshop*, Bari, 1994.

[DH93]   D.J. Duke and M.D. Harrison. Abstract Interaction Objects. *Computer Graphics Forum*, 12(3):25–26, 1993.

[DH95]   D. K. Duke and M. D. Harrison. Event model of human system interaction. *Software Engineering Journal*, January 1995.

[FP90]   G. Faconti and F. Paterno. An approach to the formal specification of the components of an interaction. In *Proceedings of the Eurographics 90 Workshop*, 1990.

[GMM90]   Carlo Ghezzi, Dino Madrioli, and Angelo Morzenti. Trio: A logic language for executable specifications of real-time systems. *Journal of Systems Software*, 12(2), 1990.

[HCRP91]   Nicolas Halbwachs, Paul Caspi, Pascal Raymond, and Daniel Pilaud. The synchronous dataflow programming language Lustre. In *Proceedings of IEEE*, number 9 in 79, pages 1305–1320, September 1991.

[MC99]   I MacColl and D Carrington. Extending the Test Template Framework for specification-based testing of interactive systems. In *Proceedings of the Australasian Computer Science Conference (ACSC99)*. Springer, 1999.

[MMG92]   A. Morzenti, D. Mandrioli, and C. Ghezzi. A model-parametric real-time logic. *ACM Transactions on Programming Languages and Systems*, 14(4), 1992.

[MMSP96]   S. Morasca, A. Morzenti, and P. San Pietro. Generating functional test cases in-the-large for time-critical systems from logic-based specifications. In *International Symposium on Software Testing and Analysis*, 1996.

[Mor91]   A. Morzenti. Validating real-time systems by executing logic specifications. In *REX Workshop "Real-Time Theory in Practice"*, volume 600 of *LNCS*. Springer Verlag, 1991.

[PS97]   J. Peleska and M. Siegel. Test automation of safety-critical reactive systems. In *Proceedings of Wofacs '96*. SACJ/SART No 19, 1997.

[SC96]   P Stocks and D Carrington. A framework for specification-based testing. *IEEE Transactions on Software Engineering*, 22(11):777–793, November 1996.

A   Another specification of the bank application

```
signature
        temporal domain: 0..12 ;
domains
        buttons:{display_credit, display_debit, quit_control,
                quit_debit, quit_credit, yes_quit, no_quit, help_quit};
        toggles:{notification};
        fields: {client, account, debit, credit};
        screens:{control_scr, debit_scr, credit_scr, quit_scr};
        areas:  {b,t,f,nowhere};
TD Items
    consts total selector_on: areas;
                selected_b : buttons;
                selected_f : fields;
    propositions credited;
                click;
                typein;
    predicates   filled(fields);
                ticked(toggles);
                displayed(screens);
                move_selector_on_b(buttons);
                move_selector_on_f(fields);
                move_selector_on_t(toggles);
formulae    axioms

start_control : Past(selector_on = nowhere & click,1)
            & Becomes(displayed(control_scr));

selected_display_credit: displayed(control_scr)
  & (  (selector_on = b & selected_b = display_credit)
    & ( Past(~(selector_on = b & selected_b = display_credit),1)
        <-> Past(move_selector_on_b(display_credit),1)));
act_push_display_credit : Becomes(displayed(credit_scr))
                        -> Past(selected_display_credit & click,1);

selected_display_debit: displayed(control_scr)
  & (  (selector_on = b & selected_b = display_debit)
    & ( Past(~(selector_on = b & selected_b = display_debit),1)
        <-> Past(move_selector_on_b(display_debit),1)));
act_push_display_debit : Becomes(displayed(debit_scr))
                        -> Past(selected_display_debit & click,1);

selected_client_field : displayed(control_scr)
  & (  (selector_on = f & selected_f = client)
    & ( Past(~(selector_on = f & selected_f = client),1)
        <-> Past(move_selector_on_f(client),1)));
act_fill_client_field : Becomes(filled(client))
                        -> Past(selected_client_field & typein,1);
```

```
selected_account_field : displayed(control_scr)
  & (   (selector_on = f & selected_f = account)
      & ( Past(~(selector_on = f & selected_f = account),1)
          <->Past(move_selector_on_f(account),1)));
act_fill_account_field : Becomes(filled(account))
                           -> Past(selected_account_field & typein,1);
/* ------------------------------------------------------------ */
dc_constraint :
  Alw(displayed(debit_scr) -> SomP_e(filled(account) & filled(client)
                                   & displayed(credit_scr)));

spec : Alw(act_push_display_credit &  act_push_display_debit
           & act_fill_client_field & act_fill_account_field);

prop1: SomF(displayed(debit_scr));  .
```

B   An example of generated model

```
click                                :0               (1)
move_selector_on_f(account)          :7               (2)
move_selector_on_f(client)           :8               (3)
typein                               :[8..9]          (4)
move_selector_on_b(display_credit)   :9               (5)
click                                :[10..11]        (6)
move_selector_on_b(display_debit)    :10              (7)

selector_on = nowhere                :0               (8)
selector_on = _203513{b, nowhere, t} :7               (9)
selector_on = f                      :[8..9]          (10)
selected_f = client                  :9               (11)
selected_f = account                 :8               (12)
selector_on = b                      :[10..11]        (13)
selected_b = display_credit          :10              (14)
selected_b = display_debit           :11              (15)

not displayed(control_scr)           :0               (16)
not displayed(credit_scr)            :[0..10]         (17)
not displayed(debit_scr)             :[0..11]         (18)
displayed(control_scr)               :1               (19)
displayed(control_scr)               :[8..11]         (20)
displayed(credit_scr)                :11              (21)
displayed(debit_scr)                 :12              (22)
not displayed(credit_scr)            :12              (23)

not filled(account)                  :[0..8]          (24)
filled(account)                      :[9..11]         (25)
not filled(client)                   :[0..9]          (26)
filled(client)                       :[10..11]        (27)
```

Using automated reasoning in the design of an audio-visual communication system

José C. Campos and Michael D. Harrison

Human-Computer Interaction Group
Department of Computer Science, University of York
e-mail: {Jose.Campos,Michael.Harrison}@cs.york.ac.uk

Abstract. Formal reasoning about how users and systems interact poses a difficult challenge. Interactive systems design provides a context in which the subjective area of human understanding meets the objectivity of computer systems logic. We present results of a case study in the use of automated reasoning to aid the formal analysis of interactive systems. We show how we can use human-factors issues to generate properties of interest, and how we can use model checking and theorem proving to analyse our specifications against those properties. This is part of ongoing work in the development of a tool to allow the automatic translation of interactor based specifications into SMV, and in the analysis of the role which different verification techniques might have during the development of interactive systems.

1 Introduction

In this paper we present results of an ongoing case study in the use of automated reasoning to aid the formal analysis of a proposed design of an interactive system. This case study is being undertaken as part of the development of a tool to allow the automated verification (through model checking) of interactor specifications: a "MAL-based interactors" to SMV compiler (cf. [5,4]). We are also interested in discussing the role which different verification techniques might have during the development of interactive systems.

When reasoning about models of systems, we can identify important classes of properties, including:

1. the coherence of the model (for example, type checking), used to answer questions of the type: "are we building the model right?";
2. the functional behaviour of the system (for example, safety properties), used to answer questions of the type: "are we modelling the right functionality?";
3. how will system and users interact, used to answer questions of the type: "will the system be easy to use?".

While properties of type 1 and 2 are, obviously, important, our research deals with properties of type 3. The ability to identify and verify this type of property is fundamental, as is confirmed by the recognition that even the best functionality can be rendered useless by a badly designed user interface.

Formal (mathematically based) methods have proven useful in dealing with class 1 and 2 properties. This is specially true when we can resort to automated tools to aid reasoning. It is natural therefore to consider the applicability of such methods and tools to the development of interactive systems. This has been an active area of research in recent years (see, for example, [18,2,6]).

Formal reasoning about how users and systems interact poses a difficult challenge. Interactive systems design provides a context in which the subjective area of human understanding meets the objectivity of computer systems logic. In order to analyse, in a formal context, aspects of system design which have a degree of subjectivity, we must find some way to merge both areas. In this paper we show how we can use human-factors issues to generate properties of interest. We build an interactor based model of a system, and use the interactors to SMV compiler to enable us to check those properties against the model, using the SMV [16] model checker. The use of PVS [17], a theorem prover, is also illustrated. We will also point out how the results of such analysis can then be fed back into a human-factors context for subjective analysis.

1.1 The case study

We selected for this case-study the ECOM system [1]. ECOM is a audio-visual communication system. Audio-visual communication systems attempt to enhance collaboration and awareness between a community of users distributed over a number of distinct physical locations. This is done by offering a number of means of contact between users. These will include audio, video, and any other form of exchange of information that might be judged appropriate for a specific system.

This type of system presents a tension between the need to promote a sense of awareness between users, and the need to preserve individual privacy. In order to address the privacy issue users are offered some mechanism to control how/by whom they can be contacted (their accessibility).

One of the features that makes ECOM interesting from a design analysis point of view is the attempt at integrating two different such mechanisms. ECOM integrates features from both CAVECAT and RAVE, two previous media space systems (see [1] for a description). In CAVECAT accessibilities are represented by a door state. There are four such door states (open, ajar, closed, and locked), each representing a different accessibility level, with its associated set of allowed connections. Users can select an appropriate door state and can see the doors states of other users in the system. In this way users can select an appropriate level of accessibility. If, for example, some user is in an important meeting, and does not want to be interrupted, he can *lock the door* thus preventing connections to him. At the same time users can have a notion of how accessible other users are, by looking at each other's door state.

In RAVE accessibilities are set on a per user basis. Users can select a specific type of connection and specify which users are allowed to establish it. Awareness is promoted by a panel showing periodically updated snapshots of all users. The idea being that these snapshot will give an idea of how busy (or not) a user is and hence how receptive to connections.

CAVECAT allows for an easy change in the accessibility level. However it does not include the possibility of exceptions to the general setting: you might want the meeting not to be interrupted *unless* it is the boss! On the other hand, RAVE allows a better tailoring of the accessibility setting, but makes it harder to make a global change since the accessibility setting of every user will have to be updated manually.

ECOM proposes the integration of both mechanisms. Users can set a general accessibility level using the door state metaphor, but a mechanism for exception setting is introduced that allows for specific users to have different accessibility rights.

Setting exceptions is done by selecting a user, a specific type of connection and the most conservative door state that still allows the user to connect (see Figure 1). Hence, if the exception level is set to *when Door Open*, the connection will also be allowed when the door is ajar. We will call this the cumulative nature of exceptions. Additionally the

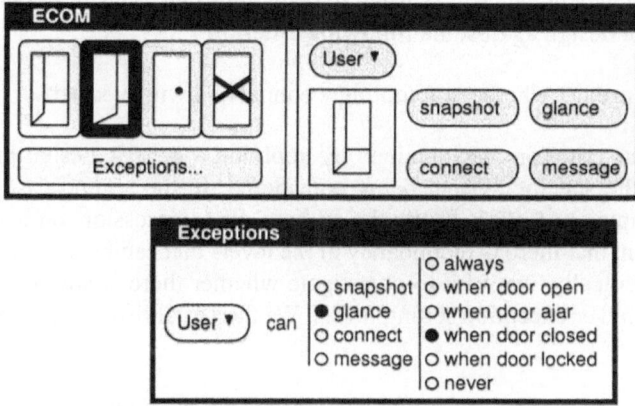

Fig. 1. The ECOM system (adapted from [1])

exception can be set to *always* or *never*.

By merging both designs, the designers hope to improve on the previous systems by incorporating the best features of each.

So far we have only described how each individual user sets an accessibility level. As in CAVECAT, awareness is promoted by presenting the door state of each user to all other users. One interesting question is whether this mechanism is still valid in the new system.

2   Checking the Proposed Design

To study the applicability of automated reasoning techniques to this case study, we must start by selecting some candidate features of the system, that we wish to analyse. We can resort to a number of sources to aid us in this process:

— *off-the-shelf* catalogues of design principles — these can be found in the literature on human computer interaction (see, for example, [7, Chapter four]);

— the results of other approaches to the analysis of the system — in the present case, some of the decision that were made regarding what properties to check were informed by the results of previous cognitive and formal analysis reported in [1];
— past experience in the development of systems — the *critical eye*.

We will look at two particular aspects of the system, because they seem interesting, and also because we hope they will allow us to illustrate the application of different reasoning techniques. First we will look at the issue of predictability. Being a general principle, predictability might be looked at from a variety of angles. We will consider the following angle: "the user should understand from the interface if an operation they might like to invoke cannot be performed" [7]. This is particularly relevant since we are attempting to promote a sense of awareness of how available other users are in the system: if the mechanism to establish connections is not predictable, then users will lose faith in the state they perceive the system to be in, thus defeating awareness. Hence, we will evaluate the design against the following criterion:

Can a user predict whether attempting a connection will succeed?

The previous criterion was obtained by applying a generic design principle (predictability) to the specific system being considered. In the second case we base our analysis on simple *gut feeling*. It was the authors' first impression, on reading the systems description, that there is redundancy in the levels that can be used to set an exception. More specifically, we want to investigate whether there is any real need to have the *always* and *never* exception setting levels. We then establish another two criteria for analysis:

— The effect of setting the exception level to *always* cannot be achieved by setting it to some other level.
— The effect of setting the exception level to *never* cannot be achieved by setting it to some other level.

We will now try to assess the proposed design against the criteria enumerated above. To do that we develop models that focus on those aspects of the system that are most relevant to the principles being analysed (cf. [13,5]). Note that this is yet another instance of the general process of model building: we abstract away what is considered to be accessory, and focus on what is considered to be relevant. As with any other model, care must be taken that all which is relevant is conveniently included.

2.1 Predictability

We will now look at the first criterion:

Can a user predict whether attempting a connection will succeed?

We start by building a model of the proposed system. To do that, we have to identify those aspects of the system which relate to the property we want to investigate. In the present case we have to model:

— the mechanisms for accessibility and exceptions setting — they have an impact on which connections can be established;

— the mechanism for establishing connections — it is what we are looking at;

— the mechanism for promoting awareness — it gives users information about other users.

The model is loosely based on one presented in [1]. We will consider a user panel representing the interface to a single user, and the system core representing the remainder of the system. The user accesses the system core through the user panel.

We will use interactors [12,10] to write the model. Modal Action Logic (MAL) [19] will be used to specify interactor behaviour. First, some types are introduced:

types
User   # all users
Service   # available services
Door   # door states
Conn = User × Service × User # connections

The type names should be self explanatory. Services represent possible connection types, and connections are defined as tuples built with two users (the caller and the callee), and a service (the type of connection).

The system core model is presented in figure 2. Its main task is to manage connections. At each instant there are a number of connections in progress (attribute current). Two actions manipulate current: action establish initiates a given connection, and close ends it. Attribute default associates, with each door state, the valid services for that state. The validity of a specific connection depends on the level of accessibility of the callee (which, in turn, is determined by the callee's door state — cf. attribute accessibility). However, this mechanism can be overridden by setting exceptions. These are registered by associating the desired connections with the most conservative door state that still allows each connection to take place (attribute exceptions).

To simplify reading the specification, a further attribute is used which represents the allowed connections at each moment (attribute allowed). The process of determining if a connection is allowed (i.e. the value of attribute allowed) is specified by axiom (5). It mimics the reasoning just described.

Two more actions are considered: action setexcep introduces an exception into the system, and action setacc sets the accessibility of a given user. Note that the behaviour of establish and close has been left deliberately under-specified (see axioms 1 and 2). The axioms state what happens if the parameters to the actions are valid, action behaviour under invalid conditions is left unspecified. It would have been possible to specify that the actions can only happen when the parameters are valid, but that would have been too restrictive, as it would limit further development of the model: for example, we might wish to add later that an error message should be generated when an illegal action is attempted.

The user panel is built on top of the core, its model is presented in figure 3. Since, in the present case, we are looking at a situation where one user is trying to establish a

interactor core
attributes
allowed: $\mathbb{P}$ Conn
accessibility: User $\to$ Door
current: $\mathbb{P}$ Conn
default: Door $\to$ $\mathbb{P}$ Service
exceptions: Conn $\to$ Door
action
establish(Conn) close(Conn)
setexcep(User,Service,User,Door) setacc(User,Door)
axioms
(1) c $\in$ allowed $\to$ [establish(c)] current' = current $\cup$ {c}
$\wedge$ unchanged(accessibility, default, exceptions)
(2) c $\in$ current $\to$ [close(c)] current' = current - {c}
$\wedge$ unchanged(accessibility, default, exceptions)
(3) [setexcep(u1,s,u2,d)] exceptions'=exceptions+[(u1,s,u2) $\to$ d]
$\wedge$ unchanged(accessibility, default, current)
(4) [setacc(u,d)] accessibility'=accessibility+[u $\to$ d]
$\wedge$ unchanged(exceptions, default, current)
(5) (caller,type,callee) $\in$ allowed $\leftrightarrow$
(((caller,type,callee) $\notin$ dom(exceptions) $\to$
type $\in$ default(accessibility(callee)))
$\wedge$
((caller,type,callee) $\in$ dom(exceptions) $\to$
exceptions((caller,type,callee)) $\geq$ accessibility(callee)))

Fig. 2. Core

connection, the model of the user panel is developed only so far as to make the analysis possible. Hence, the model includes the buttons that are used to request connections (attribute buttons), the user that has been selected as callee (attribute chosen), and its door state (attribute door-icon). The callee is set by action select. Finally, the user panel has an owner, the caller (attribute owner). The axioms should be self explanatory. Axiom 3 defines that then a button is pressed (buttons(s).$>_{action}$=pressed) a request to establish the corresponding connection is originated ($>_{action}$=request(owner, s, chosen)). The special attribute $>_{action}$ represents the action that has taken place (see [4]).

In the present context we will use SMV [16] to perform the verification. Since SMV is a model checker, the analysis of SMV specifications is completely automated. To make the model checking of interactor specifications easier, we are developing a compiler that generates SMV code directly from interactor specifications. An initial version of the compiler was introduced in [5]. In [4] the tool is further developed and the correctness of the translation process from the interactor language to SMV is demonstrated.

Having a compiler to SMV means that, given an *appropriate* interactor specification, we can check properties automatically. In the context of model checking, an *appropriate* interactor specification means one that can be expressed as a finite state machine, and ideally with a minimum of states. In order for that to be true of our specification, some adjustments must be made. The first step is to make all types finite. From Figure 1 it can be seen that there are four possible connection types (snapshot, glance, connect,

interactor userpanel
importing core
attributes
owner: User
vis chosen: [User]
vis buttons: Service → button
vis door-icon: [door] # door state of selected user
action
vis select(User)
axioms
(1) chosen ≠ nil → door-icon=accessibility(chosen)
(2) chosen = nil → door-icon=nil
(3) buttons(s).$>_{action}$=pressed ↔ $>_{action}$=establish(owner,s,chosen)
(4) per(buttons(s).pressed) → chosen≠nil
(5) [select(u)] chosen=u

Fig. 3. User Panel

and message), and also four possible door states (open, ajar, closed, and locked). Since door states are also used to set exceptions, all and none are added as possible door states (and all attributes except exceptions are restricted to the original four values). The number of users in the system is arbitrary, three users are used. The types become:

types
User = {user1, user2, user3}   # all users
Service = {snapshot, glance, connect, message} # available services
Door = {all, open, ajar, closed, locked, none}   # door states

Since all other types are defined on top of these three, they become finite by definition. Finally, all structured types have to be rewritten as arrays. Type $\mathbb{P}$ Conn, for example, becomes:

PConn = array user1 .. user3 of
                    array snapshot .. message of array user1 .. user3 of boolean

The same process is applied to all other structured types present in the specification.

We now rewrite the specification to take into consideration these concrete definitions of the types. As an example we show the new version of axiom 5 in interactor core (compare with figure 2):

allowed[caller][type][callee] ↔
(exceptions[caller][type][callee]=null →
default[accessibility[callee]][type])
∧ (exceptions[caller][type][callee]≠null →
exceptions[caller][type][callee] ≥ accessibility[callee])

Inspection of the axiom above, however, reveals an error in the specification: in the presence of an exception, allowed is calculated by seeing if the door level set for

174

the exception is greater (more conservative — look at the enumeration order in the definition of Door) than the accessibility level set by the callee. However, since in the definition of Door we have all as the smallest value, and none as the greatest, then setting the exception level to all/none prohibits/allows all connections! This behaviour is exactly the opposite of what is the reasonable interpretation of both value names. We need to exchange the position of all and none.

Since the order in which the values were enumerated was based on the order they appear in the proposed presentation, this might mean that there is some problem with that aspect of the interface. We will see how to investigate this further in Section 2.2.

In order to verify the proposed design against the criterion set forth above, that criterion needs to be defined as a CTL formula. Looking at the specification of the user panel, it can be seen that the user gets information on the callee's accessibility level through its door state. We will suppose that the user can *remember* which connections are valid for each door state (it could be argued that this information should be encoded in the interface by disabling *illegal* buttons for the given door state, as it will be shown this is not enough). If that is assumed, then the system is predictable if all valid button presses for each door state result in the corresponding connection being established, i.e. all valid button presses *to the user*, are valid button presses *to the system*. This can be expressed as a family of CTL formulae:

$$\forall_{d \in \text{Door}, s \in \text{default}(d)}.$$
$$\text{AG}(\text{chosen} \neq \text{nil} \land \text{door\_icon} = d \land \text{buttons}(s). >_{\text{action}} = \text{press} \rightarrow$$
$$(\text{owner}, s, \text{chosen}) \in \text{current})$$

While looking at how the property is expressed might already give some notion of the type of problems that the system would suffer from, we will go on and show how the problem can be detected by model checking the specification.

To make sure the property holds we have to test it for all possible users, and all types of connections that are valid for each door state. If it fails for any given combination, then clearly the property does not hold. A problem now arises. The finite state machine generated by the specification is too *big* for model checking to be practical. In order to reduce the size of the finite state machine generated by our specification, we can do two things: eliminate state variables, and decrease the size of the state variables domain [11]. It should be stressed that this must be done carefully, in order not to affect the meaning of the specification. More specifically, the simplified version of the specification must preserve all the behaviour of the original specification regarding the property that we are checking. Several simplifications were introduced:

- only two types of connection were considered — this is valid since the specification/property does not depend on the number of services available;
- the number of door states was reduced to four (all, open, ajar, none) — note that all and none had to be kept since they are special cases;
- attributes default, owner and callee were *hard-coded* into the specification — this is valid since changes in those values are not being considered (i.e. they are thought of as constants).

With these alterations the specification becomes model checkable. We try the following instance of the property:

$$AG(\text{door\_icon} = \text{open} \wedge \text{button\_snapshot. } >_{\text{action}} = \text{press} \rightarrow$$
$$(\text{snapshot}, \text{user1}) \in \text{current})$$

and SMV's reply is (after some editing for readability):

```
-- specification AG (door_icon = 2 & do_snapshot.ac... is false
-- as demonstrated by the following execution sequence
state 1.1:
allowed[snapshot][user1] = true
current[snapshot][user1] = false
door_icon = open

state 1.2:
action = setexcep(snapshot,user1,none)
allowed[snapshot][user1] = false
current[snapshot][user1] = false
door_icon = open

state 1.3:
button_snapshot.action = press
action = establish(snapshot,user1)
current[snapshot][user1] = false
door_icon = open

resources used:
user time: 8.58 s, system time: 0.09 s
BDD nodes allocated: 206873
Bytes allocated: 4521984
BDD nodes representing transition relation: 47519 + 409
```

It can be seen that the property does not hold. What the counter example shows is that the callee might set an exception for the particular connection being tried. This is done in state 1.2, and the connection becomes not allowed. Unfortunately the caller has access only to the callee door state (see visibility annotations in the specification), so the user is unable to predict whether a connection is going to be accepted or not.

The analysis above tells us that the system is not predictable. The user can not tell whether a request for connection will be successful or not. From the user's point of view, this happens because the information that is displayed regarding the callee's receptiveness to connections is inappropriate.

Since exceptions can override the accessibility level, what should be presented to the caller is not the general accessibility level of the callee, but the result of applying the exceptions regarding the caller to the callee's accessibility level (and, for instance, disabling inappropriate buttons). In fact, it could even be argued that the general accessibility level of the callee should not be displayed at all, so as to avoid callers detecting that they were being in some way *segregated*. Note how this shows that the initial suggestion of disabling buttons according to the door state only would be inappropriate.

The problem is that two mechanisms with different philosophies are being integrated. Determining what is the best compromise solution falls outside the scope of formal/automated verification. What these techniques offer is a way to study the different proposal against specific criteria of quality.

Going back to SMV's answer, and looking at it from the specification side, we can see that the property fails because there is a mismatch between the precondition of the core level action that establishes the connection (action establish), and the preconditions (in the user's head) of the user interface commands that trigger that action (the buttons). It is easy to see that a necessary condition for a user interface to be predictable is that the preconditions at the two levels match. Although this is an indirect test, it still allows us to detect if a system will not be predictable.

State exploration type properties, like the first property checked above, demand that the system be reduced to a finite state machine. It is clear that as our specifications grow in complexity this becomes increasingly hard. Moreover, even if we can express the system as a finite state machine, it can also happen that this machine is too big and model checking is not feasible. Checking for the satisfaction of preconditions, on the other hand, can be done by hand or using a theorem prover. Hence, even if the specification is too complex for model checking, we can still analyse it regarding predictability, verifying if all preconditions at the user interface level match the corresponding system level ones. Similarly we can think of analysing if the result of system level actions matches what the user expects.

2.2 Checking the Presentation

In the previous Section we have seen how we can use model checking to analyse predictability in ECOM. In this Section we look at two aspects of the proposed presentation. The properties that we will be interested in lend them selves more naturally to theorem proving, so we will be using PVS.

At this stage we do not yet have a tool to automatically translate our interactor specifications into the PVS notation. Hence, we had have to perform the translation manually. This is not hard, as each interactor can be expressed as a PVS theory with relative ease.

Cumulative exception setting As we have seen, there was an error in the order in which we first enumerated the door states, and this had influence on how the cumulative nature of exceptions worked. Since we were using the same order which is used at the interface, we have reason to suspect that the presentation used for the exceptions might not be in agreement with the abstract model. More specifically, we want to guarantee that the proposed interface conveys the notion of cumulative exception setting.

In order to verify this we follow the same process as already applied in [8]. We develop a model of the proposed interface presentation, and a function (ρ) which builds a presentation from an abstract specification. We then develop two operators capturing the relevant concepts we want to analyse, one for each model. Since we want to study how the cumulative nature of exceptions is conveyed by the presentation, we will consider how a user determines if a connection is allowed by its current exception setting. We then have to show that using the operator at the abstract level yields the same result as mapping the abstract state into a presentation and using the operator defined in the presentation level (see Figure 4). This type of problem is better solved using theorem

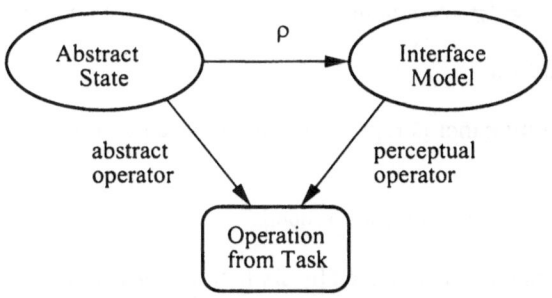

abstract operator = perceptual operator o ρ ?

Fig. 4. Verifying presentation issues (adapted from [9])

proving (see [3]), so we choose to use PVS [17], a theorem prover.

As stated above, we will consider the case where a user is setting the exception level for some other given user and specific type of connection service (since those are fixed, we can omit them from now on). The task is to predict whether the selected exception level will allow the connection or not.

Since we are only looking at a single user, we can use a simplified version of the model developed previously. Also, because we will be looking only at how attributes are mapped in the presentation, we don't include actions in this restricted version of the model. At the abstract level we need the accessibility, and exceptions attributes. We can begin to model this in the PVS notation as the theory:

```
restrictedpanel : THEORY
    BEGIN
    Attributes :
    TYPE  =  [# accessibility : {d :  Door |  d ≠ none ∧ d ≠ alld}, exceptions :  Door#]
    ...
    END restrictedpanel
```

In the presence of an exception, whether or not a request for establishing a connection will succeed can be modeled by the following operator, which we add to the theory above:

```
willsucceed : [Attributes → bool]  =
    (λ (a : Attributes) : exceptions(a) ≥ accessibility(a))
```

This definition is easily deduced from axiom 5 of core (remember that we are considering that the user has set an exception).

We now build a model of the actual interface that is being proposed for the system. For the current purpose we are only interested in the level of accessibility and exception setting:

```
rho_restrictedpanel : THEORY
    BEGIN
    Attributes : TYPE = [# accessibility : AccPanel, exceptions : ExcepPanel#]
    ...
    END rho_restrictedpanel
```

where the accessibility panel is represented by an array of four buttons (one for each door state):

```
AccPanel : TYPE = ARRAY[DoorIcon → bool]
```

and the exceptions panel is represented by six buttons (one for each possible level):

```
ExcepPanel : TYPE = ARRAY[ExcepItem → bool]
```

In order to model the order in which the buttons are present in the interface, we introduce the operator:

```
isabove : [ExcepItem, ExcepItem → bool]
```

We can now write a function that builds a concrete interface from an abstract state:

```
ρ : [restrictedpanel.Attributes → rho_restrictedpanel.Attributes] =
  (λ (rp : restrictedpanel.Attributes) :
    (#accessibility := rho_accessibility(accessibility(rp)),
      exceptions := rho_exceptions(exceptions(rp))#))
```

where rho_accessibility and rho_exceptions perform the translation of each of the door states (accessibility and exceptions setting) to the corresponding array of buttons.

In order for the presentation to convey the notion that exceptions accumulate (i.e. when an exception level is set, all door states up to that one are allowed) the exception setting level must vary progressively along the column of buttons. If that happens, the user will be able to know if a request for a service will succeed based on the relative position of the current accessibility level and current exception setting level. The request is allowed if the exception setting is equal or *bigger* than the current accessibility (for example, the situation illustrated in Figure 1 allows for glance to happen). This is conveyed by the following operator, which compares the exception level with the accessibility setting:

```
rho_willsucceed : [nonempty_Attributes → bool] =
  (λ (a : nonempty_Attributes) :
    (set_access = set_excep ∨ isabove(set_access, set_excep))
      WHERE
      set_access : DoorIcon = identify_access(accessibility(a)),
      set_excep : ExcepItem = identify_excep(exceptions(a)))
```

where identify_access and identify_excep model the cognitive tasks of identifying which button is selected in each of the panels.

If we try to prove that this is an adequate operator to check for permissions:

equivalence : THEOREM
  $\forall$ (rp : restrictedpanel.Attributes) : willsucceed(rp) = rho_willsucceed(ρ(rp))

we end up in a situation where the theorem prover asks us to show that:

$\vphantom{|}$
|——————————————————————
| [1] isabove(maptoexceplist(OpenDoor), Always)

That is, the prover tells us that, in order for the theorem to be true, the button for *when Door Open* must be above the button for *Always*. This is clearly not true (look at Figure 1). The problem is that, as with the definition of Door in the previous Section, Never and Always are placed the wrong way around. The order of the buttons in the interface should be:

1. Never
2. (only if) Door Open
3. (up to) Door Ajar
4. (up to) Door Closed
5. (up to) Door Locked
6. Always

This problem was initially reported in [1]. There, PUM analysis was used to model the system from an human-factors perspective. Here we show how in the context of a more software engineering oriented approach, the selection of appropriate abstractions allows us to reach the same conclusion.

Analysing Redundancy We will now look at the second and third criteria set forth initially. More specifically, we want to investigate whether there is any difference between:

— setting the exception level to always or to when door locked;
— setting the exception level to never or to when door open.

This analysis has been prompted by two factors: as a general principle, redundancy should be avoided at the interface; it is the authors impression that there is redundancy in the number of buttons used to set the exception level. In order to corroborate/discharge this suspicion, we will try to prove that there is no difference between the pairs of buttons mentioned above. For the first case we write:

alwaysvslocked : THEOREM
  $\forall$ (a_1, a_2 : Attributes) :
    ((exceptions(a_1) = alld$\land$
      exceptions(a_2) = locked$\land$
      accessibility(a_1) = accessibility(a_2)) $\Rightarrow$
    willsucceed(a_1) = willsucceed(a_2))

We are trying to show that given two situations where the accessibility is the same, and the exception is set to always in one case, and locked in the other, then if a connection succeeds in one case it will succeed in the other.

Similarly for the second case we write:

nonevsopen : THEOREM
   $\forall\,(a_1, a_2 :$ Attributes) :
    $((\text{exceptions}(a_1) = \text{none}\wedge$
       $\text{exceptions}(a_2) = \text{open}\wedge$
         $\text{accessibility}(a_1) = \text{accessibility}(a_2)) \Rightarrow$
      $\text{willsucceed}(a_1) = \text{willsucceed}(a_2))$

In the first case we are able to prove the theorem. What this points out/proves is that there is no difference between setting the exception level to Always or to Locked. Whence, we do not need both levels in the system.

In the second case the proof fails (i.e. we cannot perform it). This happens because setting the exception level to open still allows some connections while setting it to never allows no connections at all.

In the light of the results above, we can propose another change to the design of exception setting:

1. never
2. only if door open
3. up to door ajar
4. up to door closed
5. up to door locked (always)

3   Discussion

3.1 On the tools

We have seen how we can use automated reasoning techniques to help the formal analysis of interactive systems designs. Two techniques have been used: model checking, and theorem proving. Traditionally theorem proving is considered more difficult to use, however the case study shows that this is not necessarily always the case.

In using these tools to analyse interactive systems we are putting them to uses that were not initially envisaged. This is specially true of model checking. Interactor specifications have proven brittle in terms of the time taken to perform the model checking step: small changes in the interactor specification can produce huge differences in the time taken to get an answer. This is aggravated by the fact that it is not easy to predict how long the model checking process of a particular specification is going to take. While these problems are inherent to model checking in general, the fact that we are using such concepts as parametrised actions and sets in our specifications (remember that each parameter in an action means that the action will originate a number of actions at the SMV level) seems to make our specifications more susceptible to them. Additionally, bringing the specification down to a model checkable size is a step that must be done with care and in a stepwise manner..

On the other side, the proofs turned out to be easy to perform, as PVS solved most of the situations. In general, the sub-cases that were left to prove were easily solved. The PVS learning curve is not easy though.

In the end, the decision on which is the best tool to apply will always depend on the style of property we are looking at.

3.2 On the analysis

It is not realistic to assume we can analyse all aspects of an interactive system with one single model. Hence, the first step in an analysis process must be to decide which aspects are worth looking into. We have illustrated different possibilities for this step.

The analysis in Section 2.1 was based on a generic design principle: predictability. We analysed whether the commands to establish connection were predictable. To perform this analysis we used SMV, a model checker. We concluded they were not predictable since there was a mismatch between the actual accessibility settings of a user and the information made available to the community. Once a problem, and its causes, are identified, it usually falls out of the scope of the formal approach to decide the best solution. That solution will have to be reached in collaboration with other user centered approaches. What formal methods have to offer is the possibility of, given a set of quality measures, comparing the different proposals.

During the modelling process for the analysis above, our attention was drawn to the importance of the ordering of the different door states. Here we see how the modelling process can, in itself, be useful at raising issues. In Section 2.2 we investigate whether the proposed presentation is coherent with the underlying semantics of the door states. This analysis is done with PVS, a theorem prover.

Finally, the properties analysed in Section 2.2 are the result of a critical look at the proposed system. As a generic principal, redundancy at the interface should be avoided. It was the authors' impression that redundancy existed in the number of buttons available for exception setting. A formal analysis, performed with the theorem prover, enabled us to determine a situation where in fact there was redundancy, and another where that didn't happen.

Several approaches to the analysis of the ECOM system were used in [1]. Comparing our analysis with those, we see that our approach can be used to complement the formal system analysis performed there. We are using automated tools exactly to perform that kind of analysis. Regarding the cognitive user modelling approaches (PUM and CTA), we can see that we were able to reach similar results. However, our results were obtained while still in the context of a software engineering approach. PUM and CTA demand human-factors expertize. We see our approach as being complementary to those in the sense that they can be used to define a set of quality measures which can then be rigorously analysed using formal methods. Furthermore, they can help in interpreting the results of such analytic process.

A fourth analysis (PAC-AMODEUS) of the case study is reported. The PAC-AMO-DEUS analysis is architecture oriented, hence not so much interested in usability issues, but more in implementation issues.

4 Conclusion

We looked at the use of automated reasoning tools in the formal analysis of an interactive system design. While mastering the use of the tools will inevitably take some effort, they enable us to be more confident of the results of the analysis.

Unlike other approaches to the use of automated reasoning in HCI, we do not focus on the tool, instead we focus our approach on integrating verification with the development process (cf. [5]). Once an interesting aspect of the system has been identified, we investigate which type of tool will fit best to its analysis. In this way, we are not tied to a particular type of model, and we have greater freedom in terms of what we can model and reason about.

Our long term objective is to develop a framework enabling us to integrate formal software engineering (automated reasoning in particular) with the other disciplines involved in HCI.

Acknowledgements

José Campos is supported by Fundação para a Ciência e a Tecnologia (FCT, Portugal) under grant PRAXIS XXI/BD/9562/96.

References

1. Victoria Bellotti, Ann Blandford, David Duke, Allan MacLean, Jon May, and Laurence Nigay. Interpersonal access control in computer-mediated communications: A systematic analysis of the design space. *Human-Computer Interaction*, 11:357–432, 1996.
2. Peter Bumbulis. *Combining Formal Techniques and Prototyping in User Interface Construction and Verification*. PhD thesis, University of Waterloo, 1996.
3. José C. Campos. *Automated Reasoning and Interactive Systems Development*. DPhil thesis, Department of Computer Science, University of York, 1999. in preparation.
4. José C. Campos and Michael D. Harrison. Detecting interface mode complexity with interactor specifications. submitted, 1998.
5. José C. Campos and Michael D. Harrison. The role of verification in interactive systems design. In Markopoulos and Johnson [15], pages 155–170.
6. Bruno d'Ausbourg. Using model checking for the automatic validation of user interfaces systems. In Markopoulos and Johnson [15], pages 242–260.
7. Alan Dix, Janet Finlay, Gregory Abowd, and Russell Beale. *Human-Computer Interaction*. Prentice-Hall, 1993.
8. G. Doherty, J. C. Campos, and M. D. Harrison. Representational reasoning and verification. In J. I. Siddiqi, editor, *Proceedings of the BCS-FACS Workshop: Formal Aspects of the Human Computer Interaction*, pages 193–212. SHU Press, 1998. ISBN 0 86339 7948.
9. Gavin Doherty and Michael D. Harrison. A representational approach to the specification of presentations. In Harrison and Torres [14], pages 273–290.

10. David J. Duke and Michael D. Harrison. Abstract interaction objects. *Computer Graphics Forum*, 12(3):25–36, 1993.
11. Matthew B. Dwyer, Vicki Carr, and Laura Hines. Model checking graphical user interfaces using abstractions. In Mehdi Jazayeri and Helmut Schauer, editors, *Software Engineering — ESEC/FSE '97*, number 1301 in Lecture Notes in Computer Science, pages 244–261. Springer, 1997.
12. G. Faconti and F. Paternò. An approach to the formal specification of the components of an interaction. In C. Vandoni and D. Duce, editors, *Eurographics '90*, pages 481–494. North-Holland, 1990.
13. Bob Fields, Nick Merriam, and Andy Dearden. DMVIS: Design, modelling and validation of interactive systems. In Harrison and Torres [14], pages 29–44.
14. M. D. Harrison and J. C. Torres, editors. *Design, Specification and Verification of Interactive Systems '97*, Springer Computer Science. Springer-Verlag/Vien, June 1997.
15. P. Markopoulos and P. Johnson, editors. *Design, Specification and Verification of Interactive Systems '98*, Springer Computer Science. Springer-Verlag/Vien, 1998.
16. K. L. McMillan. *The SMV system*. Carnegie-Mellon University, draft edition, February 1992.
17. S. Owre, N. Shankar, and J. M. Rushby. *User Guide for the PVS Specification and Verification System*. Computer Science Laboratory, SRI Internatinal, Menlo Park CA 94025, USA, (beta release) edition, March 1993.
18. Fabio D. Paternò. *A Method for Formal Specification and Verification of Interactive Systems*. PhD thesis, Department of Computer Science, University of York, 1995.
19. Mark Ryan, José Fiadeiro, and Tom Maibaum. Sharing actions and attributes in modal action logic. In T. Ito and A. R. Meyer, editors, *Theoretical Aspects of Computer Software*, volume 526 of *Lecture Notes in Computer Science*, pages 569–593. Springer-Verlag, 1991.

A ECOM model (model ckeckable)

```
define
  none    = 1
  open    = 2
  locked  = 5
  all     = 6
  snapshot = 1
  glance   = 2
  user1 = 1
  user2 = 2
  null = 0

types
  Door = {none, open, locked, all}
  OptDoor = {none, open, locked, all, null}
  Service = {snapshot, glance}
  PConn = array snapshot..glance of \
                array user1..user2 of boolean
  ConnDoor = array snapshot..glance of array user1..user2 of \
                                     {none, open, locked, all, null}
  User = {user1, user2}
  UserDoor = array user1..user2 of {open, locked}
```

```
interactor core
# core modelled from the view point of a caller
attributes
  allowed: PConn
  accessibility: UserDoor
  current: PConn
  exceptions: ConnDoor
actions
  establish(Service,User) close(Service,User) \
  setexcep(Service,User,OptDoor) setacc(User,Door)
axioms
# (1)
  allowed[s][u] -> [establish(s,u)] \
          current[s][u]' = 1 & current<s><u>' = current<s><u> \
        & unchanged(accessibility, exceptions)\
  !allowed[s][u] -> [establish(s,u)] \
          unchanged(current, accessibility, exceptions)
# (2)
  per(close(s,u)) -> current[s][u]
  [close(s,u)] \
          current[s][u]'=0 & current<s><u>'=current<s><u> \
        & unchanged(exceptions, accessibility)
# (3)
  [setexcep(s,u,d)] \
     exceptions[s][u]'=d & exceptions<s><u>'=exceptions<s><u> \
   & unchanged(current,accessibility)
# (4)
  [setacc(u,d)] \
     accessibility[u]'=d & accessibility<u>'=accessibility<u> \
   & unchanged(current,exceptions)
# (5)
  allowed[snapshot][user1] <-> \
     (exceptions[snapshot][user1]=null -> \
                accessibility[user1] in {open, locked}) \
   & (exceptions[snapshot][user1]!=null -> \
        exceptions[snapshot][user1] >= accessibility[user1])
  allowed[snapshot][user2] <-> \
     (exceptions[snapshot][user2]=null -> \
                accessibility[user2] in {open, locked}) \
   & (exceptions[snapshot][user2]!=null -> \
        exceptions[snapshot][user2] >= accessibility[user2])
  allowed[glance][user1] <-> \
     (exceptions[glance][user1]=null -> \
                accessibility[user1] in {open}) \
   & (exceptions[glance][user1]!=null -> \
             exceptions[glance][user1] >= accessibility[user1])
  allowed[glance][user2] <-> \
     (exceptions[glance][user2]=null -> \
                accessibility[user2] in {open}) \
   & (exceptions[glance][user2]!=null -> \
```

```
                  exceptions[glance][user2] >= accessibility[user2])
# initial state
  []    exceptions[snapshot][user1] = open \
     & exceptions[glance][user1] = open \
     & exceptions[snapshot][user2] = open \
     & exceptions[glance][user2] = open \
     & !current[snapshot][user1] & !current[glance][user1] \
     & !current[snapshot][user2] & !current[glance][user2] \
     & accessibility[user1] = open & accessibility[user2] = open

interactor button
attributes
  enabled: boolean
actions
  press
axioms
  per(press) -> enabled
  [press] enabled' = enabled

interactor main
importing
  core
includes
  button via do_snapshot
  button via do_glance
attributes
  door_icon: Door
axioms
# (1) hard-code user1 as callee
  door_icon=accessibility[user1]
# (3) we have to
  do_snapshot.action=press <-> action=establish_1_1
  do_glance.action=press <-> action=establish_2_1
# initial state
  [] do_snapshot.enabled
test
  AG(door_icon=open & do_snapshot.action=press -> \
                                current[snapshot][user1])
```

B PVS model

```
ecom : THEORY
   BEGIN

   IMPORTING restrictedpanel, rho_restrictedpanel

   rho_accessibility : [{d : Door | d ≠ none ∧ d ≠ alld}  →  AccPanel] =
     (λ (d : {d : Door | d ≠ none ∧ d ≠ alld}) :
       COND
```

$d =$ open $\rightarrow$ $(\lambda$ (di : DoorIcon) : di $=$ OpenDoor),
$d =$ ajar $\rightarrow$ $(\lambda$ (di : DoorIcon) : di $=$ AjarDoor),
$d =$ closed $\rightarrow$ $(\lambda$ (di : DoorIcon) : di $=$ ClosedDoor),
$d =$ locked $\rightarrow$ $(\lambda$ (di : DoorIcon) : di $=$ LockedDoor)
ENDCOND)

rho_exceptions : $[d :$ Door $\rightarrow$ ExcepPanel] $=$
$(\lambda$ $(d :$ Door) :
COND
$d =$ none $\rightarrow$ $(\lambda$ (ei : ExcepItem) : ei $=$ Never),
$d =$ open $\rightarrow$ $(\lambda$ (ei : ExcepItem) : ei $=$ whenOpen),
$d =$ ajar $\rightarrow$ $(\lambda$ (ei : ExcepItem) : ei $=$ whenAjar),
$d =$ closed $\rightarrow$ $(\lambda$ (ei : ExcepItem) : ei $=$ whenClosed),
$d =$ locked $\rightarrow$ $(\lambda$ (ei : ExcepItem) : ei $=$ whenLocked),
$d =$ alld $\rightarrow$ $(\lambda$ (ei : ExcepItem) : ei $=$ Always)
ENDCOND)

ρ : [restrictedpanel.Attributes $\rightarrow$ rho_restrictedpanel.Attributes] $=$
$(\lambda$ (rp : restrictedpanel.Attributes) :
(#accessibility := rho_accessibility(accessibility(rp)),
exceptions := rho_exceptions(exceptions(rp))#))

equivalence : THEOREM
$\forall$ (rp : restrictedpanel.Attributes) : willsucceed(rp) $=$ rho_willsucceed(ρ(rp))

END ecom

restrictedpanel : THEORY
BEGIN

Door : TYPE $=$ {none, open, ajar, closed, locked, alld}

door_order : [Door $\rightarrow$ int]
door_order_none : AXIOM $(\forall$ $(d :$ Door) : $d =$ none $\Rightarrow$ door_order$(d) = 1$)
door_order_open : AXIOM $(\forall$ $(d :$ Door) : $d =$ open $\Rightarrow$ door_order$(d) = 2$)
door_order_ajar : AXIOM $(\forall$ $(d :$ Door) : $d =$ ajar $\Rightarrow$ door_order$(d) = 3$)
door_order_closed : AXIOM $(\forall$ $(d :$ Door) : $d =$ closed $\Rightarrow$ door_order$(d) = 4$)
door_order_locked : AXIOM $(\forall$ $(d :$ Door) : $d =$ locked $\Rightarrow$ door_order$(d) = 5$)
door_order_all : AXIOM $(\forall$ $(d :$ Door) : $d =$ alld $\Rightarrow$ door_order$(d) = 6$)
CONVERSION door_order

Attributes :
TYPE $=$ [# accessibility : $\{d :$ Door $\mid$ $d \neq$ none $\wedge$ $d \neq$ alld$\}$, exceptions : Door#]

willsucceed : [Attributes $\rightarrow$ bool] $=$
$(\lambda$ $(a :$ Attributes) : exceptions$(a) \geq$ accessibility(a))

alwaysvslocked : THEOREM
$\forall$ $(a_1, a_2 :$ Attributes) :

$((\text{exceptions}(a_1) = \text{alld}\wedge$
$\quad \text{exceptions}(a_2) = \text{locked}\wedge$
$\quad\quad \text{accessibility}(a_1) = \text{accessibility}(a_2)) \Rightarrow$
$\quad \text{willsucceed}(a_1) = \text{willsucceed}(a_2))$

nonevsopen : THEOREM
$\quad \forall (a_1, a_2 : \text{Attributes}) :$
$\quad ((\text{exceptions}(a_1) = \text{none}\wedge$
$\quad\quad \text{exceptions}(a_2) = \text{open}\wedge$
$\quad\quad\quad \text{accessibility}(a_1) = \text{accessibility}(a_2)) \Rightarrow$
$\quad\quad \text{willsucceed}(a_1) = \text{willsucceed}(a_2))$

END restrictedpanel

rho_restrictedpanel : THEORY
$\quad$ BEGIN

$\quad$ DoorIcon : TYPE = {OpenDoor, AjarDoor, ClosedDoor, LockedDoor}
$\quad$ AccPanel : TYPE = ARRAY[DoorIcon $\rightarrow$ bool]

$\quad$ AccPanel_is_RadioBox : AXIOM
$\quad\quad \forall (ap : \text{AccPanel}) : \neg\exists (di1, di2 : \text{DoorIcon}) : di1 \neq di1 \wedge ap(di1) \wedge ap(di2)$

$\quad$ ExcepItem : TYPE = {Always, whenOpen, whenAjar, whenClosed, whenLocked, Never}
$\quad$ ExcepPanel : TYPE = ARRAY[ExcepItem $\rightarrow$ bool]

$\quad$ ExcepPanel_is_RadioBox : AXIOM
$\quad\quad \forall (ep : \text{ExcepPanel}) : \neg\exists (ei1, ei2 : \text{ExcepItem}) : ei1 \neq ei1 \wedge ep(ei1) \wedge ep(ei2)$

$\quad$ isabove : [ExcepItem, ExcepItem $\rightarrow$ bool]
$\quad$ isabove_transitive : AXIOM
$\quad\quad \forall (ei1, ei2, ei3 : \text{ExcepItem}) :$
$\quad\quad (\text{isabove}(ei1, ei2) \wedge \text{isabove}(ei2, ei3)) \Rightarrow \text{isabove}(ei1, ei3)$
$\quad$ isabove_antisymmetric : AXIOM
$\quad\quad \forall (ei1, ei2 : \text{ExcepItem}) : (\text{isabove}(ei1, ei2) \Rightarrow \neg\text{isabove}(ei2, ei1))$
$\quad$ isabove_Never_whenOpen : AXIOM
$\quad\quad (\forall (e_1, e_2 : \text{ExcepItem}) :$
$\quad\quad (e_1 = \text{Never} \wedge e_2 = \text{whenOpen}) \Rightarrow \text{isabove}(e_1, e_2))$
$\quad$ isabove_whenOpen_whenAjar : AXIOM
$\quad\quad (\forall (e_1, e_2 : \text{ExcepItem}) :$
$\quad\quad (e_1 = \text{whenOpen} \wedge e_2 = \text{whenAjar}) \Rightarrow \text{isabove}(e_1, e_2))$
$\quad$ isabove_whenAjar_whenClosed : AXIOM
$\quad\quad (\forall (e_1, e_2 : \text{ExcepItem}) :$
$\quad\quad (e_1 = \text{whenAjar} \wedge e_2 = \text{whenClosed}) \Rightarrow \text{isabove}(e_1, e_2))$
$\quad$ isabove_whenClosed_whenLocked : AXIOM
$\quad\quad (\forall (e_1, e_2 : \text{ExcepItem}) :$
$\quad\quad (e_1 = \text{whenClosed} \wedge e_2 = \text{whenLocked}) \Rightarrow \text{isabove}(e_1, e_2))$
$\quad$ isabove_whenLocked_Always : AXIOM
$\quad\quad (\forall (e_1, e_2 : \text{ExcepItem}) :$

$(e_1 = \text{whenLocked} \wedge e_2 = \text{Always}) \Rightarrow \text{isabove}(e_1, e_2))$

Attributes : TYPE $= [\# \text{ accessibility} : \text{AccPanel}, \text{exceptions} : \text{ExcepPanel}\#]$

nonempty_AccPanel : TYPE $= \{ap : \text{AccPanel} \mid \exists\,(di : \text{DoorIcon}) : ap(di)\}$

nonempty_ExcepPanel : TYPE $= \{ep : \text{ExcepPanel} \mid \exists\,(ei : \text{ExcepItem}) : ep(ei)\}$

nonempty_Attributes :
  TYPE $= \{a : \text{Attributes} \mid$
    $(\exists\,(di : \text{DoorIcon}) : \text{accessibility}(a)(di)) \wedge$
      $(\exists\,(ei : \text{ExcepItem}) : \text{exceptions}(a)(ei))\}$

maptoexceplist : $[\text{DoorIcon} \rightarrow \text{ExcepItem}]$
maptoexceplist_OpenDoor : AXIOM maptoexceplist(OpenDoor) = whenOpen
maptoexceplist_AjarDoor : AXIOM maptoexceplist(AjarDoor) = whenAjar
maptoexceplist_ClosedDoor : AXIOM maptoexceplist(ClosedDoor) = whenClosed
maptoexceplist_LockedDoor : AXIOM maptoexceplist(LockedDoor) = whenLocked
CONVERSION maptoexceplist

identify_access : $[\text{nonempty\_AccPanel} \rightarrow \text{DoorIcon}] =$
  $(\lambda\,(ap : \text{nonempty\_AccPanel}) :$
    COND
    ap(OpenDoor) $\rightarrow$ OpenDoor,
    ap(AjarDoor) $\rightarrow$ AjarDoor,
    ap(ClosedDoor) $\rightarrow$ ClosedDoor,
    ap(LockedDoor) $\rightarrow$ LockedDoor
    ENDCOND)

identify_excep : $[\text{nonempty\_ExcepPanel} \rightarrow \text{ExcepItem}] =$
  $(\lambda\,(ep : \text{nonempty\_ExcepPanel}) :$
    COND
    ep(Always) $\rightarrow$ Always,
    ep(whenOpen) $\rightarrow$ whenOpen,
    ep(whenAjar) $\rightarrow$ whenAjar,
    ep(whenClosed) $\rightarrow$ whenClosed,
    ep(whenLocked) $\rightarrow$ whenLocked,
    ep(Never) $\rightarrow$ Never
    ENDCOND)

rho_willsucceed : $[\text{nonempty\_Attributes} \rightarrow \text{bool}] =$
  $(\lambda\,(a : \text{nonempty\_Attributes}) :$
    $(\text{set\_access} = \text{set\_excep} \vee \text{isabove}(\text{set\_access}, \text{set\_excep}))$
      WHERE
      set_access : DoorIcon $= \text{identify\_access}(\text{accessibility}(a)),$
      set_excep : ExcepItem $= \text{identify\_excep}(\text{exceptions}(a)))$

END rho_restrictedpanel

Analysing User Deviations in Interactive Safety-Critical Applications

F. Paternò [(1)], C. Santoro [(1)], B. Fields [(2)]

[(1)] CNUCE-C.N.R., Pisa, Italy
[(2)] University of York, York, United Kingdom

Abstract. Usability and safety problems have often been addressed separately in designing interactive safety-critical applications thus obtaining fragmented results. In this paper we present a method to analyse possible deviations of users in performing their activities in order to elicit safety requirements and to improve design of interactive safety-critical applications. An application of the proposed method to a case study in the Air Traffic Control domain is discussed.

1 Introduction

Interactive safety-critical applications are an interesting field for the application of structured and formal methods because the cost of learning and using formal approaches can be justified by the potential benefits in terms of reducing the possibilities for human-machine interaction problems that can result in disasters. Thus one key problem is to understand how to reach such positive results using formal approaches.

Task models can be used to describe activities that have to be performed to reach a goal. In the HCI field, task models have been recognised as one relevant model in the design of user interfaces [14]. In safety critical sectors, however, specific issues arise that are not so readily captured by traditional methods for user interface design. For instance, in safety critical domains, sometimes user actions cannot be undone (for example, if an irreversible physical process is being controlled), so the issue of 'user errors', and how to predict and design so as to avoid them, acquires a special importance. In other words, it becomes especially important to provide designers with tools, techniques and methods to help consider erroneous actions as well as correct ones, in systems and situations where 'error' can result in injury or loss of human life. In the approach proposed here, task models are advocated as the basis of a technique to assist designers in analysing the possible user behaviours and potential 'deviations' for normative courses of action in order to understand how current designs support them and provide possible further suggestions for improvements.

In doing so, we build upon the HAZOP family of techniques, originally developed for investigating hazard and operability issues in the chemical process industry, and which have been applied in a number of other spheres including software development. Traditionally, the goal of a HAZOP Study [7] is to identify what potentially hazardous situations could arise in the operation of some system, as a result of possible deviations from design intent in the interactions between system's components. The purpose of this article is to present a method based on the application of HAZOP-like techniques to task models [12, 16] in order to assist a designer in making improvements to the design of interactive safety-critical applications [8]. We show examples of the application of the resulting method on an Air Traffic Control Application.

The motivation for the development of this new method is threefold:
- As a means of providing a more structured and systematic way of identifying user interface requirements, with particular attention to those which can have an impact from both usability and safety viewpoints;
- To provide a means of progressing from an "initial" task model to an "improved" one, broader in scope, on which we wish to place greater reliance, since it describes activity in abnormal as well as normal situations. Such a task model may relate to a refined user interface design that includes features that tend to discourage user actions with negative system consequences;
- To give the analyst or designer a means of recording the justification or rationale for decisions that have been made.

In almost all safety-critical systems (such as Air Traffic Control, railway systems, industry control systems) it is clear that central to the humans' activity is a high degree of co-operation with other workers. The system as a whole typically relies on the successful co-ordination of the activities of individuals [13]. These co-ordinations are often achieved as a result of communications taking place in a variety of media. This suggests a need for an integrated analysis of usability, safety and co-operation in the design of work and associated user interfaces, since many of the possible safety and usability problems are related to how the various agents work together to reach the common goals. Therefore we have attempted to provide guidance in the form of a structured method to support this analysis. One interesting component is the application of structured techniques for analysing what hazard situations could result from deviations from design intent in the co-operative and communicative activities between different agents.
In the following sections we present our proposal for a method in which HAZOP techniques with task modelling co-exist. First we introduce HAZOP techniques and discuss how they can be introduced in the design process. Then we describe how to tailor these techniques for improving user interface design in interactive safety-critical applications. We provide one example of the technique's deployment in the Air Traffic Control domain, as a partial demonstration of the extent to which these techniques could aid in the requirements elicitation and design phases. Finally, some concluding remarks are made.

2 Design process context

Traditionally, the purpose of a HAZOP Study is to identify potentially hazardous situations that may arise in the operation of a system, by analysing possible "deviations from design intent" in the interactions between components [5, 10]. A HAZOP Study systematically examines possible deviations from design intent of the attributes of the system components or of the attributes of the interconnections between components.

The procedure for identifying such deviations (for instance, excursions of a value outside its normal operating envelope) from the design intent is facilitated by the application of a number of *guidewords*. A *guideword* is a word or phrase that expresses and defines a specific type of deviation. On applying a guideword to an attribute, the team of analysts enquire into possible *causes* and *consequences* of the deviation for the system as a whole. Mechanisms that aid the *detection* or *indication* of any hazards are also examined and the results are recorded.

It is important to note that the presence of protection mechanisms must not stop identified hazards being explored and listed. If such mechanisms exist, you may explore their efficacy in reducing the probability or mitigating the consequences of the hazard, if this is appropriate. The conclusion or recommendation shall be noted in the HAZOP Study documentation. Variants of the basic HAZOP techniques have been used for analysing software-based systems (e.g. see [10] and human factors aspects of interactive technology [2, 3]). However we note a lack of proposals to introduce them in structured methods for user interface analysis and design with the support of task models.

It is worth mentioning that the work described in this paper bears some similarities to other projects and approaches. In the CREWS method [9] a systematic 'walkthrough' is conducted of a scenario in which a proposed system is being used. At each stage in the scenario, a number of 'what if' questions may be posed, encouraging the analyst to consider 'non normal' sequences of events, and ask whether the requirements for the new system will cope adequately with exceptional circumstances and usages. Similarly, the THEA technique [4] proposes a scenario-based enquiry that encourages an analyst to consider ways in which interface design features contribute to a scenario occurring in unintended, erroneous ways. As well as the similarities, both of these pieces of work differ from the current approach in that they rely on relatively informal models. By the use of formality, the current approach opens the way for more sophisticated tool support for the analysis, and a tighter integration with the detailed design process.

A HAZOP Study may be carried out at various stages of a system's life cycle and at any level of design representation. A number of HAZOP Studies should contribute significantly in order to refine and extend the identification of hazards by means of a systematic examination of the design intentions of parts of a system to identify hazards, mal-operations or malfunctions of individual entities within the system, evaluate the consequences on the system as a whole and on its environment and reduce their associated risks to a tolerable level.

However, our intentions go beyond only safety and hazard features. It is our opinion that a HAZOP-like "what if" approach could have a broader goal, stimulating a deeper exploration of the application domain and the space of design requirements. In other words, such a method can support the requirements elicitation and design phases by prompting discussions when there are uncertainties which have to be resolved, raising questions for further study, and helping to shape subsequent analysis work.

One approach to user interface design that has been used in requirements elicitation is task analysis, where the goal is to identify the principal tasks users are to perform while interacting with the system, and their relevant properties. Thus we think that a technique for analysing deviations can be used during the task modelling phase, when the tasks identified are structured in a model, to provide an awareness of the possible hazards and safety problems, and to provide recommendations for user interface design so as to prevent, discourage, or contain and mitigate the effects of erroneous actions. Once a good understanding of tasks and user interface dialogues to support them has been reached, this knowledge can be captured in a formal model [6], which can be used for checking whether formal properties are discharged and interface requirements are satisfied [1, 11].

In the remainder of this paper, the analysis technique will be applied to task models, with a particular emphasis on tasks related to communication between distributed users, with a view to making recommendations about the design of communication technologies. It is important to note that although we consider deviations in communication tasks, it will be of vital importance to retain the task context surrounding an individual communicative act, and it will also be important when applying the guidewords to look for deviations in structures larger than a single isolated communication. As part of the analysis, it will be important to mention (when possible) the type of indication that can be provided (when warning messages should be provided, when problematic task sequencing should be prevented, etc.).

3 Analysing user deviations for improving user interface design

The HAZOP approach is described in detail in a number of other books and standards [5, 7], where a generic collection of guidewords is presented, covering a large class of deviation types. A more specific set of guidewords may be drawn up for a particular study and application domain. We have selected a small set of guidewords which represents a flexible and general tool for paying attention to the possible deviations. The set of guidewords identified are indicated in Table 1. Some of them can be further refined: for example, *Other than* could be further refined in *Less*, *More*, or *Different* depending on less, more or different information has been used in performing the tasks. Likewise *Ill-timed* can be refined in *Early* or *Late* depending on the task is performed too early or too late.

In particular, this set of guidewords has shown to be useful to analyse ATC applications whose main activity to support is the exchange of messages between controllers and pilots. The selected guidewords in the ATC application domain are relevant to consider the eventuality that no communication occurs (*None* guideword), or that some different communication is exchanged between the involved partners

(*Other than*), or —as the time is a highly critical parameter in such system— that the right communication occurs but at the wrong time (*Ill-timed*).

None	The task has not been performed or it has been performed but it has not produced any result.
Other than	The task has been performed using the wrong data or producing wrong data
Ill-timed	The task has been performed at the wrong time.

Table 1. Guidewords for analysing interaction failures

Having identified the set of guidewords that drive the hazard analysis, we must now describe how they will be used and the resulting analysis incorporated in a structure documenting it. The resulting representation can be used also for design rationale purposes. The results of the analysis will be recorded in a tabular form containing the following elements:*Task*, indicating the activity which is being analysed;

- *Guideword*, indicating the type of deviation which is considered;
- *Deviations*, indicating the specific problems detected — or how the guideword is interpreted in the context of the task;
- *Causes*, indicating hypotheses about the ways in which how the problem might arise;
- *Consequences*, indicating the possible effects of the deviation for the system as a whole;
- *Protections*, indicating how (within the current design) it is possible to protect from the deviation
- *Recommendations*, indications for an improved design in order to prevent the deviation.

In addition to provide guidewords to indicate prompts during the analysis process for the different types of deviations that may occur, it will also be useful to do something similar for the possible causes of deviations. Four keywords that can help analysts to consider possible cognitive causes of deviations are:

- Intention (i.e., the intention is in some sense faulty),
- Action (i.e., the actions are carried out incorrectly),
- Perception (i.e., a deviation results from an incorrect perception),
- Understanding (i.e., the deviation results from a mis-understanding of perceived information).

The difference between deviations of intention and action is roughly the mistake/slip distinction made in [15].

The technique proposed helps to identify potential hazards. However, a designer's decision about what to do about a potential failure will depend on a deeper assessment of the hazard, its causes and its consequences. As a very simple example, consider the following two "errors" that can be made by the user of a word processor:

- In order to make a region of text bold, the text is first selected, and then the "Command-B" key combination is pressed. An incorrect performance of this task can be to press "Command-B" before having selected the text.
- In order to quit normally from the word processor, the current file is first saved, and then the "Quit" command is invoked. An incorrect performance occurs if "Quit" is invoked before having saved the document.

Superficially, at least, these two "errors" seem very similar: they both arise when the order of a pair of actions is reversed (or the first action in the pair is omitted); it may even be the case that both are equally likely. However, an important difference is the consequences of the first (where it is possible to select the correct text then complete the task) are far less severe than the second (where work may be lost).
What this suggests is that a designer's response to an identified hazard may be guided by an informal assessment of risk as a location in two-dimensional space. The dimensions are an estimate of the likelihood of the hazard arising (ranging from probable to improbable), and an assessment of how serious the impact of the hazard can be (ranging from inconsequential to severe). The resulting obligations on the designers range from no response being necessary, to a requirement to take action to mitigate the consequences of possible user errors.

4 The initial task model of the example

In this section we consider a case study taken from the Air Traffic Control domain. In particular, we consider communications that take place between controllers and pilots, and the design of an interactive application supporting "datalink" communications (electronic exchange of data).

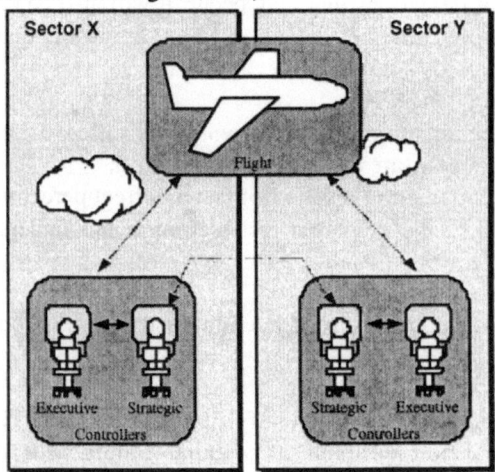

Fig. 1. The EnRoute Air Traffic Control Application

In general, airspace is subdivided into a number of *sectors*, and for each sector a team of controllers (usually two controllers, strategic and executive) is in charge of communicating with the pilots of the flights crossing it in order to assist them in the achievement of safe and expeditious flight (see Figure 1). The example considered here takes place in a region of airspace where two adjacent sectors meet, and analyses some of the tasks involved in the management of aircraft passing from one sector (and therefore one team of controllers) to another one.

Figure 2 shows a model of some of the tasks carried out by controllers as aircraft are transferred between sectors. The notation used is based on the ConcurTaskTrees task modelling notation [12], which has been extended for describing tasks in cooperative rather than "single user" settings [13]. The model is actually a somewhat simplified presentation of a model of the overall tasks concerning the cooperations occurring when the control of an aircraft is transferred between sectors in a datalink environment.

Before attempting any analysis of the task model, we briefly explain the meaning of the graphical specification in Figure 2 for the reader unfamiliar with this notation. Figure 2 describes some of the activities carried out by the controller of one sector as aircraft's transfer in and out of that sector. Parts of the task are concerned with the way in which a controller must coordinate their activities with those of the controllers of adjacent sectors to reach agreement on how the transfer of aircraft may take place, and — of course — with the activities of pilots. These coordinations are captured in the *ChangeSector* task, which is decomposed into three sub-tasks:

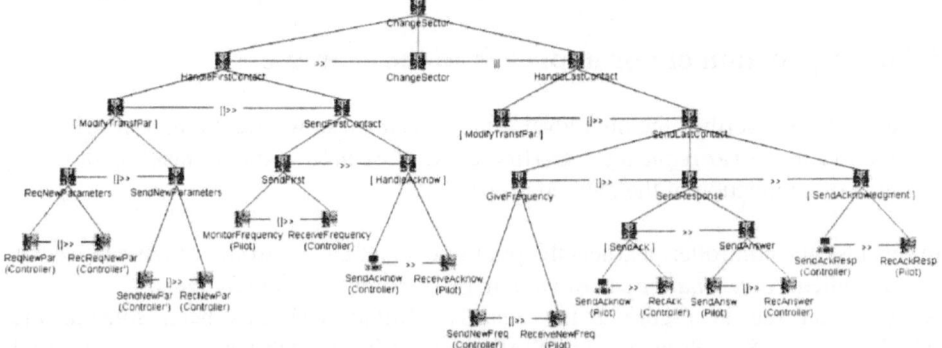

Fig. 2. ConcurTaskTrees model of the example

- *HandleFirstContact* models the tasks carried out when a pilot initiates communication with the controller as the aircraft enters the sector.
- *ChangeSector* models the possibility of performing recursively the parent task before it has been completely terminated. Having as a sub-task another occurrence of the parent task represents recursion in the graphical notation, and is used to capture the dynamic situation where it is not possible to know in advance how many flight will be entering in the sector and what is the order among flights entering and leaving the sector. Since there is no predefined maximum number of flights in a sector we did not include a termination condition for the recursion.
- *HandleLastContact* captures the tasks related to the last message exchange occurring between the pilot and the controller of a sector. This task has been decomposed into two subtasks. First, *ModifyTransfPar*, a possible negotiation

between the controllers involved in the sector's transfer (the same task occurs also as child of the *HandleFirstContact* task). Second, *SendLastContact* task — the last messages exchanged between the controller and the pilot, in which the controller informs the pilot about the frequency for voice communication in the new sector, the system acknowledges the receipt of the information from the pilot's side and the pilot send the operational answer.

For clarity, it is worth noting the use of the *Enabling with information passing* operator (T1 []>>T2) when T1 provides some information to task T2 other than enabling it (">>" operator is used for only *Enabling*, without information passing). T1 ||| T2 indicates that the two tasks can be performed concurrently and it has higher priority than the enabling operator. Tasks with their name enclosed in squared brackets are optional tasks (for example [*ModifyTransfPar*]). Expressions of the type [T1] []>> T2 mean that it is possible either to perform T1 and then T2 or to perform immediately T2, in other words the performance of T1 before T2 is optional.

The different types of icon give some indication of where the responsibility for performing the task lies. A number of allocation possibilities include an icon with a user interacting with a system to indicate interaction tasks, an icon with two users to indicate cooperative tasks requiring actions from several parties, and a computer icon indicates tasks performed only by the computer system.

5 The application of our approach to the example

Once we have described the high level *ChangeSector* task we are going to restrict our attention to the *GiveFrequency* task (first child of *SendLastContact* task) to show an example of application of the method proposed.

In this task the controller instructs the pilot to contact the controller of the next sector (the so-called *Voice Change Instruction* or *VCI*), giving the new frequency.

As you can see in Figure 2 the *SendLastContact* task has been split in the *GiveFrequency, SendResponse* and *SendAcknowledgment* sub-tasks. If we ignore all the optional sub-tasks appearing in the model's lower levels, (*SendAck* and *SendAcknowledgment*), the *SendLastContact* task can be reduced to one that has as children *GiveFrequency* and *SendAnswer* (see Figure 3).

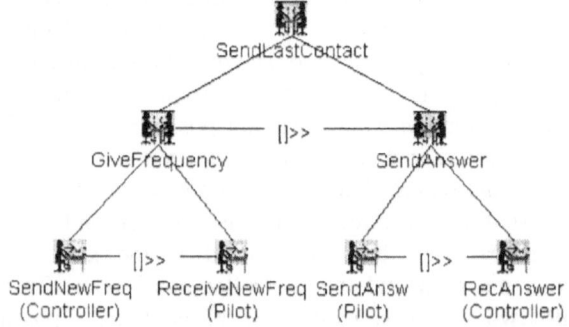

Fig. 3. *SendLastContact* task without optional subtasks

In Figure 4 each of these tasks is further elaborated by splitting them into two subtasks performed by each of the communicative partners. For example, the *GiveFrequency* co-operation is shown as two separate arrows — one for the *SendNewFreq* task, (the arc exiting from controller's circle) and the other one for the *ReceiveNewFreq* task (on the previous one's same direction, entering pilot's circle).

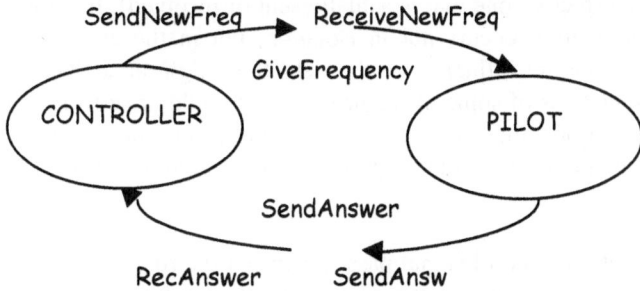

Fig. 4. Communicating a new frequency

If we analyse each of these sub-tasks we note that they allow the two roles to exchange messages with each other. The reason for decomposing communication into two separate items is not simply to improve the 'accuracy' of the model. For example, the messages sent from the controller to the pilot might not necessarily coincide with the messages *actually* received by the pilot. For our purposes this point should not be ignored, so we decided to illustrate the co-operation in a way that emphasises the fact that messages that are sent are not necessarily received. In this way, we have highlighted the need to analyse and reason about these "messages" (e.g. we would like to specify the information contained, the time when the communication occurs, etc.), and therefore will employ a more specialised, though still comprehensible, notation for describing communications.

If we focus for the moment on the *GiveFrequency* task, we observe that each part of communication can be specified by the agents involved (sender and receiver), the information contained in the message, and the time when the communication occurs. For *GiveFrequency*, the correct sub-tasks performed by each role involved (pilot and controller) should be as follows:

- First, for *SendNewFreq*, at *t* time the controller (***Controller)*** gives the pilot (***Pilot***) approaching the exit point of the sector the new frequency (***freq***), which we write as: ***Controller: send(t, Pilot, freq)***.
- Second, for *ReceiveNewFreq*, the pilot receives this communication, that is: ***Pilot: receive(t, Controller, freq)***. Although transmission delays may occur, for the moment at least, they will be ignored.

To summarise, then, the communication that takes place when a new frequency is issued to a pilot (*GiveFrequency*) can be seen as having two parts corresponding to the two communicative participants:

1. ***Controller: send(t, Pilot, freq)***
2. ***Pilot: receive(t, Controller, freq)***.

Taking this as a basis, we can now begin to discuss the kinds of deviations that can (reasonably) happen, by comparing the *effective* (eventually *not* correct) send/receive interactions performed by each role with the *correct* previous ones showed above (1. and 2.). We can perform this analysis by considering possible deviations in attributes of the actions (for example, a frequency value *freq* may differ between the intended message and the effective one that is actually sent or received). It is important to note that this communication occurs not in isolation, but in the context of other tasks, which have an important influence on the risks that might arise. The sections below record a partial analysis of some of the hazards that could arise from failures in these communicative actions that was gained by considering potential failures in our communication example corresponding to each of the guidewords in Table 1.

5.1 None

In this case no data or control signal passes between the roles, because the controller does not send the message or the message has been sent, but it is not received by the pilot (for example, as a result of some hardware fault or environmental interference).

Task: GiveFrequency			Guideword: None	
Deviations	Causes	Consequences	Protections	Recommendations
No message is sent by the controller	Controller fails to recognise the need for giving a new frequency (e.g. mistake dues to failing to note a/c location or proximity to sector boundary) Perception problem	No new frequency received by pilot — a/c may enter the sector without having contacted the new controller	(i) If a/c enters next sector without making a call, the next controller will call the current one.	Provide an indication when a/c within threshold distance of sector boundary Such an indication would persist until electronic system updated
	Controller recognises need, but fails to send message (e.g. memory lapse or high workload-induced slip) Action problem		(ii) Pilot calls ATC	
No message is received	Pilot fails to perceive message (e.g. inattention, high workload) Perception problem		(i) Controller expects answer; lack of it may prompt a second call.	If there is no answer within a quantity of time an alarm message (e.g. an audible signal) should be automatically activated
	Total failure of communication technology or corruption of messages		(ii) Pilot calls ATC	

Table 2. Table for "None" guideword

The most immediate consequence is that the pilot does not know the new frequency for communicating with the controller of the new sector. In cases where no message is received by the pilot, a possible indication to signal this situation is the lack of the Acknowledgement required for this message. If after some time period no acknowledgement has been received, the controller may become suspicious. A possible recommendation is that, after an appropriate "timeout", if no reply has been received, then the message should be re-sent. To this end, a safety requirement could be to decide upon a reasonable threshold time and provide the controller with an automatic alert if messages are unacknowledged.

Another possible (though for various reasons, implausible) protection is that if the pilot is aware of the sector boundary and the aircraft's proximity to it, then it should be possible for the pilot to request the sector and frequency change. In any case, the message concerning the new frequency should be sent several minutes before the aircraft leaves the sector, so as to allow plenty of time for repair actions.

5.2 Other than

The task is performed by using a set of data complete but incorrect. Two possible interpretations of this deviation exist.

1. *Controller: send(t, Pilot, freq'),   Pilot: receive(t, Controller, freq')*

that is, the controller sends wrong frequency to the right aircraft. "Wrong" in this context could refer to two different situations. First, it is possible that *freq' ∉ Freqs* (*Freqs* is the set of available and correct frequencies: if freq' $\notin$ *Freqs* it means that is not a valid frequency, because it does not exist). Secondly, the frequency may be perfectly valid, but *freq≠freq'* (it exists but it is not the right one). We only analyse the second situation.

What are the consequences? The pilot receives an erroneous frequency, and is then potentially unable to speak to the controller of the new sector.

What are the possible indications / protections? The (wrongly) contacted controller should notice that a pilot that is not in his sector is contacting him.

Are there possible recommendations? A possible safety (and usability) requirement could be to provide pilots and controllers with a convenient, or even automatic, way to check the correctness of a frequency. A possible implementation would be a user interface component such as a menu, from which only valid choices can be made. Is this deviation safety-critical? It does not seem to be particularly safety-critical since, in the worst case it will tend to lead to a delay in establishing the right frequency.

2. *Controller*: send(t, *Pilot'*, freq) , *Pilot'*: receive(t, *Controller*, freq)

that is the controller gives the right frequency to the wrong pilot because of some kind of mistake. As for the frequency case above "wrong" breaks down into two cases depending on whether or not the message refers to an aircraft that actually exists. We only analyse the case where the wrong pilot does exist.

What are the consequences? The pilot approaching to change sector does not receive any new frequency, whereas another pilot in the sector —who may not be changing sector and if they are, are necessarily moving into the same sector — is going to change the frequency because of an erroneously address message.

A possible recommendation is that the computer system should provide an alert if a flight that is far from the sector boundary has received the frequency of a new sector.

Task: GiveFrequency			Guideword: Other Than	
Deviations	**Causes**	**Consequences**	**Protections**	**Recommendations**
Controller allocates wrong frequency in communicat ion	Controller holds faulty belief about correct frequency (e.g., a mistake about which sector a/c will be entering, or about what the correct frequency for that sector is) Intention problem	(i) Valid frequency The pilot can not communicate with the right controller (ii)Invalid frequency The pilot can not communicate with any controller	Valid (but wrong) frequency may not be detected immediately. Invalid frequencies easily detected by pilot	Ensure the user interface provides controllers with representations of associations between sectors and frequencies immediate to be interpreted
	Controller knows frequency, but makes a slip Action problem			Design user interface which prevents from slips
Controller uses incorrect callsign	... as a result of a mistake .. Intention problem	The new frequency is given to the wrong flight	Controller should check the flight which receives the new frequency	The application should warn that a flight far from the sector boundary has been selected
	... or a slip. Action problem			Design user interface which prevents from slips
Wrong frequency received	Pilot mis-reads frequency , because of inattention, poor video quality, or being biased by a preconception. Perception problem Or Understanding problem		When the pilot detects that he is using a wrong frequency he should contact immediately the old controller	The application should detect automatically that a wrong frequency is used and inform the old controller in order to send again the right frequency
Wrong pilot receives	System's mal- function	Wrong pilot receives, right pilot doesn't	Check that the pilot answering is really that who has to change sector	The application automatically detects that the pilot answering is not that foreseen

Table 3. Table for "Other than" guideword

5.3 Early

The flow of information occurs before it was intended. If we interpret this in the context of our example, the associated deviation will be that the controller gives pilot the new frequency when the pilot is still far from the sector's boundaries.

Controller: **send(t', *Pilot,* freq),** *Pilot:* **receive(t', *Controller,* freq)** with **t'<t**

The controller sends pilot the order of changing the frequency when the aircraft is still far from the boundaries line, resulting in an aircraft become no longer in communication with the old (but for the time being still *current*) controller and in contact with the new (but wrong since it is too early and the aircraft has not crossed the sector line yet) controller.

Task: GiveFrequency				Guideword: Early
Deviations	Causes	Consequences	Protections	Recommendations
Message issued before than optimum time	Controller's slip or mistake Action/Intention Problem	No more communications with the controller of the current sector	The pilot should check his position inside the sector	(i)Disabling the controller to issue this instruction to a/c still inside the sector or (ii) provides a warning to controller when he tries to communicate the new frequency to a/c still far a defined margin from the boundaries

Table 4. Table for "Early" guideword

A possible protection mechanism could rely on pilots checking their actual position before changing the frequency channel. A design possibility would be to prohibit controllers issuing such instructions to an aircraft that is far from the sector boundaries. To this aim, an appropriate 2D margin should be defined so that the interface can issue the warning in appropriate situations.

5.4 Late

The flow of information occurs after it was intended.

Controller: **send(t', *Pilot,* freq),** *Pilot:* **receive(t', *Controller,* freq)** with **t'>t**

Translating it in terms of our domain, the associated deviation should be that the controller gives the pilot the new frequency when the pilot's aircraft is already entered in the new sector. In this way, the pilot is informed to change the frequency later than the right time.

No specific indication / protection is made provision for indicating the problem and for mitigating the consequences, except than the new controller calls the old controller as soon as s/he sees the aircraft is entered in his sector without the previous required first contact. From a theoretical point of view in some situations this deviation might constitute a hazard: however, this will depend on how large the delay is, and how far the aircraft travels before the situation is rectified.

Task: GiveFrequency			Guideword: Late	
Deviations	Causes	Consequences	Protections	Recommendations
Message issued later than optimum time	Controller's slip or mistake Action/Intention Problem	Issues are much the same as for "None"		

Table 5. Table for "Late" guideword

6 Conclusions and future work

This work presents a method for analysing deviations in performing activities represented in task models in order to provide recommendations to improve the user interface design. The aim is to help designers to understand what properties and behaviours their user interface design should exhibit to avoid wrong safety critical user interactions or to limit the possibility that they can occur, or, at least, to mitigate the consequences.

We have discussed an example of application of the method proposed to a case study taken from the Air Traffic Control domain to describe the type of results that can be achieved. The shown example has demonstrated the rich set of indications useful to obtain safer design of the user interface that it is possible to gather by applying such a method. As this work is being carried out as part of the Esprit MEFISTO Project, which is an interdisciplinary project involving designers, cognitive experts and software developers, we took into consideration the discussions that we had with other members of the project and such discussions were stimulated by our method.

In the future we plan to perform more structured collective exercises using our method. This will give us the possibility to better compare the results of our approach with other approaches such as the "phenotype" framework of [17] and scenarios' analysis of [18]. We also aim at producing formal properties that capture the user interface requirements identified by our method. These properties can be verified on formal task models by using model-checking techniques.

Acknowledgements

We wish to thank Stéphane Chatty and Sophie Tahmassebi and their group from CENA (Centre d'Etudes de la Navigation Aerienne, Toulouse, France) for useful information on the En Route Air Traffic Control case study. This work has been supported as part of the Esprit LTR MEFISTO project (http://giove.cnuce.cnr.it/mefisto.html).

References

1. Abowd G., Wang H., Monk A.; 1995; "A formal technique for automated dialogue development", Proceedings Designing Interactive Systems'95, August'95, pp.219-226, ACM Press.

2. Burns, D.J. and Pitblado, R.M. A Modified HAZOP Methodology For Safety Critical System Assessment. Directions in *Proc. of the Safety-Critical Systems Symposium*, (Bristol, 1993), Springer-Verlag.

3. Chudleigh, M.F. and Clare, J.N. The benefits of SUSI: Safety Analysis of User System Interaction. In *Proc. of the 12th International Conference on Computer Safety, Reliability and Security*, (Poznan-Kiekrz, Poland, 1993), Springer-Verlag.

4. Fields, R.E., Harrison, M.D. and Wright, P.C. (1997). *THEA: Human Error Analysis for Requirements Definition.* University of York, Department of Computer Science, Technical Report YCS-97-294. http://www.cs.york.ac.uk/~bob/papers.html

5. HAZOP Studies on Systems Containing Programmable Electronics. UK Ministry of Defence Interim Def Stan 00-58, (1996), Issue 1. Available from http://www.dstan.mod.uk/dstan_data/ix-00.htm.

6. Jacquot, J.P., Quesnot, D., Early Specification of User-Interfaces: Toward a Formal Approach. In *Proc. ICSE'97*, (Boston, USA, 1997).

7. Kletz, T. HAZOP and HAZAN: Identifying and Assessing Process Industry Hazards, (1992), *Institution of Chemical Engineers*.

8. Leveson, N.G. Safeware: System Safety and Computers – A guide to preventing accidents and losses caused by technology. Addison Wesley.

9. Maiden, N.A.M. (1998). *CREWS-SAVRE: Scenarios for acquiring and validating requirements.* City University, CREWS Report Series 98-27.

10. McDermid, J.A. and Pumfrey, D.J. A Development of Hazard Analysis to aid Software Design. Proc. COMPASS'94, *IEEE Press*. ftp://ftp.cs.york.ac.uk/ hise_reports/safety/develop.ps.Z

11. Paternò, F., "Formal Reasoning about Dialogue Properties with Automatic Support", Interacting with Computers, 9 (1997), pp.173-196, Elsevier

12. Paternò, F., Model-Based Design and Evaluation of Interactive Applications, Springer Verlag, 1999.

13. Paternò, F., Santoro, C., Tahmassebi, S. Formal Models for Cooperative Tasks: Concepts and an Application for En-Route Air Traffic Control. In *Proc. DSV-IS '98*, (Abingdon, U.K., June 1998).

14. Puerta, A. A Model-Based Interface Development Environment, IEEE Software, pp.40-47, July/August 1997.

15. Reason, J. Human Error. Cambridge University Press, (1990).

16. Wilson S., Johnson P., Kelly C., Cunningham J. and Markopoulos P. (1993). Beyond Hacking: A Model-based Approach to User Interface Design. *Proceedings HCI'93*. In: *People and Computers VIII, Proc. of HCI'93 Conf.,* Cambridge: CUP.

17. Hollnagel E., Human Reliability Analysis, Academic Press, 1993.

18. Carrol J, Rosson M., Getting around the task-artefact cycle: how to make claims and design by scenario, ACM Transactions Information System, 10, 2, 1992 pp.181-212.

Dialogue Validation from Task Analysis

Francis JAMBON, Patrick GIRARD and Yohann BOISDRON

LISI / ENSMA[1], Téléport 2, B.P. 109
F-86960 Futuroscope cedex, France
E-mail: {girard, jambon}@ensma.fr
Web: http://www.lisi.ensma.fr/ihm.html

Keywords: Dialogue Validation, Task Analysis, ARCH Architecture Model, H^4 Architecture Model, Dialogue Component.

Abstract:

Up today, formal methods have mainly been used to allow designers to *verify* that software conforms to its specification. In this article, we propose a *validation* method and a tool to analyse whether the design actually fulfils the original requirements for the system. The principle of our validation method is to generate the complete set of possible user interaction sequences from the task analysis. Then, this set is injected in the Dialogue Controller Component of the application. At last, the Dialogue Controller Component's calls to the Functional Core are intercepted, and compared with the user's goals. Our case study is in the general Computer-Aided Design area, in which systems support a huge number of tasks.

1. Introduction

As it is stated in [Fields, Merriam, & Dearden 1997], in recent past years, formal methods have mainly been used to allow designers to *verify* that software conforms to its specification. By the use of a single notation, many authors intended to demonstrate that some properties of the specification –more precisely, that would have to be in the specification– can be enforced by formal study, by the way of model checking or theorem proving.

Today, the field seems to be mature enough to reach a second step that deals with *validation*. It consists in analysing whether the design actually fulfils the original requirements for the system. In the article above mentioned –[Fields, Merriam, & Dearden 1997]– the authors suggest combining different formalisms which are right for some classes of properties. From descriptive and prescriptive viewpoints, the authors propose using formal methods as communication artefacts in the design process. At the end of their analyses, they conclude with a necessary focus shift from a semantic level to a methodological level.

---

[1] Laboratory of Applied Computer Science, National School of Engineers in Mechanics and Aerotechnics

Nevertheless, the focus of these approaches is always the design process. Even when requirements are explicitly involved, as for example when task analysis is emphasised, the goal is to provide more formal descriptions of these requirements, and to help analysis and design. This approach might be interesting in domains were tasks are well-defined. Unfortunately, that is not always the case. In the Computer-Aided Design area, systems cannot be described as a global task analysis. The reasons are twice. On the one hand, these systems must support a huge number of possible tasks –for example, some systems contain thousands of primitive functions, whose assembly generates up to a hundred of thousand tasks. On the other hand, "designers" are people whose creativity is a major characteristic. So doing, they cannot be restricted to a finite number of diagrams embedded in constrained tasks.

By the way, validation may be required for systems that cannot be exhaustively described by classical task analysis. Let us give two examples of such validation needs: (1) Choosing an existing system requires the purchaser to evaluate the possibilities of the system against his needs, when basic evaluation of every function of the system is not possible, the definition of scenarios to test on the system may be a solution. An "ad hoc" validation would be a good solution. (2) When a new release is distributed, it is important to know whether the system, despite of its new capabilities, is always capable to do what the users made with the previous release. So, an automated validation would be very interesting.

Our aim in this paper is to describe a method, which includes a task definition grammar and automated tools, in order to provide the designer of a CAD system for a practical validation of use cases. This paper is organised as follows: in Section 2, we explore some related approaches. In Section 3, we describe the context of Computer-Aided Design. In Section 4, we detail what kind of validation we want to achieve. At last, Section 5 focus on our case study.

2. Related Work

Many works in HCI use formal methods to check models of the actual systems. Model checking methods are a good illustration of this point. They are based on the evaluation of logical properties on the state transition system obtained from the evolving variables. Among these techniques, we can find temporal logics, Petri nets and so on. In the area of interactive systems, these methods are assumed to have first been used in formal verification of interactive systems [Campos & Harrison 1997]. For example, [Abowd, Wang, & Monk 1995] verify user interfaces with SMV (Symbolic Model Verifier) using CTL (Computational Tree Logic), while [Paternó & Faconti 1992] uses LOTOS to write interactors specifications, and analyse translated finite state machines using ACTL (Action-based Temporal Logic). [Brun 1997] develops a new temporal logic based on formalism, named XTL (eXtended Temporal Logic), to address interruptions in interactive systems' specification. Model checking is also used by Palanque et al. who model user and system by the way of object-oriented Petri nets –ICO– [Palanque, Bastide, & Sengès 1995]. The weakness of these approaches is that the running system has to be proved to conform to the model. More recently, [D'Ausbourg 1998] used the Lustre language for the automatic validation of user interface systems. In this case, the formal model is deducted from the UIL[2] description of the interface. Assuming the translator is proved, we can consider that we are really working on the actual system. Nevertheless, in most cases, formal models are only "modelling" the system, with no proof of the equivalence between the model and the system.

Using proof systems have quite similar drawbacks. They are systems where the model is described by variables, operations and invariants. The operations must preserve these invariants and a set of other properties (preconditions and/or post conditions). To ensure the correctness of these specifications, a set of proof obligations are generated and they must be proved. The proof system can achieve some of the proofs automatically. Among these techniques, we can mention Z, based on set theory [Spivey 1988], VDM, based on preconditions and post-conditions calculus [Andrews & Ince 1991], and B, based on the weakest precondition calculus [Abrial 1996 ; Dijkstra 1976]. In the Human-Computer Interaction field VDM and Z have been used to define atomic structures like interactors [Duke & Harrison 1993], and Z and Object-Z are now used more extensively [Hussey & Carrington 1997]. HOL (a Higher Order Logic Theorem Prover) has been used in the verification of User Interface specifications [Bumbulis, et al. 1996]. In these methods, we generally have the same problem of separating specifications and models of the system –on which proofs are conducted– from the actual system –which is only supposed to conform to the models. An exception can be found in [Aït-Ameur, Girard, & Jambon 1998], which uses the refinement methodology to reach the code level: the application itself is proved.

Despite this large number of studies, formal methods are not largely used in HCI. One of the reasons is the *formality gap* [Dix 1991], i.e., the mapping from the requirements of the users and the formalism. In fact, even if we assume that formal models used for reasoning are relevant with final applications, formal methods suffer from a lack of readability and usability for non-specialists. Reading formal models is always hard, and the transition between the informal state of requirements and the formal model is quite difficult. Whenever formal approaches address task analysis [Markopoulos, Johnson, & Rowson 1997], such as ConcurrentTaskTree [Paternò, Mancini, & Meniconi 1997] or [Palanque & Bastide 1995], constructed models are very far from task analysis models such as MAD [Scapin & Pierret-Golbreich 1990] or HTA [Shepherd 1989]. Moreover, while these methods are devoted to analysis and design, no real method or tool is developed to allow system users or experts in human factors to directly validate the systems.

Obviously, a strong need exists for validation techniques, able to ensure that a system "is really able to do that". We describe hereafter a couple of method and tool that allows it in the particular domain of Computer-Aided Design.

---

[2] User Interface Language

3. Computer-Aided Design Context

Our work has been made in the context of Computer-Aided Design. In this area, systems have specific topics like a huge number of functions, strong relations between functional core and presentation layer, and complex dialogues. In fact, they constitute one of the worse case of applications according to the taxonomy of interactive systems [Pierra 1995]. In this taxonomy, seven criteria have been developed to classify applications' needs. They deals with task arity (1) and structuring (2), domain objects autonomy (3) and structuring (4), source of control (5), mono/multi-user (6) and mono/multi modal (7) applications. The first four criteria are specially relevant for CAD applications. In this section, the terminology conforms to the Arch model [Bass, et al. 1992].

3.1 Task arity

Applications support different kinds of tasks. They can be mono-object tasks –each user task involves only one domain object– or multi-object tasks –each task involves several domain objects. Mono-object tasks may be supported by direct manipulation techniques, whatever multi-object tasks must be represented independently from the domain objects. Some dialogue component, of which the structure is independent from the object structure, must exist. As an example, MacDraw™ only supports mono-object tasks. Examples of multi-object tasks are provided by the drafting systems that enable creating lines as tangential to two circles.

3.2 Task structuring

Applications support atomic tasks when users must specify independently each of their tasks, the result of these tasks are recorded in the state of the domain-specific component. Conversely, applications support structured tasks when users may input in pre-order their task/sub-task hierarchy [Norman 1986]. The support of structured tasks needs recording the state of the dialogue independently from the state of the domain-specific component and the interaction component. Atomic tasks may be encapsulated either in domain objects or in interaction objects.

The following example (fig. 1) shows a typical structured task in which commands are in bold and <> represents conceptual objects that are picked up by the user.

```
create_circle_centre_radius
        projection
                    <point_1>
                    <line_2>
        distance
                    <point_3>
                    <point_4>
        /
                    2.0
```

Figure 1: A structured task

We call *create_circle_centre_radius* a **terminal task**: it corresponds to one of the goals of the application, and *projection* a **production sub-task**: its role is to *produce* some information token, e.g., a position computed by projecting *<point_1>* on *<line_2>*, for the higher level terminal task.

3.3 Domain objects autonomy

The domain objects are autonomous when their presentation is mainly dependent on their state. In the opposite, they are relational when their presentation depends on the state of other domain objects. If these objects are autonomous, each of them may be mapped onto one interaction object that supports its rendering function. In the other case, rendering spaces must be provided. CAD objects are relational since that they are parts of complex models whose visualisation depends on the view the user selects.

3.4 Domain objects structuring

Domain objects are structured when several levels of objects, structured by aggregation, may be accessed by the user, whenever they are simple when domain objects are not part of other domain objects. When they are highly structured, designing one domain object may only be interpreted by the domain-side components. It requires a complete traversal of the system by the user-defined events.

3.5 Designing a specific model for CAD systems

So, complex interactive graphic applications are systems that support multi-object structured tasks and of which the conceptual objects are structured and relational objects. CAD systems are good examples of such applications. In these systems, conceptual objects are very precise: line are defined by their two end points and sweeps by their sweeped face and sweeping vectors. The tasks are multi-object tasks, users know these constraints and the system must provide for the specification of these constraints [Roller 1990]; the system supports expressions and the tasks are structured.

The conceptual objects are highly structured –a solid is the part inside of a closed shell, a shell consists of faces, etc.– and relational objects –the visibility of a point depends on every entity involved in the hidden surface process. Therefore, it does not exist any one to one mapping between conceptual objects and presentation objects, and when the designer picks up some graphical position, in order to designate some conceptual object, its intent may only be interpreted by querying the functional core.

Such systems are complex software systems, and it is well known, in Software Engineering, that these systems, whether they are designed according to object oriented techniques or not, must be first split into sub-systems. The Arch [UIMS 1992] model provides for such a macro-structuring of the system. But Software Engineering principles also require the interfaces, specification and relationships between these sub-systems, to be precisely defined, and require each system to map to one unique abstraction. We have developed a specialisation of the Arch model for CAD systems, called the H^4 architecture [Guittet 1995].

The macro-structure of this model (fig. 2) conforms to the Arch model. Regarding its macro-structure, each component, but the domain-adaptor, is based on a specific hierarchy of units. Their role, interface and structuring criteria, have been precisely defined.

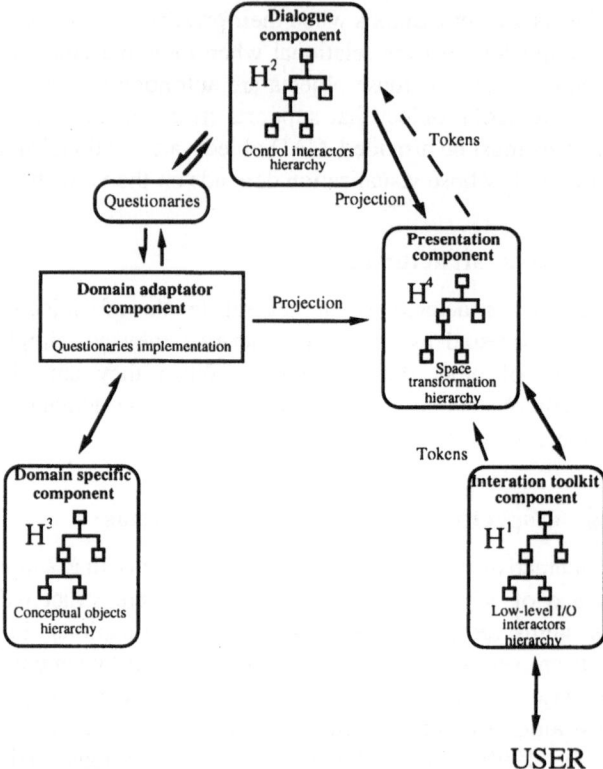

Figure 2: The H^4 architecture model

In our purpose, let us emphasise the dialogue component. The only role of the *dialogue component* is to support the structured and multi-object task-level protocol. When using a multi-agent approach to specify this component, the agents involved in this component are very different from the classical interactive agents such as interactors [Duke & Harrison 1993]. They do not only differ by the abstraction they implement –dialogue component agents implement one task or one category of related tasks such as defining geometrical 3D entities, defining 2D drafting presentation, producing geometric positions from geometric expressions, and so on)– but they also differ by their *interface* with the remaining part of the system. The main role of these agents, that we call *control interactors,* is to control, i.e., to trigger the functional core procedures. The only exchange of events is not sufficient to achieve this goal.

The state of the dialogue does not depend upon the output data that are issued by the functional core as a feedback of the triggered procedures: it only depends on whether or not the procedure fails. Therefore there is no reason to justify that the output flow from the domain adaptor component to the user should go through the dialogue component. This fact was acknowledged by the Seeheim model [Pfaff 1985], and it is still required by the class of applications we discuss in this paper.

Therefore, a control interactor does not provide rendering functions. To ensure the independence between tasks and sub-tasks, a special kind of event dispatcher –called a *monitor*– is needed to realise the circulation of events. It must be noticed that the development of dialogue interactors is completely different from the one of I/O interactors. Intended to support application specific tasks, they cannot be found in any predefined standard toolkit. Fortunately, they may be specified either by using a language approach [Olsen 1992], using an ATN approach [Woods 1970] or Petri Nets [Palanque 1992] in a pure declarative way. Therefore, they may be automatically generated and the different models proposed for dialogue specification [Green 1986] may be used to specify, *in a modular way*, each dialogue interactor behaviour. Do notice that this approach is close to the "transducer" approach from [Accott, et al. 1997]. The major difference consists in the main structure and the global behaviour of our model, which involves elementary "bricks", such as transducers.

Thanks to this architecture, the composition of complex dialogues is straightforward. Organising functions in separate dialogue interactors according to global levels of functions –picking, graphical expressions, geometrical creations, structuring, etc.– allows a good modular decomposition of the application. Then, the hierarchical organisation of the dialogue interactors, under the control of a monitor, allows free compositions of task/sub-tasks provided they do not belong to the same dialogue interactor.

3.6 A strong need for validation

Unfortunately, task analysis is very difficult in CAD systems. Because of the strong hierarchy of goals and sub-goals, which leads to strong hierarchy of tasks and sub-tasks. Task analysis of such systems leads to extremely large and flat trees. Reaching a given goal may be made by several methods with an equivalent result. Defining every possible path is unrealistic. In practice, the definition of CAD systems is made by incremental adjunction of new functions, which are integrated into the dialogue. A design lifecycle starting from a task analysis does not apply.

So, the need for validation is different from systems with well-characterised tasks, as for example air-traffic control or database management. In our approach, we do not address any ergonomic aspect of HCI applications. In the opposite, we focus on dynamic dialogue control. The question is "Is the system able to do *that*", in which "*that*" is expressed in a user-comprehensible way. We choose a notation that is in fact a restriction of MAD [Scapin & Pierret-Golbreich 1990]. This method allows us to define abstract scenarios of dialogues to be validated on the system.

A second requirement is to automate the validation. So, our objective is to produce test sequences from the scenarios' descriptions, and then, to validate the global execution of these test sequences onto the system itself. Test sequences are not an example of system execution, because no real value is provided. The test generation only produces dialogue tokens without associated value. In fact, we are only able to *validate* the dialogue of the

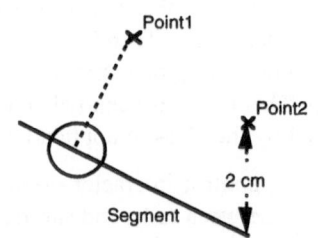

Figure 3: Creation of a circle

interactive system. Let us give an example. Assume we need to test if creating a circle, which centre is the projection of a point on a segment, and which radius is half the distance between a second point and the extremity of the segment, is still possible in a new release (Fig. 3).

For user convenience, we want the system to allow either entering first the centre or the radius of the circle. The task is well-defined: the main goal may be split in two sub-goals, defining the centre and defining the radius, with no sequential relation between them. Each of them must then be expressed by a projection and a distance calculus. Expressing this task in MAD is straightforward. Of course, in real world applications, a huge set of these complex tasks may have to be checked, and so, the validation cannot be hand-performed. From this description, our system must be able to automate the generation of tests sequences and their validation on the system.

At this point, we can list the major requirements for our validation system: the designer's needs, expressed in terms of a goal and sub-goals hierarchy, lead us to use a task analysis as the main data input for our validation system. In addition to this, the designer should want to be sure that the user's goals are really achieved, i.e., correct side effects are the consequences of the user's actions. So, we have to check the system's links to the functional core of the system too. On a more technical point of view, the need for a complete coverage and the huge set of possible user interactions with the target system force us to develop an automated tool to ensure a realistic validation. We will show in the next section our validation principles, and their application on our case study in section 5.

4. Validation Principles

This section deals with the validation principles, whereas the next one (5) is dedicated to the tools used to ensure the validation of our case study –a prototype of a CAD application. In this section, we first detail the HCI properties we want to validate, and then, we describe the validation methodology starting from task analysis to interaction sequence generation.

4.1 Usability Properties

As detailed in the previous section of this paper, our research focuses on CAD systems. These systems usually gather a very important set of functions. In such context, our aim is twofold: we want to make sure that all these functions are reachable for the user, and consistent with the domain objects. So, following Dix and al. [Dix, et al. 1998] in §4.3.3, we have to check both *Reachability* and *Task completeness*.

Reachability

On the one hand, our goal is to check that the system implements the full set of user's tasks given in the user interface specifications. More precisely, we want to make sure that the system accepts and recognises the sequence of user interactions –command selection, object designation, etc.– used to perform each task given in the specifications, and each of its variants. So, from the A. Dix and al. point of view, we want to ensure *Reachability* which "refers to the possibility of navigation through the observable system states".

Reachability is a common usability principle. This principle may be checked by the way of verification of formal specifications. As for example, P. Palanque et al. use an object-oriented Petri nets formalism and a model checking method to prove some Reachabily properties [Palanque, Bastide, & Sengès 1995]. The Y. Aït-Ameur et al. approach is quite different: they use the B method and theorem proving to ensure this principle [Aït-Ameur, Girard, & Jambon 1998].

Our approach in this paper is significantly different: we want to validate the Dialogue Controller of an existing application. We do not provide any model of the final system –in fact we use the binary code of the Dialogue Controller itself. We just need a model of the user tasks performed in an independent way by a specialist of human factors. Another difference is in the scale: we need a complete coverage validation of the system, not only partial proofs.

Task completeness

On the other hand, we want to ensure that the modifications of the domain objects are consistent with the user's tasks. In other words, we must show that the side effects of the user's tasks on the Functional Core can be linked with the user's goal, i.e. the system does exactly what the user wants it to do. So, from the A. Dix and al. point of view, we want to ensure *Task completeness* which "refers to the level to which the system services can be mapped onto all the user tasks".

Task completeness is a usability principle rather difficult to prove, because one has to bridge the gap between user's goals and system Functional Core. In our approach, we want to check that the Functional Core methods called by the Dialogue Controller during user interaction are consistent with the goal and sub-goals defined in the task analysis. This way, we only make the validation on the Dialogue Controller. So, to ensure full Task completeness, we make the assumption that the Functional Core methods are functionally correct. Such validation of the Functional Core can be carried out separately.

4.2 Task Model

The first step of our validation method is a task analysis, which is supposed to be performed by a specialist in human factors. This task analysis gathers all the possible interactions performed by the user to achieve his goal. And in CAD systems, these user's goals are creations of conceptual objects in the model, modifications or requests for information on these objects.

Typical user's tasks of CAD systems –see §3– are structured. They can be modelled by a classical task/sub-task tree corresponding to a goal/sub-goal hierarchical analysis. In our task model, as in MAD, sub-tasks can be re-used, but cycles and recursivity are forbidden. Moreover, the set of temporal relationships between tasks is restricted to sequence, alternative, and order independence. So our task model is limited to this set of relationships.

We defined a new and simple task model for our kind of applications. This model can be considered as a simplified version of HTA [Shepherd 1989] or MAD [Scapin & Pierret-Golbreich 1990] notations underlying model. The resulting task model will enable us to generate all the possible user's interaction sequences.

4.3 User's Interaction Sequences

It is not straightforward to validate the Dialogue Controller directly from a user's tasks model. However, it is easy to check if a sequence of user's interactions is valid: one just have to do it with the system and see what happened. Our validation method follows a similar principle: we validate the user's interaction sequences one by one.

To do so, we use the task analysis to generate all the possible interaction sequences. These sequences are automatically generated by the way of a classical tree traversal –cycles and recursivity are forbidden from our task model. All the possible sequences are generated, so, we ensure a complete coverage validation of the application. These sequences are finally sent to the system to be validated.

4.4 Dialogue Component Validation

We assume that the target system has been implemented with the Arch architecture model [Bass et al. 1992]. In fact, our case study has been implemented with the H^4 architecture model –see §3.5– which is a variant of the Arch model. Our aim is to validate the Dialogue component of the final application.

As shown on figure 4, the principle of our validation method is to generate the complete set of possible user interaction sequences from the task analysis. Then, this set is injected in the Dialogue Component of the real application via a modified Presentation Component. Then, the application is launched and the Dialogue

Component calls to the Domain Specific Component –the Functional Core– via the Domain Adaptor Component are intercepted, and compared with the user's goal. If they match exactly, the sequence of interactions is assumed to be valid.

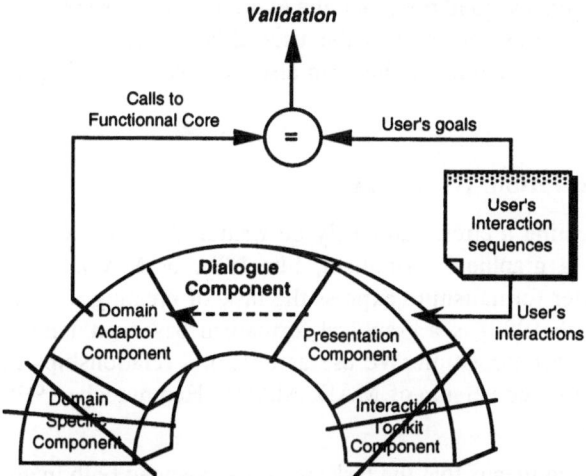

Figure 4: Dialogue component validation principle in the Arch model

This validation principle considers the Dialogue Component as a black box. No assumptions are made about the internal architecture of this component. It must onlyto respect the Application Programming Interface of both the Presentation and the Domain Adaptor Components which is reused by the modified components. So, it is possible to use the binary code of an existing application directly, provided the programming language accept post-compilation linkage.

5. Case study

This section deals with a validation example. We apply the validation principles exposed in the previous section (4) to a case study: MiniCAD, an application of the GIPSE system. In this section, we first describe the main features of MiniCAD, and then we relate the validation process from task analysis to error trace generation.

5.1 Test Application

The GIPSE system is a prototype of a CAD application with an integrated Programming by Example Interface Generator [Patry & Girard 1997]. GIPSE is implemented with the H^4 architecture model described in §3.5. We use a part of this system, called MiniCAD, as our case study. Briefly speaking, the MiniCAD application implements basic CAD functions –objects drawings, objects selections, etc.– and enables structured dialogue modes, but does not include any programming by demonstration generator.

Although MiniCAD is a prototype with very little functions available –compared with a real world CAD system– a huge set of user interactions are possible. As a

216

consequence, the system cannot be validated "by hand". So, we develop a tool to do so. We test this tool on the complex structured task previously described: «creating a circle, which centre is the projection of a point on a segment, and which radius is half the distance between a second point and the extremity of the segment» (see fig. 3). For user convenience, the system allows the user either entering first the centre or the radius of the circle. The circle's radius can also be given in a simpler way by typing directly its value.

5.2 Task Description Grammar

The task of creating a circle can easily be written down by a specialist in human factors thanks to a graphical formalism, like HTA or MAD. We use a simplified version of this latter formalism to express the task of creating a circle. MAD [Scapin & Pierret-Golbreich 1990] is a graphical formalism based on temporal relationships and task/sub-task decomposition. We use as temporal relationships the more relevant operators of an enhanced version of MAD, MAD* [Hammouche 1995]. Among these operators, we use:

- AND which means that the tasks must be executed both in any order ;
- OR which means that only one of the tasks must be executed ;
- SEQ which means that the tasks must be executed both, and in sequence.

The figure 5 shows the resulting specification. In this diagram, the sentences in rectangles are tasks whereas sentences in *Italics* are final atomic tasks directly executed by the user on the interface, as selecting an object by a mouse click or a typing of a number with the keyboard.

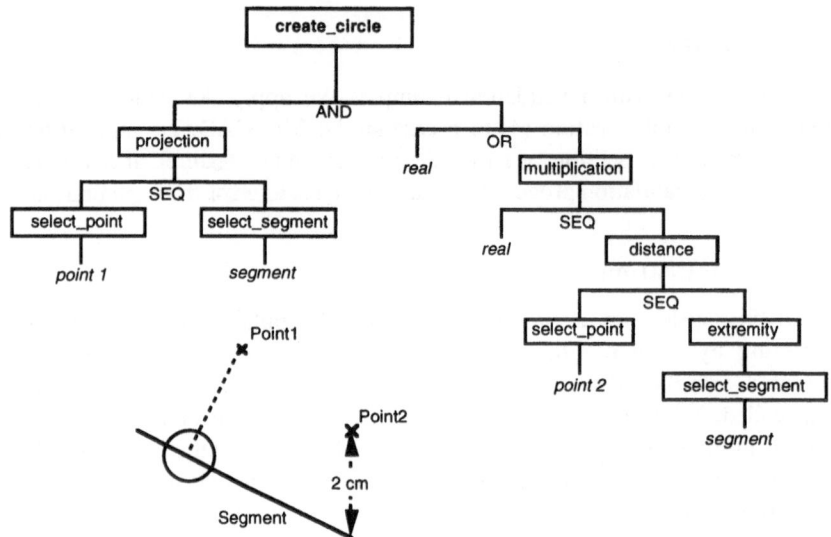

Figure 5: Task of creating a circle in a simplified version of the MAD formalism.

Of course, our sequence generator cannot directly interpret the diagram on figure 5. So, we define a task grammar. Both representations –graphical and text– are equivalent. The tool to translate the graphical representation to the textual one is not yet implemented. Consequently, the task description shown on figure 6 has been translated manually from the MAD description (fig. 5).

```
## task 1

    command : create_circle
    result : circle
    parameter : position=<11>
    & parameter : real=a_real / <13>

    # sub-task 11
            command : projection
            result : position
            parameter : point=<111>
            parameter : segment=<112>
    # end sub-task

    # sub-task 13
            command : multiplication
            result : real
            parameter : real=a_real
            parameter : real=<12>
    # end sub-task

# sub-task 12
            command : distance
            result : real
            parameter : point=<121>
            parameter : position=<122>
    # end sub-task

    # sub-task 122
            command : extremity
            result : position
            parameter: segment=<1221>
    # end sub-task

    # sub-task 111
            command : select_point
            result : point
            parameter: position=a_position
    # end sub-task

    # sub-task 112
            command : select_segment
            result : segment
            parameter : position=a_position
    # end sub-task

    # sub-task 121
            command : select_point
            result : point
            parameter : position=a_position
    # end sub-task

    # sub-task 1221
            command : select_segment
            result : segment
            parameter : position=a_position
    # end sub-task

## end task
```

Figure 6: Task of creating a circle in our task grammar.

In our task grammar, the tasks and sub-tasks are numbered. Each task (resp. sub-task) description begins with the keyword *task* (resp. *sub-task*) and ends with the same keyword with the word *end* before. Then, three types of fields must be fulfilled:

- The *command* field refers to the command activated by the user, for example, the menu's item he must select in order to accomplish his task ; this field is also used to check the Functional Core calls ;
- The *result* field is the type of conceptual object the task or sub-task is supposed to produce, for example, the sub-task extremity (of a segment) command returns a position;
- The *parameter* field gives information about the sub-tasks of the present task:
    - First, it gives the type of the expected conceptual object (*position* or *real* for example);
    - Second, it gives the possible sub-tasks, which can be either the number of a sub-task (*<11>* for example) or an atomic action (*a_position* or *a_real* for example); these sub-tasks are supposed to produce the conceptual object type expected ;
    - Third, a temporal operator can be used to set the relationships among the order of parameters –in fact sub-tasks– or the use of more than one sub-task as a parameter. These operators are equivalent to MAD operators: "&" is equivalent to AND, "/" is equivalent to OR, and the SEQ operator is default.

5.3 Dialogue Sequences Generator

From the task analysis, we can extract the user's interaction sequences. Our task model does not allow neither recursivity nor cycle, so, the task/sub-task analysis specify a finite number of user's interaction sequences. Consequently, we can achieve a complete coverage validation of the Dialogue component of the MiniCAD application.

We develop a tool to extract automatically all these possible interaction sequences. The task analysis (fig. 6) gives four possible interaction sequences. We reprint two of them on figure 7. The syntax of the interaction sequences in similar to the task grammar syntax, except that each sequence begins with the keyword *SEQUENCE* and ends with the keyword *END_SEQUENCE*. When commands are issued by the user (*create_circle* or *select_point* for example) the "COMMAND :" sentence is added before the command name. When the user's actions are atomic actions (*a_position* or *a_real* for example), their names are directly printed.

```
SEQUENCE
    COMMAND : create_circle
    a_reel
    COMMAND : projection
    COMMAND : select_point
    a_position
    COMMAND : select_segment
    a_position
END_SEQUENCE
```

```
SEQUENCE

    COMMAND : create_circle
    COMMAND : projection
    COMMAND : select_point
    a_position
    COMMAND : select_segment
    a_position
    COMMAND : multiplication
    a_reel
    COMMAND : distance
    COMMAND : select_point
    a_position
    COMMAND : extremity
    COMMAND : select_segment
    a_position
END_SEQUENCE

    ...
```

Figure 7: Interaction sequences.

5.4 Test Platform

Our case study is the MiniCAD application (fig. 8). MiniCAD was developed in the ADA95 language with the H^4 architecture model. Our test platform re-uses the Dialogue Component of the MiniCAD application to validate it.

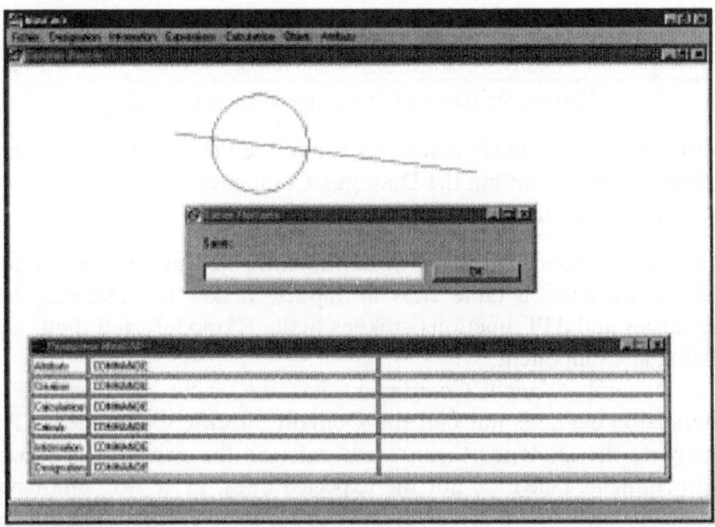

Figure 8: MiniCAD application after the completion of the task "drawing a circle".

In order to make the mapping between the command names of the task analysis done by the human factors specialist –in English in our case study– and the names of functions implemented by the MiniCAD programmer –in French in our case study–

we need an association table. This table embodies the links between terminal tasks and functions of the CAD system. This table is in fact the only formal link between the human factor domain and the Application Programming Interface (API). The filling of this table needs cooperation between the designers. This table are to be filled only once in the design process, because the task names as well as the API are usually reused for new application versions. It must be update if new tasks are added or API are changed. Figure 9 gives an excerpt of the table we use, in which task analysis command names are on the left side of the "=" symbol, whereas the API methods are on the right one.

```
command : create_circle = COMMANDE : creation.cercle
command : create_segment = COMMANDE : creation.segment
command : create_point = COMANDE : creation.point
command : multiplication = COMMANDE : calc.multiplication
command : projection = COMMANDE : calculs.projection
command : distance = COMMANDE : calculs.distance
command : select_circle = COMMANDE : designation.cercle
command : select_segment = COMMANDE : designation.segment
command : select_point = COMMANDE : designation.point
command : extremity = COMMANDE : information.extremite

...

a_reel : = REEL :
a_position : = POSITION :
a_segment : = SEGMENT :
a_point : = POINT :
a_circle : = CERCLE :

...
```

Figure 9: Excerpt from the association table.

For the test platform, we made a new version of the Presentation component and the Domain Adaptor Component but the Dialogue Component is exactly the same as the one of the MiniCAD application (fig. 10):

- The *Presentation Component* takes the simulated user's interaction sequences and the association table files as inputs, makes the mapping between the sequences and API functions –tokens in the H^4 model– and then, activates the Dialogue Component.
- The *Domain Adaptor Component* has the same API as the MiniCAD application but does not call the Domain Specific Component. This module compares the Dialogue Component calls to the expected commands. When the command called are not the expected ones, or if no command has been called, the test system produces an error for the corresponding sequence. Every error is written in the output file.

221

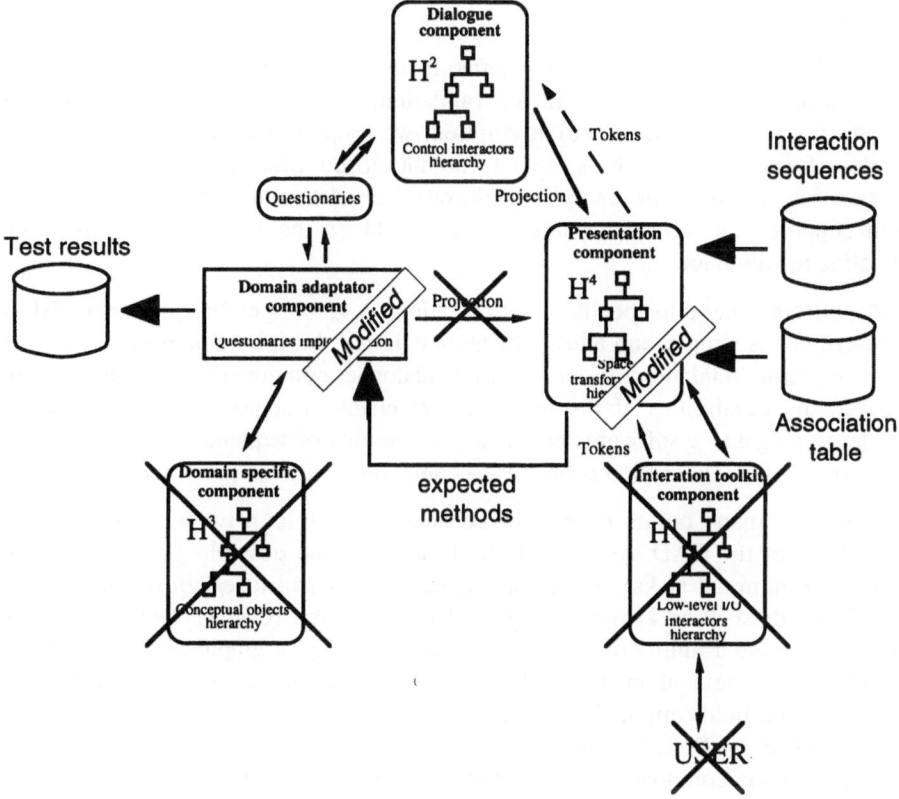

Figure 10: Test platform architecture.

5.5 Execution Traces

We have identified three major validation errors:

- The method called by the Dialogue Component via the Domain Adaptor Component does not exist in the Domain Specific Component API ;
- The method called is not the expected one, e.g., a rectangle is created, whereas a circle is expected.
- No method is called by the Dialogue Component at the end of the sequence.

These errors may be symptoms of either task analysis error or Domain Specific Component bugs. So, they can be rather difficult to interpret by the design team. However, our main goal is to check a huge number of interaction sequences to validate the system as a whole, i.e., to answer the designer "yes all is OK" or "no, there is a problem".

6. Conclusion

[Fields, Merriam, & Dearden 1997] define focus shifts as new trends for works in DSV-IS papers. In the specific point of validation, our proposal addresses many of them. Shifting from prescription to description, we propose a simple way to describe examples of tasks we want the system to be able to do. Starting from that point, a validation can be done: the analysis performed can determine whether or not the system supports the task. So doing, we also address the need for shifting from verification to validation.

Shifting from general to specific notations allows a great operability. Our model of task description is simple, and allows the automation of the validation process. We are able to perform validation of an existing dialogue component after its design. Moreover, the capabilities of the test platform enable designers to check quickly, while developing a new software version, a huge number of sequences. Doing so, they might prove that a new version is backward compatible with the previous one.

Nevertheless, many points have to be enhanced. The link between terminal tasks and functions of the CAD system is hand-made. With the possible great number of functions (so terminal tasks), a more automated mechanism to establish this link is needed. Methods such as Programming by Demonstration [Cypher 1993] might be used to enforce the usability of our tools. In the same way, a graphical tool might be preferable to pure textual methods. At last, the adaptation of this methodology to other application fields might also be interesting. We also plan to generate interaction sequences not at the Presentation Component level but at a lower level, i.e., at the Interaction Toolkit Component level in order to reduce system code modifications.

7. Bibliography

[Abowd, Wang, & Monk 1995] Abowd G.D., Wang H.-M., & Monk A.F. A Formal Technique for Automated Dialogue Development. *DIS'95, Ann Arbor, Michigan*, August 23-25 1995. p. 219-226.

[Abrial 1996] Abrial J.-R. *The B Book: Assigning Programs to Meanings*. Cambridge University Press, 1996.

[Accott et al. 1997] Accott J., Chatty S., Maury S., & Palanque P. Formal transducers: Models of devices and building bricks for the design of highly interactive systems. *Eurographics Workshop on Design, Specification, Verification of Interactive Systems, Granada, Spain*, June 4-6 1997. p. 143-160.

[Aït-Ameur, Girard, & Jambon 1998] Aït-Ameur Y., Girard P., & Jambon F. Using the B formal approach for incremental specification design of interactive systems. *IFIP Working Conference on Engineering for Human-Computer Interaction (EHCI'98), Heraklion (Crete), Greece*, 14-18 September 1998. p. {to be published}.

[Andrews & Ince 1991] Andrews D. & Ince D. *Practical Formal Methods with VDM*. McGraw-Hill, 1991.

[Bass et al. 1992] Bass L., Faneuf R., Little R., Mayer N., Pellegrino B., Reed S., Seacord R., Sheppard S., & Szczur M.R. A Metamodel for the Runtime Architecture of an Interactive System. *SIGCHI Bulletin*, 1992. vol. 24, n° 1, p. 32-37.

[Brun 1997] Brun P. *XTL: a temporal logic for the formal development of interactive systems.* Formal Methods for Human-Computer Interaction, Springer-Verlag, 1997. p. 121-139.

[Bumbulis et al. 1996] Bumbulis P., Alencar P.S.C., Cowan D.D., & Lucena C.J.P. Validating properties of component-based graphical user interfaces. *Third International Eurographics Workshop on Design, Specification, and Verification of Interactive Systems (DSV-IS'96), Namur, Belgium,* 5-7 June 1996. p. 347-365.

[Campos & Harrison 1997] Campos J.C. & Harrison M.D. Formally Verifying Interactive Systems: A Review. *Eurographics Workshop on Design, Specification, Verification of Interactive Systems, Granada, Spain,* June 4-6 1997. p. 109-124.

[Cypher 1993] Cypher A. *Eager : Programming Repetitive Tasks by Demonstration.* Watch What I Do, Cambridge : The MIT Press, 1993. p. 205-217.

[D'Ausbourg 1998] D'Ausbourg B. Using Model Checking for the Automatic Validation of User Interface Systems. *Eurographics Workshop on Design, Specification and Validation of Interactive Systems (DSV-IS'98), Abingdon, UK,* 1998. p. 242-260.

[Dijkstra 1976] Dijkstra E. *A Discipline of Programming.* Englewood Cliff (NJ), USA : Prentice Hall, 1976.

[Dix et al. 1998] Dix A., Finlay J., Abowd G., & Beale R. *Human-Computer Interaction.* Prentice Hall, 1998.

[Dix 1991] Dix A.J. *Formal Methods for Interactive Systems.* London, UK : Academic Press, 1991.

[Duke & Harrison 1993] Duke D.J. & Harrison M.D. *Towards a Theory of Interactors.* Amodeus Esprit Basic Research Project 7040, 1993 System Modelling/WP6.

[Fields, Merriam, & Dearden 1997] Fields B., Merriam N., & Dearden A. DMVIS: Design, Modelling and Validation of Interactive Systems. *Eurographics Workshop on Design, Specification, Verification of Interactive Systems, Granada, Spain,* June 4-6 1997. p. 29-44.

[Green 1986] Green M.W. *A Survey of three Dialogue Models.* ACM Transactions on Graphics. 1986. vol. 5,n° 3, p. 244-275.

[Guittet 1995] Guittet L. Contribution à l'Ingéniérie des Interfaces Homme-Machine - Théorie des Interacteurs et Architecture H4 dans le système NODAOO. Thèse de Doctorat : Université de Poitiers, Poitiers, 1995.

[Hammouche 1995] Hammouche H. De la modélisation des tâches utilisateurs à la spécification conceptuelle d'interfaces Homme-Machine. PhD : Paris VI, 1995.

[Hussey & Carrington 1997] Hussey A. & Carrington D. *Specifying a Web Browser Interface Using Object-Z.* Formal Methods for Human-Computer Interaction, Springer-Verlag, 1997. p. 157-174.

[Markopoulos, Johnson, & Rowson 1997] Markopoulos P., Johnson P., & Rowson J. Formal Aspects of Task Based Design. *Design, Specification and Verification of Interactive Systems (DSV-IS'97), Granada, Spain,* June 4-6 1997. p. 209-224.

[Norman 1986] Norman D. *User Centered System Design.* Lawrence Erlbaum Associates, 1986.

[Olsen 1992] Olsen D.R. *User Interface Management Systems: Models and Algorithms.* San Mateo (CA), USA : Morgan Kaufmann, 1992.

[Palanque 1992] Palanque P. Modélisation par Objets Coopératifs Interactifs d'interfaces homme-machine dirigées par l'utilisateur. PhD : Toulouse I, Toulouse, 1992.

[Palanque & Bastide 1995] Palanque P. & Bastide R. *Task Models - System Models: a Formal Bridge over the Gap.* Critical Issues in User Interface Engineering, London : Springer-Verlag, 1995. p. 65-80.

[Palanque, Bastide, & Sengès 1995] Palanque P., Bastide R., & Sengès V. Validating interactive system design through the verification of formal task and system models. *IFIP TC2/WG2.7 working conference on engineering for human-computer interaction (EHCI'95), Grand Targhee Resort (Yellowstone Park), USA,* 14-18 August 1995. p. 189-212.

[Paternó & Faconti 1992] Paternó F. & Faconti G.P. *On the LOTOS use to describe graphical interaction.* Cambridge University Press, 1992. p. 155-173.

[Paternò, Mancini, & Meniconi 1997] Paternò F., Mancini C., & Meniconi S. ConcurTaskTrees: A Diagrammatic Notation for Specifying Task Models. *IFIP TC13 human-computer interaction conference (INTERACT'97), Sydney,* 1997. p. 362-369.

[Patry & Girard 1997] Patry G. & Girard P. From Adaptable Interfaces to Model-Based Interface Development: The GIPSE Project. *Third Annual ERCIM Workshop on "User Interfaces for All", Obernai, France,* 3-4 november 1997. p. 127-133.

[Pfaff 1985] Pfaff G.E. User Interface Management Systems, Proceedings of the Workshop on User Interface Management Systems held in Seeheim. Eurographic Seminars. Berlin : Springer-Verlag, 1985.

[Pierra 1995] Pierra G. Towards a taxonomy for interactive graphics systems. *Eurographics Workshop on Design, Specification, Verification of Interactive Systems, Bonas,* June 7-9 1995. p. 362-370.

[Roller 1990] Roller D. *Dimension-Driven Geometry in CAD: a Survey.* Theory and Practice of Geometric Modeling, Springer-Verlag, 1990. p. 509-523.

[Scapin & Pierret-Golbreich 1990] Scapin D.L. & Pierret-Golbreich C. *Towards a method for task description : MAD.* Work with display units 89, Elsevier Science Publishers, North-Holland, 1990.

[Shepherd 1989] Shepherd A. *Analysis and training in information technology tasks.* Task Analysis for Human-Computer Interaction, Chichester, USA : Ellis Horwood, 1989. p. 15-55.

[Spivey 1988] Spivey J.M. *The Z notation: A Reference Manual.* Prentice Hall Int., 1988.

[Woods 1970] Woods W. *Transition Network Grammars for Natural Language Analysis.* Communications of the ACM. 1970. vol. 13,n° 10, p. 591-606.

Task- and Object-Oriented Development of Interactive Systems – How many models are necessary ?

Peter Forbrig

Fachbereich Informatik, Universität Rostock,
Albert-Einstein-Str. 21, 18051 Rostock, Germany
Peter.forbrig@informatik.uni-rostock.de

Abstract: In the field of model-based development of interactive systems, several approaches have been proposed to integrate task and object knowledge into the development process and its underlying representations. Within the paper different types of models are classified according to their importance for the development process. The relation between existing, envisioned and programming models are discussed and a task driven approach for object-oriented programming is suggested.

1   Model-Based Development of Interactive Software

Up to now, there have been different points of view on how to develop interactive software. On one hand, the community of traditional software engineers insisted and part of it still insists in a more or less complete and more or less formal specification of the functionality of an application in the course of design that has finally to be implemented. After finishing these steps the programming (hard coding) rather than the specification of user interfaces is performed, thus leading to a more or less complete integration of the user interface into the application (in this context to be understood as a set of functions). As an example have a look at [21] or at most of the papers concerning UML.

On the other hand the community of software ergonomists mostly pursues a completely orthogonal strategy: The user interface is designed and specified before the functionality of an application is going to be specified. As a consequence, the desired functionality of a software system has to be derived from more or less complex interaction feature and modality specifications. As an example we only refer to the MAD*-system [16]. However, in this case the authors are aware of the limitations of their approach: 'One should also state some of the limitations of the approach: it is not explicitly linked to traditional software design processes and methods, it does not incorporate organisational characteristics, nor software requirements.'([16] p. 224).

Both approaches, in case of strictly following their concepts, might lead to cumbersome interactive systems that might either fail to support the tasks that should be accomplished or fail to provide user-adequate features for navigation and dialog control. In order to prevent both types of failures there has to be an exchange of views of both communities. In any case, the proper functionality has to be considered as a prerequisite for user-centred interaction at the user interface. Hence, the functionality of a system has priority in software development from the technical perspective. Customer still primarily pay for software because the offered functionality is assumed to solve some problems in their enterprise.

Rapid development of user interfaces, as it is performed in the course of prototyping, helps developers to understand the functionality and facilitates the participation for end users. As a consequence, software developers have to study the work of potential users: They have to analyse the tasks users are performing and to specify the functionality of software according to the results of this analysis, e.g. [12]. In taking into account end user tasks and the way how they accomplish their tasks, design of software becomes design of work: "From the point of view of the user interface, designing systems for users means designing a task world in the first place." [20]

However, in most of the cases the development of interactive systems starts either from a data model, such as described in [3, 4; Janssen et al. 93], or from an functional application model, in order to separate the user interface from the application, such as described in [4, 19]. In both cases, object representations for user interfaces tend not to model how a system might be used by users in accomplishing their work tasks. They rather attempt to provide the designer with existing software architectures to implement user interfaces. The structuring facilities are termed models, in order to express the proposed design at a high level of abstraction, however, focusing on the functional behaviour of the interface without end user task context.

In parallel to the model-based approaches, task-based techniques have evolved, such as ADEPT [22] and MUSE [15]. Their prime concern is to improve design by enhancing its suitability for end user tasks, and the organisation they are part of. Task-based techniques focus on the process of creating design representations, not necessarily object representations, from information about the user's tasks, thus increasing confidence that the interactive system is compatible with the work places it is intended to support. However, model-based and task-based approaches have several features in common [23], such as:

1. They both focus on the use of models to represent the various sorts of information that contribute to the design of user interfaces.
2. Both approaches discuss issues pertaining to the use of the models in design activities (e.g. further analysis, evaluation, and generation).
3. They might be supported through tools to automate the design activities or to assist designers in their work.

The main difference between the two approaches is that model-based approaches focus on the tools that support the design whereas task-based approaches focus on the design process. In this paper we discuss fundamental approaches that try to bridge the gap between model- and task-based approaches using object-oriented development techniques. We are going to question the mutual relationships involved in model-based development based on end user tasks (section 2). We then proceed with discussing the role of the existing and envisioned models with respect to model- and task-based development approaches (section 3). We will finally give a strategy to support implementation, i.e. straightforward programming without reducing contextual information (section 4). Section 5 concludes the paper summarising the achievements and identifying topics for further research.

2 When and How to Focus on a Model of the Dialog

In this section we are going to develop an understanding on

(i) how many models developers actually require for task- and model-based development, and

(ii) how many steps have to be performed before a dialog or application model can be specified in the context of end user tasks.

Interactive system development that takes into account end user tasks has to comprise some representation of these tasks. In order to develop software based on end user task representations in a structured way model-based reference models and frameworks have been introduced. For instance, in the approach by [18] interactive software development is based on the methodological integration of a task model, a user model, a problem domain model (data model) and an interaction model (see also figure 1).

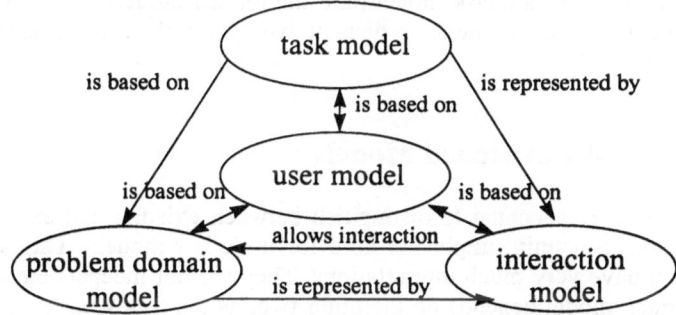

Fig. 1. Relations between models according [18].

1. Task model: Describes the static and dynamic organisation of the work.

2. User model: Characterises the users and specifies their perception of tasks and the organisation of work, the access rights to data, and their preferences for interaction modalities.

3. Problem domain model: Specifies objects of the problem domain with attributes, methods and relations, as well as the behaviour of these models.

4. Interaction model: Describes the structure and behaviour of interaction devices, features, and modalities.

The relationships between these models are also presented in figure 1. They demonstrate that any data model of interaction model, in order to represent or present end user tasks, has to be based on the task model of the application. In addition, the task model have to be modelled in mutual relationship to the user model, representing the functional roles users have to play for task accomplishment, as well as their individual perception of the tasks. The user model is also related to the data model and the interaction model, since according to the tasks users perform they might have to be provided with certain views on the data, and the interaction model has to reflect the abilities, skills, and preferences of end users. The mutual relationship between the problem domain and the data model is required, since on the one hand, the problem domain data have to be presented to the end users for interactive task accomplishment, and on the other hand, the interaction model might enable multiple presentations facilities for data.

Since the framework is model-driven, designers may handle interaction and data modelling separately as long as required. However, finally a single (object) architecture remains that is the result of several modelling activities. The design process is then a loose order of specification activities and mutual adaptation procedures in and between different models. This approach still enables designer to start either with the interface specification or the data modelling activities, based on a task model.

Now the question is: Does a task model (and the related models) reflect the existing tasks (and interaction modalities) or does it have to reflect envisioned tasks, as claimed by [13]?

3   Existing and Envisioned Models

Although it is widely accepted to distinguish between existing and envisioned task models, the same constraint might not hold for the other models. The task, object, and user model have very much interrelations. They are not independent dimensions of a system. Each model depends on the other two, as the following examples try to demonstrate:

(i)   A multimedia application cannot be built without media players.
(ii)   An expert in data base development has not to be an expert in compiler construction
(iii) A data base is very useful tool for data management but it makes not much sense to use it for the development of a text editor.

Once we assume that the development of interactive systems might be based on envisioned task models, the consequences of this assumption have to be elaborated: Due to the close interrelationship of the models each modification of the task model and an envisioned task model has to be reflected by the other models. Hence, changes to an envisioned task model leads to changes in all the other models. They might become or be envisioned, too. As a consequence, we do not only have to distinguish between an existing and envisioned task model, but also between an existing and envisioned user and object model (see also [6] and figure 2).

229

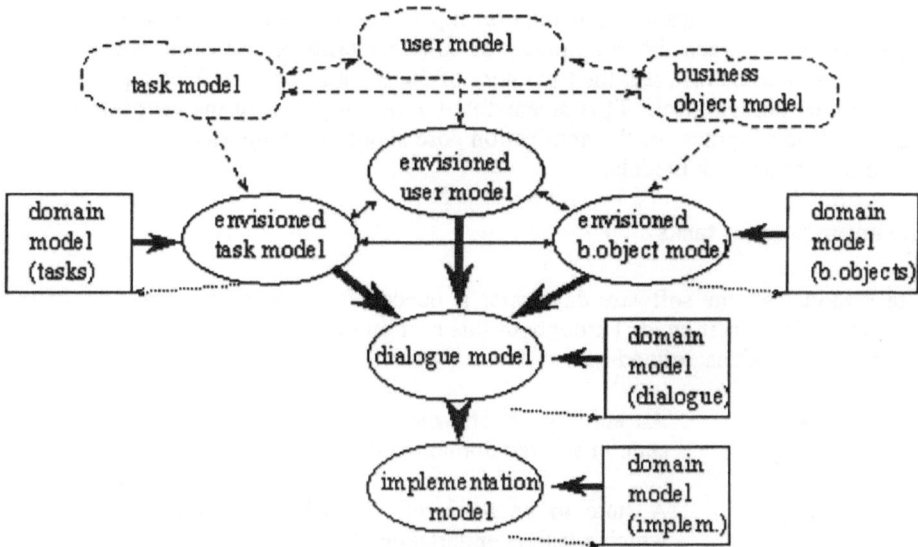

Fig. 2. Relationships between models in case of existing and envisioned models.

In addition to the different kinds of each category of models in figure 2 different terms according to the previous figures are used. The role of the previous problem domain model is now played by the object model. The problem domain model is now defined in a broader sense. It contains tasks and objects. Originally it has been defined for objects exclusively. However, it makes sense to incorporate into the development of envisioned task models and envisioned object models the specifications of already implemented models. This could significantly increase the reuse of parts of existing models and it could be supported by tools directly. Figure 3 visualises the domains of the different models and their relationships.

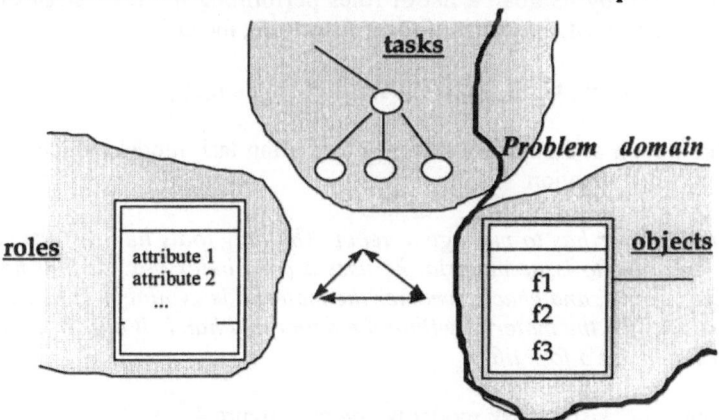

Fig. 3. Relationships between models and problem domain.

3   Models to Support Programming

In the following we discuss the relationship between design and implementation. Since the gap between the community of software ergonomic people and software engineers should be bridged, the treatment of the models has to reflect support to the development process itself. That means that the development of the user interface as well as the development of the application core should be supported. We will at first have a look at the task models.

The importance of tasks

A task model for the software developer is needed for proper understanding of the application domain at hand. Throughout this section the following terms will be used in specifying tasks as defined below:

Task	An activity which when undertaken results in a change of state in a given domain and satisfies a main goal.
Goal	A state to be achieved; a goal provides the purpose for which a task is undertaken.
Role	Characterises the skills and abilities of a group of users.
Artifact	An object which is essential for a task. Without this object the task can not be performed. The state of this artifact is usually changed in the course of task performance.
Tool	An object which supports the performance of a task. Such a tool can be substituted without changing the intention of a task.

A task is described by its goal, a list of roles performing the task, a list of artifacts which were manipulated, and a list of tools supporting the task.

$$\text{Task} = (\text{ Goal, Role(s), Artifact(s), Tool(s) })$$

We first take a look at a part of a simplified existing task model, which is based on the following work situation.

An administrator has to manage a depot. The only tools he uses are paper and pencil. In order to issue material he uses a card index box. At first he receives the requirements, and checks whether the material is available. If he can find it a worker looks for the material within the depot and hands it out. If required this worker might use a fork lift.

The corresponding existing task model is given in Figure 4.

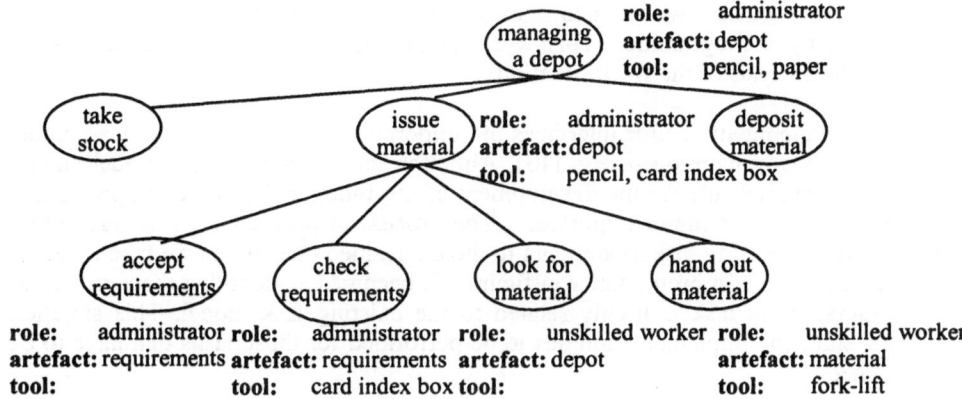

Fig. 4. Part of an existing task model.

After analysing this tasks some ideas of a computerised support are obvious. In the future a software system should support the work of the administrator. The application should execute some of the manually performed tasks (check requirements, look for material) automatically. The following task-model gives some hints how work could be organised in the future.

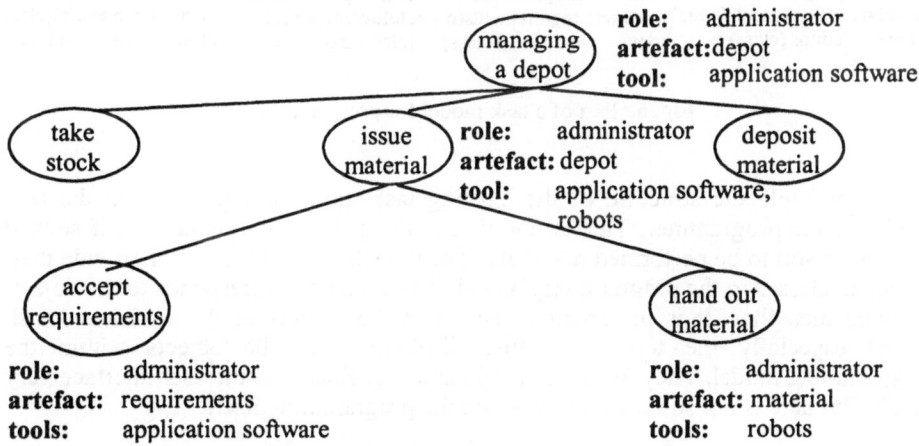

Fig. 5. Part of an envisioned task model.

Figure 5 demonstrates the different tasks, goals, roles, artifacts and tool within the envisioned environment. The checking of environments and the looking for material are done automatically using the application. The tasks 'accept requirements' and 'hand out material' are supported in an interactive way by the forthcoming software.

232

As software engineers we are also interested in some hints how the software can be developed by a programmer. This work should be guided by models developed during the analysis of the work situation.

For the development of user interfaces the importance of the envisioned task model has been already mentioned, e.g. [13]. Although the envisioned task model should also play a crucial role for the development of the functional core of an application, surprisingly, it is of minor importance: The process of programming is much more related to the existing task model than to the envisioned one. When we take a deeper look at the tasks of a programmer in figure 6 it becomes evident that the structure of the programming task is highly related to the existing task model. This situation occurs, since the implementation has to be performed for those tasks that have to be automated.

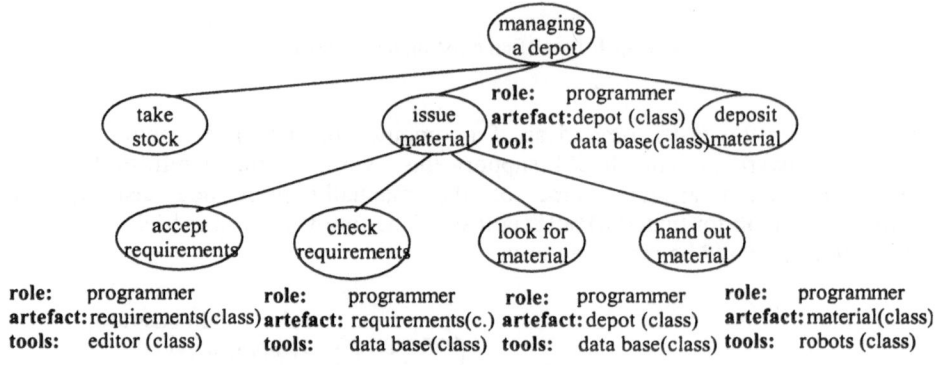

Fig. 6. Part of a task model for programming.

In this example the structure of the existing task model is equivalent to the task model of the programmer. This is not always the case. In particular not, if several tasks have still to be performed manually. The objects of the task model provide their names to classes in the programming model. This situation corresponds to the object-oriented metaphor. It is important to note that the objects of the envisioned task model especially the tools are quite different from the objects within the programming model. They influence the interaction objects of the user interface very much. But here is not so much influence on the programming itself.

At the first moment we were surprised that the programming model is more oriented to the existing task model than to the envisioned task model. But after careful consideration it was clear that the envisioned task model can not drive the implementation process in detail. This could be done by the existing task model exclusively. This model could be a guide line for the development of the task model for the programmer. It contains the information of the task, which have to be implemented by functions of the system. One of these functions is e.g. "check requirements", which is no more available within the envisioned task model.

The importance of objects

We have already mentioned the object-oriented metaphor. Our approach is a unified strategy of structured and object-oriented ideas. Focussing our first analysis on task descriptions does not imply to ignore the importance of defining objects: There are special relationships between artifacts, parts of artifacts and tools, which are specified within the object model. These relationships can be extracted from the task model but they can also guide the development of the task model, in case they already exist. Possible relationships are association, message connection or part of relation.

There exists always a message connection or an association between artifacts and tools. If not, a failure occurred, the models have one or more bugs. An artifact can be composed of parts. In case, this fact becomes evident in the course of task analysis it may drive the detection and definition of subtasks.

Figure 7 tries to visualise the relations between the suggested models during software development.

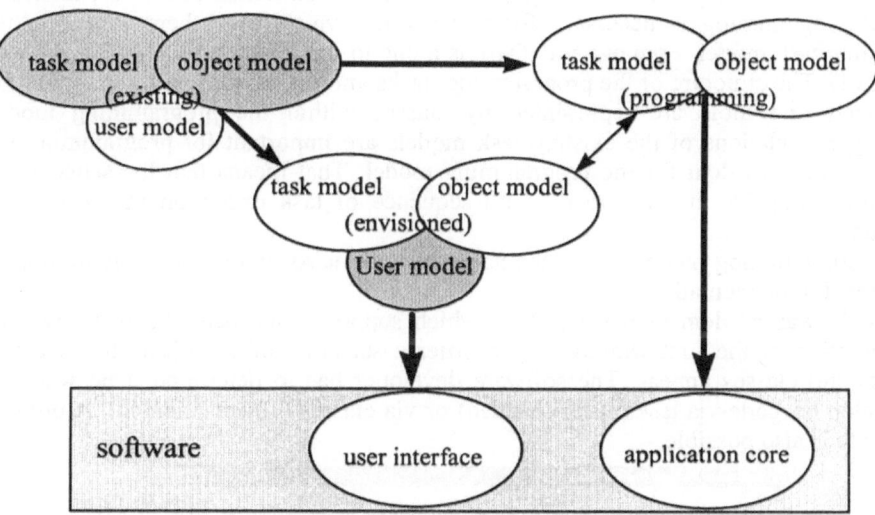

Fig. 7. Relations between all suggested models.

The models of the envisioned work are influenced by the models of the existing work, but they are quite different. But leaves in the tree structure of the envisioned model have often a relation to an inner node in the exiting task model. In this case the corresponding sub-tree is inserted at the leave to get a model for programming. Figure 4 tries to visualise this fact.

234

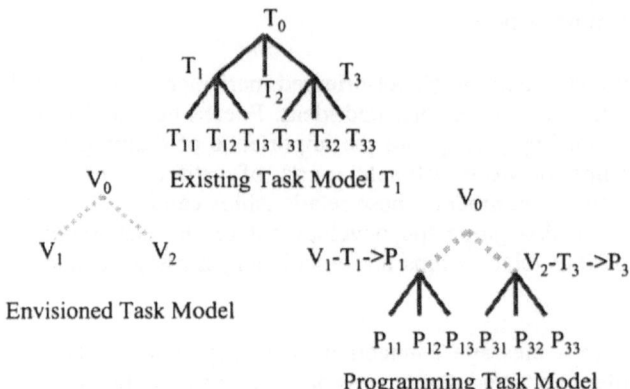

Fig. 8. Possible Relations between Models

It is the aim of Figure 8 to show, that the rough structure of the programming model is constructed according to the envisioned task model. This part of the programming model is used for administrative (navigation) purposes only. The corresponding software supporting these tasks is generated during construction of the user interface. Real programming is necessary for those tasks, which have their origins in the existing task model. Fore every P_i there is a one to one relation to a T_i (But not vice versa !). The structure of the programming tasks and the existing tasks is similar but artifacts and tools are represented by classes within the programming model. Temporal relations of the existing task models are important for programming but they are not evident for the programming model. That means that the sequence of programming has nothing to do with sequence of task execution in the existing model.

The programming model allows the navigation via tasks across the evolving object-oriented implementation.

A tool was implemented using Java which supports this idea. Figure 9 gives an impression of the first window, where after a selection of a project all associated tasks and classes appear. The software developer has to determine if he wants to develop his code via tasks (task-oriented) or via classes (object-oriented). A mixture of both is also possible.

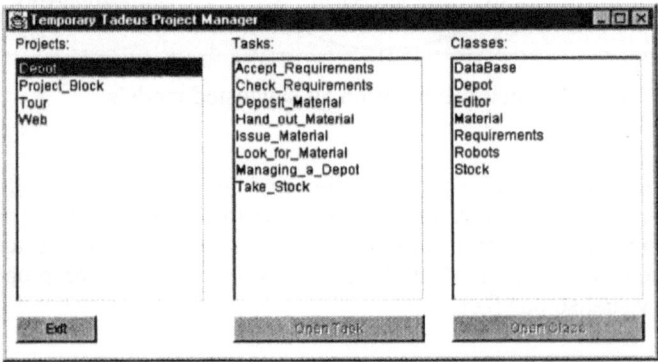

Fig. 9. First View on a Project during Implementation.

Let us first have a look at the "task-oriented" way. A window appears where the selected task (issue) is presented. It is the method of an artifact (Material). All the other method of this artifact are presented under own methods. These methods, methods of artifacts in subtasks and services of tools can be called in the body of the actual method. This can be done by double clicking the corresponding elements of lists. A navigation to subtasks, artifacts and tools is possible. It is also possible to introduce new tools and new classes as part of an artifact in the course of implementation. In this case, the corresponding models have to be updated automatically. The source code itself is shown in a very simplified form at the left of the window in figure 10.

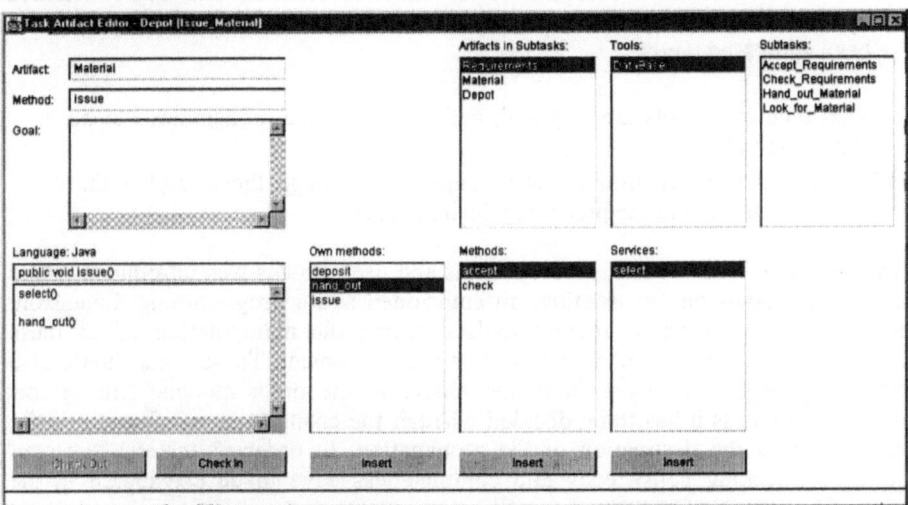

Fig. 10. Tool supporting the suggested kind of programming

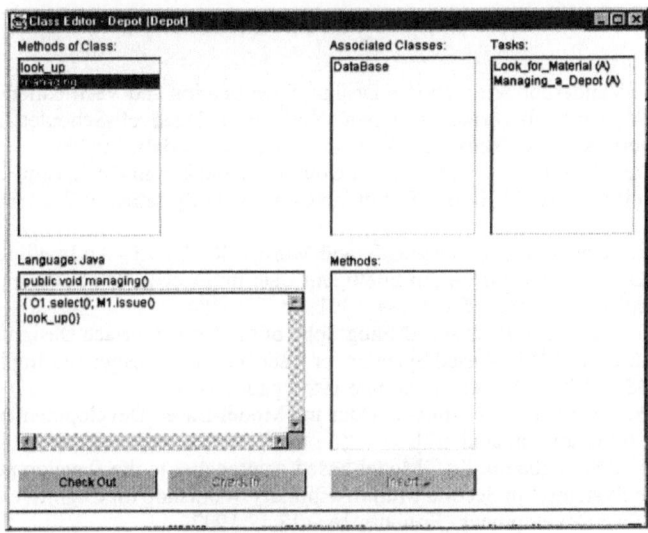

Fig. 11. The view of a class

If the software developer navigates via tools, artifacts or classes the window of figure 11 appears. It allows the coding of methods in the classical form, but additionally navigation via tasks is possible.

4. Conclusions

In this paper we have revealed the origins and different applications of model-based development approaches with respect to task-oriented user interface and general software development. A combination of function-oriented and object-oriented development techniques has been suggested. The crucial issues in this context that have been addressed were:

(i) What type of models are required, and how do these models have to be related mutually.
(ii) How can the programming task be supported through those models that have been defined in the preceding design phase.

A framework of task models, object models and user models was introduced where each of the models has an existing, an envisioned and a programming dimension. These multiple dimensions require tools enabling the manipulation of all these models along the different phases of software development. These tools should also enable to propagate changes from one model to the other models. During this propagation process it has to be decided whether the changes have influence on the model which is the destination of the propagation. In order to achieve this goal algorithms checking consistency and completeness have to be considered in the course of further developments.

References

1. Bodart, F.; Vanderdonckt, J. (Eds.): Design, Specification and Verification of Interactive Systems'96, Springer-Verlag, Wien New York, 1996.Breedvelt-Schouten, F. D.; Paterno, F. D., Severijns, C. A.: Reuseable Structures in Task Models, In:[10].
2. deBaar, D.J.M., Foley, J., Mullet, K.E.: Coupling Application Design and User Interface Design, in Proc. CHI'92 Human Factors in Computing Systems, ACM, 1992, pp. 259-266.
3. Foley, J.D., Kim, W.C., Kovacevic, S. and Murray, K.: UIDE - An Intelligent User Interface Design Environment, in Intelligent User interfaces, J.W. Sullivan, S.W. Tyler (Eds.), Addison Wesley, ACM Press, 1991, pp. 339-384.
4. Foley, J.D, History, Results and Bibliography of the User Interface Design Environment (UIDE), an Early Model-based Systems for User Interface Design and Implementation, in Proc. of DSV-IS'94, Carrara, 8-10 June 1994, pages 3-14.
5. Forbrig, P., Elwert, T: ``Multimedia Data and Model-Based Development of Interactive Systems," In: [Harrison et al. 97].
6. Forbrig, P., Schlungbaum, E.: ``Model-based Approaches to the Development of Interactive Systems," In Second Multidisciplinary Workshop on Cognitive Modeling and User Interface Development, Freiburg 16. - 18.12.1997.

7. Forbrig, P., Stary, C.: "From Task to Dialog: How Many and What Kind of Models do Developers Need ?" CHI Workshop "From Task to Dialogue: Task-Based User Interface Design", 1998, Los Angeles.
8. Elwert et al. 95] Elwert, T., Schlungbaum, E.: Modelling and Generation of Graphical User Interfaces in the TADEUS Approach , In: P. Palanque, R. Bastide (Eds.): Designing, Specification, and Verification of Interactive Systems. Wien, Springer, 1995, S. 193-208.
9. Gorny, P.: EXPOSE - HCI-Counseling for User Interface Design, In K. Nordby et al. (Eds.): Human Computer Interaction, Interact'95, Chapman & Hall, London 1995, p. 297-304.
10. Harrison , M.D.; J.C. Torres (Eds.): Proceeedings of the 4th Eurographics Workshop on Design, Specification and Verification of Interactive Systems, University of Granada, p. 427-440, 1997.
11. Janssen, Ch., Weisbecker, A., Ziegler, J.: Generating User Interfaces from Data Models and Dialogue Net Specifications, in Proc. INTERCHI'93 Human Factors in Computing Systems, ACM/IFIP, 1993, pp. 418-423.
12. Johnson, P.: Human Computer Interaction: Psychology, Task Analysis and Software Engineering, McGRAW HILL BOOK COMPANY, 1992.
13. Johnson, P.; Wilson, S.: Bridging the Generation Gap: From Work Tasks to User Interface Design, in [1].
14. Makopoulos, P.; Johnson, P. (eds): Design, Specification and Verification of Interactive Systems '98, Springer-Verlag, Wien New York, 1998.
15. K.Y. Lim, J. Long, The MUSE Method for Usability Engineering, Cambridge University Press, Cambridge, 1994.
16. Rodriguez, F. G.; Scapin, D. L.: Editing MAD* task descriptions for specifying user interfaces, at both semantic and presentational levels, In: [11].
17. Paterno, F.; Santoro, C.; Tahmassebi, S.: Formal Models for Cooperative Tasks: Concepts and an Application for En-Route Air Traffic Control, in [14].
18. Stary, C.; Vidakis, N.; Mohacsi, St.; Nagelholz, M.: Workflow-Oriented Prototyping of Interactive Systems, Proceedings IEEE COMPSAC'97, 1997.
19. Szekely, P., Luo, P., Neches, R. Beyond Interface Builders: Model-Based Interface Tools, in Proc. INTERCHI'93 Human Factors in Computing Systems, ACM/IFIP, 1993, pp. 383-390.
20. van der Veer, G. C.; van Vliet J. C.: Team Design for Groupware - a View on Structure, 15th Interdisciplinary Workshop on "Informatics an Psychology", Schärding, May 24 - 26, 1994.
21. Waldén, K.; Nerson J.-M.: Seamless Object-oriented Software Architecture, Analysis and Design of Reliable Systems, Prentice Hall, 1995.
22. S. Wilson, P. Johnson, C. Kelly, J. Cunningham, P. Markopoulos, Beyond Hacking: A Model-Based Approach to User Interface Design, in Proc. of HCI'93, pp. 217-231.
23. S. Wilson, P. Johnson, Bridging the Generation Gap: From Work Tasks to User Interface Design, in Proc. of CADUI'96, Namur, Belgium, 5-7 June 96, pp. 77-94.

Usability Properties in Dialog Models

Martijn van Welie, Gerrit C. van der Veer, Anton Eliëns

Vrije Universiteit, Department of Computer Science
De Boelelaan 1081a, 1081 HV Amsterdam, Holland
+31 20 4447788, {martijn,gerrit,eliens}@cs.vu.nl

Abstract. Usability has gained a lot of attention in the design community and it is one of main goals of every design project. Evaluating usability is usually done with end-users after a prototype has been built and there are not many techniques available that allow usability evaluation during the early design phases. Current dialog modeling techniques generally do not deal with usability aspects, as they are often functional based models, dealing only with states and state changes. This paper investigates how usability aspects can be incorporated into dialog models so that usability can be evaluated during the design process without doing usage tests. A set of measurable properties is given which together could give an indication about the usability of the design, This way, some usability aspects can be covered early in the design process without the need for an executable prototype or end-users.

Keywords. Usability, Verification, Validation, Dialog Models.

1   Introduction

In every design, the dialog between the user and the systems needs to be designed. The dialog is concerned with the structural aspects of the communication between the user and the system. At the dialog level, we are not dealing with presentational aspects such as layout and color usage. Many methods and techniques to model the dialog have been proposed but most dialog models can hardly deal with usability aspects. In [1][8]a set of properties for dialog models is given but the focus is only on aspects such as state reachability and interaction-paths. Although some of those properties can be very useful to evaluate, they only cover a very small aspect of usability. Most dialog models are state-based and do not contain information for evaluating other usability properties.

Usability is concerned with many aspects that cannot all be covered by state based models. For instance, the usability of a design strongly depends on the cognitive and motor abilities of the users together with the tasks and the goals they have to achieve. User centered design focuses on the user by involving the user heavily into the iterative design process, thereby ensuring usability. An iterative design process can be very useful but is essentially a trial-and-error kind of process and does not address the underlying problem of how to ensure usability *during* the design process itself. Formal dialog modeling could be very useful for evaluating usability early in the design process without the need of some kind of prototype or end-users. This would allow a more objective evaluation that is not highly dependent on the expertise of a usability expert. However, if a formal dialog model is used with the purpose of early usability evaluation, the dialog model and the properties to be checked *must* give a valid indication of usability. Consequently, there needs to be relation between a framework for usability and the dialog model. Obviously, not all aspects of usability can possibly be evaluated using a dialog model, so it is important to understand how much early usability evaluation is possible using dialog models.

The next sections will first sketch a framework for looking at usability and the relationship with dialog models. Then we will investigate what aspects of usability can be quantified and which cannot, in relation to a dialog model. In the last sections a new dialog modeling technique is presented that allows some usability properties, other than concerning states, to be checked. A small example is given to show what is possible.

1.1 Related Work

Usability evaluation can be done at several stages of design. Approaches such as EMA[2] and ERGOVAL[10] can be applied once a prototype exists and evaluation is done by means of real usage test. Consequently, such approaches cannot be used early in the design process when prototypes do not exist yet. Several techniques exist that model the dialog part of a design and those are used very early in the process. However, most of those techniques only allow a small set of usability properties to be evaluated. GOMS[14] is a technique that focuses on the performance by evaluating the structure of the dialog. It is based on counting the number of steps needed to perform a task and the time required for each task. The properties defined by Abowd[1] are derivable from a state based dialog model and concern state reachability. In our opinion, this is not directly related to usability but more to the correctness of the specification. ETAG[24] addresses consistency by using grammars although the focus is not on determining the level of consistency. In the following sections we also will try to define additional properties to those mentioned in the related work so that dialog models can offer more effective possibilities for early usability evaluation.

2 Usability during Design

User centered design mainly uses iterative design/prototyping as the main driving force. In itself this is a very poor method and is characterized by the "trial and error" principle. It prohibits the preservation of "design knowledge" and the same mistakes could be made repeatedly. In real-life design projects, there are many factors that influence the design process. Time and money are often constraints that prevent iteration in the design process, making the evaluation of usability during the early design stages even more important. When a project is running out of time, the last activities in the design process such as user testing are likely to be skipped. In practice, the skills and experiences of the designers and design guidelines are the main sources for design knowledge. Guidelines preserve design knowledge but skill and experience are easily lost. In [3] it is suggested that *design patterns* may capture some of this design knowledge similar to patterns in Software Engineering. The idea of capturing knowledge of good designs may be attractive but there is no agreement on what *good* design is. A good design can be defined as a design that maximizes the goals of the design within a set of given constraints. Maximizing usability may not always be the main design goal and in practice, money and marketing strategies may dominate the constraints which may lead to less attention to the usability aspects. In each design project there will be conflicting requirements, a well-known fact in requirements engineering. Therefore, it is important that the design which *is* produced and that can not be evaluated as much as desired, is still as good as possible. This can only be achieved if design knowledge is structurally incorporated into design methodology. It is a challenge for formal methods to adequately formalize this knowledge in a way that makes it easy for designers to use and facilitates early usability evaluation.

3   A View on Usability

Before usability aspects are incorporated into dialog modeling, it needs to be clear what usability is and how usability is related to the dialog part of a system. Several authors have given definitions or categorizations of usability alongside guidelines, heuristics, principles and criteria [4,8,21,22]. All the different definitions and principles make usability a confusing concept when actually designing a new system. Usually authors spent a lot of effort trying to find out what is the "best" set of principles or to define a "complete set of heuristics". Although these "aids" are useful, it remains unclear how they are related and they lack a theoretical underpinning. In [26] we introduced a model that gives more structure to the concept of usability. It is a theoretical view on usability that integrates several well-known definitions of usability and puts them into a structure. Although it is a theoretical model, it can also be of practical value when designers have to deal with actual usability problems. We will briefly summarize the structure of the model since the model helps to understand the possibilities and limitations of usability evaluation.

Figure 1 shows the layered model of usability that helps understanding the various aids. On the highest level, the ISO definition of usability is given split up in three aspects: efficiency, effectiveness and satisfaction. This level is a rather abstract way of looking at usability and is not directly applicable in practice. However, it does give three pillars for looking at usability that are based on a well-formed theory[4]. The next level contains a number of *usage indicators* which are indicators of the usability level that can actually be observed in practice when users are at work. Each of these indicators contributes to the abstract aspects of the higher level. For instance, a low error-rate contributes to a better effectiveness and good performance speed indicates good efficiency.

One level lower is the level of *means*. Means cannot be observed in user tests and are not goals by themselves whereas indicators are observable goals. The means are used in "heuristics" for improving one or more of the usage indicators and are consequently not *goals* by themselves. For instance, consistency may have a positive effect on learnability and warnings may reduce errors. On the other hand, there may be good reasons for not complying completely with a platform style.

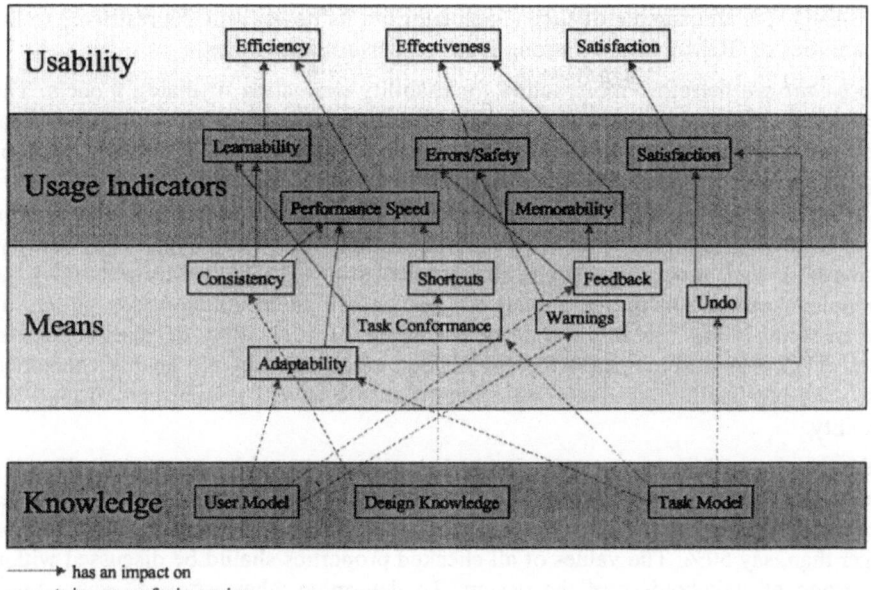

Figure 1 A layered view of usability

Each means can have a positive or negative effect on some of the indicators. The means need to be "used with care" and a designer should take care not to apply them automatically. The best usability results from an optimal use of the means where each means is at a certain "level", somewhere between "none" and "completely/everywhere/all the time". It is up to the designer to find those optimal levels for each means. In order to do that the designer has to use the three knowledge domains (humans, design, and task) to determine the appropriate levels. For example, when design knowledge is applied by using *guidelines,* it is clear that the guidelines should embody the knowledge of *how* changes in use of the means affect the usage indicators.

The means and usage indicators of **Figure 1** are examples and stem from literature[8,17,22]. All of the guidelines and heuristics can give suggestions for other useful means and usage indicators. More research is needed to determine which means are most effective for improving usability. Knowing the impact of a means on usage indicators could then lead to more effective usage of the means.

4 Dialog Modeling and Verification

If a dialog model is to be verified on usability, the *usage indicators* in principle cannot be used since their evaluation is not possible yet, as there is no prototype. However, model based approaches *can* generate a prototype from a collection of models that among other things describe the dialog. In addition, evaluating usability with prototypes is a form of model validation and not model verification. A simulation based on the dialog model can give data about *some* of the usage indicators but there is not much foundation for conclusions; it remains unclear how aspects such as learnability or memorizability can be measured during simulations. The tool

GLEAN[13] is an example of such a simulator but its power remains restricted to the capabilities of GOMS, hence a strong focus on performance times.

The *means* are therefore more suited for usability evaluating of dialog models. The means are not directly in the right "form" because they are often in an intangible form and need to be translated into usability properties. For instance, if consistency helps improving (among others) learnability, then a property could be that "confirmation tasks" are always handled in the same way. Several of such properties can be given for each means. The properties should be measurable, either relatively or absolutely. In addition, such properties should be restricted to properties that are related to the dialog level and not the presentation level. So, "consistent use of colors for buttons" is not an appropriate usability property for usability evaluation of dialog models. Abowd[1] presents some properties for dialog models but they are mainly concerned with state reachability and they consequently do not have a strong relationship with usability.

Although the usability properties should be measurable, their values typically only have a meaning in the context of that design. Some properties may also have a general meaning like a property, "Percentage of Undoable functions" should in any design be larger than, say 50%. The values of all checked properties should be discussed within the group of stakeholders of the design. To determine what a "good" value for a property is, designers need to look at the three knowledge domains that are the basis for the *means*. For instance, a task model is a good source of knowledge in order to determine task conformance and knowledge of the cognitive processes of humans can be used to evaluate memory load or the need for feedback. As can be seen from **Figure 1** each of the knowledge domains discussed in section 3 is important for usability. Case specific attributes such as giving appropriate warnings and task conformance cannot be checked without a formal task model. Other human aspects concerning efficiency are easier to check and can even be measured using current state based models. Effectiveness and satisfaction are harder to measure than efficiency and more information concerning application functionality or the specific case is needed.

5   Dialog Models and Validation

Formally verifying a dialog model alone takes a design out of its context. The design is verified without looking at the tasks users need to do, conventions and styles that are posing constraints, or specific aspects of the intended user group. Validation of a dialog includes the context of the design and opens the possibility to look at other important usability aspects, especially concerning the effectiveness and satisfaction of a design.

5.1 Validating against User Models

Checking a dialog against a user model means looking at the dialog aspects where cognitive and motor skills and limitations are involved. Some aspects of user modeling are easier to deal with than other aspects. Considerable research into user modeling has been done to capture relevant aspects of user behavior when interacting with s system. PUMs[27] is a technique that uses both a user model and a system model to evaluate usability. PUMs does not clearly define any general usability properties and the actual formal proof of properties remains difficult[5].

5.2 Validating against Design Models

Design models only sparsely exist. Source for design knowledge can be found in guidelines, style definitions, standards and design heuristics. For formal evaluation purposes these sources are usually not formal enough and can only be used by humans, as they require a lot of interpretation. However, some attempts have been made to formalize design knowledge and "connect" it to dialog models, see EXPOSE[18] and DIADES-II[7]. The knowledge is usually a mix of dialog and presentation aspects with a strong focus on presentation aspects. Such tools can be very useful in assisting designers very early in the design process. Some tools such as ERGOVAL[10] do an automatic evaluation of a prototype using ergonomic rules. The disadvantages are that a limited amount of information can be extracted out of an executable and the necessity of an executable.

5.3 Validating against Task Models

Verifying a dialog model against a task model is not straightforward. First of all because of the diversity of task models it is not guaranteed that they model the same thing. An important issue in discussions about task models is the question what exactly they describe. Task models for model based systems and other methods like GOMS[14] and ConcurTaskTrees[19] are *prescriptive* task models. Other task models such as TKS[12] and GTA[25] are *descriptive* and focus on modeling the user's task knowledge. A consequence of this distinction is that the meaning of task and object is different. In a system's task model the objects are all part of the system which is not necessarily true for a user task model. Also with a system's task model usually the focus is on *one* user interacting with the system instead of taking into account other users and stake holders, other roles and the environment in which a user may interact with a system.

It is clear that a task model's most obvious contribution is in checking task conformance although this may not be easy to do. However, for other usability means the task model can also be a valuable source. For instance, when determining when and how often warnings should be given by the system the task model should have information about critical tasks and the frequency of those tasks. In order to make a dialog more usable for both novices advanced users, information about the tasks and the different types of users is needed from the task model. Unfortunately, not all task-modeling methods describe all those aspects of the task world[25].

Other approaches such as EMA[2] and USINE[15] use a combination of a task model or interface models and actual usage logs. The actual usage logs are analyzed against the task model. The outcome of the analysis is an annotated user log that still needs to be interpreted by an expert. The properties that are found are mainly related to deviations of user actions compared to the *prescriptive* task model. Such an evaluation is still highly subjective and the method does not provide direct clues on causes of usability problems nor on possible improvements. That has to be done by the expert. A requirement for these approaches is a prototype where logging code has been added. The models used are models that contain both dialog *and* presentational aspects. When analyzing the results it is difficult to assess whether causes of the deviations are related to the presentation aspects, to the dialog, or to the task model.

6 Towards Usability Properties for Dialog Models

In the remainder of the paper, we will focus on automatic usability evaluation based on models that describe the dialog solely and *without* doing any user testing. This will allow very early evaluation by constantly evaluating properties of dialog models that are explicitly related to usability. It would not require any software prototype and designers could make a clear distinction between dialog and presentation aspects. Before we can define any usability properties for dialog models, we need to determine what reasonable usability measures for dialog models are. As said before, usability measures need to be derived from the *means* of **Figure 1** for improving usability. A usability measure says something about the usage of a means by evaluating properties that express the means. In order to define such usability properties we have to look closer at the possible usability measures. There are several restrictions that need to be made. First of all, the usability measures need to concern the dialog only and secondly the assumptions about the behavior of the dialog components need to be restricted in order to keep evaluation as simple as possible. Some approaches such as [11] give a formal definition of the behavior of the components of the dialog. Such a definition would need to describe the complete windowing toolkit that is used and the additional project specific controls that were needed. Using that formal description, more claims can be made than without this knowledge. The connection of components to the system is however important because the basic application functionality is very relevant for usability on the dialog level. A formal description of the application functionality is not considered at the moment and only some properties of functions that are directly relevant for usability evaluation are included.

Since we are interested in expanding the use of dialog modeling for usability evaluation, we need to look further than measures that deal with interaction paths and measures such as reachability of states. In order to define properties for dialog models, it needs to be known which basic concepts should be present in a dialog model.

6.1 Some usability measures for the Dialog

This section will give a list of possible measures. Each measure is informally explained and discussed in the context of a dialog model. The measures are mostly taken from literature on usability, guidelines and modeling techniques together with some new measures. The aim was to come up with a comprehensive list of dialog related usability measures.

Interface feedback

Different functions require several kinds of feedback in response to user actions. Actually, the term feedback is not very good because it implies that all the interactions are initiated by a user, which is not true. A better term would be *interface actions* indicating that the interface acts just as well as a user, sometimes in reaction to user actions but also on its own initiative. Especially in a windowing environment, the system often initiates interaction. Consider an email program that pops up a window notifying the user a new email has arrived in which case the system needs to give feedback because of events that have occurred. For some cases of interaction, it could be stated what kind of feedback is needed.

- A calculation task requires feedback that the system is busy and the user needs to be informed of its progress.

- Functions that cannot be undone should warn the user that the result cannot be undone.

- The goal of the function is to display information.

- A function changes the system state with respect to possible next user actions.

- The system needs input so it has to indicate what user actions are needed.

- The system is in a complex activity with time characteristics that relate to temporal aspects of user input enabling/disabling

In relation to a dialog model, it is clear that it has to be identifiable when feedback or system actions occur, preferably in relation to the function type or the task type.

Forgiving the user

A user should not be punished for unintended actions, for instance when it is not directly clear to the user what a function does. Basically this means that the consequences can be undone either directly using an undo function or indirectly by going through a sequence of actions. Undo could mean that the user can go back to a previous *interface state* but also that the user goes back to the previous *application state*. Being able to go back to the previous interface state does not say too much about "forgiving the user" because the application state may not have been undone. Offering the possibility to undo complete actions may strongly impact learnability and error rate as well as the satisfaction of the user. In terms of the dialog model, it has to be known if a function is (or will be) undoable and if the previous interface state can be reached. In addition, it needs to be known if the function has *side-effects* that are not undone if the function is undone.

Consistency and platform conformability

Being consistent within one application and being consistent with a platform style also helps improves learnability and the error rate. It makes a system more predictable for the user. Consistency could be found in many aspects of a dialog:

- A message window always contains an OK button.

- Every confirmation window always contains an OK and CANCEL button

- Functions on the same object are selected in the same way.

Each platform has its own style definitions, the Apple, Windows, and Motif standards explicitly define their styles. Some aspects of a style are shared between styles and others are style specific. Concerning the dialog one could verify several properties such as:

- The number of levels of submenus. In the Apple guidelines it is stated that there should not be more than one level of submenu's

- Closing a document window should ask for saving when needed.

- Menu entries that require additional input before execution should have (…) added to the text.

In order to find out if similar tasks are handled the same way, it has to be possible to identify small structured sequences in the dialog model. For other aspects the interactors would need to be of a certain widget type, allowing platform rules to be checked.

Total number of enabled visual functions

There is a clear difference between the number of functions that are enabled at one point and the functions that have an access path of length one. In a complex application, the number of active functions can be quite large while the number of directly accessible functions should not be very high, perhaps maximally 50. For example, imagine Word with all the toolbars active. This obviously violates this rule and is bad for usability. Reducing the number of directly accessible functions reduces the cognitive load of the user. When the user has to compare things the number 7 plus or minus 2 is a good guideline [6] but for localizing tasks where the user knows what to look for this number can be much higher, assuming the search space is in some way structured and the user knows or understands the structure[23]. The question remains if the concept of having many toolbars is bad per se or that users are just not prevented from abusing them. In a WIMP interface the fact that the button is visible is the only guarantee that the button can be selected so visibility is closely related to enabling or disabling of functions.

Interaction Path Length

Each function has a path of interactions before it is selected. The path can be a number of keypresses or mouse movement and mouseclicks. Methods such as GOMS have already tried to make prediction about the user performance based on the path length. The path length is a good indicator for the speed of performance (efficiency) and is also of interest in determining how usable the system can be for novices and experts. If shortcuts are added more paths of different length are available.

Modalness of windows

Modal windows are windows that get all device inputs so that no other windows get input. The modal window is then the active window and the user cannot change focus to another window that belongs to the same application. When a task has parallel subtasks, none of the subtasks is allowed to be modal since that would violate the parallelism. When a window is modal only the contained widgets are enabled and the rest is disabled. Modal *non-movable* windows should probably always be avoided since they even prevent the user from looking at possibly relevant information elsewhere on the screen. Modal windows are often the result of platform limitations on multitasking capabilities or because of limitations in the toolkit that is being used. They force the user into a certain state that does not allow them to do anything else and should therefore be used with caution. Although non-modal dialog windows increase the cognitive load of the user, it depends on the task whether this is desired or not. In a dialog model modalness can be detected when one component or function disables all components that are not part of it.

Preventing errors

In certain tasks it may be good to warn the user for the consequences. Typically, these are tasks that cannot be undone by the application such as tasks or actions towards the network or any other external process. For instance, opening a valve in an oil refinery is not simply undone by closing the value and the operator has to use other means to deal with the resulting situation. When the task can be undone, no warning is necessary in general. When dealing with critical task a warning is also good to make the user more aware of his decision. In such a task undoing the function may take to much time and lead to hazardous situations. When a warning is needed depends on the task of the user, the type of user and the system function.

Task type classifications and interface feedback

Both tasks done by the user and tasks done by the system can be classified. Paterno gives a classification of task types in his TLIM[19] method. For instance a calculating task may involve progress feedback. Similar a formfilling task may involve help on the meaning of the form fields. Application tasks types include report, compare, give information, locate, group of data, control, store/retrieve etc. User task types could be to select, edit, control (confirm), ask for help, navigate etc.

Adaptability of function access

A simplistic view on an application would regard an application as a collection of functions that can be used. Interaction styles make these functions available. However, it may often be wise to provide more than one access path to the function so that for instance advanced users can bypass a menu using a shortcut. Even better would be to have functionality to change the contents of toolbars so that the user can adapt his access paths.

6.2 Extracting the concepts

A dialog model that allows usability to be evaluated needs to be based on a set of concepts that enable the usability to be evaluated. Basically every formal method has a set of concepts that it uses and those concepts should be exactly what is needed in terms of the purpose of the modeling technique. The usability measures that were described show that more concepts than bare states and state changes are needed. The following aspects seem important for usability evaluating of a dialog model:

- Task/Function Typing
- Interaction paths
- Feedback
- Enabling and disabling of interaction objects
- Visibility of interaction objects
- The type of an interaction object
- Function undo-ability and side-effects

Once a dialog model can describe these aspects, we can define usability properties concerning those concepts.

7 DIMUSE

In this section a first sketch of a new dialog modeling method is given that allows some usability properties to be evaluated. DIMUSE (DIalog Modeling for USability Evaluation) is based the concept of interactors[9] and is extended to be able to deal with usability evaluation. The purpose of this dialog modeling technique is to allow usability evaluation so that design choices can be evaluated by their impact on usability properties. The concepts and relationships of DIMUSE were based on the list of possible usability measures that were described in the previous section.

7.1 Basic Concepts

The basic concepts of DIMUSE are interactors, functions, events, and actions. The dialog consists of a structure of interactors on which the user can perform actions. In the end, the actions lead to the execution of a function. In return a function can also perform actions and thereby give feedback to the user. Both functions and interactors are typed. An event is given by the system but is not directly triggered by an action of the user. Essential for the evaluation is that the actions are specified in sufficient detail to determine the usability properties. In addition some extra information about the functions is also needed such as the possibility to undo this function. Sometimes the possibility to undo a function is a design choice but sometimes it may be a given constraint; sending an email just cannot be undone. In other cases it may be undoable but the side effects are not, consider closing/opening a valve in an oil refinery; closing the valve does not undo the fact that fluid has passed through.

7.2 An Example

In order to give an idea of what could be evaluated using DIMUSE a small example will be given. **Figure 2** shows a fraction of a dialog model that describes an email program similar to most commonly found email programs. There is a list of all emails and an email can be viewed by clicking on a list item, which causes a new window to appear: the email viewer. The email viewer has several buttons which lead to the selection of a function.

Interactors can handle several *actions* such as activation and deactivation. One of the parameters of actions is the input device action that triggered the activation and deactivation. In other cases it can be a condition of the application state or interface state. Both the user and the application can be the initiator of interface changes. User initiated changes are actions starting in interactors and application initiated changes start in events or functions.

Figure 2 is a sketch of how a graphical representation could look like. At this point, we are still in the process of determining the exact definitions of the concepts and attributes that are needed to enable usability evaluation. After that, a formal definition of the modeling language and the usability properties can be given.

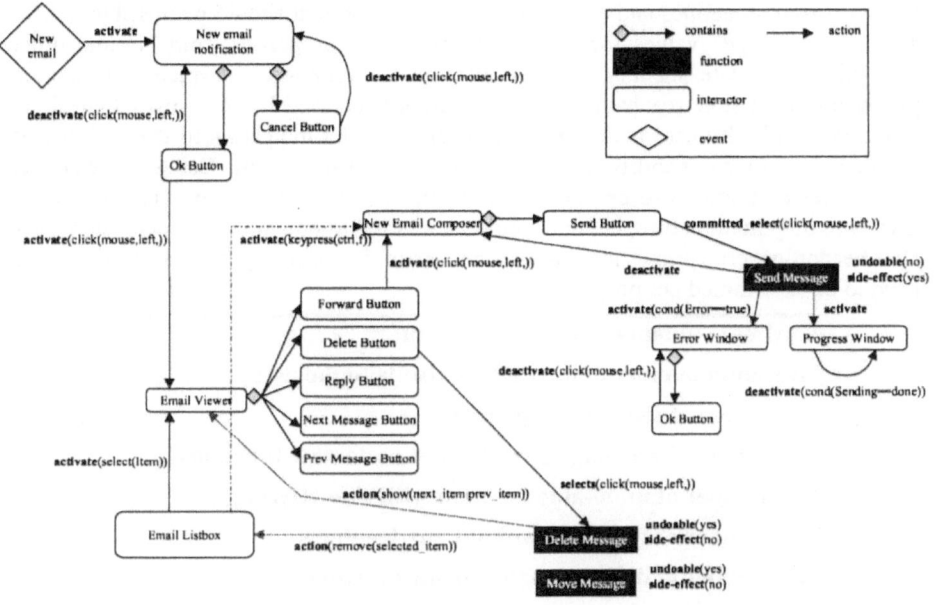

Figure 2 Part of the dialog of an email progam

Using **Figure 2** we can define how the properties of section 6.1 can be detected. For instance, interaction path can be determined by counting the number of action arrows from one interactor to a function. By inspecting activations of interactors, following actions selecting a function we can give meaning to feedback. Re-use of interactors in multiple locations of the dialog together with the containment structure of interactors, can be used to determine consistency properties. Because the dialog model also contains basic information about functions, it is also possible to detect if warnings are given for functions that have side effects.

7.3 Static Property Evaluation

One way of evaluating this dialog model is by determining static properties. The model is taken "as-is" and the value of a property is checked. Checking static properties says something about the "value" of the *means* as described in section 3. It is therefore not valid to make assumptions about the usage indicators, and consequently usability itself. However, such properties can be useful to *compare* design variants. For most means, it is intuitively clear that their value should be within certain ranges. For instance, most designers would agree that it is better to have the possibility to undo "some" actions than no such possibility. Properties can also concern structures within the dialog model. For instance, TAG[20] addresses consistency by using feature grammars; tasks that have a similar structure only differ in features and the user only has to learn the structure once to use all of the similar tasks.   From guidelines and experiences from designers, it should be possible to give some "on average" values for most properties. The properties from [1] and other evaluations of state models only evaluate static properties. Typically these are properties about state reachability which is often supported by some model checking tools. The difficulty here is that in order to give a *valid* indication of the usability of the design, state-reachability does not give much justification. Using the example some other properties can be checked as well, see Table 1. The properties that are given are of general nature, i.e. they could be applied to any dialog model. There may also be non-general properties that can be useful for usability evaluation but those need to be determined per project.

Maximum number of items in a menu
Maximum number of interactors visible to the user
Percentage of undo-able functions
Percentage of warnings given for not undo-able functions
The number of undo-able function with side-effects
The number of functions without any feedback
The number of different paths to one function
The minimum path length to a function
The number of functions reachable without using the mouse
Number of possible deadlocks
The number of unreachable functions

Table 1 Examples of static usability properties

It is clear that it is possible to evaluate more usability properties than only those concerning state reachability. The examples given are still rather simple but they give an indication of what is possible. None of the examples has taken advantage of interactor typing or function typing. Especially using interactor typing, some of the design guidelines concerning for instance menu structuring could be defined as properties.

7.4 Dynamic Property Evaluation
Although it seems to be problematic to make predictions about the usability of a dialog, it is possible to get some data about more dynamic properties related to usage indicators. One way is by making some basic assumptions about users' behavior. Essentially this is what GOMS[14] was based on; the assumption that tasks take an average amount of time depending on the type of task. Using that assumption, a prediction about the speed of performance could be made. Again the absolute value was always under discussion but at least designs could be compared using this assumption and the most favorable could be chosen. Other assumptions could concern the differences in behavior of novices and expert users. A novice uses less shortcuts than an expert and for each a ratio could be defined between shortcut use and menu usage. Using that assumption one can calculate the expected number of interaction

steps needed to perform and action and consequently the performance gain. Going even further one could make assumptions about the chances that a user selects the wrong menu or button. Consequently, one could calculate how often one would select a function that cannot be undone. For those kind of functions extra warnings could be useful.

Estimated path-length for an novice/advanced user
Estimated time to complete a task
Estimated number of errors that are not undo-able
Estimated memory load

Table 2 Examples of dynamic properties

However, assumptions underlying dynamic properties must be approached with caution. Such assumptions must be validated empirically before simulations are possible. Ideally, one would like to have a *simulator* that can be used to evaluate dialog models on a large set of properties both static and dynamic. However at this point it is too early to construct such a simulator and as long as there is not enough information about human behavior to make valid assumptions for a simulator, there cannot be a valid simulator.

8 Discussion

The proposed model is essentially an extension to the existing dialog models. It allows somewhat more verification than plain state based models although it still questionable how good the properties are as an indicator of usability. Usability has many aspects and if we *only* look at the dialog level we certainly do not cover all aspects of usability. At the presentation level there are also a lot of details that can be checked and even some tools have been produced[16]. Especially a style definition can help in checking the platform style conformance which is an important aspect of usability when it comes to aspects such as predictability and learning time. Besides the fact that presentation contributes a lot to usability, dialog and presentation are not completely independent. Consider a dialog describing is a menubar with 8 menu's in a window but the font size is large and it is used on a handheld PC with a resolution of 320x200 pixels so that only the first 5 menus are visible. In that case, there is no problem that may be detected on the dialog level or on the presentation level but together there is a problem.

For all of the static properties it holds, that their absolute value does not give a valid usability indication. Interpretation would become easier if we would know more about their values because of lessons learnt in practice. Such knowledge could be captured in heuristics that would help interpret static properties. Another possibility is to relate the static property to other models such as a user or a task model. How to do this is unclear and especially when relating to for instance *descriptive* task models.

Modeling the dialog remains a very time consuming and nontrivial task but if the resulting dialog model can be used for usability evaluation, the usability of the final outcome is definitely improved and the development time could be shortened, making it worth to engage in the modeling activity.

9 Conclusions

This paper has discussed the possibilities for early usability evaluation of dialog models without the need for prototypes. Using a framework of usability, we have argued that it is possible to do early usability evaluation by determining usability properties in dialog models. Although these properties can be objectively determined, there is still little ground for valid conclusions since their values need to be interpreted in their context. Consequently, the usability properties are more valuable when comparing alternative dialog models than for determining the absolute level of usability. In order to determine the usability properties, a suitable dialog modeling technique is needed since none of the existing techniques fully allow the properties to be determined. We have outlined such a new modeling technique which we will develop further in the near future.

References

1. Abowd, G. D., Wan, H. M., and Monk, A. F. (1995), *A Formal Technique for Automated Dialogue Development*, DIS '95, Ann Arbor MI.

2. Balbo, S. (1994), *EMA: Automatic Analysis Mechanism for the Ergonomic Evaluation of User Interfaces*, CSIRO Technical report 96/44.

3. Bayle, E. (1998), *Putting it All Together: Towards a Pattern Language for Interaction Design*, SIGCHI Bulletin, vol 30, no. 1, pp.17-24.

4. Bevan, N. (1994), *Guidance on Usability*, ISO 9241-11 Ergonomic Requirements for Office Work With VDTs..

5. Butterworth, R., Blandford, A., and Duke, D. (1998), *The Role of Formal Proof in Modeling Interactive Behavior*, DSV-IS, Abingdon, UK, Springer-Verlag.

6. Card, S.K., Moran, T.P. and Newell, A. (1983), *The Psychology of Human-Computer Interaction*, Lawrence Erlbaum Ass, Hillsdale.

7. Dilli, I. and Hoffmann, H. J. (1994), *DIADES-II, a multi-agent user interface design approach with an integrated assesment component*, CHI'94 HCI Bibliography, SIG on Tools for Working with Guidelines.

8. Dix, A., Abowd, G., Beale, R. and Finlay, J. (1998), *Human-Computer Interaction*, Prentice Hall Europe, 1998

9. Duke, D., Faconti, F., Harrison, M. D., and Paternó, F. (1994), *Unifying Views of Interactors*, Proceedings of the Workshop on Advanced Visual Interfaces, Bari, ACM Press.

10. Farenc, C., Palanque, P., and Vanderdonckt, J. (1995), *User Interface Evaluation: is it still usable ?*, Proceedings of 6th International Conference on Human-Computer Interaction HCI International'95, Yokohama, Elsevier Science, Amsterdam.

11. Hussey, Andrew and Carrington, David (1998), *Which Widgets? Deriving Implementations from User-Interface Specifications*, DSV-IS, Abingdon, UK, Springer Verlag.

12. Johnson, P., Johnson, H., Waddington, R. and Shouls, A. (1988), *Task-Related Knowledge Structures: Analysis, Modeling and Application*, in: Jones, D. M. and Winder, R., People and Computers IV pp. 35-62, University Press, Cambridge.

13. Kieras, D. E., Wood, S. D., Abotel, K., and Hornof, A. (1995), *GLEAN: A Computer-Based Tool for Rapid GOMS Model Usability Evaluation of User Interface Designs*, Proceedings of UIST '95, Pittsburgh, PA, ACM Press.

14. Kieras, D. and Polson, P.G. (1985), *An approach to the formal analysis of user complexity*, International Journal of Man-Machine Studies, vol 22, no. 365-394.

15. Lecerof, A. and Paterno, F. (1998), *Automatic Support for Usability Evaluation*, IEEE Transactions on Software Engineering, vol 24, no. 10, pp.863-888.

16. Mahajan, R. and Shneiderman, B. (1995), *A Familiy of User Interface Consistency Checking Tools*, CS-TR-3472.

17. Nielsen, J. (1993), *Usability Engineering*, Academic Press, London, 1993

18. P. Gorny (1995), *EXPOSE, HCI-Counseling for User Interface Design*, Human Computer Interaction - Interact '95, Lillehammer, Norway, Chapman & Hall.

19. Paterno, F. D., Mancini, C., and Meniconi, S. (1997), *ConcurTaskTrees: A Diagrammatic Notation for Specifying Task Models*, Proceedings of Interact '97, Sydney, Chapman & Hall.

20. Payne, S.J. and Green, T.R.G. (1989), *Task-Action Grammar: the model and its developments*, in: Diaper, D., Task Analysis for Human-Computer Interaction, Ellis Horwood, Cambridge MA.

21. Scapin, D.L. and Bastien, J.M.C. (1997), *Ergonomic criteria for evaluating the ergonomic quality of interactive systems*, Behaviour & Information Technology, vol 16, no. 4/5, pp.220-231.

22. Shneiderman, B. (1998), *Designing the User Interface*, Addison-Wesley Publishing Company, USA, 1998

23. Smith and Mosier (1986), *Guidelines for Designing User Interface Software*, MITRE, 1986

24. Tauber, M. J. (1990), *ETAG: Extended Task Action Grammar - a language for the description of the user's task language*, Proceedings of INTERACT '90, Amsterdam, Elsevier, Amsterdam.

25. van Welie, M., van der Veer, G. C., and Eliëns, A. (1998), *An Ontology for Task World Models*, Proceedings of DSV-IS98, Abingdon UK, Springer-Verlag, Wien.

26. van Welie, M., van der Veer, G. C., and Eliëns, A. (1999), *Breaking down Usability*, Proceedings of Interact '99, Edinburgh, Scotland.

27. Young, R. M., Green, T. R. G., and Simon, T. (1989), *Programmable user models for predictive evaluation of interface designs*, CHI '89 Conference Proceedings: Human factors in Computings Systems, ACM Press.

Cross-Contextual Reference in Human-Computer Interaction

Jon Rowson, Peter Johnson, Graham White

Department of Computer Science
Queen Mary & Westfield College, University of London
London E1 4NS, UK

email: {jon,pete,graham}@dcs.qmw.ac.uk

1 Introduction

One of the themes of this year's workshop is the challenge of designing usable systems that make use of shared environments. Based on this, one of the scenarios selected for discussion by the working groups consists of "genuinely co-operative applications, involving concurrent interaction between multiple parties in some form of shared world".

This position paper deals with just one aspect of this envisaged interaction across contexts with other artefacts or people; namely how both users and interface software refer to shared entities from their own various contexts. These entities (which may be objects, processes or tasks) can often be referred to by users and interfaces by means of full, unambiguous descriptive terms but it is usually the case that these are far too elaborate for normal use. Much more frequently references to entities are made via incomplete descriptions or using no description at all (e.g. by a gesture).

In this paper we hope to demonstrate that such 'cross-contextual reference' in general, and 'non-descriptive reference' in particular, is an important class of problem common to many kinds of human-computer interaction. The paper includes a preliminary analysis of some of the main issues surrounding the problem including a simple classification of some common classes of referential device. The rest of the paper consists of a discussion of the themes and aims of our research and an account of the multi-disciplinary research methodologies we are employing.

2 Description and reference in human-computer interaction

To introduce the problem of reference in human-computer interaction, consider the following two simple events that may occur when browsing a web site.

- We select a link to indicate to our web browser that we wish to view a new page. The link may present a brief description of the content of the page but typically does not contain any information about its location.

- We issue the browser command 'Back' to re-visit the previous page without explicitly stating which page it is.

If we now remember that web pages themselves may contain links for navigating within a web site (one of which may be labelled 'Back' perhaps?), then it should be apparent that there is at least the potential for confusion in even the simple use of non-descriptive references. Still more potential problems emerge in the following scenario.

- In opening a page we indicate to our web browser that we wish to view it in a new window. In this new window we find that there is no previous page to go back to.

This situation arises because the web browser creates not just a new window but a new browsing context with its own, initially empty, history list of previous pages visited. So, to understand the meaning of 'Back' in particular, and to navigate successfully in general (e.g. to know how to visit in one context a page already visited in another), the user must be quite aware of these local browsing contexts. But the way the local and global histories are managed by the browser and the facilities for sharing items between these contexts may be quite unclear. One well-known program, for example, allows the user to view the local histories but not the global one and another allows precisely the opposite. In both cases though, the meaning of 'Back' becomes still more opaque when frames are involved (more hidden contexts)!

The examples used above are, we believe, neither contrived nor constrained to the sometimes innocuous activity of web browsing. On the contrary, we claim that the use of non-descriptive reference has become pervasive and ubiquitous throughout user interfaces of all kinds including those to operating and file systems, databases, generic office tools and special-purpose applications (especially those involving multi-media interfaces or virtual environments).

We claim further that the treatment of cross-contextual reference plays an extremely sensitive and important role in the usability of an interface and yet has, so far, received virtually no systematic attention from HCI researchers and designers. One reason we suggest for this is that the extent of such referencing is strongly dependent on the number and range of contexts in which people are enabled to work while using interactive systems. It is only quite recent developments in generic interactive computing technology (e.g. GUIs, multi-media interfaces, virtual environments) that have enabled the production of working environments involving multiple contexts and until now this has mostly been constrained within the boundaries of individual applications. It is more recently still that the potential inherent in the technology for linking and sharing information across different applications and tasks has been envisaged, let alone exploited in any systematic way.

As we suggested in our introduction the development of mobile computing is now producing a similar demand for linking information across devices as well. The scenarios included in working group problem 2 of this workshop raise the issue of how to enable various co-operating parties to refer non-descriptively but unambiguously, perhaps through the use of gestures, to a common piece of information whose representation is dependent on the device in question. A further example of this requirement for linking of information across devices can be found in the design of interfaces for hand-held devices that enable access to larger, existing systems. Here the applications and interface mechanisms of the original systems need to be re-contextualized to suit the very different characteristics of these mobile devices.

3 Issues in cross-contextual reference

The range of entities referred to across contexts cannot easily be delimited (it includes files, programs, commands, documents, drawings, videos and multi-media objects) and neither can the range of items used as references (names, aliases, hyperlinks, graphical objects, agents and gestures). What can be observed though is that cross-contextual references generally employ one of a small class of referential devices for their effect as illustrated by the following examples:

- There may be a description which is sufficient to identify the referent and which does so in any context. For example, a full pathname uniquely identifies a file within a filestore. We will call terms like this *fully descriptive*.

- There may be a description which identifies the referent on the first occasion of use, whereas on subsequent occasions some other referential device refers to the same object, whether or not the original description now applies to it. For example, while word-processing we may insert a bookmark to the last paragraph in the document. The bookmark will subsequently refer precisely to that paragraph, whether or not it is still the last. These subsequent references are typically not fully descriptive and we say that they are of *anaphoric type*.

- We may refer to an item by a demonstrative (or some other gesture) with no overt descriptive content at all. An example of this is a hyperlink on a web page (labelled, perhaps, 'Click here'). Because we do not have a description of the page location, the dichotomy given in the previous example does not arise and subsequent references will be to that object. We say that references like this are of *demonstrative type*.

- *Mixed types* are also possible. For example, we may open a program for editing using only its name in the current working directory; this is an example of a partially descriptive reference. Subsequently, the editor will still display the same file and will save it to the directory which was current when it was opened, even if the current working directory has since changed.

The spectrum of referential devices described above is common to many different media of interaction and we find similarly structured distinctions employed in language, for example. In considering human-computer interaction though, both descriptive and non-descriptive forms of behaviour can be directly motivated in terms of task performance. We want to find entities conforming to descriptions because these descriptions may relate to the requirements of a task (the end of a document, say, because we want to add a final paragraph). On the other hand, we want to refer to persistent entities (e.g. 'the place where we still have to insert a reference to the literature' because we want to return to 'that place' at a later date, even though its position in the document may change due to subsequent editing). Similarly, in computer-supported collaborative work different people have their own view of the environment and that may differ from their co-worker's view. When they need to refer jointly to objects identified purely demonstratively (e.g. by pointing on the desktop) the two workers must evolve an acceptable form of reference across their own working environments to support this communication.

A central issue in cross-contextual working is the identity of objects. When we use computer systems we are encouraged, partly by many of the metaphors of the user interface, to think of objects as having a persistent identity across contexts. We can, for example, move a file around between windows and we think of it as being 'the same file' in these different locations. Referential devices such as aliases (in the Macintosh file system) or bookmarks (in web browsers) may often assist this process of re-identification. Sometimes, of course, the practical realization provided by the software will fall short of the intuitive concept being appealed to by the metaphor. For example, MacOS aliases track files very well so long as they move within a single volume but as soon as they are copied across volumes the identification breaks down. Identifying web pages is even more problematic as there is currently no support other than URLs and these identify pages only so long as they are not moved or renamed. Users, on the other hand, often want to keep track of a page under these circumstances.

4 Research programme and methodology

Our research is initially aimed at developing a theoretical framework that provides an explanatory understanding of how cross-contextual reference can work as intended in a range of situations and also how it can break down. The work is multi-disciplinary and draws on diverse theories and models from HCI, linguistics, psycholinguistics, logic and computer science. The focus of the empirical research required for the construction of the theory is mobile medical applications with which we are involved in other research work. This includes diabetes patient care across clinicians and patients and the remote, in-home monitoring of patients with heart and respiratory conditions along with the interaction with clinicians at a medical centre.

This framework will subsequently provide the basis for deriving two applied representations of the theory; a formal semantics of cross-contextual reference and a collection of user interface design principles. Both of these are designed to support the practical application of the theory to the design of human-computer interaction. Further empirical work will evaluate the practical applicability of these derived forms.

The following sections introduce a small number of selected aspects of the research.

4.1 A theory of cross-contextual reference

Task Knowledge Structures The theory of Task Knowledge Structures (TKS) [1] forms the underlying basis for our research. In particular, we are using the TKS principles of 'categorical structuring' and 'procedural dependency' to relate references and contexts to user tasks. The former of these principles is derived from the notion of similarity between concepts and predicts that users will group actions on the same object to form subtasks. This puts an emphasis on the taxonomy that these concepts inhabit and, consequently, on the assignment of the objects occurring in a task knowledge structure to some appropriate conceptual taxonomy. The principle of procedural dependency concerns actions and predicts that users form conceptual structures by grouping actions that are related by goal dependencies. In turn this new research is extending and generalizing TKS via the development of a richer semantics.

Scope, contexts and tasks   The members of a pair of contexts such that a referential device used in one of them can also be referred to in the other are generally closely related. This relation is usually referred to as 'scope' and we say that a context is or is not in the scope of a device used in another context.

Scope is particularly relevant to the semantics of demonstrative and mixed type references. Suppose, for example, that we refer to 'the last paragraph in the document' at some time and later refer to 'that paragraph' when it is no longer the last one. The two instances define two different contexts and the scope of the original description cannot be extended to the later context (because the item it refers to fails to be 'the last' there). A demonstrative reference to 'that paragraph', however, will still (provided it has not been erased) be in scope in the later context. In the linguistic case a systematic account of the semantics of demonstrative and descriptive expressions has also been given in terms of scope [2] but it should be noted that, in contrast to this, we do not necessarily have a linear time line and that scope in the HCI case may be strongly task-related. We may, for example, have several windows open simultaneously as part of a single user task. Here, scope for the application is window-related, for the user it is task-related and we usually require a correspondence between the two.

4.2 Supporting the application of the theory

Formal semantics   Much related work has been done in other areas, particularly in logic, semantics and programming languages, to show that the development of a formal semantics for cross-contextual reference in human-computer interaction is a plausible goal. There are, however, sufficient differences from these other domains that results from them cannot simply be transcribed into the HCI field.

One requirement will be to provide both procedural and denotational descriptions of the referential devices. Procedural accounts are necessary in order to describe the role of the devices in user interaction while denotational accounts allow us both to compare different procedural solutions to the same task and to reason about the correctness of an interface. Indeed, these issues arise particularly acutely in human-computer interaction since interfaces can be used in many different ways and there may be many different procedures which accomplish the same task. What is required, therefore, is to be able to reason uniformly about the semantics of references both within and across tasks. This type of reasoning will generally relate to what are called 'reliability' properties in the classification given in [3].

The standard treatment of textual anaphora, due to Kamp [4], gives an informal, narrative description of how anaphora resolution takes place during text processing. In addition, there have been several recent suggestions (e.g. [5], [6]) for relating the procedural treatment of anaphora with a compositional, denotational semantics, generally using linear logic. We aim to formulate this relationship in a novel way by treating the procedural semantics in the π-calculus and then by using the known connections between the π-calculus and linear logic [7].

Design principles Our second applied representation consists of a collection of design principles which directly address user interface designers.

Consider the following use of an anaphoric type reference in mixed form.

- We open a folder that contains a file and then open the file in a word-processor, which now refers to the file just by its name. This extremely frequent procedure can, however, lead to ambiguity and confusion since we may have other folders open which also contain files of the same name. Conversely, we can have several documents of a given name open in our word-processor and yet be unable to know which one corresponds to a file in an open folder that is visually present in an open window.

Support for disambiguation in this and similar cases, if provided for at all by an operating system, is usually asymmetrical. For example, disambiguation may be supported when we have many files with the same name open in an application but does not seem to be explicitly supported in the opposite direction. A user interface design principle that would promote support of a symmetrical approach though could be "*There should always be a perceptible connection between the visible referents of visible references*". This time we have an example of a 'visibility' property in the classification of [3] and clearly the work of [8] on the specification of visual presentations is relevant here.

4.3 Usability

One further aspect of our research concerns the usability of interface techniques to support cross-contextual reference. Usually we would expect a correspondence to be maintained between the user's conceptual scheme and that presented by the user interface. Apparent divergences between them, however, may sometimes be desired. For example,

- I may be presented with a view that includes some descriptive component and perform some operation on it. When presented with the view again, perhaps slightly changed this time, I may not re-read the descriptive component but may simply remember its general appearance and select an area in a similar location to the previous one.

When the interface presents the view again then, it takes care to maintain the general layout as well as the explicit descriptive content in order to allow the use of location as a cue. Such re-use, however, may not always be desired, perhaps because the view has changed more than the user realizes, in which case the presentation should be such as to prevent this kind of re-use. Considerations such as these concern the 'reachability' properties of the interface [3].

5 Conclusion

We have referred above to the dependence of multi-context working environments on quite recent developments in interactive computing technology. Where efforts have been made to provide some sharing of information across tasks this has so far generally been achieved by incorporating the separate functions into a single program (e.g. internet applications with their component web browser, e-mail handler etc.). Unfortunately this turns out to be merely a convenient but unsustainable fix for the underlying problem of how to link information across contexts in general. Future areas of growth that we can expect to benefit especially from effective techniques for providing this linking include mobile, web-based and CSCW applications, especially those employing multi-media interaction since this usually implies an increase in the amount of cross-contextual working.

The issue we raised concerning the identity of objects across contexts can also be shown to be of particular importance in current and future developments in cross-contextual working. Our aims here are to provide a coherent account of how the identity of objects is, or can be, maintained across changes of context during interaction and to indicate what is required of practical implementations to support these concepts of, say, 'the same file', 'the same email message' or 'the same web page'. This, however, might imply significant changes in the methods of support (just as the introduction of aliases into the Macintosh operating system itself required the creation of the concept of a file identification number). The recent IMAP protocol anticipates some of this by identifying email messages globally by a unique identifier rather than by a position in the mail queue on a particular computer. In the case of web pages though, there are rather different problems since pages that come with frames or that are constructed by scripts are virtual entities created in real-time. Some browsers do attempt to provide partial support for this, via the bookmarking of framesets together with their state, but they still lack a clear, task-related semantics that tells us what it is to be 'the same web page'.

Other research of importance and relevance to us that has demonstrated awareness of the significance of contexts in interaction is that of Dix (e.g. [9] which concerns the semantics of some selected context-dependent operations). Our research in general also shares many of the wider aims of the 'syndetic modelling' approach (e.g. [10]) which is concerned with combining cognitive models of the user with formal system models. We hope that our work will complement these approaches and be able to extend them with useful methods and results.

6 References

[1]   H.Johnson, P.Johnson "Task knowledge structures: psychological basis and integration into systems design", *Acta Psychologica* **78** (1991), pp. 3-26

[2]   L.Linsky (ed.) *Reference and Modality*, Oxford Readings in Philosophy, Oxford University Press, 1971

[3]   J.C.Campos, M.D.Harrison "Formally verifying interactive systems: a review". In M.D.Harrison, J.C.Torres (eds.) *Design, Specification and Verification of Interactive Systems '97, Proc. of the 4th. International Eurographics Workshop*, Granada, Spain, Springer (1997), pp. 109-124

[4]   H.Kamp "A theory of truth and semantic representation", in J.A.G.Groenendijk, T.M.Janssen et al. (eds.) *Formal Methods in the Study of Language Part 1*, Amsterdam: Mathematisch Centrum, (1981) no. 135 in Mathematical Centre Tracts, pp. 277-322

[5]   J. van Eijck, H.Kamp "Representing discourse in context". In J.van Benthem, A.ter Meulen (eds.) *Handbook of Logic and Language*, Elsevier, 1997, chapter 3

[6]   K.Terui "Anaphoric linking at run time: a type-logical account of discourse representation", Tech. Rep. LP-1997-17, Institute for Logic, Language and Computation, Amsterdam, 1998

[7]   G.Bellin, P.J.Scott "On the π- calculus and linear logic", *Theoretical Computer Science* **135** (1994), pp. 11-65

[8]   G.Doherty, M.D.Harrison "A representational approach to the specification of presentations". In M.D.Harrison, J.C.Torres (eds.) *Design, Specification and Verification of Interactive Systems '97, Proc. of the 4th. International Eurographics Workshop*, Granada, Spain, Springer (1997), pp. 273-290

[9]   A.J.Dix "Moving between contexts". In P.Palanque, R.Bastide (eds.) *Design, Specification and Verification of Interactive Systems '95, Proc. of the 2nd. International Eurographics Workshop*, Toulouse, France, Springer Wien (1995), pp. 149-173

[10]   D.J.Duke, P.J.Barnard, D.A.Duce, J.May "Systematic development of the human interface". In *APSEC'95: Second Asia Pacific Software Engineering Conference*, IEEE Computer Society Press, 1995, pp.313-321

Modelisation of Co-operative Work

M. Gea, F.L. Gutierrez, J.C. Torres, N. Padilla, M. Cabrera
Dpto. Lenguajes y Sistemas Informáticos. University of Granada
E.T.S.I. Informática. Av. Andalucía, 38. 18071. Granada. Spain.
<*mgea,fgutierr,jctorres, mcabrera*>@ugr.es, npadilla@ualm.es

Abstract: Nowadays, there is an increasing interest in user co-operation and the different ways of accomplishing user tasks. Users share a common scenario simultaneously. In such systems, we must take into account technological aspects as well as human factors. Characteristics involved with users (such as usability and performance) as well as the social and contextual organisation must be studied. By doing so, an abstract model, regarding design and implementation details, allow us to contemplate the efficiency of these properties.

1   The Scenario

Co-operative work allows several users to communicate among themselves while sharing a common scenario. Examples of such systems can be found in the virtual reality environment, where different persons share the virtual space. The co-operative framework has been described in[1] as several participants (P) sharing a common artefact (A). Problems arise from the control of multiple participants over the same artefact, and the underlying user communication process, which is established in the scenario.

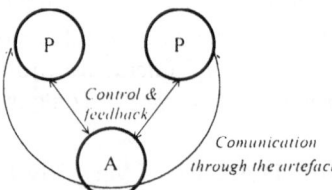

Figure 1. A CSCW system

Collaborative virtual environment involves several participants in the interaction process. For example, on a virtual CAD studio we may find several people taking part of the design process: the architect, the engineer and the client. They share a VR world (a model of a building), and each one plays different *roles*. The architect is responsible for the design of the model (aesthetic appearance as well as its comfort); the engineer is in charge of its robustness while the client is merely an observer of the final result (walking through out the entire virtual model). We must take into account these different user perspectives and different devices (media) of the same fact. In fact, a *media* (a CAD workstation, a palmtop connected by modem to the Internet studio server, a videoconference system, etc.) gives us a partial information of the shared environment. Usually, the network bandwidth is not enough to have a high quality communication or in other cases, the device which is being used has not 3D realistic graphic capabilities. Therefore, we have to infer the underlying co-operative behaviour from the knowledge obtained with these devices.

Some important considerations must be taken into account within this work context.

1. Users share the workspace with other participants. The user is working with the computer as well as others people, thus mixing human-computer and human-human interactions.

2. These participants co-operate to perform the user tasks (*"join to win"*). The main aim of these applications is communication improvement and consequently, works performance through the direct communication among participants.

3. These participants may have different privileges within the workspace (the architect can modify buildings, but the client can only go through it). Different privileges represent different social organisations of the work assessment)

4. Different ways to perform tasks. A user has different devices (audio, gesture, manipulative) to communicate, and different devices for input (CAD workstation, PDA, text-based display, etc.).

5. Synchronisation. The co-operation is done interactively. Network delays and devices response must be overridden. Each user *"should see the same world at the same time"*

These considerations make the study of these systems more difficult. Within the same scenario we have different mental models (one for each participant), and in some cases, these models may be inconsistent one each other's.

For such scenario, we must look for a model that allows us to contemplate these properties without regarding on internal details. Several approaches can be found on the bibliography. For example, Coutaz[2] proposes an architecture to develop multi-user systems, whereas Paternó[3] establishes a unified framework to capture the co-operative tasks of a collaborative environment in a single concurrent tree model. However, problems with these systems arise from technological and social point of view. The first one focuses on concurrency and synchronisation problems whereas the second one is related with human factors regarding differences in interpretation of any given aspect, the suitability of these tasks and whether this new model establishes an effective work scenario. For the second approach, an abstract model which focuses on relevant systems properties, may be suitable for this purpose.

2 From user to groups: Extending the PIE model

We have focused on an abstract model of the scenario in order to formalise system properties, and one well known is the PIE model[4].

$$P \xrightarrow{\quad I \quad} E$$

Figure 2. The PIE model

A system is viewed as a triple <P, I, E> as follows. **P** denotes the set of sequences from the set of possible commands (**C**) what the user can do. That is:

$$p \in P = seq(c_i \mid c_i \in C)$$

The set **E** denotes the effect space (the set of all possible effects on the system, and finally, **I** is the interpretation function representing the mapping of command sequences to system responses. Some keypoints of this model are:

a) The artefact abstraction. That is, for each input sequence (P), an effect (E) is obtained which will be interpreted as the system state after the command sequence has been performed.

b) The description is abstract enough to allow us to obtain conclusion of the system properties without having to be aware of the internal representation.

This model has been extensively studied. However, it cannot reflect the possibility of co-operation among different participants for any given task. In accordance with the objective presented above, we propose an extension of the PIE model (denominated as the **Extended PIE model**) based on the following relationships.

1. **User-Media mapping**. This function represents the correspondence among users (U) and their available command set. Although the set C denotes the command domain, users may have restricted their participation to a subset of C. Therefore, the command domain may be partitioned as $\wp(C)$, and each partition describes the available command set for a participant. The **m** function represents the mapping from user to their corresponding command set.

$$U \xrightarrow{\quad m \quad} \wp(C)$$

Figure 3. The user media

Therefore, each user (u) has access to a subset of commands $C_u \subseteq C$. Note that devices are used in order to perform commands, and these devices are implicitly captured in the m-function.

2. **The User-PIE model**. The input of a PIE model must take into account the user responsible of it. For that purpose, we can redefine the input sequence P as a sequence of tuples Π (called *user inputs*) as follows:

$$\Pi = (C \times U)^*$$

That is, any input command ($c \in C$) is associated with the user ($u \in U$) responsible for performing it. A valid sequence of inputs is a correlation of pairs represented as follows:

$$C = \{c_1, c_2, .. \ c_n\}, U = \{u_1, u_2, .. \ u_m\}$$

$$\Pi = (\ C_{i_1}, U_{j_1}\ ) \circ (\ C_{i_2}, U_{j_2}\ ) \circ .. \circ (\ C_{i_k}, U_{j_k}\ ), \quad \forall k, \ i_k \in 1..n, \ j_k \in 1..m \ / \ C_{i_k} \in \wp (C u_{j_k})$$

Trivially, in a single-user system, the Π sequence is equivalent to the P sequence (always represents the same user U = {u}, and it can be overridden).

$$\Pi \xrightarrow{\quad I \quad} E$$

Figure 4. The User-PIE model

The command set in this scenario (a co-operative system based on a VR world) would be composed as follows: walk until location, look at *position*, turn *direction*, pick *something*, move *something*, etc. Restrictions for participant may occur, for example, the client has not privileges to move anything in the model (he cannot change the space), but he can walk and open door picking the door knob.

One important aspect of the effect of a shared environment is to know what each participant is seeing. For example, the client can't see the intrinsic model of such building (skeleton structure, pipes, etc.). PIE model can be extended to a Red-PIE model to describe the display effect. In such a case, the result (**R**) obtained from the interpretation function and the visible appearance on the display (**D**) can be distinguished. In our approach, each user has his own device (in order to simplify the notation, we consider that each user has only one device). At this point, an array of displays D = {d_0, d_1, .. d_i} appears, where the subscript i denotes the device for the i-user. Therefore, the display function is now a collection of functions originating from the current effect (the internal state of the system) to each user display.

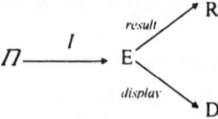

Figure 5. The extended PIE model

It is important to take into account that the result is unique (independent of the number or kind of users) whereas the displays are directly related to users (each user possesses at least one display in the shared environment).

3 Properties

In the VR world, some interesting properties should be studied:

- Users have different display to see the VR world. How can they see "the same" if not everyone has the same graphic capabilities? This may be considered as a display-effect relationship.
- How can they interact with different devices? Is that restriction a constraint in the communication? This subject is related with command availability for users (reachability).
- The users have different roles on the scenario. How can they communicate each other? How can we describe co-operative task or a collaborative system? Does everybody know his functionality (responsibility) on the shared system?
- How can affect the presence of other participants in the single-user tasks? This is related with system properties like predictability.
- What is thinking other participant, or at least, what are they looking at? This may be considered as a human synchronisation problem.

These questions can be formalised on an abstract model. We informally revise some of them. An interesting point is the user accessibility restricted to a subset of devices (also related with **reachability**). For that purpose, this property can be formalised relating users, devices, and input commands; that is, the user performs a command using a device. This relationships is described as follows:

$$C \xrightarrow{\;\delta\;} \Delta$$

Figure 6. The δ-function

The δ-**function** maps commands to devices (where Δ is the domain of input devices, as mouse, keyboard, gestures, speech, etc.). Therefore, we can partitionate the C domain according to a particular device. The following set represents the subset of command that can be performed using the mouse as device:

$$C_{mouse} = \{\, c \in C \mid \delta(c) = mouse \,\} \subseteq C$$

By doing so, the effect of using a particular device can be analysed. For example, a user (u_i) can perform anything in the system with a particular device (in the case study, a hand-held device) if the command set attached with that device allows him to fully reach the space effects (E), that is:

$$I(u_i \times C_{move})^* = I(u_i \times C)^* = E$$

That is, defining $E_{move} = I(u_i \times C_{move})^*$, this is equivalent to say that

$$E_{move} - E = \varnothing$$

Other interesting property is the preservation of the user intentions. **Predictability** is focused on goal that the user wanted to achieve, without affecting the participation of other users in the scenario. For example, the user is preparing to "walk" while engineer and architect discusses technical details. This situation can be expressed as follows:

For any given $r \in R$, representing the effect of a u_i task, the following relationship must be satisfied:

$$\forall u_j \in U, c_k \in C$$
$$r = result(\ I\ (p_1 \circ p_m)\ ) = result\ (\ I\ (p_1 \circ (c_k, u_j) \circ p_m)\ )$$

That is, the interference of other participants does not affect the expected result for a particular user.

The artefact must promote the group task. We characterise user collaboration on this scenario based on the notion of co-operative task. A **task** t is a sequence of input commands that allows us to achieve a desired result in the result (R) domain. That is:

$$t = p \in \Pi \mid\ result(I(p)) = r \in R$$

Therefore, a **co-operative task** is a task that must involve more than one participant in order to achieve the goal. A co-operative task $t_c \in T$ is defined as follows:

$$t_c = (p_0 \circ (c_k, u_i) \circ \ ...\ (c_l, u_j) \circ p_n) \in \Pi \mid u_i \neq u_j$$

A system can be defined as *co-operative* when at least one co-operative task exists.

4 Bibliography

1. A. Dix, J. Finlay, G. Abowd, R. Beale: "Human Computer Interaction, second edition". Prentince Hall, 1998.
2. J. Coutaz: *"PAC-ing the Architecture of Your User Interface"*. In Design, Specification and Verification of Interactive Systems'97. Springer Computer Science, 1997.
3. F. Paternó, C. Santoro, S. Tahmassebi. *"Formal Models for Cooperative Task: Concepts and Application for En-Route Air-Traffic Control"*. In Design, Specification and Verification of Interactive Systems'98. Springer Computer Science, 1998.
4. A. Dix: *"Formal methods for Interactive Systems"*. Academic Press, 1991.

Discussion topics for the DSV-IS'99 working groups

D.J. Duke

Dept. of Computer Science, The University of York, Heslington, York, YO10 5DD, UK
Email: duke@cs.york.ac.uk

As part of the DSV-IS workshop, participants are split randomly into working groups. For the 1999 workshop, three groups were organised and were given two design scenarios as a starting point for discussion. Each group was free to work on either or both of the scenarios. A Rapporteur was appointed for each of the groups, and the following three chapters of these proceedings contain a summary of the points that were raised within the groups.

Two scenarios were chosen, one concerned with haptic interaction, the second with telecollaboration. These reflected the theme for the 1999 workshop, "extending the mind by enriching the senses", and were linked to the research areas of the invited speakers. The purpose of the discussion groups was not to design an interface or artefact, but rather to use the scenarios to generate discussion about the challenges presented to interface design by emerging technologies and trends.

1 Scenario One: Haptic Rendering

Hardware for haptic rendering has advanced to the stage where it is priced within reach of many individuals and research groups. The role of haptics in virtual environments was for example explored in a paper by Srinivasan and Basdogan in a special issue of the journal "Computers & Graphics"[1]. At a time when interface designers are discussing increasing the use of 3D worlds for common interface tasks, for example file-space management, what are the implications of the emergence of haptic devices as a widely available technology? Possible questions include:

- Is haptic feedback simply valid for highly specialised domains such as CAD/CAM and surface modelling, or does it have something to offer end users in more elementary tasks, such as managing their desktop?
- What further advances might be needed in haptic technology before it becomes acceptable to a wide range of end users (apart, that is, from cheap mass-production)?
- How would the availability of haptic rendering techniques affect the design process for interactive systems; what new questions might have to be addressed?
- How well, if at all, can HCI modelling techniques be extended to deal with haptic interaction? There are models of efficiency and workload for visually driven direct manipulation tasks. Are equivalent models emerging for haptics-based tasks? Does the use of haptics have implications for the likelihood of user error, or the kinds of errors that users might make?

---

[1] M.A. Srinivasan and C. Basdogan, *Haptics in virtual environments: taxonomy, research status, and challenges*, Computers & Graphics, Vol. 21, No. 4, pp. 393–404, Pergamon Press, 1997

This last was not intended to be exhaustive, and it was expected that participants would identify further issues related both to haptic rendering in particular, and the introduction of new hardware technology into interaction in general.

2 Scenario Two: Supporting Distributed Collaboration

Although HTML/XML pages on the World Wide Web are probably the most visible and well known manifestation of the Internet, other technologies have also matured to utilise the powerful infrastructure provided by digital networks. Teleconferencing and video-on-demand have been widely discussed, but in both cases the scope for interaction is limited. Genuinely "cooperative" applications, involving concurrent interaction between multiple parties in some form of shared world (for example, "virtual realities" defined in VRML) are largely either research prototypes or of novelty value. One of the many problems that exists is how to support in some sense fair cooperation when different parties may have access to quite different display and input technologies. For example, one person may be using a workstation connected directly to a high-performance network, while a second participant may be using a hand-held or portable device linked to the same network via a mobile telephone. As a concrete example, the two people may be an architect in her office, and a structural engineer on the site of a proposed building. The architect and engineer are attempting to interact with a model of the building in order to accommodate changes. Unable to resolve a design problem, they ask a representative of the client to join the interaction, and attempt to explain the problem. The architect has access to a high-performance CAD workstation with input devices with 6 degrees of freedom. The client has a standard PC equipped with a mouse. The engineer has a mobile machine with limited display space and a touch screen / pen as input device. The following questions were given to the groups as a starting point:

– What modelling techniques exist that would allow the design of such a system to represent and understand the trade-offs involved in supporting the interaction needed to allow a participant to annotate and modify a shared graphical model in this context?
– Does this kind of technology have implications for empirical approaches to usability assessment? Does the fact that the engineer might be working in poor light and a device that is slippery from drizzle make a difference, or is ever considered?
– How well do existing software architectures and development tools cope with the need to (i) support multiple access to shared data, and (ii) work with the limitations imposed by sometimes unreliable communications infrastructure?

As with the first scenario, the groups were free to develop and address their own set of concerns.

Working Group 1 Report

S.P. Smith

Department of Computer Science, University of York
Heslington, York, YO10 5DD, U.K.
shamus@cs.york.ac.uk

1 Participants

Marcelino Cabrera
David Duke
Nicholas Graham
Panos Markopoulos
Miguel Gea Megias
Carmen Santoro
Shamus Smith (Rapporteur)
Martijn van Welie

2 Problem Domain

Working group one focused on problems associated with the use of distributed applications. Initially several possible topics of discussion were considered including the growth of the world wide web (WWW), problems of lag across networks, the high resource requirements of particular tasks in distributed collaboration and the impact on current theories and techniques for design and modelling. The focus was on looking at ways that the use of distributed applications could be improved, especially in the light of new developments in both technology and cognitive science.

The group decided that a concrete example would allow the discussion to proceed in an appropriate context. Figure 1 shows a representation of a group of people collaborating over a network. P1 and P2 are connected by a high speed network link and P3 is connected by a slow speed network link. Two initial problems identified were fragmented communication and lack of update consistency.

Fragmented communication occurs when one of the users on the high speed link (P1) tries to communicate on a channel that is not quickly received by the slow speed user (P3), for example, gesturing (e.g. circling an object) in a shared working space with the mouse pointer. P2 may see and understand the gesture and continue communicating with P1. However, P3 has not seen the gesture and has therefore lost part of the communication. If P1 and P2 are unaware that P3 has not seen the gesture then they may continue communicating and effectively cut P3 out of the collaboration.

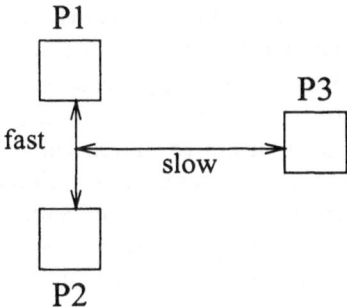

Fig. 1. Problem domain example

A possible solution to this problem would be for each participant to get imme-diate feedback of their actions from the other participants. Therefore each user could verify that their actions were getting received by all the other participants of the collaboration. However this solution requires overheads of both techno-logical (more data to transmit/receive) and cognitive (more data to interpret) natures.

If two participants are using a shared drawing environment and both try to manipulate the same object within the environment, who should get prior-ity? This could cause a problem with updating the consistency of the shared workspace. Typical systems work on time information but if P3 has network lag, their timing information will always be delayed. Therefore the slow updates never get through, due to the slow propagation of events from P3 and again, P3 is cut out of the collaboration.

It was proposed that showing the state of the network to the participants would allow each person in the collaboration to explicitly consider the possible problems that the other participants may be having. Therefore users on a fast link may see that the network is currently slow and take this into consideration when trying to communicate. However, one issue that was raised was that of how this would effect the working environment in terms of the transparency of the network. The group was concerned that the addition of network state information may be seen as an intrusion to the collaborative environment.

These problems then led the discussion to two related issues, fairness and equality in collaborative environments and the effects of degrading the quality of communication channels to promote fairness and equality.

3 Fairness, equality and changing the environment

In an ideal situation, all participants would be in direct communication over a transparent medium. However, what are the effects on the communication as the separation between the users becomes less and less transparent? This may be in consideration of timing concerns, e.g. lag times across a network, or technology associated problems, e.g. one user with a high performance workstation and another with a hand held device. In both cases, there is the problem of how to support some sense of *fair* cooperation when different users are communicating.

An obvious but clumsy way to try and provide a sense of fairness in a collaboration is to enforce equality between the participants. In most cases this would require slowing down the faster users to match the speed of the slower users. However, this was considered an unacceptable solution by the group as in many domains this would make the communication unusable at some minimum levels. For example, collaborations that require video streams as a minimum communication channel could not operate when degrading to just an audio channel.

One solution was to not only slow down the faster users but to try and speed up the slower user. This may involve the use of alternative networks (e.g. closer to the slow user). Also the communication could be split over existing channels. For example, the audio could be moved to a standard telephone/speaker-phone link and the network link reserved for the visual channel, e.g. a shared white-board space. However, if a particular channel is deemed essential for a communication, the pursuit of fairness may lead to the exclusion of slow users.

Another suggestion was that instead of degrading the fast users, allow the slower users to use an alternative mode of communication on a higher bandwidth channel. From the example in Figure 1, P1 may transmit a picture of the town Braga to the other participants. P2 receives the full colour picture while P3 receives a text message "A picture of Braga, Portugal". In this case, P3 suffers a downgrading of modality but only in the output channel. Depending on the context of the collaboration, the modification of the content may be an acceptable alternative.

It was identified early in the discussion that the context and content of the collaborations and the collaborative tasks involved play an important role in deciding how to support/ensure fairness and equality in a distributed working environment and the extent to which the degradation and/or switching of particular communication channels are feasible and acceptable to users.

If equality and a sense of fairness are to be supported, could it be automated by the systems involved? The concern here is whether the separation can be made more transparent by automating the way in which the communication is organised. However, automatic degrading of channels has its' own associated problems.

Users typically adapt to the environment that they are currently faced with. For example, P1 and P2 may identify the problem of the slow link to P3 and socially adapt (e.g. communicate more on the audio channel) to allow P3 to participate. However, if the system has also determined that there is a problem with the environment, it may automatically change the environment setup. This may involve more user adaptation once they realise the change. Therefore there are associated problems with users needing to know the *mode* of the system and what mode they are currently in.

Also there may be important tradeoffs to be considered before any particular channel is re-configured. These can be in the quality of service provided for each channel and the associated input and output overheads that particular technologies require. Therefore the group then began to look at a way of defining the collaborative space.

4 Defining the space

The Clover model [1] was proposed as a basis to define a taxonomy for comparing how different configurations within distributed environments could be compared. The Clover model defines three spaces, the production, the communication and the coordinate spaces. Issues of unfairness, equality and different input/output device all impact on these spaces in different ways. For example, how does degrading the communication space effect the other two spaces and how does coordination get affected when systems lose some of their transparency.

With the first question, the degrading of a communication channel may make the use of particular production spaces unusable e.g. if the visual channel is removed, common workspaces (e.g. virtual white-board) may become effectively impossible for an environment. While the second concern, awareness of the network and/or awareness of what other people in the collaborative space know about the environment may effect the modes of communication which are used.

One overshadowing concern over much of the discussion is the importance of content and whether lower quality content can be used in particular contexts. This is decided by the domain of application. If we are using the distributed environment to collaborate we may have more flexibility in the quality of the content if alternative communication methods can be matched with the systems current performance, while if we are interested in broadcasting specific content on a particular communication channel then the amount of degradation we will tolerate may be less.

The selection of input and output devices was also identified as an important consideration when looking at the degradation, or quality of service, of an environment. If output is degraded how does this impact on the input? For example if we degrade to an audio only communication and my input device is a 6DoF (degrees of freedom) Spaceball, how does that effect my ability to communicate. This will effect the transparency of the communication within the environment. Therefore there may be serious tradeoffs that need to be considered before degradation is implemented.

Other related questions are who decides whether the tradeoffs involved with a degradation are acceptable and when are they carried out. As mentioned earlier, there is the possibility of automatic system degradation with the associated problem of mode changes for the users.

An extension to the Clover model was then developed as the basis for a framework for both the classification and comparison of different environments. This can be seen in Figure 2.

Again, the three constraint spaces, production, communication and coordination, are presented and example configurations are placed on the horizontal axis. On the left of Figure 2 are the 'ideal' elements, for example 3D, fast, big and colour for production and normal social protocols for coordination, while moving to the right is the degrading of the environment, e.g. to 2D, slow, small and black and white. The ideal for each system can be plotted on the three rows. The vertical column (funnel) represents the coverage that a particular configuration may have. This allows a technology constraint space to be defined over the three Clover spaces. This can be useful for two reasons.

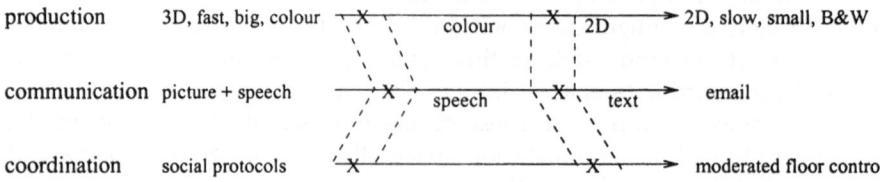

Fig. 2. Extended Clover model

Firstly, the relations between the three spaces can highlight important issues in a systems configuration. For example, if the production value is moved from left to right, how does that effect the values on the other two spaces. More specifically, how is the coverage of constraint spaces effected? Secondly, with multiple systems defined on the diagram, where do their columns overlap. This can be used to measure the ease of collaboration within different environments.

The tradeoffs of altering different environments can be defined in terms of the whole distributed system. This can allow the users in these environments to re-configure their systems as to maximise the components of the three spaces which are deemed most important. For example, if one user is on a fast machine and sees that other participants are on slower machines 1) there is no point in him speeding up his system and 2) he can see the tradeoffs of either degrading a particular channel in the communication or reducing the production overhead.

5 The future

As technology matures and the new generation of integrated services are developed, there is increasing scope for collaborative work over distributed applications. The group discussed new technologies such as cell phone/hand-held computer combinations and how communication can move from telephony to email to video conferencing and sharing/sending documents of different media types (through attachments and WWW based media).

The overriding motivation is that we want access to shared workspaces and we therefore need a way of managing the tradeoffs that are necessary when working with mobile and small scale systems. An important consideration is knowledge of what others are perceiving and how that information can be integrated into the way users communicate.

One issue that kept appearing throughout the discussions was the consideration of context dominance. If the context is well defined then the quality of the content can be downgraded. If the content is not important, then it may be possible to discard that media channel or to look at the available tradeoffs of discarding the channel. In some contexts, even if users are only getting a limited experience, they may still wish to participate. Also knowledge of the content may allow users to adapt to the degraded modalities.

Seeing the tradeoffs of different technology may allow minimum requirements for particular tasks, especially in terms of interaction, to be identified. Also base configurations for distributed environments could be defined in terms of the users, the technology and the methods of communication required.

However, the new generation of portables do not have enough resources to provide quality of service on some communication channels. Therefore there is the need to degrade some part of those channels. The identification of tradeoffs may provide motivation to push for the improvement of particular technologies, for example, 3D high resolution displays on mobiles and better protocols for error-prone communication links.

The session concluded by noting that the overwhelming problem of trying to collaborate over distributed applications is finding a common base configuration for a particular task in terms of the quality of service, desire for fairness based shared workspaces and the best usage of the available resources.

6 Acknowledgements

Thanks to Panos Markopoulos and Martijn van Welie for their useful comments on the first draft of this report.

References

1. D. Salber, J. Coutaz, D. Decouchant, and M. Riveil. De l'observabilite et de l'honnetete: le cas du contre d'acces dans la communication homme-homme mediatis. In *Proc. IHM'95, 7emes journees de l'Ingenierie de l'Interaction Homme-Machine*, pages 27–35. CEPA, 1995.

Working Group 2 Report

G. White

Department of Computer Science, Queen Mary and Westfield College, London, UK
Email: graham@dcs.qmw.ac.uk

1 Participants

Jose Campos
Peter Forbrig
Francis Jambon
Mario Martins
Mieke Massink
Tore Urnes
Graham White (Rapporteur)
Charles Wüthrich

2 Definition of Haptics

Srinavasan defines it as "the use of hands to explore and manipulate". This definition seems a little biased towards the direct manipulation uses of this technology; we are somewhat more interested in its possible uses for communication and data representation, and thus in what might be called the "haptic rendering" of information. question of haptic rendering.

3 Factors for Haptic Interaction

Some of the factors marking out a "haptic space" for this form of interaction are as follows:

contact Whether or not there has been contact
quality There are various haptic *modalities* (tactile, kinaesthetic and temperature sensing), and with these modalities we explore various haptic qualities of the sensed objects: shape, texture, elasticity, and friction.
quantity Several of these qualities – for example, force, temperature, and frequency – can vary in quantity; this allows a continuous variation along several dimensions of the haptic space.

4 Kinds of Interaction

We can use haptic interaction in several ways: both

passive sensing, in which we are simply exposed to incoming stimuli, and

active exploration, in which we can ourselves perform direct manipulation, either merely for exploration of the felt object, or in some sort of communicative context.

5 Peculiarities

Haptic interaction with objects functions with an extremely tight feedback loop (of the order of milliseconds). This clearly poses problems for standard telecommunications channels, where such rapid communication may not be available. Furthermore, standard models of interaction may well not be accurate; most models of computer-aided communication are either asynchronous or assume some sort of alternating protocol, in which the parties take turns to communicate with each other. Haptic interaction is synchronous, but cannot be subsumed under an alternating communication protocol; in most of the interesting cases there is continuous feedback, and we cannot naturally partition either information stream into discrete chunks.

There is also the issue of coding. Suppose, as an example, that we have a cellphone which vibrates, or which emits some other haptic stimulus, instead of giving an audible ringing tone. Suppose that we want to encode more information than merely the presence or absence of a signal. Now there is clearly enough room in haptic space to encode considerable quantities of information: the fact that people can, with training, read braille, or understand speech using purely haptic capabilities, shows that we can extract complexly structured information from haptic stimuli. However, as soon as we move beyond the merely technical possibities, there are many human interface problems. What tasks would such an interface be suitable for? What sort of information needs to be communicated in these tasks? How can codings be devised that are either intuitively comprehensible, or easy to learn?

Working Group 3 Report

D.A. Duce

Rutherford Appleton Laboratory, Chilton, Didcot, OX11 0QX, UK
Email: D.A.Duce@rl.ac.uk

1 Participants

Pablo Castells
Jacques Cazin
David Duce (Rapporteur)
Michael Harrison
Mike Hollier
Chris Roast

2 Introduction

The working group focused on the second problem - cooperative applications in an environment where different partners may be connected by different bandwidth communications links, or may be using equipment with differing processing power or input/output capabilities - for example, an office workstation environment, desktop virtual reality environment or hand-held device.

3 Observations

The first observation was that different devices and different operating environments lead to the need to employ different representations for information. A photorealistic rendering of an architectural model in a desktop workstation environment is infeasible in a hand-held device with a small monochrome display. In the latter environment plan and elevation drawings might be the most that is feasible, or perhaps some form of non-photorealistic rendering such as a sketch rendering.

When different partners have different operating environments, it is important for all partners to understand the environment in which each person is operating, in order to tailor dialogue to a level which is comprehensible to all participants. The display of status and context information is very important in such situations in order to keep track of how other people will interpret one's utterances and actions.

It was recognized that there is a high degree of task dependency in this, and what is appropriate will vary from one work situation to another. Work and task analysis is therefore very important in designing systems for such applications. One example discussed in the working group was that of a police helicopter following the evolution of a crime. The officers in the helicopter have an overview of the situation and may be giving directions to officers on the ground giving chase to the criminals. The officers on the ground do not have an overview, nor do they need one - the local context and next step is sufficient. This is typical of command and control situations, or hierarchically structured work, where roles and tasks are well-defined and the information required by each task is well-defined.

It is important to establish synchronization relationships amongst partners, so that, for example, partners whose equipment is connected by slow links are not left behind by participants connected by faster links. This is also important if different participants are using different modalities, for example because of their operating environment. Presentation of textual information on and display and through a speech synthesizer have different synchronization properties and requirements.

The working group noted that the architectural work at Queen's University addresses some of these issues.

There is a sense in which all participants could use the same "lowest common denominator" representations. Whether this is sensible is a function of the work to be done or task to be performed (however that is understood). Participants with access to richer representations should not be denied such access. It might be sensible for all participants to be able to access the same lowest common denominator representations, for example as an aid to resolving misunderstandings arising from the use of different representations.

In many collaborative settings there is a distinction between shared information that is to be made available to all partners, and private information which is local to particular partners. Representation considerations are most acute for shared information.

4 Mini-scenarios

The working group considered some specific scenarios in the architecture area. One was inspired by a programme shown on television in the UK about people who had built their own houses. The programme looked at the relationship between client and architect. In one programme, the clients decided they wanted a large patio in front of their house, a decision made as the house was being constructed. The architect tried to persuade them that this would distort the harmony of the design and have a negative aesthetical impact. Because the house was being built on a slope, the structural engineers were concerned at the height and thickness of wall required to retain the earth packed behind.

In a second scenario the working group thought about building an extension to a house, in which as construction work is proceeding, the electricity company inform the architect that the power cable needs to be rerouted, the routing proposed by the architect in the original design is not in fact technically permissible.

5 Insights

The working group explored how these negotiation scenarios might be played out with the players in different locations with different equipment, for example the architect and structural engineer or electrical engineer in offices with powerful desktop workstations, but different representations of the building (either model or plans) and the client on site with hand held or low performance laptop computer. The notion of "fair cooperation" in these settings was explored.

It was recognized that it is important that statements made in the context of one representation have to have an interpretation in the other representations - for example, a statement such as "the red one other there" may be meaningless for a participant with a monochrome display and no notion of where "there" is.

At times it is necessary for all participants to be able to share a common view (even if it is in different representations such as model and plan), i.e. to be viewing the situation from the same position. "That's what I am looking at now" has to be possible. This implies that there needs to be a common geometric shared frame of reference for all participants. Coherence needs to be maintainable as the viewpoint is changed.

It was recognized that there is much that can be learnt from work on human error recovery and repair - for example when a statement is misunderstood by a participant working with a different representation. To enable communication, participants need to build up a shared vocabulary. How this happens and what can be done to facilitate it, are interesting questions when participants are working with different representations and perhaps with representations that change over time if the participant's environment (e.g. quality of communications connection) is changing over time.

SpringerEurographics

Nadia Magnenat-Thalmann,

Daniel Thalmann (eds.)

Computer Animation
and Simulation '99

Proceedings of the Eurographics
Workshop in Milano, Italy,
September 7–8, 1999

1999. X, 230 pages. 148 partly coloured figures.
Softcover DM 89,–, öS 625,–
ISBN 3-211-83392-7. Eurographics

The 20 research papers in this volume
demonstrate novel models and concepts in
animation and graphics simulation. Special
emphasis is given on innovative approaches
to Modelling Human Motion, Models of Collision Detection and Perception, Facial Animation and Communication, Specific Animation Models, Realistic Rendering for Animation, and Behavioral Animation.

Dani Lischinski,

Ward Larson (eds.)

Rendering Techniques '99

Proceedings of the Eurographics
Workshop in Granada, Spain,
June 21–23, 1999

1999. XI, 382 pages. 212 partly coloured figures.
Softcover DM 118,–, öS 826,–
ISBN 3-211-83382-X. Eurographics

The papers in this volume present new
research activities in the "classical" rendering workshop topics:
radiosity and Monte Carlo global illumination
algorithms and illumination models, alongside papers on near-interactive ray tracing,
hardware-assisted rendering algorithms,
techniques for acquisition and modeling
from images, image-based rendering, novel
shadow algorithms, and inverse lighting and
design.

All prices are recommended retail prices

SpringerWienNewYork

Sachsenplatz 4–6, P.O.Box 89, A-1201 Wien, Fax +43-1-330 24 26, e-mail: books@springer.at, **Internet: http://www.springer.at**
New York, NY 10010, 175 Fifth Avenue • D-14197 Berlin, Heidelberger Platz 3 • Tokyo 113, 3–13, Hongo 3-chome, Bunkyo-ku

SpringerEurographics

Eduard Gröller,

Helwig Löffelmann,

William Ribarsky (eds.)

Data Visualization '99

Proceedings of the Joint EUROGRAPHICS
and IEEE TCVG Symposium on Visualization in Vienna, Austria, May 26–28, 1999

1999. XII, 340 pages. 230 partly coloured figures.
Softcover DM 118,–, öS 826,–
ISBN 3-211-83344-7. Eurographics

In the past decade visualization established
its importance both in scientific research and
in real-world applications.
In this book 21 research papers and 9 case
studies report on the latest results in volume
and flow visualization and information visualization.
Thus it is a valuable source of information not
only for researchers but also for practitioners
developing or using visualization applications.

Michael Gervautz,

Axel Hildebrand,

Dieter Schmalstieg (eds.)

Virtual Environments '99

Proceedings of the Eurographics
Workshop in Vienna, Austria,
May 31–June 1, 1999

1999. X, 191 pages. 78 figures.
Softcover DM 85,–, öS 595,–
ISBN 3-211-83347-1. Eurographics

The special focus of this volume lies on
augmented reality. Problems like real-time
rendering, tracking, registration and occlu-
sion of real and virtual objects, shading and
lighting interaction and interaction techniques in augmented environments are
addressed. The papers collected in this book
also address levels of detail, distributed
environments, systems and applications and
interaction techniques.

All prices are recommended retail prices

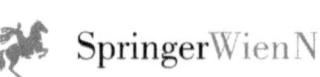 SpringerWienNewYork

Sachsenplatz 4–6, P.O.Box 89, A-1201 Wien, Fax +43-1-330 24 26, e-mail: books@springer.at, **Internet: http://www.springer.at**
New York, NY 10010, 175 Fifth Avenue • D-14197 Berlin, Heidelberger Platz 3 • Tokyo 113, 3–13, Hongo 3-chome, Bunkyo-ku